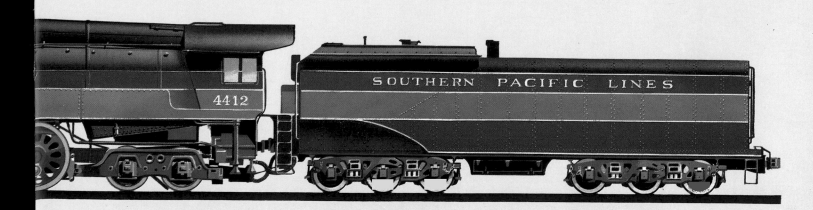

The Illustrated Encyclopedia of the World's

STEAM
Passenger Locomotives

TIGER BOOKS INTERNATIONAL
LONDON

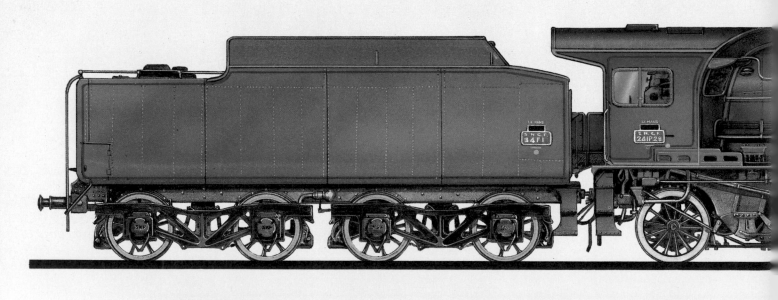

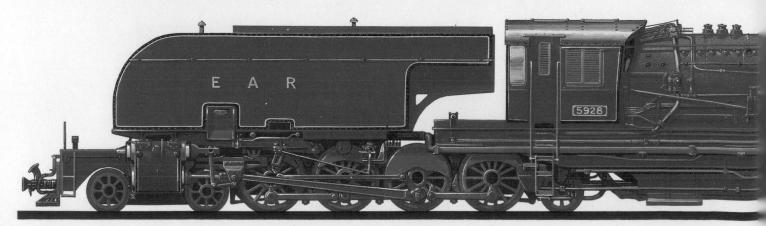

The Illustrated Encyclopedia of the World's
STEAM
Passenger Locomotives

A technical directory of major international express train engines from the 1820s to the present day

Brian Hollingsworth

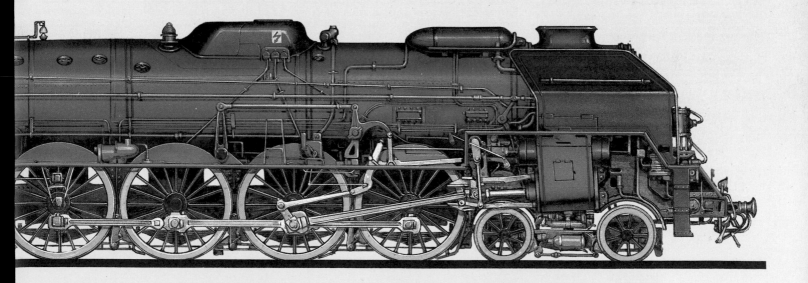

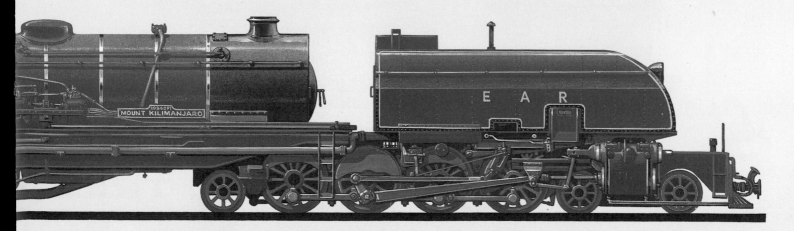

A Salamander Book

This edition published in 1989 by Tiger Books International PLC, London.

© Salamander Books Ltd 1982

ISBN 1 85501 030 5

Credits

Editor: Ray Bonds

Designer: Philip Gorton

Colour artwork: Terry Hadler, David Palmer, Dick Eastland, Michael Roffe, and TIGA Ltd. (© Salamander Books Ltd.).

Picture research: Diane and John Moore *(full picture credits are given at the back of the book)*

Filmset: Modern Text Ltd.

Colour and monochrome reproduction: Rodney Howe Ltd.

Printed in Belgium by Henri Proost et Cie.

The author

BRIAN HOLLINGSWORTH, M.A., M.I.C.E.

Brian Hollingsworth has had an extravagant passion for railways ever since he can remember. After qualifying in engineering at Cambridge University, and after a brief excursion into the world of flying machines, he joined the Great Western Railway in 1946, his mathematical background leading him into British Rail's computers and also to a heavy involvement with BR's TOPS wagon and train control system.

He left British Rail in 1974 to take up writing and has published nine major books on various aspects of railways besides contributing to technical railway periodicals.

He is a director of the Romney, Hythe and Dymchurch Railway and civil engineering adviser to the Ffestiniog Railway. He has a fleet of one-fifth full size locomotives which run on his private railway in his own 'back garden' (actually a portion of a Welsh mountain!), and he actually owns the full-size LMS 'Black Five' Class 4-6-0 No.5428 *Eric Treacy,* which operates as a working locomotive on the North Yorkshire Moors Railway for tourists and rail enthusiasts.

The consultant

PATRICK B. WHITEHOUSE, O.B.E., A.R.P.S.

Patrick Whitehouse is the author of some 30 books on railway subjects, and has been editor of and consultant to several national railway magazines. He has also been active in steam preservation, becoming the secretary of the very first British line to be rescued by amateurs, the Talyllyn Railway in North Wales. In addition, he is a patron of the world-famous Ffestiniog Railway and has a direct involvement in the preservation and indeed ownership of several main line steam locomotives.

An Associate of the Royal Photographic Society, Patrick Whitehouse has been taking photographs of railway subjects since the age of eleven, and over the years has built up a picture library of approximately 100,000 railway subjects worldwide. To keep himself up-to-date he sets aside at least a month in every year to travel the world not only to look at the main lines but also to poke into the corners to seek out what is left of steam.

Author's acknowledgements

The author wishes to express his special thanks to Arthur Cook who contributed 22 of the locomotive descriptions, including all the German entries, most of those concerned with the Pennsylvania Railroad, and a number of others. His gratitude is also due to Peter Kalla-Bishop who checked the manuscript, making many valuable suggestions, and who prepared the index, as well as to Margot Cooper who took the main burden of the typing.

As regards all the wonderful artwork and rare photographs in the book, the author would also like to pay tribute to the team of artists, to Diana and John Moore, and to all those people and institutions who have scoured their archives and treasured photo collections to help make the book one of the best illustrated on the subject of steam locomotives.

Brian Hollingsworth

Contents

Locomotives are arranged in chronological order, except where production problems have prevented it.

Introduction

THE PURPOSE of this book is to tell the story of the birth, development, triumph and, finally, slow extinction of that best-loved of all mankind's mechanical creations, the steam express passenger locomotive. It attempts to do so by describing and illustrating individually over 150 outstanding examples of the breed arranged (in general) chronologically.

The story begins over 150 years ago when those legendary "Rocket" class locomotives were built by George and Robert Stephenson for the world's first inter-city railway between Liverpool and Manchester. All England held its breath as these little fire chariots began to annihilate space and time at speeds up to 35mph (56km/h). In this way journey times were reduced by a factor of three or more, in comparison with those achieved by road carriages hauled by the flesh-and-blood kind of horse. Within a dozen years even these speeds had doubled, while locomotive weights had trebled, power outputs had quadrupled and a fair degree of reliability had been achieved. In addition, two quite separate lines of development had emerged on either side of the Atlantic Ocean.

Even nowadays, when far more wonderful examples of man's mastery over Nature's physical forces are commonplace, we find a working steam locomotive a thrilling sight, but for people living then it must have been awesome indeed. No wonder people expected the cattle to be made barren, the crops to fail, hens to cease laying and fruit to rot on the trees when a steam locomotive thundered by.

None of these things happened but, nevertheless, the coming of the steam locomotive changed the world in a few short years by reducing both the cost as well as the speed of travel again by a factor of three or more. No longer did all but a favoured few among people living in inland regions need to spend all their lives in the same place. Of course, in the wilder parts of the world the coming of steam locomotion often marked the very start of civilisation: the railway actually opened up and built many countries, the United States of America being the most prominent example.

But there is another side to steam on rails and, surprisingly, it was a young actress called Fanny Kemble who is the first person (and both the first and almost the last woman) on record as having realised that here was a new art-form to thrill the senses. On 26 August 1830 she wrote to a friend that "...a common sheet of paper is enough for love but a foolscap extra can alone contain a railroad and my ecstasies". She went on to speak of "this brave little she-dragon...the magical machine with its wonderful flying white breath and rhythmical unvarying pace" and finally she felt as if "no fairy tale was ever half so wonderful as what I saw". True, not everyone was conducted by George Stephenson personally the first time they met a steam locomotive but, even so, this perspicacious lady really rang the bell in speaking of the iron horse the way she did.

Many of the rest of us are only beginning to realise the value of what we used to have now that it has been or is being snatched away. In most

Above: *Southern Railway "West Country" class 4-6-2* Blackmore Vale *hauls a train on the Bluebell Railway in 1981.*

Above: *A construction train on the Mexican Railway is pulled across a spindly steel viaduct behind a Fairlie articulated locomotive.*

countries one can no longer stand beside the railway line and listen to the *thrum, thrum, thrum* of a steam locomotive as an express train comes up fast towards us, then watch it go by with rods flailing and a white plume of exhaust shining in the sunshine; or maybe stand at the carriage window and listen to the chimney music and the patter of cinders on the roof as a mighty steam locomotive up front pounds up some long hard grade in the mountains.

But this steam locomotive worship thing has much more to it than that and for pointing this out we again owe Miss Kemble our gratitude. Almost without realising it—not being familiar with today's railway locomotives which are just noisy boxes on wheels—she pin-pointed one of the other great charms of the steam locomotive, the fact that most of its secrets are laid bare for those who have eyes to see. Fanny wrote "...she (for they make all

Above: *"Duchess" class 4-6-2* Duchess of Hamilton *leaves York, England, on her first trip after restoration.*

Left: *"A4" class 4-6-2 No.60025* Falcon *bursts from Gasworks Tunnel, Kings Cross with the* Flying Scotsman.

these curious little firehorses mares) consisted of a boiler, a stove, a small platform, a bench . . . she goes on two wheels which are her feet and are moved by bright steel legs called pistons; these are propelled by steam and in proportion as more steam is applied to the upper extremeties (the hip-joints, I suppose) of these pistons, the faster they move the wheels . . . The reins, bit and bridle of this wonderful beast is a small steel handle, which applies and withdraws the steam from the legs or pistons, so that a child might manage it. The coals, which are its oats, were under the bench and there was a small glass tube fixed to the boiler, with water in it, which indicates by its fulness or emptiness when the creature wants water . . ."

Although steam locomotives up to six times larger, forty-six times heavier and with a nominal pulling force sixty times that of Fanny's locomotive

steam locomotives as, say, the *Niagara* 4-8-4s of the New York Central Railroad.

Efforts have been made to make the geographical coverage as wide as possible; some priority has been given to including examples from all those nations—some of them surprisingly small and agricultural—which built their own steam express locomotives. At the same time the examples chosen are intended to have as wide a coverage as possible in a technical sense: taking express trains across high passes in the North American Rockies needed a different sort of animal to doing high speeds across the Plain of York in England.

Finally, not forgotten have been some brave attempts to advance the technology of the steam express locomotive beyond the original Stephenson concept. Some of the most promising among compound, articulated, condensing and turbine locomotives are included with the sole proviso that the examples chosen did at least run in traffic on important trains, even if they did not represent the main-stream of development.

Further difficulties arose over drawing the line between express passenger locomotives and others. Apart from such obvious signs as coloured liveries and the carrying of names to help one to decide, the principal question asked has been, "Was this machine intended to be used on one of the world's great trains?" If the answer was "yes", then we had a candidate for inclusion.

The Descriptions

The individual descriptions which form the body of the book attempt to look at each locomotive in several different ways. First, one must take a glance at its nuts-and-bolts—that is, weights, pressures, sizes, etc. Second, comes the bare bones of its history—how many there were, when they were built, who designed and built them, how long they lasted and the like. Thirdly, perhaps more interestingly, there are the technical aspects. The steam locomotive came in fascinating variety and, with most of its mechanism being visible, even the smallest details have always attracted attention from professional and amateur alike.

Next comes the tale of what the class of locomotive was built to do as well as how (and whether) if fulfilled its designers' aspirations. Then something has to be said about the way it looks—its success or failure as a work of art if you like. Lastly, a brief mention is made of any that survive today.

As regards individual items on the description, the heading of each one begins with the class or class name. Different railways had different systems; many of the designations were designed to tell you something about the locomotive. For example, the British London & North Eastern Railway used a letter which told you the wheel arrangement, followed by a number which identified the actual class within that type. Hence the "A4" class were the streamlined 4-6-2s (of which the record-breaker *Mallard* was the outstanding example), the fourth class of 4-6-2 introduced by the LNER or its predecessors.

Other railways used class numbers which were as random as those applied to some modern aircraft or computers. Yet others (and these included such opposite ends of the spectrum as feudal Great Western of Britain as well as the Railways of the Chinese People's Republic) had names—"King" and

Above: *A German Federal Railways class "01" 4-6-2 makes a fine show of exhaust smoke setting out with an express.*

(it was *Northumbrian*, by the way) are included in this book, her enchanting description fits them too. All the elements mentioned are similarly visible to the casual observer in the same way; and whether their maximum speed is 25mph (40km/h) or 125mph (200km/h), their working follows exactly the same principles.

However much the steam locomotive's vital statistics may vary—and this is reflected in extremes of shape as well as size—one thing does not, and that is its degree of attraction for us. Whether it is elaborately painted and lined or just coated with bitumen (or even rust), or whether given a brass-plate complete with romantic name or simply a stencilled-on number, the result is the same—it instills in us a desire to find out everything there is to know about each and every one of these wonderful machines.

In respect of the writing of this book, the most difficult problem has been to select the best examples from among so many well-qualified candidates. Naturally, the first choice has been those that represent major steps along the road of evolution from Stephenson's *Rocket* to such ultimate

Type Designations for Steam Express Passenger Locomotives

Configuration	British and N. American	Continental European	Name
	0-2-2	A1	—
	2-2-0	1A	—
	2-2-2	1A1	—
	4-2-0	2A	—
	4-2-2	2A1	—
	4-2-4	2A2	—
	0-4-2	B1	—
	2-4-0	1B	—
	2-4-2	1B1	—
	4-4-0	2B	American
	4-4-2	2B1	Atlantic
	4-4-4	2B2	(Jubilee)*
	2-6-0	1C	Mogul
	2-6-2	1C1	Prairie
	2-6-4	1C2	(Adriatic)*
	4-6-0	2C	Ten-wheeler
	4-6-2	2C1	Pacific
	4-6-4	2C2	Hudson, Baltic
	2-8-0	1D	Consolidation
	2-8-2	1D1	Mikado
	4-8-0	2D	(Mastodon)*
	4-8-2	2D1	Mountain
	4-8-4	2D2	Northern (Confederation)*
	4-6-6-4	2CC2	Challenger
	4-6-2 + 2-6-4	2C1 + 1C2	Garratt
	4-8-2 + 2-8-4	2D1 + 1D2	Garratt

These names were never frequently used.

"Castle" for the former and "March Forward" and "Aiming High" for the latter—to distinguish different designs in their locomotive fleet.

There then follows the type, the country of ownership, the railway . . . . .

As regards individual items in the descriptions, in general they are arranged as follows. The heading tells of the class (or name) and type, the country, the railway and the date of introduction of the particular locomotive in question. For steam locomotives, "type" has a special meaning and refers to the arrangement of driving wheels. Many common types have names; others are only referred to by code. The list of types mentioned in this book is given in the table in this introduction.

Locomotive Particulars

Each individual description begins with a list of dimensions, areas, weights, loads, forces and capacities applicable to the locomotive class in question. Naturally these are offered to the reader in good faith, but it must be realised that only one of them—the length of the stroke of the cylinders, is at all precise. Some vary as the engine goes along and coal and water in the boiler and in the tender is consumed or taken on. Others vary as wear takes place and there are one or two which were often deliberately falsified. Usually, too, there are some members of a class which differ from the others in various particulars.

All these things mean that the information is offered with a certain reserve. To emphasise this uncertainty, most of the figures have been suitably rounded. The first figure in each case is given in English gallons, pounds, feet or inches as appropriate; then comes (in brackets) the figure in metric measure. Where capacities are concerned there is an intermediate figure in US gallons. It should be noted that, since both the imperial and the metric figures have been appropriately rounded they are no longer the precise equivalent of one another. This applies particularly in respect of weights; it is a point that the metric ton and the imperial ton differ by far less (2%) than the amount the attributes they are used here to quantify can vary. This will be 10% more. The individual entries are as follows.

Tractive Effort This is a nominal figure which gives some indication of the pulling force ("drawbar pull") which a locomotive can exert. It assumes a steam pressure of 85 per cent of the maximum steam pressure in the boiler acting on the piston diameter. The figure takes into account the leverage implicit in the ratio between the distance from the axle to the crank-pin and the distance from the axle to the rail. In locomotives with more than two cylinders the valve found is multiplied by half the number of cylinders. For compound locomotives none of the formulae available give results that are meaningful in comparative terms, so this entry is omitted in such cases. The value is specified both in pounds and kilograms.

Axle load This figure gives the highest static load applied by any pair of wheels to the rails. For any particular line the permanent way department of the railway places a limit on this value dependent on the strength of the rails and the sleeper spacing. Mechanical departments who control the use of the weighing apparatus usually cheat by understating

Above: *Indian Railways' metre-gauge class "YP" 4-6-2 No.2539 at Agra Fort station.*

Above: *The famous preserved locomotive* Flying Scotsman *near Clapham, Yorkshire, England. Note auxiliary water tender.*

the amount, but the other side usually specify the limits with some margin to allow for this. Axle load also varies according to the amount of coal and water in the boiler and, in addition, there are the dynamic effects while the engine is moving. The axle load is specified in pounds and tons; but note that the variability is far greater than the difference between imperial tons of 2,240lbs and metric tonnes of 2,204lbs.

Cylinders The number of cylinders as well as their diameter and stroke are given; the latter can be relied upon for accuracy, but the former will increase as the cylinder is re-bored to counteract wear. When new cylinders or liners are fitted the diameter returns to that specified. Compound locomotives have high-pressure (HP) and low-pressure (LP) cylinders which differ in size and may differ in

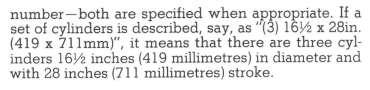

number—both are specified when appropriate. If a set of cylinders is described, say, as "(3) 16½ x 28in. (419 x 711mm)", it means that there are three cylinders 16½ inches (419 millimetres) in diameter and with 28 inches (711 millimetres) stroke.

Driving wheels The diameter of the driving wheels might be thought to be reliable—but they are turned in a lathe from time to time in order to counteract irregular wear. So the actual diameter may be up to 3in (75mm) less than the nominal amount recorded, specified in inches and millimetres. The difference in weight between wheel sets with new tyres and with tyres turned to the permitted limit would reduce the axle-load by ½ ton.

Heating surface The heating surface area of a locomotive (specified in square feet and square metres) is a measure of the size of its boiler and is made up of the surface area of the fire-tubes, of the fire-box and of any water tubes etc. in the firebox.

Superheater The area of the superheater elements is specified in square feet and square metres.

Steam pressure The steam pressure at which the boiler is intended to work is given here. It is also the pressure at which the safety valves should be set to open, but of course at any given moment during a run the steam pressure may be less than this, sometimes considerably less if things are not going well. Steam pressure is specified in pounds per square inch and kilograms per square centimetre.

Grate area This is a particularly important figure because it represents the size of the fire, and the

because it represents the size of the fire, and the fire is the source of a steam locomotive's power. It is specified in square feet (square metres).

Fuel Unless otherwise stated, the fuel used in a particular locomotive can be assumed to be coal. The nominal amount which can be carried is specified in pounds (lb) and tons. If liquid fuel is used the capacity is specified (with greater confidence than for coal) in British gallons, US gallons and cubic metres.

Water The amount of water carried in tender and/or tanks is specified in British gallons, US gallons and cubic metres.

Adhesive weight A locomotive can only exert the pulling power implicit in its nominal tractive effort if there is adequate adhesion between its driving wheels and the rails. The amount of adhesive weight (often described as "weight on coupled wheels") is specified in pounds and tons. The figure quoted must be regarded as a nominal one.

Total weight The total weight of the engine *and* tender fully loaded is specified in pounds and tons. It is another figure (specified in pounds and tons) whose variability is affected by the same factors as the axle-load.

Overall length This is the length either over the buffers of engine and tender, or over the coupling faces where centre buffers are used, and it is specified in feet and inches as well as in millimetres.

Abbreviations The usual abbreviations are used both in these lists and in the text; lb=pounds, ft=feet, in=inches, sq ft=square feet; gall=gallons, US=United States gallons, psi=pounds per square inch, mph=miles per hour, kg=kilograms, t=tons, mm=millimetres, m=metres, m²=square metres, m³=cubic metres, kg/cm²=kilograms per square centimetre, km=kilometres, km/h=kilometres per hour, hp=horsepower.

A less common measure which appears from time to time is the *chain,* used for specifying the radii of curves. A chain (abbreviated as "ch") equals 66ft, the length of an English cricket pitch, 1/80th mile and, for practical purposes, 20 metres.

How a Steam Locomotive Works

The steam locomotive is often derided for its modest efficiency; yet few realise that its elegant simplicity betokens a *mechanical* efficiency that even today makes it a viable proposition in many circumstances in spite of what those who have a vested interest in its successors have to say.

The principle on which the steam locomotive works is that water heated above boiling point tries to become steam and thus expands to a volume 1,700 times greater. Inside the boiler it remains confined and therefore the pressure rises. Once steam is transferred to a cylinder with a piston, therefore, it will push. If the push from the piston is transferred by a system of rods to the wheels, then steam from the boiler will produce movement.

The steam engine consists of these two quite separate parts—the boiler part and the engine part. The boiler is a closed vessel which in most locomotives contains a *fire-box* at the rear and tubes to

Above: *An American engineer at the throttle of a Denver & Rio Grande Western 2-8-2 locomotive.*

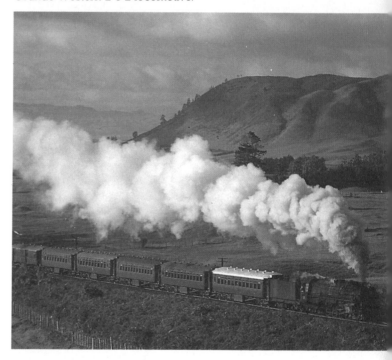

Above: *New Zealand Railways class "K" 4-8-4 No.905 near Rotorua on an Auckland express, July 1956.*

lead the hot gases from the fire to a *smoke-box* attached at the front. Hundreds of rods called *stays* are provided inside the boiler in order to resist this pressure. A valve, known as the *regulator (throttle)* is provided to control the flow of steam down the main steam pipe to the engine part. Once the steam has done its work there, it is exhausted through the *blast-pipe* into the smoke-box and up the chimney. The so-called blast-pipe is arranged so that the steam issuing from it produced a partial vacuum in the smoke-box and hence draws the fire (in the fire-box) proportionately to the amount of steam being used. Hence the more steam is used the more steam is made. Other types of boiler have from time to time been tried but rarely adopted.

Most steam locomotives are coal-burning and in these the fire burns on a *grate* formed of iron *fire-bars.* As the coal burns, ashes fall through these

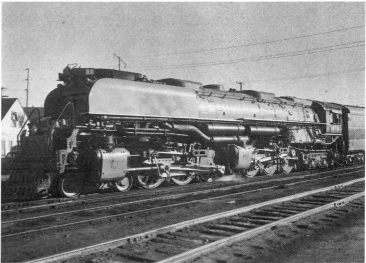

Above: *The biggest and most powerful steam locomotive ever used in passenger service—a Union Pacific "Challenger" 4-6-6-4.*

Above: *German Federal Railways class "01" 4-6-2 No.001-187-4 at Neuenmarkt Würzburg with a train to Hof, April 1970.*

Left: *The last steam locomotive built for British Railways, 2-10-0 Evening Star, at Didcot, Berkshire.*

into an *ash-pan* underneath. Means of putting water into the boiler have to be provided, as well as a store of water to replace that which gets used as steam. If the water tank is on a separate vehicle it is called a *tender* (and the locomotive a tender loco-motive). A *tank locomotive* has the tank or tanks on the locomotive.

The engine part consists of *frames* which can be built up from iron or steel plates or bars, or may be a one-piece steel casting. In this are formed slots for *axle-boxes* which carry the *wheel sets* consisting of pairs of wheels mounted on axles. The axleboxes are connected to the frame by a system of springs. The *cylinders* are fixed to the frames and each one contains a *piston*. The piston forces which result from the admission of steam to these cylinders (it is done alternately at either end) are transmitted to the wheels by a system of rods and guides, the

latter consisting of *cross-head* and one or more *guide bars.* A circular *piston rod* connects the piston to the cross-head via a steam-tight *gland,* while a *connecting-rod* connects the crosshead to the *driving wheels.* Further pairs of wheels may be driven by means of *coupling rods.*

In order to lead the steam into or out of the end of the cylinder when and—according to the direc-tion and speed of movement—where it is required, a valve or valves are provided. These are linked with the wheels by means of *valve gear.* The types of valves and valve gears used down the years have been many and varied as the narrative to follow bears witness. But all of them exploit the principle that if steam is admitted to one end of a cylinder with a piston inside it, that piston will be pushed with a force dependent on the pressure of the steam and the area of the piston.

Glossary

Notes — American Railroad English and British Railway English differ slightly. Where this is the case the fact is noted thus: Bogie (US=truck) or Truck (Br =bogie). Both entries appear but the definition is given only against the British one.

Where appropriate, items are referenced to the cut-away drawing below, viz Clack valve or Check valve *72*.

Adhesive weight — the weight on the driving wheels of a locomotive. On its amount depends the frictional grip between wheels and rail and hence the drawbar pull which a locomotive can exert.

Arch tubes — tubes connected to the water-space of the boiler provided in and across the firebox in order to add extra high-temperature heating surface. They also serve to support the brick arch or equivalent.

Articulated locomotive — a locomotive whose driving wheels are in distinct sets one or more of which are hinged or pivoted. Fairlie, Beyer-Garratt and Mallet types form the subject of individual descriptions which follow.

Ash-pan *52* — a feature of a locomotive which has the same form and purpose as the domestic variety, ie., to collect the ashes which fall through the bars of the grate. The only significant difference is the size, measured in feet rather than inches.

Axlebox *28, 44* — the axle bearings of a locomotive are known as axleboxes. It is usually convenient to make them box-shaped to suit the guides and openings in the frames which should constrain movement in the horizontal plane but allow freedom vertically.

Balancing *88* — the reciprocating and revolving masses of any steam (or diesel) engine need balancing, if it is to work smoothly. Revolving masses can easily be balanced by counterweights, but the balancing of reciprocating parts is a matter of compromise and judgement.

Bar frames — see frames.

Beyer-Garratt locomotive see "231+132BT" class, pages 150-151.

Blast pipe *7* — the exhaust pipes of a steam locomotive are arranged so that the steam emerges as a jet through a nozzle in the smokebox below the chimney. This creates a partial vacuum in the smokebox, which draws air through the boiler tubes and through the fire, so enabling combustion to take place.

Blower *2* — a steam jet in the smokebox or at the base of the chimney which can be used to draw up the fire when the loco-motive is not being run under steam.

Blowdown valve — a means of releasing water, plus impurities contained therein, from the lowest water space of the boiler.

Boiler tubes *75* — see fire tubes.

Bogie (US=truck) *24, 27, 29, 30* — a pivoted truck, usually four-wheeled, provided at the front or rear of a locomotive to give guidance and support. Most items of rolling stock and many steam locomotive tenders.

Brakes — locomotives usually (but not always) have a hand brake and (also usually) some form of power brake. Power brakes can be actuated by compressed air, steam or vacuum. Air and vacuum brakes normally can be applied throughout the train by using the controls on the locomotive.

King Class 4-6-0
Great Britain:
Great Western Railway (GWR), 1927

The drawing shows the working parts of a King Class 4-6-0 (see page 122), senior member of a unique family of standard engines. This uniqueness appears on the drawing in many ways: e.g., the mouth of the main steam-pipe (67) is placed at the highest point of the boiler instead of inside a separate raised dome on top of the boiler as is more usual.
(Drawing reproduced with acknowledgements to Railway Wonders of the World.)

1 Chimney	14 Steam Chest	28 Outside Bogie Axlebox
2 Blower Connection	15 Piston Valve	29 Bogie Spring
3 Smoke-box Door Baffle	16 Valve Rod	30 Bogie Side-Control Spring Housing
4 Door-fastening Dart	17 Piston	31 Crosshead
5 Smoke-box Door	18 Piston Rod	32 Inside Cylinder Steam Chest
6 Smoke-box	19 Stuffing Gland	33 Valve Spindle Rocker
7 Blast Pipe	20 Front Cylinder Cover	34 Guide Bars
8 Steam Port	21 Buffer	35 Guide Bar Bracket
9 Outside Steam-pipe	22 Screw Coupling	36 Bogie Bearing Angle
10 Steam-pipe from Superheater	23 Life Guard	37 Engine Main Frame
11 Superheater Header	24 Bogie Frame	38 Crank Pin
12 Regulator Valve	25 Cylinder Drain Cocks	39 Coupling Rod
13 Jumper Top	26 Cylinder	
	27 Bogie Wheel	

Air Brake — the commonest form of train brake, using compressed air as the medium of application.

Vacuum brake — the alternative to an air brake is a vacuum brake. For steam locomotives the vacuum is much simpler than the air brake, mainly because a vacuum can be generated from any steam supply by a simple static ejector, whereas compressed air needs a relatively complex pump. The objection to the vacuum system is that the pressure available is limited to about three-quarters of the atmospheric pressure, that is, some 12psi (0.8kg/cm²). This means either very large cylinders or a limited brake force.

Brick arch *79* — a brick or concrete baffle provided at the front of a locomotive firebox below the tubes, in order to extend the flame path. Early locomotives burnt coke; pro-

vision of a brick arch was necessary before coal could be used without producing excessive smoke.

Chimney (US/Smokestack) — the orifice through which the exhaust steam and the gaseous products of combustion are dispersed into the atmosphere.

Clack valve or Check valve *72* — a non-return valve attached to the boiler at the points where feed water is admitted.

Coal pusher — a steam-operated device in the tender intended to push coal forward to a point where it can be shovelled directly into the fire.

Combustion chamber — a recessing of the firebox tubeplate inside the boiler in order to increase the firebox volume at the expense of reducing the length of the tubes — in order to promote better combustion in

long-barrelled boilers.

Compensated springing — the inter-connection, by means of equalising levers, of the springs of adjacent axles. The idea is to avoid individual axles being over — or under — loaded by irregularities in the track.

Compound — a compound steam engine has its cylinders arranged so that one or more take high-pressure steam from the boiler as usual, then the remainder take the low-pressure steam exhausted from the high-pressure cylinders and use that to produce further useful work.

Conjugated valve-gear — more than two cylinders were often used in order to provide smoother running and also where an adequate total cylinder volume could only be provided in this way. In order to reduce complication, the valves of all the cylinders could be arranged to

be worked by conjugating levers from the valve gears of two of them.

Connecting rod (US=Main rod) *41* — these connect the piston rods to the crank pins of the driving wheels or crank-shaft.

Coupler — (Br-Coupling).

Coupling (US=Coupler) *22* — couplings join the vehicles of a train. Non-automatic couplings on passenger locomotives are usually of the screw pattern, formed of two links connected by a screw. Vehicles are coupled by placing the coupling of one over the hook of the other and tightening the screw, so that the buffers are in contact. Automatic couplings are designed to couple when, usually after the jaws have been opened, the vehicles are pushed gently together. The couplings then engage and lock.

Coupling rod *39* — connects ▶

40 Leading Driving Wheel	53 Fire Bars	71 Safety Valves	88 Balance Weight
41 Connecting Rod	54 Damper Doors	72 Clack Box	89 Fusible Safety Plug
42 Sand-boxes	55 Ash-pan Damper	73 Water Delivery Trays	90 Foundation Ring
43 Driving Wheel Springs	56 Cylinder Drain Handle	74 Longitudinal Stays	91 Tender Wheel Spring
44 Axle-box Horns	57 Sand Gear Handle	75 Fire Tubes	92 Spring Hanger
45 Sand-pipes	58 Fire Door Handle	76 Superheater Elements	93 Brake Block
46 Brake Blocks	59 Cab Side	77 Superheater Flue Tubes	94 Brake Rod
47 Middle Driving Wheel	60 Footplate	78 Firebox	95 Water Scoop
48 Vacuum Brake Train Pipe	61 Reversing Gear Handle	79 Brick Arch	96 Water Inlet Pipe
49 Trailing Wheel Spring	62 Fire Door	80 Firebox Back Plate	97 Deflector Dome
50 Covers for Indiarubber Pads	63 Regulator Handle	81 Firebox Crown	98 Rear Buffer
51 Equalizer Guards	64 Blower Valve	82 Firebox Tube Plate	99 Tender frame
52 Ash-pan	65 Whistle	83 Firebox Stays	100 Front Tender Buffer
	66 Regulator Rod	84 Firebox Throat Plate	101 Water Scoop Handle
	67 Mouth of Steam-pipe	85 Expansion Bracket Position	102 Brake Handle
	68 Vertical Stays	86 Splashers	103 Axlebox
	69 Boiler Casing	87 Smoke-box Tube Plate	104 Vacuum Brake Reservoir
	70 Internal Steam-pipe		

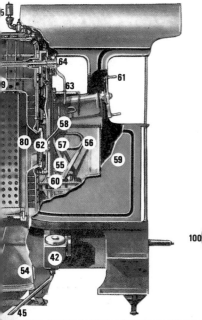

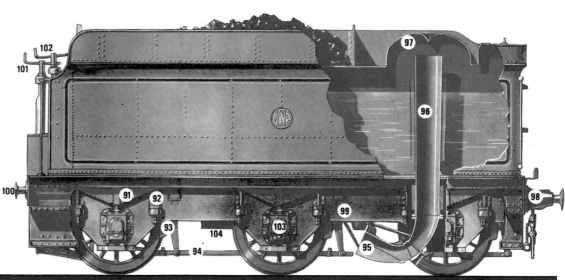

together the crank-pins of the driving or coupled wheels on one side of a locomotive.

Counter-pressure brake — using the pumping action of the cylinders to brake the train. Great heat is generated and the cylinders are kept from overheating dangerously by the injection of water, which instantly flashes into steam, thereby absorbing the energy generated.

Crank axles — the inside cylinders of locomotives drive on to axles with sections off-set to form cranks.

Crank-pins *38* — locomotive wheels are driven by rods which transmit the driving force to the driving wheels through these large steel pins fixed in the wheels.

Crosshead *31* — in conjunction with the guide-bars the crosshead guides and constrains the piston rod to keep in line as it moves in and out of the cylinder.

Cut-off — the point during the cylinder stroke at which steam is cut off by the valves. It is usually expressed as a percentage of that stroke. Typically, a steam locomotive would be set to cut-off at 75% when starting and at between 15% and 40% when running.

Cylinders *26* — in a steam locomotive the energy contained in steam is turned into mechanical force in the cylinders. Each cylinder contains a piston and the pressure of the steam on this piston produces the force.

Dampers *54, 55* — the amount of heat produced by a fire is governed by the amount of air admitted to it. This can be adjusted by opening or closing damper doors in the ashpan assembly. These are worked by levers in the locomotive cab.

Deflector dome *97* — This is provided in or on the tender in connection with the water pick-up apparatus. Water scooped from a set of troughs between the rails is first fed skywards up a vertical pipe; the deflector dome at the top of this pipe then turns the flow downwards so that the tender is filled.

Dome — the steam is usually taken from the boiler at its highest point. Where height is available, a chamber known as the dome is provided above the top of the boiler barrel in order to collect the steam.

Draincocks *26, 56* — when a locomotive is starting from cold the first steam which enters the cylinders condenses to water. Draincocks are provided, worked from the cab, to allow this water to escape. Otherwise the cylinder would be burst by

the pressure of trapped water when the piston reached the end of its stroke.

Drawbar—horsepower hour — a unit of work done by a locomotive in hauling a train. One of these units represents the exertion of a single horse-power at the locomotive drawbar for an hour.

Driving wheels *40, 47* — the driven wheels of a locomotive, sometimes referred to as coupled wheels.

Drop-grate or **Dump-grate** — when disposing of a locomotive after use the residue of the fire needs removing. Traditionally this was shovelled out through the fire-hole door, but an arrangement to allow the whole grate to be dropped or dumped was sometimes provided.

Eccentric — a device consisting of an eccentrically-bored sheave and a metal strap, having the purpose of converting revolving to reciprocating motion and used for valve-gears and pumps.

Equalisers — see compensated springing.

Fairlie locomotive — see pages 92-93.

Feed-pump — a pump to feed water into the boiler; either driven from the motion or independently by steam from the boiler.

Firebox *80-84* — made of steel or copper and fixed inside the boiler. The box in which the fire burns.

Fire door or **Fire-hole door** *58, 62* — the entrance to the firebox, through which coal is shovelled is closed by a fire door.

Fire tubes *75* — the hot gases from the fire pass through these fire tubes (often, *boiler tubes* or simply *tubes*) in the boiler between the firebox and the smoke box, so heating the water with which they are surrounded.

Flange lubricators — on sharp curves, wheel flanges bear heavily against the rails. To ease wear and reduce friction, devices to lubricate these flanges are provided on the locomotive. More usually, though, they are attached to the rail.

Flues *77* — large fire tubes, often referred to as superheater flues, which contain the superheater elements.

Footplate *60* — the surface on which a locomotive crew stands. In fact it usually extends all round the engine, but the term is now taken to mean the floor of the driving cab.

Foundation ring *90* — the rectangular ring which connects

the firebox to the boiler at the lowest point of both.

Frames *37* — often **main frames** — are the foundation upon which the locomotive is built. In British practice the frames are generally formed of plates; USA practice orginally favoured bars, but cast-steel was used generally in later years.

Fusible plugs *89* — a last-ditch defence against the consequences of boiling the top of the firebox dry, consisting of screwed brass plugs with a lead core. If there was no water present the lead would melt and the leakage of steam would (to some extent) douse the fire.

Grate *53* — usually formed of cast-iron bars and on which the fire burns.

Guide bars *34* — see *crosshead.*

Indicated horsepower — the power developed in the cylinders of a locomotive.

Horns *44* — these are guides, attached to the frames, in which the axleboxes can move vertically when running.

Injector — a static device for feeding water into the boiler by means of a series of cones. It is driven by a supply of live steam taken from the boiler or (in the case of an exhaust-steam injector) from the locomotive's exhaust when running.

Jumper blast-pipe *13* — this device was sometimes attached to the blast-pipe in order to limit the draught when the engine is working hard.

Lead — the amount which a main steam port of a locomotive cylinder is open when the appropriate piston is at its limit of travel.

Life guard *23* — Provided in front of the leading wheels of a locomotive with the idea of throwing aside objects encountered on the rails. Often also called a guard iron.

Low-water alarm — an automatic device to warn the crew that boiler-water level is getting dangerously low.

Main rod (BR=connecting rod) — see connecting rod.

Mallet — see Union Pacific 'Challenger', page 170.

Manganese steel liners — hard wearing lining surfaces used to minimise wear on the horns.

Motion — a generic term used to describe the moving parts (other than the wheels and axles) of the engine.

Nosing — an oscillating movement of a locomotive about a

vertical axis.

Piston *17* — see cylinders.

Piston rod *18* — the rod connecting the piston to the crosshead.

Piston valve *15* — see valves.

Pony truck — a two-wheel pivoted truck provided at the front or rear of a locomotive to provide guidance and support.

Poppet valve *15* — see valves.

Port *8* — see valves.

Priming — this occurs either when the water level in the boiler is too high or when impurities which cause foaming are present. It means that water is carried over down to the cylinders.

Radial axles — provide the effect of a pony truck but without a separate pivoted frame. The horns and axleboxes of a radial axle are made to allow sideways movement and are shaped so that such movement is sensibly radial about a vertical axis.

Regulator (US=throttle) *12* — serves the same purpose as the accelerator pedal on a car; in the case of a locomotive, though, it is a large and usually rather stiff steel handle.

Return crank — a revolving lever fixed on the end of a driving crank-pin so that it provides the reciprocating motion, of correct magnitude and phase, to drive the valve gear.

Reversing wheel or handle *61* — the wheel provided to alter the cut-off point of the valve gear and to move it between forward and reverse.

Reversing lever — a lever used for the same purpose as the reversing wheel, but not often found on express passenger locomotives.

Rocking grate — an arrangement to enable the grate bars to be rocked or shaken, to encourage the residues of combustion to fall down into the ash-pan.

Safety valves *71* — allow steam to escape if pressure exceeds the safe limit.

Sanding gear *42, 45* — a device to put sand on the rails to improve adhesion, particularly in damp conditions. It is worked from the cab, and the sand is either allowed to fall by gravity, or is sprayed into position with steam or compressed air.

Slide-bars *34* — see crosshead.

Slide valves — see valves.

Smokebox *6* — a chamber at the front end of the boiler which

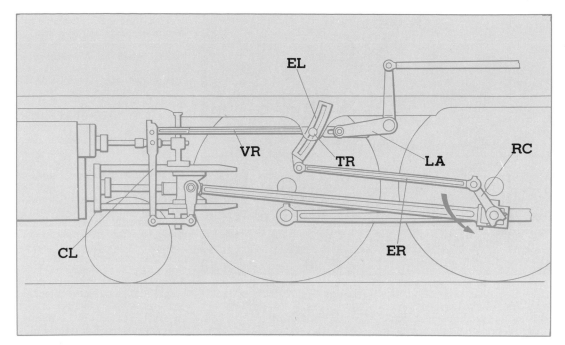

Above and below: *The parts of Walschaerts valve gear. The letters are referred to in the glossary description under* **Valve gears.** *(The diagram was produced from reference © Eleanora Steel.)*

serves to collect ashes drawn through the tubes. A partial vacuum formed in the smoke box by a jet of exhaust steam emerging from the blast pipe provides a flow of air from and through the fire.

Snifting valves — have the same function as by-pass valves but function by admitting air to the steam circuit at an appropriate point when a vacuum is formed in them.

Spark arrester — a device in the smokebox or chimney to prevent sparks being thrown.

Splashers *86* — Provided to cover the portion of large driving wheels if they protrude through the footplate or running board.

Spring hangers *92* — The tips of leaf springs on a locomotive are connected to the frames by links known as spring hangers.

Stays *68, 74, 83* — by its nature, the firebox of a locomotive cannot be circular like the front part of the boiler barrel. Its shape, therefore, needs retaining and this is done by a mass of rods known as stays connecting the firebox to the boiler shell.

Stuffing gland *19* — where a moving piston rod emerges from a cylinder in which steam at high pressure is contained, a form of gland containing packing is needed to prevent leakage.

Tank locomotive — one which carries supplies of fuel and water on its own chassis rather than on a separate tender.

Tender — a separate carriage for fuel and water attached to a locomotive.

Thermal efficiency — the proportion of the heat value of the fuel consumed which appears as useful work.

Thermic syphon — vertical or near vertical water ducts in the firebox provided with the idea of adding heating surface and improving circulation in the boiler.

Throttle (BR=regulator) — see regulator.

TIA — a form of water treatment, developed by Louis Armand of the French Railways, known as *Traitemant Intégral Armand.* It involved dosing the water in the tenders, regular tests of the acidity or alkalinity of the water in the boilers and decimated boiler repair costs in France and elsewhere.

Top feed — feed water is relatively cold and is best fed into the top of the boiler, with clack or check valves fitted there. Hence the term 'top feed'.

Tractive effort — this a theoretical figure which indicates how hard a locomotive can pull when 85% (usually) of full-boiler pressure is applied to the pistons.

Tubes — see firetubes.

Tyres — the wearing surfaces of locomotive wheels are steel tyres separate from the wheel centres.

Valves — three types of valves were used on steam locomotives. The **slide valve** was virtually universal during the first 75 years of steam construction. It consisted of a flat valve which slides on flat port face in the steam chest. A recess in the valve face connects the exhaust port with one or other cylinder according to the position of the valve. Also, according to the position of the valve, one or other cylinder port is exposed by its edge as it moves in time with the movement of the piston; steam can then flow into the appropriate end of the cylinder.

In the later years of steam **piston valves** became almost universal. The steam chest is cylindrical; boiler steam and exhaust steam are divided by two pistons which cover and uncover the cylindrical ports as the valves move. The boiler steam can be admitted either in between or outside the pistons; these arrangements are known as *inside admission* or *outside admission* respectively, the former being the most usual one.

A few steam locomotives used **poppet valves,** not dissimilar to those fitted to the family motor car.

Valve gears — provided in order to move the valves of a locomotive to a precise timing in relation to the movement of pistons. It is necessary to cope with requirements for early and late cut-off, as well as forward and reverse working. Numerous linkages have been devised to do this. Walschaert's gear became almost universal in the later days of steam. With reference to the diagram herewith, its working is as follows:—

A return crank RC is fixed to the main crank-pin so that its little end revolves 90° out of phase with the main motion. By means of the eccentric rod ER, a curved slotted link EL is oscillated about a centre TR. A die-block which slides in this link is pivoted to the Valve-Rod VR. It can be lowered by the lifting arm LA, in which case the fore-and-aft movement of the eccentric rod ER is transmitted to the valve rod VR. If LA is raised the movement of VR is reversed. In this way forward and reverse timing of the valve is catered for. By a partial movement of the lifting arm LA a reduced opening of the valve is provided. A combination lever CL serves to bias the opening of the valve towards the beginning of the stroke by, as it were, injecting a dose of the movement of the cross-head into the movement of the valve rod.

Baker valve gear is a version of Walschaerts which replaces the curved slotted link EL with a series of plain links and this was used to some extent in the USA in recent times.

Stephenson's gear would certainly rival Walschaerts if a count of the total number of sets fitted was the criterion. Other gears such as Allan, 'gab' and Gooch were used in small numbers and references are made to these linkages in the body of the book, as follows:

Stephenson see Beuth, page 30.
Gooch see 'Rover' class, page 46.
Allan see '79' class, page 40.
'Gab' see Beuth, page 30.

Water gauge — a glass tube fixed to the boiler to allow the water level to be seen — This is the most important indication that there is on a steam locomotive and hence the gauge is usually duplicated.

Westinghouse brake — see air brake.

Northumbrian 0-2-2 Great Britain: Liverpool & Manchester Railway (L&M), 1830

Tractive effort: 1,580lb (720kg).
Axle load: circa 6,500lb (3t).
Cylinders: (2) 11 x 16in (280 x 406mm).
Driving wheels: 52in (1,321mm).
Heating surface: 412sq ft (38m²).
Superheater: None.
Steam pressure: circa 50psi (3.5kg/cm²).
Grate area: circa 8sq ft (0.75m²).
Fuel (coke): circa 2,200lb (1t).
Water: circa 400gall (480 US) (1.8m³).
Adhesive weight: circa 6,500lb (3t).
Total weight: 25,500lb (11.5t).
Length overall: 24ft 0in (7,315mm).

Readers might be surprised that Stephenson's immortal *Rocket* does not lead this book's cavalcade of passenger-hauling steam locomotives. The reason for this is that between Rocket's triumph at the Rainhill trials in October 1829 and the opening of the world's first inter-city steam railway on 15 September 1830, there had been as many fundamental changes in steam locomotive design as were to occur over all the years that were to follow. Steam locomotives built in 1982 are no further from those built in 1830 than are those built in 1829—at any rate in fundamentals. Of course they got a little bigger and heavier—by a factor of 40 or thereabouts.

Northumbrian, which hauled the opening train on that disastrous opening day in 1830, had several important things which *Rocket* had not; first, she had a smokebox in which ashes drawn through the boiler tubes could accumulate. Second, the boiler was integrated with the water jacket round the firebox. These two things meant that the locomotive-type boiler, fitted to 99.9 per cent of the world's steam locomotives to be built over the next 150 years, had now fully arrived. The third thing was that the cylinders had now come down to the horizontal position —the axis of *Rocket's* cylinders were fairly steeply inclined at 35°

to the horizontal and not surprisingly the out-of-balance forces caused the locomotive to rock badly. Moreover, *Northumbrian's* cylinders were fitted in an accessible position, attached to but outside the wheels although, it is true, still at the wrong end. The *Northumbrian* weighed 7.35 tons less tender, nearly double the 4.25 tons of *Rocket* and her destructive forces were recognised by the provision of a front buffer beam complete with leather buffers stuffed with horse-hair. Another quite important improvement was the use of vertical iron plates as the main frames and a proper tender—rather than a barrel on wheels—was provided.

The features that made *Rocket* a success at the trials were continued in *Northumbrian*, but in larger and stronger form. The multi-tubular boiler—that is to say one which had numerous tubes instead of one big flue for the hot gases to pass through while they exchanged their heat with the water in the boiler. Numerous little tubes have a much greater surface area than one big flue of equivalent size and so heat is passed across to the water at a higher rate; hence such a boiler has high steam-raising capacity in relation to its size.

Below: *An early replica of Rocket before rebuilding.*

Above: *1980 replicas of 1829 locomotives. Rocket to left, Sans Pareil to right.*

The other important feature of *Rocket* was the blast-pipe, once more something that was fundamental to the success of 99.9 per cent of the steam locomotives ever built. By arranging that the exhaust steam was discharged through a jet up the chimney, a partial vacuum was set up at the chimney end. Air would rush in to fill this vacuum and the only way (it was hoped) it could do so was through the fire grate at the other end of the boiler. Hence there was a situation where the amount of air being drawn through the fire and thus the amount of heat produced would depend on the amount of steam being used. More than anything else, this automatic connection between the amount of heat needed and the amount supplied

Below: Northumbrian *depicted (so far as is known) in new condition, as the "brave little she-lion" so admired by Miss Kemble.*

was what gave the Stephensons, father and son, their triumph.

It also says enough that the boiler fitted to *Northumbrian* came to be known as the locomotive-type boiler. Of all the locomotives described in this book, only one (London & North Eastern No.10,000) had another type of boiler and only one (South African Railways' class "25") failed to have the blast-pipe. This was not through the lack of trying for something better, for many attempts were made to introduce new ideas. But only very few prevailed far enough to enter revenue service at all and, of course, none has managed to topple the Stephenson boiler from its throne whilst steam traction exists. Incidentally, credit for suggesting the multi-tubular boiler was attributed by Robert Stephenson to a Mr Henry Booth, treasurer of the L&M Company.

As regards the mechanical part of *Northumbrian*, the principle of having two and only two cylinders outside the frames and directly connected to the driving wheels became more and more the world standard as the years went by. Towards the end of steam this principle became virtually universal, apart from articulated locomotives. Even so, the actual *layout* of Northumbrian's machinery had serious drawbacks.

Because the driving wheels were at the front, the heavy firebox and the heavy cylinders were at the end where the *carrying* wheels were. There was only a box full of smoke at the other end and yet the driving wheels needed all the weight the track could stand to keep them from slipping Moreover, when the

Top right: *A contemporary engraving of the Stephenson* Northumbrian. *Note the headlights, and the crew's attire.*

Above: A dubious wooden replica of Northumbrian constructed in 1930 for the L&M centenary celebrations.

engine began pulling the force on the drawbar tended to lift the front end of the engine, thereby further reducing the weight available for adhesion.

Another problem arose through the combination of outside cylinders with a short wheelbase. The alternate piston-thrusts tended to swing the engine about a vertical axis so that it proceeded with a boxing motion and in a serpentine manner. It was not until the *Northumbrian* layout was considerably altered by having an extended wheelbase and moving the cylinders to the front that these problems were solved. In the meantime the route of development left the main line for a branch, as we shall see.

A rather dubious feature of *Northumbrian* was the primitive means of reversing. An eccentric —a device to convert rotation to oscillation — was provided on the driving axle in order to move the valve of each cylinder. To reverse the direction of rotation, the eccentric on each side has to be turned nearly 180 degrees relative to the crank. It is easy to leave the eccentrics loose on the axle and provide stops so that they take up the correct position whichever way the wheels turn. The drawback to this simple and excellent valve gear is that it is difficult to devise an arrangement to move the eccentrics upon the axle while the engine is stationary that is not complicated and inconvenient. Otherwise the locomotive can only be reversed by giving a push.

Both *Rocket* and *Northumbrian* had such an arrangement; one snag was that it could not be used while in motion. This was vividly demonstrated on that opening day. When William Huskisson MP, stepped out into the path of *Rocket*, Joseph Locke who was driving had no means of *breaking* (to use the spelling of the day) and the famous accident took place. *Northumbrian* covered herself with glory in rushing the fatally injured man to medical aid, but to no avail.

Northumbrian is regarded as belonging to the "Rocket" class, seven examples of which had previously been delivered to the Liverpool & Manchester Railway in 1829 and 1830. *Rocket's* immediate successors, *Meteor, Comet, Dart* and *Arrow,* were delivered with the cylinders in an almost horizontal position, while *Rocket* was so altered very quickly. *Phoenix* also had a smokebox and so did *North Star. Majestic,* which followed *Northumbrian,* also had all the new features. Only *Rocket's* remains survive, in London's Science Museum, but in fact they come much closer to the later engines than *Rocket* as delivered.

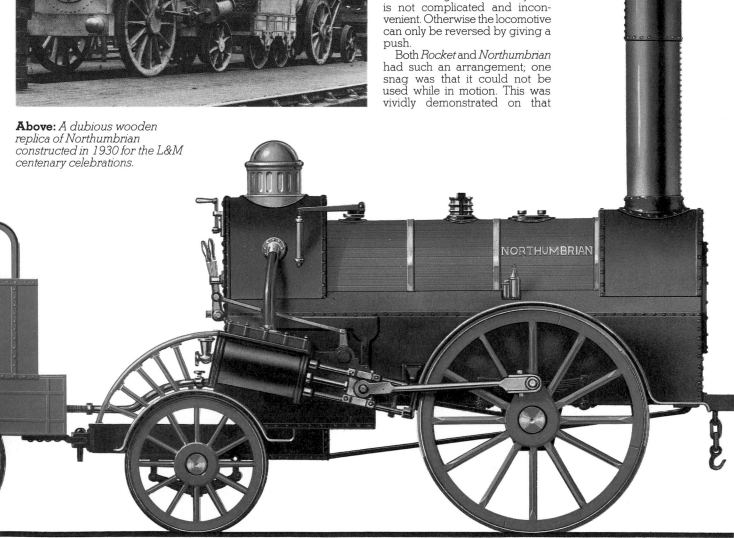

Planet Class 2-2-0
Great Britain: Liverpool & Manchester Railway, 1830

Tractive effort: circa 1,450lb (660kg).
Axle load: 11,250lb (5t).
Cylinders: (2) 11½ x 16in (292 x 406mm).
Driving wheels: 62in (1,575mm).
Heating surface: 407sq ft (38m²).
Superheater: None.
Steam pressure: circa 50psi (3.5kg/cm²).
Grate area: 7.2sq ft (0.67m²).
Fuel (coke): circa 2,200lb (1t).
Water: circa 400gall (480 US) (1.8m³).
Adhesive weight: 11,250lb (5t).
Total weight: 29,500lb (13.5t).
Length overall: 24ft 4in (7,420mm).

Planet arrived on the Liverpool & Manchester Railway in October 1830, soon after it was opened. The Stephensons had changed two things since they completed *Northumbrian* only a few weeks before. The first one was to put the cylinders at the front end instead of the back. This helped to get a good weight distribution; the drive was on to the rear pair of wheels which supported the heavy firebox, and, moreover, 99 per cent of the world's steam locomotives were to have two horizontal cylinders at the front end.

The second thing which was done was aimed at curing the "boxing" motion which plagued the earlier locomotives. This was achieved by putting the cylinders between instead of outside the wheels and connecting them to the driving wheels by making the main axle in the form of a double crank. Crank-axles continued to present a serious technical problem, not only in themselves but also because the big-end bearings of the connecting rods had to be

split—and hence weakened—so that they could be removed and replaced. Even so, some 5 per cent of the world's steam locomotives were to have two inside cylinders and crank-axles; Robert Stephenson & Co. supplied some to British Railways as late as 1953.

Planet was quite successful and many of these engines, some with four coupled wheels, were made both by the Stephensons and by others. Outstanding amongst the imitations was a 2-2-0 called *Old Ironsides*, built in Philadelphia, USA in 1832 by a Matthias Baldwin. Starting with this first full-size locomotive Baldwin went on to build up the greatest locomotive manufactory the world has ever known, with a production of 60,000 locomotives during the 130 years of its existence. It is said that Baldwin had such trouble getting payment for

his first locomotive that he declared he would build no more! The Stephensons, on the other hand, when they developed *Planet* into their celebrated six-wheel locomotives, decided that this time they would discourage imitators by taking out a patent.

Even so it was *Planet* that finally convinced a sceptical world that a form of reliable mechanical transport had arrived and that the Stephensons

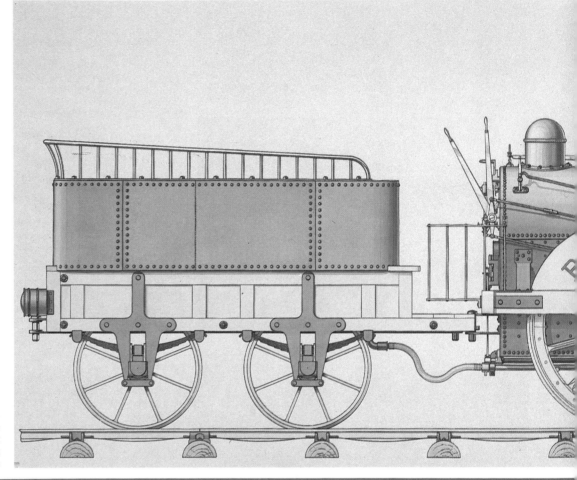

Best Friend of Charleston 0-4-0 Tank
United States: South Carolina Railroad (SCRR), 1830

Tractive effort: 453lb (206kg).
Axle load: 4,500lb (2t).
Cylinders: (2) 6 x 16in (152 x 406mm).
Driving wheels: 54in (1,371mm).
Steam Pressure: 50psi (3.5kg/cm²).
Grate area: 2.2sq ft (2m²).
Fuel (coke): not recorded.
Water: 140gall (165 US) (0.64m³).
Adhesive weight: 9,000lb (4t).
Total weight: 9,000lb (4t).
Length overall: 14ft 9in (4,496mm).

History was certainly made on 15th January 1831, the day when the first full-size steam locomotive to be built in the United States went into service. This was *Best Friend of Charleston,* running on the New World's first commercial steam railway, the South Carolina Railroad. This little contraption foreshadowed the building of 170,000 further steam loco-

were the people to provide it. Soon enough it took them from a humble cottage by the Tyne to being millionaires in the £'s of those days, as well as a name that is and will be remembered wherever and while railways exist.

Below: *A drawing of the* Planet *locomotive of the Liverpool & Manchester Railway, Stephenson's first inside-cylinder locomotive.*

Brother Jonathan 4-2-0

United States:
Mohawk & Hudson Railroad (M&HRR), 1832

Tractive effort: circa 1,023lb (464kg).
Axle load: 7,000lb (3.2t).
Cylinders: (2) 9½ x 16in (241 x 406mm).
Driving wheels: 60in (1,524mm).
Boiler: details not recorded.
Boiler pressure: circa 50psi (3.5kg/cm²).
Adhesive weight: circa 7,000lb (3.2t).
Total weight*: 14,000lb (6.4t).
Length overall*: 16ft 5½in (5,017mm).
*Engine only without tender.

Above: Brother Jonathan, a *pioneer bogie locomotive.*

As regards express passenger trains, certainly one of the great benefactors of mankind was John B. Jarvis, who in 1832 introduced the pivoted leading truck or bogie into the locomotive story, an idea suggested to him by Robert Stephenson when he visited England. Although very few particulars have survived, this little 4-2-0, originally known as *Experiment,* was the vehicle used. This pathfinding design of locomotive was built at the West Point Foundry in New York and delivered to the Mohawk & Hudson River Railroad.

Amongst the features of the locomotive, one notes that the boiler was rather small (copied from Robert Stephenson's "Planet" type) and that there was room for the connecting rods in the space between the sides of the firebox and the main frames, which were situated outside the driving wheels. These in turn were located behind the firebox, as on a Crampton locomotive.

None of these other features became the norm on the world's locomotives, but as regards express passenger locomotives, the four-wheel bogie certainly is much used. It will be found that all the classes of locomotive described in this book have leading four wheel bogies according to the principle pioneered with *Brother Jonathan.* Incidentally, Brother Jonathan was then an impolite way of referring to the English; no doubt the name was a gesture of triumph at having thrown off any possible continued dependence on English technology.

The idea was to provide guidance by having two wheels pressing against the outer rail of curves as near as possible in a tangential attitude. For any particular radius, or even at a kink in the track, the bogie would take up an angle so that the three contact points between wheel and rail on each side would lie correctly on the curve. This was particularly important on the light rough tracks of the time.

This locomotive demonstrated very clearly that the principle was a sound one and for many years thereafter the majority of American locomotives of all kinds had the advantage of this device. *Brother Jonathan* itself was successful in other ways; converted later to a 4-4-0 it had a long and useful life.

Below: *A replica of* Brother Jonathan, *alias* Experiment.

---

motives for service in the USA during the years to come. *Best Friend* was constructed at the West Point Foundry in New York in late 1830. Features included a vertical boiler, a well tank integral with the locomotive, four coupled wheels and two modestly inclined cylinders. It was built at the West Point Foundry in New York to the design of E.L. Miller, engineer of the South Carolina Railroad.

Although, apart from the coupled wheels, none of its principles of design were adopted generally, the locomotive was quite successful, but the next one built for this railroad followed the same principles only as regards mechanical parts—the later version had a horizontal boiler, the first to be built in America. Even so, the original design could

Left: Best Friend of Charleston. *Some contemporary accounts tell of additional cylinders driving the tender wheels.*

handle a train of five cars carrying more than 50 passengers at 20mph (32km/h).

In one rather tragic way, however, the locomotive did contribute to the story of steam traction development. The firemen had become annoyed with the noise of steam escaping from the safety valves and used to tie down the lever which controlled them. One day in June 1831 he did this once too often—and the boiler exploded and he was killed. In due time tamper-proof valves became the rule—people normally need shock before they take action.

Later, the locomotive was rebuilt with a new boiler and re-entered service, appropriately named *Phoenix.* By 1834, the South Carolina Railroad went the whole 154 miles from Charleston to Hamburg, just across the river from the city of Augusta, Georgia. When opened, this was by far the longest railway in the world.

Vauxhall 2-2-0
Ireland:
Dublin & Kingstown Railway, 1834

Tractive effort: circa 1,550lb (700kg).
Cylinders: (2) 11 x 18in (280 x 457mm).
Driving wheels: 60in (1,524mm).
Steam pressure: circa 50psi (3.5kg/cm²).
Overall length: circa 24ft (7,315mm).

George Forrester of Liverpool was a locomotive builder whose name is now hardly known; yet he introduced two fundamental improvements in the mechanism of the steam locomotive, one of which prevailed to the end of steam. The other was also an important move forward.

How *Northumbrian* had two outside cylinders but at the wrong end and how *Planet* had two cylinders at the front but hidden away inside, has already been described. With *Vauxhall*, constructed in 1832 for the Dublin & Kingstown Railway, Forrester

built the world's first locomotive with accessible outside cylinders placed horizontally at the leading end. Incidentally, the D&K line was built to the English standard gauge of 4ft 8½in (1,435mm); it was long before the days when the railway gauge in Ireland was standardised at 5ft 3in (1,600mm).

So already the cylinders had reached their final position with this arrangement. Since then it has been applied to most of the world's locomotives built over the subsequent 150 years, even though express passenger locomotives are the ones most prone to being given sophisticated cylinder layouts.

One way in which the Forrester engines differed from modern steam locomotives (except for those built for very narrow gauges) was that the cylinders may have been outside the frames, but the frames were outside the wheels. Separate cranks were provided at the

ends of the axles. Even so, in later years this arrangement was much used on locomotives which ran on very narrow gauges, that is, 3ft (914mm) or less.

Forrester's fundamental improvement of the valve gear was also important but as a stepping-stone rather than an arrangement which became much used in the long term. It has been mentioned that the "slip eccentric" valve gear was difficult to reverse from the cab, so Forrester provided a separate eccentric set for each direction for each cylinder—making four in all on the driving axle. The reversing lever could move the eccentric rods (which were set vertically) and engage or disengage the appropriate valve pin by means of V-shaped "gabs" fitted to the ends of the rods. No skill was required as in the previous arrangement, merely enough muscle to move the reversing lever into the appro-

priate position. But it could not be used while the engine was in motion.

Another feature of the first Forrester locomotives which was not repeated was the substitution of a swing-link parallel motion. This was intended to constrain the joint between the end of the piston rod and the little end of the connecting rod to travel in a straight line, even when the latter was at an angle and therefore trying to force the former out of line. The Stephensons had previously used a cross-head running between slide-bars for this purpose and this simple arrangement has never been displaced from its throne. The only engine apart from *Vauxhall* in this book which did not have it was the "Turbomotive" and that one only because there were no cylinders!

Wide apart outside cylinders combined with a short wheelbase was not a recipe for steady

Bury 2-2-0
Great Britain:
London & Birmingham Railway (L&B), 1837

Tractive effort: 1,386lb (629kg).
Axle load: 12,600lb (5.7t).
Cylinders: (2) 11 x 16½in (280 x 415mm).
Driving wheels: 60¾in (1,546mm).
Heating surface: 357sq ft (33.2m²).
Superheater: None.
Steam pressure: 50psi (3.5kg/cm²).
Grate area: 7sq ft (0.65m²).
Fuel (coke): c2,200lb (1t).
Water: c400gall (480 US) (1.8m³).
Adhesive weight: 12,600lb (5.7t).
Total weight: 22,000lb (10.0t).
Length overall: 26ft 9½in (8,168mm).

Edward Bury had a small engineering works in Liverpool and in 1829 he began work on a locomotive with a view to entering it for the Rainhill trials, but it was not completed in time. In the end he supplied the locomotive, which was called *Liverpool*, to the Liverpool & Manchester Railway during 1830. It had two large coupled wheels 72in. (1829mm) in diameter. It had cylinders arranged like *Planet's* but, unlike *Planet*, had frames formed of bars rather than plates. This was a significant innovation, for Bury sold some bar-framed locomotives to America and bar frames for many years became a trademark of engines built on that side of the Atlantic; this went

on until bar frames were superseded by cast steel ones. Bury managed to secure the contract for providing locomotives for the London and Birmingham Railway, by far the most important railway to be completed in the 1830s. All 58 of these passenger 2-2-0s had been supplied by 1841.

One problem with these locomotives was their small size and this was a fundamental limitation of the design, rather than something that could be overcome just by a little stretching. Bury considered rightly that pressure vessels should be circular and so his outer firebox was circular in plan and domed on top, attached to a normal cylindrical barrel by circumferential joint. The inner

fire-box was D-shaped, with the flat part facing towards the front, to allow the insertion of the tubes at right angles. The trouble was that with the circular shape the length could not be larger than the width. Since the width was also limited, because it had to go between the wheels, the size of the fire (and hence the power output) was strictly limited. Nor could the frames be extended backwards past the round firebox, so a 2-2-2 development would cause some difficulty.

So in 1837 England's first long-distance trunk railway route out of London was opened, using a fleet of locomotives that were under-powered even by the standards of the day. For

running and by 1836 these 2-2-0s, as well as others supplied to the Liverpool & Manchester, London & Greenwich and other railways had been converted to 2-2-2s. Even so, on the opening day in Ireland, 31mph (50km/h) was achieved; passengers were delighted and amazed that they could read and write with ease while moving at this stupendous speed. Few particulars of this pathfinding engine have survived, but the details missing from the specification above would approximate to those of *Planet* (see page 20).

Left: *George Forrester's* Vauxhall *locomotive built for the Dublin & Kingstown Railway in 1834. Note the horizontal outside cylinders at the front end, a mechanical arrangement which most of the world's locomotive engineers followed in time.*

example, in the same year the London to Bristol railway (then under construction) received a Stephenson 2-2-2 called *North Star* which had double the grate area and double the adhesive weight of a Bury 2-2-0.

The small size and power of these engines had advantages. They were cheap to build and reliable in service—the low stresses on the crank axles brought these always trouble-

some items more within the scope of the technology of the day. And if heavy passenger trains needed two or three locomotives (or even four) at the head, then so be it. Labour was cheap, while powerful locomotives were expensive as well as relatively untried.

Assuming that Bury was right in thinking like this in 1837—and there are many subsequent examples in locomotive history—his railway had certainly fallen behind

the times a few years later.

Below: *2-2-0 No.1 of the London & Birmingham Railway, the most important line to have been opened during the 1830s. Edward Bury designed these rather small locomotives which tended to be a little underpowered for express passenger work. Even so, they were cheap and*

reliable and Bury held on to his principles of little-and-often in locomotive design for many years, in fact until he was forced to resign in 1847. This was soon after the LNWR had been formed from the amalgamation of the Grand Junction and London & Birmingham lines.

Adler 2-2-2
Germany:
Nuremberg-Fürth Railway, 1835

Tractive effort: 1,220lb (550kg).
Axle load: 13,250lb (6t).
Cylinders: 9 x 16in (229 x 406mm).
Driving wheels: 54in (1,371mm).
Heating surface: 196sq ft (18.2m²).
Superheater: None.
Steam pressure: 60psi (4.2kg/cm²).
Grate area: 5.2sq ft (0.48m²).
Adhesive weight: 13,250lb (6t).
Total weight*: 31,500lb (14.5t).
Length overall: 25ft 0in (7,620mm).
*Engine only—tender details not available.

The first locomotive to be built in Germany was constructed in 1816, but it was unsuccessful, as was a second one built in the following year. It was not until 7 December 1835 that successful steam locomotion was inaugurated in the country, with the opening of the Nuremberg to Fürth railway, known as the Ludwigsbahn, after Ludwig I of Bavaria, who had given his royal assent to the railway in 1834.

The promoter of the railway, Herr Scharrer, tried Robert Stephenson & Co of Newcastle for the supply of material to the line, but Stephenson's prices were considered to be too high, and Scharrer therefore resolved to "buy German". Two Wurtembergers then contracted to supply an engine for the equivalent of £565, "equal to the best English engines and not requiring more fuel". Time passed and Scharrer enquired about the progress of his engine, only to find that the

contractors had decamped to Austria. He pursued them there, and was told that the price had doubled. The opening of the railway was approaching, and Scharrer had no alternative but to place an urgent order with Robert Stephenson on 15 May 1835 for a 2-2-2 locomotive, at a price of £1,750 delivered to the line.

Despite the historical importance of this engine, information about it is scanty, even its name being uncertain. Early references are to "Der Adler" (The Eagle), but more recently it has dropped the definite article, and is usually known simply as "Adler". Surviving records of the builder do not record details of the engine, but contemporary illustrations show a locomotive resembling the "Patentee", supplied to the Liverpool and Manchester Railway in 1834, developments of which figure largely amongst products of Stephenson's Newcastle works at this period.

In 1830 Robert Stephenson & Co supplied to the L&MR a 2-2-0 named "Planet", which was notable as being the first engine with inside cylinders and a crank axle. However, the art of forging axles was new, and the combination of the forces from the flanges of the wheels and from the connecting rods soon showed the vulnerability of these delicate forgings. In 1833, therefore, Robert Stephenson designed a 2-2-2 locomotive, in which the driving wheels had no flanges, so that the crank axle was relieved of flange forces. A further advantage of the extra axle was that the axle loading was reduced, a desirable measure, as the axle

loading of Stephenson's engines supplied to the L&M had been increasing steadily since "Rocket", which had been built to the severe weight restrictions which the directors of the railway deemed necessary.

The improvements incorporated in the 2-2-2 were patented, and the first engine to incorporate the patents was named "Patentee". This engine weighed 11.45 tons, but the weight of "Adler" was quoted in English sources as 6.6 tons, and in German sources as 14 tonnes, with 6 tonnes on the driving axle. A similar uncertainty applies to the boiler pressure, which has been quoted in an English source as

Campbell 4-4-0
United States:
Philadelphia, Germanstown & Norriston Railroad (PG&NRR), 1837

Tractive effort: 4,373lb (1,984kg).
Axle load: 8,000lb (3.6t)..
Cylinders: (2) 14 x 15¾in 9356 x 400mm).
Driving wheels: 54in. (1,370mm).
Heating surface: 723sq ft (67.2m²).
Superheater: None.
Steam pressure: 90psi (6.3kg/cm²).
Grate area: Circa 12sq ft (1.1m²).
Adhesive weight: 16,000lb (7.25t).
Length overall:* 16ft 5½in (5,017mm).
*Engine only—tender details not known.

Henry Campbell, engineer to the Philadelphia, Germanstown & Norriston Railroad had the idea of combining coupled wheels, as fitted to *Best Friend of Charleston*, with the leading truck of *Brother Johnathan*. In this way he could double the adhesive weight, while at the same time have a locomotive that could ride

satisfactorily round sharp or irregular curves. He patented the idea and went to a local mechanic called James Brooks (not the Brooks who founded the famous Brooks Loco Works of Dunkirk,

New York) and he produced the world's first 4-4-0 in May 1837.

Although in fact this locomotive was intended for coal traffic, it has its place here as the prototype of perhaps the most numerous

and successful of all passenger-hauling wheel arrangements.

The layout of *Brother Johnathan* was followed, the additional driving axle being coupled to the first by cranks outside the frames. The cylinders were thus inside the frames, driving the leading coupled wheels by means of a crank axle, an arrangement which was to become popular on a few railways back in Europe, even if very rarely repeated in America. The high boiler pressure is notable for the time. Whilst this remarkable locomotive demonstrated great potential, the flexibility provided in order to cope with poorly lined tracks was not accompanied with flexibility in a vertical plane to help with the humps and hollows in them. In consequence, Campbell's 4-4-0 was not in itself successful.

Left: *The world's first 4-4-0, designed by Henry R. Campbell, engineer to the Philadelphia Germanstown and Norriston Railroad. It was built in 1837 by James Brooks of Philadelphia.*

60lb/sq in (4.2kg/cm²), and in a German source as 47lb/sq in (3.3kg/cm²). Amongst details of the engine which are known are that it had 62 copper tubes, and that it had shifting eccentrics. The "Adler" was followed by other engines of similar type from Stephenson's. It remained at work until 1857, when it was sold, without wheels and some

other parts, for its scrap value.

In preparation of the centenary of the Nuremberg-Fürth Railway, a working replica of the engine was built at the Kaiserslautern Works of DR. This replica is now in the transport museum at Nuremberg. A second non-working replica was made in 1950 for use at exhibitions. Both are based on contemporary paintings.

Left: *This* Adler *replica was built for the German State Railways' centenary celebrations in 1935. It appeared in the ill-starred "der Stahltier" film, whose director was imprisoned by the Nazis for emphasising* Adler's *English origin.*

Below: Adler *was built for the Nuremburg-Fürth Railway in 1835. This was the first railway to be built in what is now known as Germany, but the locomotive was built by the famous firm of Stephenson & Son of Newcastle-upon-Tyne, England.*

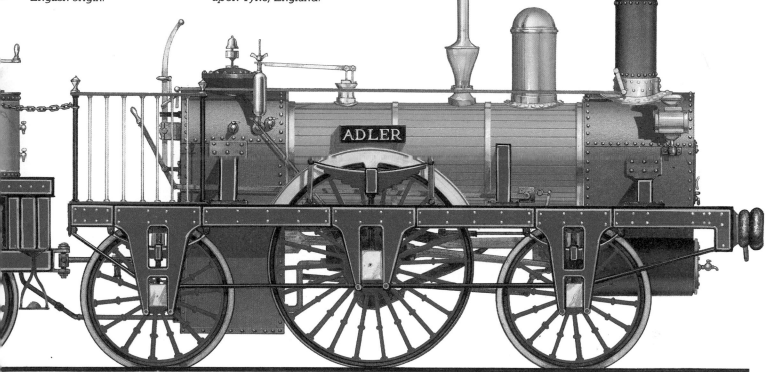

Hercules 4-4-0
United States:
Beaver Meadows Railroad, 1837

Tractive effort: 4,507lb (2,045kg).
Axle load: circa 10,000lb (4.5t).
Cylinders (2) 12 x 18in (305 x 457mm).
Driving wheels: 44in (1,117mm).
Steam pressure: 90lb/sq in (6.3kg/cm²).
Adhesive weight: circa 20,000lb (9t).
Total weight: *30,000lb (14t).
Length overall: 18ft 11in (2,564mm).
*Without tender—boiler and tender details not recorded.

In 1836, the Beaver Meadows Railroad ordered a 4-4-0 from Garrett & Eastwick, in nearby Philadelphia. The workshop foreman, Joseph Harrison, had become aware of the problems encountered by Henry Campbell in keeping all the wheels of his 4-4-0 pressing on the rail, yet he also remembered 4-2-0 *Brother Jonathan* of 1832 which sat on the rough tracks like a three-

legged stool on the floor. The saying "right as a trivet" comes vividly to mind, the three legs being, respectively, the two driving wheels and the pivot of the leading bogie or truck. There was also the example of one or two early 4-2-0s by Norris, also of Philadelphia. Harrison had the idea of making his two pairs of driving wheels into a kind of non-swivelling bogie by connecting the axle bearings on each side by a large cast iron beam,

pivoted at its centre. The pivots were connected to the main-frame of the locomotive by a large leaf spring on either side.

In this way eight wheels were made to support the body of the locomotive at three points. It was a brilliant notion which solved the problem of running on rough tracks and was the basis of the three-point compensated springing system which was applied to most of the world's locomotives from simple ones up to 4-12-2s.

Hercules was well named and many similar locomotives were supplied. Joseph Harrison was made a partner in the firm which (since Garrett was retiring) became known as Eastwick & Harrison. The famous "American Standard" 4-4-0, of which 25,000 were built for the USA alone, was directly derived from this most innovative engine.

Left: Hercules, *built by Garrett & Eastwick of Philadelphia in 1836, marked an important step forward in locomotive development.*

Lafayette 4-2-0

United States:
Baltimore & Ohio Railroad (B&O), 1837

Tractive effort: 2,162lb (957kg).
Axle load: 13,000lb (6t).
Cylinders: (2) 10½ x 18in (268 x 457mm).
Driving wheels: 48in (1,220mm).
Heating surface: 394sq ft (36.6m²).
Superheater: None.
Steam pressure: 60psi (4.2kg/cm²).
Grate area: 8.6sq ft (0.80m²).
Fuel (coke): 2,200lb (1t).
Water: 450gall (540 US) (2m³).
Adhesive weight: 30,000lb (5t).
Total weight: 44,000lb (20t).
Length overall: 30ft 40¼in (9,250mm).

The so-called Norris locomotives have a very important place in locomotive history, being a design which took steam another great step forward.

William Norris had been building locomotives in Philadelphia since 1831. Although a draper by trade, after a few years in partnership with a Colonel Stephen Long, he set up on his own and by the beginning of 1836 had produced some seven locomotives. In that year he built a 4-2-0 for the Philadelphia & Columbia Railroad called *Washington County Farmer*. In arrangement it bore some resemblance to *Brother Johnathan* with leading bogie, but the two cylinders were outside the wheels

and frames and the valves were on top of the cylinders. The driving wheels were in front of rather than behind the firebox, so increasing the proportion of the engine's weight carried on them.

In this way the final form of the steam express passenger locomotive had almost arrived. *Northumbrian* had the locomotive-type boiler and two outside cylinders; *Planet* had the cylinders at the front while Forrester's *Vauxhall* had cylinders outside and at the front. Bury's locomotives had the bar frames and *Brother Jonathan* had the bogie. Now we find outside cylinders, bar frames and a leading bogie in combination.

In 1827, the Baltimore & Ohio Railroad was the first public railroad for passengers and freight transport to receive a charter. It was opened for twelve miles out of Baltimore in 1830, but for a number of years horses provided haulage power—although there were trials with steam locomotives. Steam took over in 1834 in the form of vertical-boiler locomotives, known as the "Grasshopper" type.

The Ohio River was reached in 1842 via a route which then included a series of rope-worked inclined planes, but long before this more powerful locomotives than could be encompassed within the vertical-boiler concept were needed. The B&O management were impressed with Norris'

Washington County Farmer and asked him to build a series of eight similar engines. The first was *Lafayette* delivered in 1837; it was the first B&O locomotive to have a horizontal boiler. Edward Bury's circular domed firebox and bar frames were there and the engine is said to have had cam-operated valves of a pattern devised by Ross Winans of the B&O. It says enough that later members of the class had the normal "gab" motion of the day.

The locomotives were a great success, giving much better performance at reduced fuel consumption. They were also relatively reliable and needed few repairs. The same year Norris built a similar locomotive for the Champlain & St. Lawrence Railway in Canada. This was the first proper locomotive exported from America, and the hill-climbing ability of these remarkable locomotives led to many further sales abroad.

The first Old World customer was the Vienna-Raab Railway and their locomotive *Philadelphia* was completed in late 1837. Before the locomotive was shipped it was put to haul a train weighing 200 tons up a 1 in 100 (1 per cent) gradient, a feat then described as the greatest performance by a locomotive engine so far recorded. Railways in Austria (not the small republic we know today but a great empire also embracing much of what is now Czechoslovakia, Poland, Rou-

mania and Jugoslavia) were the best customers, but even before 1840 Norris had also sent his 4-2-0s to the Brunswick and Berlin & Potsdam Railways in Germany. A large fleet of 15 went to the Birmingham and Gloucester Railway in Britain, where they had some success in easing the problems involved in taking trains up the 1 in 37 (2.7 per cent) Lickey Incline at Bromsgrove in Worcestershire.

The demand for Norris locomotives was so great that the firm was able to offer the design in a range of four standard sizes. Class "C" had a cylinder bore of 9in (229mm), class "B" 10½in (268mm), class "A" 11½in (292mm), class "A extra" 12½in (318mm). Grate areas were, respectively, 6.4, 7.3, 7.9 and 9.5sq ft (0.6, 0.69, 0.73 and 0.88in²) while engine weights were 15,750, 20,600, 24,100 and 29,650lb (7.1, 9.4, 10.9 and 13.45t).

The Norris locomotives which came to England were particularly interesting as of course the English railway engineers were more accustomed to sending engines abroad rather than importing them. Seventeen locomotives came over from Philadelphia between March 1839 and May 1842 and they included examples of the three larger out of the four standard Norris sizes. There were nine B's, three A's and five A extras, the latter used as bankers on the heavy grade.

Certain improvements were made to reduce what was originally a very high coal consumption on the arduous banking duties. All five A-extras were converted to tank locomotives and this saved hauling the weight of the tenders. Steam blown from the safety valves and some exhaust steam was turned back into the new saddle tanks. Copper fireboxes replaced iron ones and various other examples of rather shaky workmanship replaced. The result was that a coal consumption of 92lb/mile (26kg/km) in 1841 was reduced by 53 per cent by 1843.

The best of the Norris engines remained in service until 1856.

In his native America, Norris' list of other customers in the 1830s included 27 predecessors of the railroads of the great age of steam, situated in Connecticut, Georgia, Louisiana, Maryland, Massachusetts, New York State, North Carolina, Pennsylvania, Tennessee and Virginia. One of them, the Richmond, Fredericksburg and Potomac Railroad, is even still trading under the same name today. Norris went on to become for a time the largest locomotive builder in the USA, supplying 4-4-0s, 0-6-0s and finally 4-6-0s in addition to the 4-2-0s which made his name. On the other hand the success of these engines in Europe did not bring commensurate prosperity there. Although William Norris and his brother Octavius went to Vienna in 1844 and set up a locomotive building plant, it was other builders who adopted Norris' ideas, produced hundreds of locomotives based on them, and made the money.

The first of the European builders who built Norris-type locomotives was John Haswell of Vienna. Others were Sigl, also of Vienna and Guenther of Austria, Cockerill of Belgium, Borsig, Emil Kessler and his successor the Esslingen Co of Germany. In Britain, Hick of Bolton and Nasmyth of Manchester also built 4-2-0s of this pattern. A 4-2-0 called *La Junta* supplied to Cuba circa 1840, was for many years preserved at the United Railways of Havana station in Havana. No reports have been received either of its survival or destruction. A full-size replica of an early Norris locomotive was constructed in the USA about 1941 and was reported to be preserved on the Tallulah Falls Railway in northern Georgia.

Below: *A typical standard Norris 4-2-0 locomotive is portrayed in this side view. The elementary controls of a locomotive of the 1840s can all be clearly seen. The horizontal handle behind the firebox is the throttle, while the vertical one alongside the firebox controls the "gab" reversing gear. The spring balance pressure gauge is above the firebox together with the whistle. A brake on the engine was regarded as a luxury.*

Above: *The gravestones in the churchyard at Bromsgrove, Worcestershire, in memory of a locomotive crew who were killed in a boiler explosion in November 1870. The engine concerned was not a Norris one, but nevertheless the headstones display carvings of locomotives of this type, more typical of the railway at Bromsgrove.*

Fire Fly Class 2-2-2

Great Britain:
Great Western Railway (GWR), 1840

Tractive effort: 2049lb (929kg).
Axle load: 25,000lb (11.2t).
Cylinders: (2) 15 x 18in 381 x 457mm).
Driving wheels: 84in (2,134mm).
Heating surface: 700sq ft (65m²).
Superheater: None.
Steam pressure: 50psi (3.5kg/cm²).
Grate area: 13.5sq ft (1.25m²).
Fuel (coke): 3400lb (1.5t).
Water: 1,800 gall (2,160 US). (8.25m³).
Adhesive weight: 25,000lb (11.2t).
Total weight: 92,500lb (42t).
Length overall: 39ft 4in (11,989mm).

In 1833 Isambard Kingdom Brunel was made engineer to what he referred as "the finest work in England". He was not one to be a follower and he thought little of what he called contemptuously "the coal waggon gauge". He said, "I thought the means employed was not commensurate with the task to be done . . ." and accordingly chose a gauge for his railway almost 50 per cent

Right: Centaur was one of Daniel Gooch's famous standard locomotives, and was built by Nasmyth, Gaskell & Co. of Manchester, and delivered in 1841. It ceased work in 1867.

larger than the one employed by the Stephensons. This 7ft 0¼in (2,140mm) gauge was the largest ever employed by any railway in the world.

When it came to locomotive matters the Great Western Railway was truly great, but this was not so at the beginning. Brunel perhaps a little casually had ordered a series of locomotives from various manufacturers; and it was not one of his best efforts. They were given a free hand within certain almost impossible constraints, that is, that the weight of a six-wheeled locomotive should not exceed 10½ tons and that piston speeds should not exceed 280ft per minute (85m per minute) at 30mph (48km/h). The results were totally unsatisfactory and in its earliest days the GWR had only one locomotive upon which it could rely, the fortuitously acquired Stephenson six-wheel 'Patentee' locomotive *North Star* which weighed 18.2 tons, over 75 per cent above Brunel's stipulated weight. Even the piston speed at 30mph (48km/h) was over the top at 320ft/min (98 m/min).

To take charge of the locomotives Brunel had engaged a young

man called Daniel Gooch, a north countryman who had worked with the Stephensons. Following long struggles — often all night — in the running shed at Paddington with the collection of not-too-mobile disasters which formed the GWR locomotive fleet of the time, Gooch formed some very strong views on what should have been done. In the end when it was clear that no sort of timetable could be kept to with things as they were, Gooch had to report over this chief's head upon the situation to the Directors. Brunel was angry but soon made it up and the two remained friends as well as colleagues until the older man's death in 1859.

Eventually Gooch was responsible for drawing up plans and specifications for a wholly practical fleet of more than 100 six-wheeled locomotives, based again on Stephenson's 'Patentees', and including 2-4-0s and 0-6-0s for freight work, as well as 2-2-2s for passenger traffic. Boilers, tenders, motion and many other parts were common to all the types — it was standardisation on a scale the world had never seen before. This time the manufacturers were allowed no latitude — as was to be the case so often in future years, there were only two ways to do things — the Great Western Way and the Wrong Way. As well as drawings, templates were issued to the makers; moreover, the builders were responsible for any repairs needed during the first 1,000 miles (1,600km) running with proper loads. Sixty-two of the

locomotives were for express trains and these concern us. The first of these to be delivered was *Fire Fly* which came from Jones, Turner & Evans, Newton-le-Willows, Lancashire, in March 1840, to be followed by *Spit Fire, Wild Fire, Fire Ball, Fire King* and *Fire Brand* from the same firm. On 17 March *Fire Fly* took a special train from Twyford to Paddington in 37 minutes for the 30¾ miles (49.5km). The maximum speed was 58mph (93 km/h). By the end of 1840, for the opening to Wootton Bassett beyond Swindon, a further 25 of these locomotives were available and a timetable worthy of the name could be issued at last.

None of these little fire-horses had their dignity insulted by the attachment of numbers, but there was some attempt at giving related names to the products of each supplier. The results, showing some considerable bias towards the classics, were:

Sharp, Roberts and Co, Manchester: *Tiger, Leopard, Panther, Lynx, Stag, Vulture, Hawk, Falcon, Ostrich, Greyhound.*
Fenton, Murray & Jackson, Leeds: *Charon, Cyclops, Cerberus, Pluto, Harpy, Minos, Ixion, Gorgon, Hecate, Vesta, Acheron, Erebus, Medea, Hydra, Lethe, Phlegethon, Medusa, Proserpine, Ganymede, Argus.*
G. & J. Rennie, Blackfriars, London: *Mazeppa, Arab.*
R.B. Longridge & Co., Bedlington: *Jupiter, Saturn, Mars, Lucifer, Venus, Mercury.*
Stothert & Slaughter, Bristol: *Arrow, Dart.*

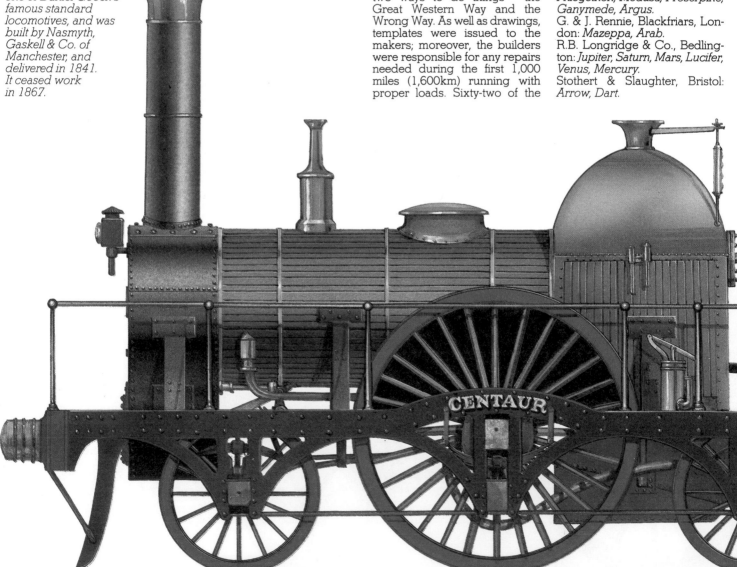

Nasmyth, Gaskell & Co, Manchester: *Achilles, Milo, Hector, Castor, Mentor, Bellona, Actaeon, Centaur, Orion, Damon, Electra, Priam, Pollux, Phoenix, Pegasus, Stentor* (which was the last to be delivered in December 1842).

Incidentally, both the custom of naming as well as the style and shape of the brass letters used persisted for the company's express locomotives until after the railways of Britain were nationalised in 1948. The frames were interesting, being of the sandwich type made from thin sheets of iron enclosing a thick in-filling of oak. The "gab" type valve gear was used. This was later altered in most cases to Stephenson's pattern, so allowing for expansive working of the steam. All the locomotives were coke burners and had large domed "gothic" type fireboxes. Both four-wheel and six-wheel tenders were attached to different members of the class at different times; the dimensions given refer to the use of the six-wheel pattern.

Phlegethon had the honour of hauling the first Royal Train, provided for Queen Victoria's first railway journey from Slough to Paddington on 13 June 1842. Gooch drove and Brunel was on the footplate with him. The journey of 18½ miles (30km) took 25 minutes and the young Queen was delighted.

Castor hauled the opening train between London and Bristol on 30 June 1841. This was the original full extent of the GWR, but at that time the associated Bristol & Exeter Railway was under construction and *Castor* was able to continue as far as Taunton.

Brunel, as is well known, had the idea of extending the GWR from Bristol to New York and it was on yet another fine summer day, 19 July 1843 that Daniel

Gooch took the Queen's husband Prince Albert down to Bristol to launch the famous steamer *Great Britain*, using an unrecorded locomotive of this class. As Gooch records in his diaries, "On the down journey we had some long stops for the Prince to receive addresses, but having no delays on the return journey it was done in 2hrs 4mins. Few runs have been made as quick as this since over so long a distance". In fact, the average speed was 57mph (92km/h) for the 118¾ miles.

There is little doubt that the stability afforded by Brunel's broad gauge tracks with 7ft 0¼in (2,140mm) between the rails, plus the remarkable running qualities of these early standard locomotives led to locomotive performances unequalled in the world at the time.

Another example was on 1 May 1844, the opening day to

Exeter, when Gooch personally drove the official party there and back with the locomotive *Orion*. The 194 miles (312km) back from Exeter to London were run in 280 minutes including several stops for water. A year later this journey was being performed by regular express trains with a schedule of 270 minutes, including stops (totalling 13 minutes) at Didcot, Swindon, Bath, Bristol and Taunton.

During the "Battle of the Gauges" in 1845, *Ixion* made test runs on behalf of the broad-gauge faction for the Government's Gauge Commissioners; runs were made from Paddington to Didcot and back. With 60 tons the 53 miles (85km) journey was performed in 63½ minutes with a maximum speed of 61mph (98 km/h), a feat far beyond anything the narrow gauge people could do on their tests between York

Above: Queen *belonged to the later "Prince" class of 1847. The main difference was the absence of outside frames.*

and Darlington. *Ixion* was the last of these famous locomotives to remain in service, ceasing to run in 1879. The class thus spanned almost 40 years, during which railways grew up as a means of transport. When *Ixion* stopped work the decision to abandon the broad gauge had been taken, although it was not to disappear finally until 13 years later.

By 1879 that young man who had (with the aid of another young draughtsman, also to be famous, called Thomas Crampton) laid out the original *Fire Fly* on his drawing board, had become Sir Daniel Gooch, MP, and Chairman of the Great Western Railway Company.

Lion 0-4-2
Great Britain:
Liverpool & Manchester Railway (L&M), 1838

Tractive effort: 1,836lb
(833kg).
Cylinders: (2) 12 x 18in
(305 x 457mm).
Driving wheels: 60in
(1,524mm).
Superheater: None.
Steam pressure: 50psi
(3.5kg/cm²).
Length overall: 33ft 9in
(10,287mm).
(Other details not available).

Whilst not strictly an express passenger locomotive, the locomotive *Lion*, built for the Liverpool and Manchester Railway in 1838, has several unusual claims to fame. She was built at a time, almost a decade after the famous locomotive trials at Rainhill, when locomotive design had begun to settle down and one could order engines for specific duties with reasonable confidence *Lion* came from Todd, Kitson & Laird

of Leeds and was one of a class of 0-4-2 locomotives named after powerful beasts. It was also a time when the L&M railway began to manufacture its own motive power, a policy that has continued through successive owners of the world's first inter-city railway — Grand Junction Railway, London & North Western Railway, London, Midland & Scottish Railway and British Railways — to this day.

A happy chance led to *Lion* being sold to the Mersey Docks & Harbour Board in 1859, for use as a shunting engine. Some years later the Board set her up as a stationary engine. In this guise the engine lasted in commercial service until 1920, when the LMS railway bought the

Right: *Liverpool and Manchester Railway 0-4-2, Lion still in running order after 140 years.*

Beuth 2-2-2
Germany:
Berlin-Anhalt Railway, 1843

Tractive effort: 4,120lb
(1,870kg).
Axle load; 20,000lb (9.5t).
Cylinders: (2) 13.1 x 22.3 in
(330 x 560mm).
Driving wheels: 60¾in
(1,543mm).
Heating surface: 500sq ft
(47m²).
Superheater: None.
Steam pressure: 78psi
(5.5kg/cm²).
Grate area: 8.9sq ft (0.83m²).
Adhesive weight: 20,000lb
(9.5t).
Total weight: *41,000lb
(18.5t).
Length overall: *20ft 2in
(6,143mm).
(—Engine only. Tender details not known).*

The year 1841 was important in the development of the German locomotive-building industry, for in that year three works delivered their first locomotives — Borsig of Berlin, Maffei of Munich and Emil Kessler of Karlsruhe. August Borsig was a man of immense ability and energy, who built an industrial empire which included an iron works and a large water works. At the time of his entry into locomotive building the 4-2-0s built by Norris of Philadelphia were being imported by a number of European railways, and Borsig's first products were 15 engines of this wheel arrangement supplied to the Berlin-Anhalt Railway. They closely resembled the Norris products in having bar frames and a large haycock fire-box, but they included a number of improvements due to Borsig. They were highly successful and further orders followed.

By 1843 Borsig had incorporated further improvements, some of his own devising and some drawn from English practice. This blending of the practices of America, England and Ger-

many was well illustrated in a 2-2-2 locomotive supplied to the Berlin-Anhalt Railway in 1843 and named *Beuth* in honour of August Borsig's former teacher, Professor Beuth of the Royal Industrial Institute of Berlin.

The equal spacing of the axles gave a better weight distribution than in the Norris 4-2-0s. The design was advanced for its day. The flat side valves above the cylinders were driven by the new Stephenson's link motion, which had been first applied in 1842. It was actually an invention of an employee of Robert Stephenson, by name William Howe, whose part in the affair was always acknowledged by his employers.

Like all great inventions it was very simple. Existing valve gears had separate eccentrics for forward and reverse, and "gabs" or claws on the ends of each eccentric rod which could engage or disengage with the valve spindle as appropriate. Howe's idea was to connect the two eccentric rods by means of a link with a curved slot formed in it. In this slot was a die-block to which the valve spindle was connected. The link now just needed to be raised for one direction of travel and lowered for the other; the arrangement worked very well and the majority of the world's steam locomotives over the next 60 years used it.

It was also possible to use intermediate positions to give cut-off of the steam at an early point in the stroke, to allow of more economical working through expansion of the steam. Borsig, however, used an auxiliary slide-valve to control expansion. The fitting of cylinder drain cocks operated from the footplate was an improvement on Norris' engines, in which the drain cocks were operated by levers on the cylinders themselves. The boiler feed pumps were driven

by levers attached to the crank pin, and extending back to a position under the cab. As in the Norris engines, bar frames were used. The firebox was elliptical in horizontal section and the upper part formed a capacious steam space. A cylindrical casing on top of the firebox housed the

remains for restoration. In 1930 *Lion* was run at the centenary celebrations of the Liverpool & Manchester Railway and afterwards the engine was preserved to what is now the Merseyside County Museum at Liverpool. *Lion* also ran in the cavalcade to celebrate the 150th anniversary of the L&M, in 1980, and is now the world's oldest working locomotive.

Interesting features of the locomotive include the impressive "haycock" shape firebox and sandwich frames enclosing the wheels.

Lion has also been a film star, playing the title role in that enchanting frolic called "Titfield Thunderbolt", still a favourite.

Right: *140 years of railway progress: Liverpool & Manchester Railway* Lion *of 1841 alongside the Advanced Passenger Train.*

steam pipe and one of the two Salter safety valves. The firebox was finished in bright metal, and the boiler barrel was lagged with wood. The six-wheeled tender had outside frames, and screw-operated brakes acted on both sides of all tender wheels.

This was the 24th engine built by Borsig, and it enhanced his growing reputation as a locomotive builder. Orders flowed in, the works expanded, and by 1846 a total of 120 locomotives had been built, a remarkable achievement for the first five years of a new works. Beuth was typical of many of the products of the works in that period.

The original engine was scrapped, but in 1921 the builders made a full-size replica which is housed in the German Museum.

Below, left: *The locomotive* Beuth *as built for the Berlin to Anhalt Railway in 1843.*

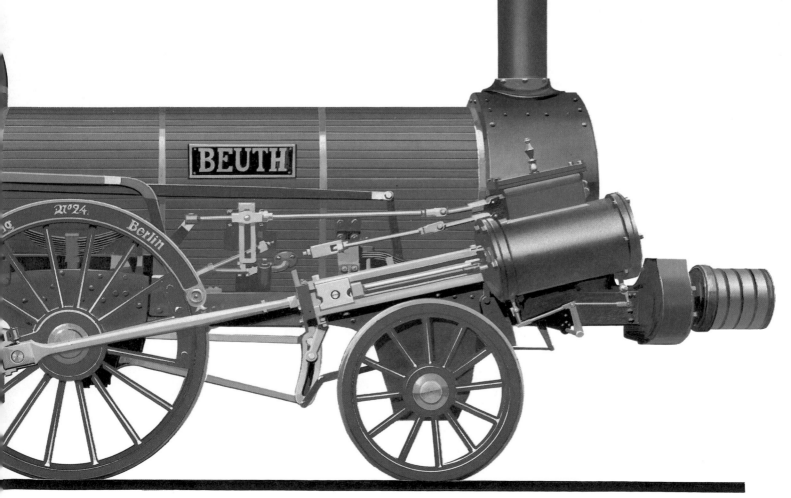

Médoc Class 2-4-0
Switzerland:
Swiss Western Railway (O-S), 1857

Tractive effort: 8,986lb
(4,077kg).
Axle load: 20,150lb (9.2t).
Cylinders: (2) 16 x 24in
(408 x 612mm).
Driving wheels: 66¼in
(1,686mm).
Heating surface: 1,023sq ft.
(95m²).
Superheater: None.
Steam pressure: 114psi
(8kg/cm²).
Grate area: 10.75sq ft (1.00m²).
Fuel: 5,280lb (2.4t).
Water: 880 gall (1,050 US)
(4.0m³).
Adhesive weight: 40,000lb
(18.1t).
Total weight: 88,500lb (40t).
Length overall: 44ft 9½in
(13,650mm).

Below: *2-4-0 No.58 Simplon of
the Jura-Simplon Railway,
previously No.11 of the Swiss
Western Railway. It ran from
1857 to 1901.*

Above: *The "longboilertyp"
2-4-0 of the Swiss Western
Railway, later the Jura-
Simplon Railway.*

Buddicom Class 2-2-2
France:
Paris-Rouen Railway, 1843

Tractive effort: 3,100lb
(1,460kg).
Axle load: 14,550lb (6.6t).
Cylinders: (2) 12.5 x 21in
(318 x 533mm).
Driving wheels: 63in
(1,600mm).
Heating surface: 534sq ft
(48.5m²).
Superheater: None.
Steam pressure: 70psi
(5kg/cm²).
Grate area: 9.5sq ft (0.86m²).
Adhesive weight: 14,550lb
(6.6t).
(Original tender details not
available).

This locomotive class is the 2nd
oldest in this book of which a
genuine survivor (not a replica)
survies in runnable condition.
French National Railways must
take the credit (together with
their predecessors the Western
Railway and the State Railway)
because it is their loving care
which has enabled this significant
and wholly delightful 139-year
old creature to be there to give us

pleasure today.
    The designer, W.B. Buddicom,
was one of that band of British
engineers who spread the gospel
according to Stephenson round
the world—though in this case
travelling his own different road
and one that in the end proved
the right one. The Buddicom
2-2-2s represent one more step
as regards the European locomotive from *Northumbrian* via
Planet and *Vauxhall* towards the
world standard steam locomotive
with two outside cylinders—
although it was a close race with
very similar and equally famous
2-2-2s built at Crewe to the
design of Alexander Allan for the
London & North Western Railway
in England and known as the
"Crewe" type. The motivation
behind the new design lay in the
constant breakages of the crank
axles of inside-cylinder locomotives.
    In addition to just two outside
cylinders, Stephenson's new link
motion was fitted, as well as a
deep firebox between the rear

two wheels. The results were
extremely successful and the
engines continued in use for
many years. Latterly 22 of them
were converted to 2-2-2 tank
locomotives, but in 1946 the last
survivor, long out of use, was

Above right: *"Buddicom" 2-2-2
as restored to original condition
at Bricklayers Arms depot,
London, 1951.*

Above: *"Buddicom" 2-2-2 as
converted to a tank locomotive.*

The Stephensons pioneered much concerning the locomotive, yet Forrester, Norris, Crampton and others were ahead in adopting what became the final arrangement of the cylinders. The famous 'long-boiler' six-wheeled design offered by Robert Stephenson & Co from 1846 onwards, with two horizontal outside cylinders at the front, was usually combined with an increased length of boiler, in an attempt to extract more of the heat from the hot gases in the tubes. Many of the earlier long-boiler engines had a raised hay-cock firebox instead of a dome.

The firebox was outside the wheel-base which was proportionately rather short. This led to a tendency for these locomotives to pitch at speed, but their other qualities led to many being built of the 2-2-2, 2-4-0 and 0-6-0 wheel arrangements, both at home and under licence (or not) in many European countries. The word *longboiler* entered the railway vocabularies of several lands.

The example depicted in the artwork below was a late *long-boilertyp* of which 15 were built in 1856-58 at Karlsruhe in Germany for the Swiss Western Railway, later the Jura-Simplon Railway. The design was known as the *Médoc*, an almost standard French type of the period. They all had long and useful lives, the last being withdrawn in 1902.

Gloggnitzer Class 4-4-0

Austria:
Vienna-Gloggnitz Railway, 1848

Tractive effort: 5,750lb (2,610kg)..
Axle load: 16,500lb (7.5t).
Cylinders: (2) 14½ x 23in (368 x 579mm).
Driving wheels: 55¾in (1,420mm).
Heating surface: 760sq ft (70.6m²).
Superheater: None.
Steam pressure: 78psi (5.5kg/cm²).
Grate area: 10sq ft (0.94m²).
Fuel: 4,500lb (2t).
Water: 1,500gall (1,800 US) (6.8m³).
Adhesive weight: 33,000lb (15t).
Total weight: 70,000lb (32t).
Length overall: 42ft 2in (12,853mm).

The story of how the Norris brothers had better-than-average technical insight but less-than-average commercial acumen has already been related. One of those who combined these qualities was a Scotsman called John Haswell who in 1836 went out to Austria to put some locomotives exported from Britain into service. He did this satisfactorily and was asked to stay on in charge of the locomotive department of the 27-mile (43km) Vienna-Gloggnitz Railway. He died in 1897 at the age of 85 having twice been knighted by the Emperor for services to Austria.

One of his most successful designs was for some 4-4-0s based on the Norris layout. They were known as the "Gloggnitzers" even though with the completion of the Southern State Railway over the Semmering Pass in 1857 their sphere of action—except over the pass itself—became extended beyond Gloggnitz to Laibach, 284 miles (460km) from Vienna. Laibach is now known as Ljublana and is situated in Jugoslavia.

Amongst the features of these locomotives should be mentioned the leading bogie, which was arranged to be able to move radially instead of merely to pivot about its centre, as in the Norris engines. Because the coupled wheels were situated close to the bogie, thus constraining the axis of the locomotive, some sideways movement of the bogie was important. Haswell introduced this device well before Levi Bissell of New York (whose name it usually bears) obtained his patent. Also interesting are the gen-u-ine Yankee pattern spark-arresting smoke stack (there was not a Norris factory in Vienna for nothing), the circular-section coupling and connecting rods, and the bundles of brushwood attached to the leading guard irons to sweep the rails clear of stones and other small obstructions.

One of these famous engines has survived and is displayed in the Vienna Railway Museum. This is the *Steinbrück,* which happily in 1860 passed into the hands of the Graz-Köflach Railway, a concern whose kindly reluctance to scrap ancient machinery is greatly appreciated by the locomotive historian.

Below: *Haswell "Gloggnitzer" 4-4-0* Steinbrück *as preserved in the Vienna Railway Museum.*

restored to near original condition.

The preserved engine is No. 33 of the Paris to Rouen Railway, named *Saint Pierre.* It visited England for the 1951 Festival of Britain and was actually steamed and run in the Bricklayers Arms Locomotive Depot, London. It was welcomed into Britain by Miss Buddicom, a descendant of the builder. Normally it is kept at the National Railway Museum at Mulhouse.

Crampton Type 4-2-0
France:
Eastern Railway (Est), 1852

Tractive effort: 5,040lb
(2,290kg).
Axle load: 27,500lb (12.5t).
Cylinders: (2) 15¾ x 21½in
(400 x 500mm).
Driving wheels: 82¾in
(2,100mm).
Heating surface: 1,059sq ft
(98.4m²).
Superheater: None.
Steam pressure: 92psi
(6.5kg/cm²).
Grate area: 15.3sq ft (1.42m²).
Fuel: 15,500lb (7t).
Water: 1,540gall (1,850 US)
(7m³).
Adhesive weight: 27,100lb
(12.5t).
Total weight: 105,000lb (47.5t).
Length overall: 41ft 9in
(12,728mm).

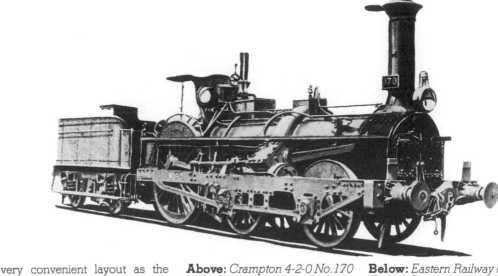

Thomas Russell Crampton's engines are a legend—the word *Crampton* for a time entered the French language to mean "train" —yet they in no way formed a step forward in the art of locomotive engineering. But they were magnificent.

Crampton was born in August 1816, the same month as Daniel Gooch. He learnt his trade as an engineer under Marc Brunel, father of the Great Western Railway's builder. In due time Crampton joined the GWR himself and worked with Gooch on the design of his celebrated standard locomotives.

In 1842, whilst still working for this company, he applied for a patent for a high-speed express locomotive with a low centre of gravity yet having an adequate-size boiler. The problem was the driving axle—if you used big wheels to permit fast running, then the bottom of the boiler had to clear the revolving cranks and had to be mounted high. So that he could set the boiler low and thus keep the centre of gravity also low Crampton put the driving axle *behind* it. The cylinders were outside the wheels and were mounted well back from the front of the engine. It was a

very convenient layout as the machinery was all accessible—in fact, in that respect (but little else) the Cramptons followed the final form of the steam locomotive.

Crampton was working on a broad gauge railway and he must have regarded standard gauge locomotives as having little better stability than the penny-farthing bicycles of the day. In the typical Crampton design illustrated here the height of the centre of the boiler was about the same measurement as the rail gauge, very similar to the same ratio for a conventional design on the 7ft 0¼in (2,140mm) gauge.

He was also concerned about pitching, which affected certain locomotives having a short wheel-base, especially if this was combined with having much of the weight of the engine concentrated on a single central driving wheel. It could be said that the idea was only dubiously original but even so Crampton got his patent and went into business. It was a case of a "prophet not being without honour save in his own country" and the first engine was the 4-2-0 *Namur* for the Namur-Liège Railway in Belgium. The builders were the little

Above: *Crampton 4-2-0 No.170 of the French Northern Railway. Note the huge single pair of driving wheels at the back.*

Below: *Eastern Railway of France Crampton 4-2-0 No.80 before restoration as the working museum exhibit we know today.*

known and long vanished firm of Tulk and Ley of Lowca Works, Whitehaven, and since the Belgian line was not complete when the locomotives was ready, trials were held in Great Britain as well as on the Belgian State Railway.

Altogether some 320 Cramp-

tons were built, most of them for various French railways, notably the Northern and Eastern companies. Amongst many notable doings of theirs in that country might be noted the haulage of the last train to leave Paris when it was besieged by the Germans in

Pearson 9ft Single Class 4-2-4
Great Britain:
Bristol & Exeter Railway (B&ER), 1854

Tractive effort: 7,344lb
(3,330kg).
Axle load: 41,500lb
(18.5t).
Cylinders: (2) 18 x 24in
(457 x 610mm).
Driving wheels: 106in
(2,743mm).
Heating surface: 1,235sq ft
(114.8 m²).
Superheater: None.
Steam pressure: 120psi
(8.4kg/cm²).
Grate area: 23sq ft
(2.15m²).
Fuel: 4,480lb (2t).
Water: 1,430gall (1,720 US)
(6.5m³).
Adhesive weight: 41,500lb
(18.5t).
Total weight: 112,000lb (49.7t).
Length overall: 30ft 9in
(9,372mm).

1870. Another Crampton belonging to the Eastern Railway and rebuilt with a strange double-barrelled boiler, was responsible for breaking the world speed record — not only for trains but for everything — when No.604 was run at 89.5mph (144km/h) with a load of 157 tons, during trials on the Paris-Laroche main line of the Paris, Lyons & Mediterranean Railway on 20 June 1890.

The main drawback of the Crampton design was the limited adhesive weight which could be applied to the rails; with a single driving axle right at the end of the wheelbase this limitation was a fundamental one. Because of this the success of the Cramptons in handling light trains at high speeds was to some extent self-defeating — because of the fast service more people used the trains, more coaches had to be added and the limit of these engines' capacity was soon reached. It is also true to say that, whilst at first sight it would appear that a low centre of gravity would make a locomotive more stable, in fact it is a case where the cure can be worse than the disease. Such locomotives may be less liable to overturn when driven round curves at two or more times the permitted speed, but liability to serious oscillation and consequent derailment from that cause is increased.

Nevertheless, other features made the Crampton engines into sound propositions. Their layout enabled bearings of really adequate size to be applied to the driving axle and this made for long periods of trouble-free running between visits to the shops. Similar advantage sprung from the fact that a rear wheel of a vehicle tends to run with its flanges clear of the rails on curves, leaving the leading wheels to do the guidance. Hence the small (and cheap) carrying wheels bore the brunt of the flange-wear, leaving the large and expensive

driving wheels to last longer.

Crampton was also one of the first locomotive engineers to understand and apply the principles of balancing the reciprocating and revolving weights of a locomotive mechanism. This also contributed to the success of his engines, as did his patent regulator or throttle valve. Crampton had clearly a most original mind, although sometimes his ingenuity outran his good sense. In addition to the well-known Crampton layout which was only secondary in the application, his original patent of 1842 claimed the idea of locomotives with a driving axle *above* the boiler. The first (and almost certainly the last) of these, named *Trevithick* after the builder

of the world's first steam locomotive, was built in 1847 by the London & North Western Railway at their Crewe Works. It had 9ft (2,742mm) diameter wheels and presented an exceedingly strange appearance. It was not a success.

Crampton took out a further patent in 1849 to cover locomotives provided with an intermediate shaft, either oscillating or revolving, between the cylinders and the driving wheels or axle. Its application to steam locomotives was brief (but not quite so brief as the underslung boiler) but after Crampton had died in 1888 and the patent had expired the idea found extensive use for the drive mechanisms of early electric locomotives.

The considerable mark which Thomas Crampton made in the world of locomotive engineering is recognised by the preservation of 4-2-0 No.80 *Le Continent,* originally of the Paris-Strasbourg Railway, later the Eastern Railway of France. This beautiful locomotive relic, superbly restored and in working order (but only steamed on great occasions) is usually to be found in the French National Railway Museum at Mulhouse. She is the subject of the vital statistics given at the head of this article.

Below: *Crampton 4-2-0 of the Eastern Railway of France as now superbly restored makes one of her rare appearances in steam.*

These remarkable tank locomotives were designed for the broad-gauge Bristol & Exeter Railway by Locomotive Superintendent Pearson and eight (running numbers 39 to 46) were built by Rothwell & Co. of Bolton in 1853 and 1854. They were intended specially for working the B&ER's section of the London to Exeter express route, including the famous train "Flying Dutchman", at that time the fastest train in the world. They had the largest driving wheels ever successfully used on a locomotive and no one has come up with an authentic recording of any higher speed

Left: *A side view of a Pearson 4-2-4 tank locomotive as used on the broad-gauge lines of the Bristol & Exeter Railway.*

previous to one of 81.8mph (130km/h) made behind a Pearson single while descending the Wellington incline south of Taunton.

The B&ER had only taken over from the Great Western the working of its own railway in 1849, a bare five years before this very original piece of locomotive thinking was turned into hardware. It says enough of the relationship between the two companies that they were as far as possible removed from the Gooch 4-2-2s first supplied. Most original pieces of thinking in respect of locomotive design spent more time in sidings than on the road, but it was not so with these so-called nine-footers. After 14 years in traffic four of them were rebuilt — to an extent that counted more as

a replacement — at the B&ER's own works at Bristol. But the so-original first design was followed.

The engines were guided by a four-wheel bogie at each end, and they were propelled along by that mighty pair of flangeless driving wheels placed more or less centrally between the bogies. As with all locomotives that ran on Brunel's broad-gauge lines, the cylinders and motion were inside the frames.

Water was carried in the tank at the rear as well as in a well-tank between the frames. Pearson's singles were untypical, though, in that they carried no names, only numbers.

In 1876, shortly after the GWR had finally taken over the B&ER, a Pearson single (No.39, renum-

bered 2001) derailed with loss of life at Long Ashton near Bristol. In consequence the remaining three locomotives were again completely rebuilt on more conventional lines as 4-2-2 singles, regarded by some as the most handsome (this was not hard to achieve) ever to run on the 7ft 0¼in (2,140mm) gauge.

Had the broad-gauge continued into the twentieth century, it would seem as though these rebuilds might have formed the basis upon which development might have taken place. The design of a modern broad gauge 4-6-0 with two large inside cylinders and a power and size similar to that of the *Saint* class 4-6-0s of the GWR would be a fascinating exercise, especially if followed up by a working model.

American Type 4-4-0

United States: Western & Atlantic Railroad (W&ARR), 1855

Tractive effort: 6,885lb (3,123kg).
Axle load: 21,000lb (9.5t).
Cylinders: (2) 15 x 24in (381 x 610mm).
Driving wheel: 60in (1,524mm).
Heating surface: 98.0sq ft (91m²).
Superheater: None.
Steam pressure: 90psi (6.35kg/cm²).
Grate area: 14.5sq ft (1.35m²).
Fuel: (wood) 2 cords (7.25m³).
Water: 1,250 gall (2,000 US) (5.75m³). ·
Adhesive weight: 43,000lb (19.5t).
Total weight: 90,000lb (41t).
Length overall: 52ft 3in (15,926mm).

The *General* was built by Thomas Rogers of Paterson, New Jersey in 1855 and it is a wholly appropriate example of the most numerous and successful locomotive design ever to have been built. The reason is that Rogers was responsible for introducing most of the features which made the true "American" the success it was. The most significant development, so far as the U.S.A. was concerned was the general introduction of Stephenson's link motion, which permitted the expansive use of steam. This was in place of the "gab" or "hook" reversing gears used until then, which permitted only "full forward" and "full backward" positions.

In other aspects of design Rogers gained his success by good proportions and good detail rather than innovation. An example was the provision of adequate space between the cylinders and the driving wheels, which reduced the maximum angularity of the connecting rods and hence the up-and-down forces on the slide bars. A long wheelbase leading truck (in English, bogie) allowed the cylinders to be horizontal and still clear the wheels. This permitted direct attachment to the bar frames, which raised inclined cylinders did not.

To allow flexibility on curves, early examples of the breed inherited flangeless leading driving wheels from their progenitors, but by the late 1850s the leading trucks were being given side movement to produce the same effect. Naturally the compensated spring suspension system giving three-point support to the locomotive was continued. Wood-burning was also nearly universal in these early years of the type, and the need to catch the sparks led to many wonderful shapes in the way of spark-arresting smokestacks.

Within two or three years other makers such as Baldwin, Grant, Brooks Mason, Danforth and Hinkley began offering similar locomotives. To buy one of these locomotives one did not need to be a great engineer steeped in the theory of design—it was rather like ordering a car today. One filled in a form on which certain options could be specified and very soon an adequate and reliable machine was delivered.

Speeds on the rough light tracks of a pioneer land were not high—average speeds of 25mph (40km/h) start-to-stop, implying a maximum of 40mph (64km/h), were typical of the best expresses. Although the 4-4-0s were completely stable at high speeds, the increased power required meant

that by the 1880s a bigger breed of 4-4-0 as well as "Ten-wheelers" (4-6-0s) were taking over from the "American".

There was another revolution taking place too. The earlier years of the type were characterised by romantic names and wonderful brass, copper and paint work, but the last quarter of the nineteenth century was a time of cut-throat competition, with weaker roads going to the wall. There was no question of there being anything to spare for frills of this kind—so it was just a case of giving a coat of bitumen and painting big white running numbers in the famus "Bastard Railroad Gothic" fount on the tender sides.

For most of the second half of the nineteenth century this one type of locomotive dominated railroad operations in the U.S.A. It was appropriately known as the "American Standard" and

Above: *The "General" as currently preserved in working order. The wood "stacked" in the tender hides an oil fuel tank.*

about 25,000 of them were built, differing only marginally in design. The main things that varied were the decor and the details. They were simple, ruggedly constructed machines appropriate for what was then a developing country; at the same time a leading bogie and compensated springing made them suitable for the rough tracks of a frontier land.

The subject of the specification above is perhaps the most famous of all the 25,000. The *General* came to fame when hijacked by a group of Union soldiers who had infiltrated into Confederate territory during the American civil war. The idea was to disrupt communications behind the lines, in particular on the 5ft (1,524mm)

Below: *Typical United States "Standard" 4-4-0 illustrating the elaborate decor that was often applied in the early years of American railroading but which was abandoned in the 1880s.*

gauge line 135 miles (216km) long connecting Atlanta with Chattanooga. The Union forces were approaching Chattanooga after their victory at Shiloh and the Confederates were expected to bring up reinforcements by rail. There was a major trestle bridge at a place called Oostenabula and the intention was to steal a train, take it to the site and burn the bridge. A replacement would take weeks to build.

The Union force, twenty in number under the command of a Captain Andrews, having stayed overnight at a place called Marietta and having bought tickets to travel on the train, took over the locomotive at a place called Big Shanty, some 30 miles (48km) north of Atlanta, while the passengers and crew were having breakfast in the depot's eating house. The conductor of the train, whose name was Fuller, gave chase first on a handcart and then on a small private ironworks loco, the *Yonah*.

The raiders' intention was to cut telegraph wires behind them, remove the occasional rail and demand immediate passage at stations they came to in the name of Confederate General Beauregard. A problem Andrews faced was the presence of trains coming the other way on the single line and perhaps the game was lost at Kingston where he had to wait an hour and twenty five minutes until one divided into two sections had finally arrived.

In the end the *Yonah* arrived there only four minutes after Andrews and the *General* had left. Here Fuller took over another "American" 4-4-0, the *Texas* and after this Andrews never got enough time to block the track

before what had now become a Confederate posse came within rifle range. In the end, after eight hours and 87 miles the *General* expired when it ran out of fuel; the Union group then scattered into the woods. All were later captured and seven of the senior men shot.

Leaving out the human drama for a moment two qualities of the "American Standards" emerge from this affair. First, in spite of the rough track high maximum speeds of around 60mph (100 km/h) were reached during the chase and both locomotives stayed on the rails. The second thing was that the range between fuel stops was very short. A full load of two cords of wood fuel (a cord is 128cu ft or 3.62m²) would last for a mere 50 miles (80km).

Both the *General* and the *Texas* (or what purports to be them) have survived. The former, normally in store at Chattanooga, is occasionally run. Oil fuel is used, the tank being concealed under a fake woodpile. The *Texas,* as befits a Confederate conqueror, has an honoured place in Grant Park at Atlanta. Both were converted from the 5ft (1,524mm) gauge of the Western & Atlantic Railroad after the war was over.

The American Civil War was one of the first great wars to be fought using railway transportation, most of which was provided on both sides by this "American" type. The earliest transcontinental railroads were first built and then operated by them; the well-known picture of the last spike ceremony at Promontory, Utah, has placed the Cental Pacific's *Jupiter* and the Union Pacific No.119 second only to the *General* on the scale of locomotive fame. It is said that

"America built the railroads and the railroads built America"; substitute "American 4-4-0" for "railroad" and the saying is equally true.

The "American" type was a universal loco; the only difference between those built for passenger traffic and those for freight was between 66in (1,676mm) diameter driving wheels and 60in (1,524mm). It also served all the thousands of railroad companies who then operated America's 100,000 miles (160,000km) of line, from roads thousands of miles long to those a mere ten.

The last "American" class in the U.S.A. did not retire from normal line service for more than

Above: *American Standard 4-4-0, as refurbished to resemble the Cental Pacific RR's* Jupiter, *ready to re-enact the completion ceremony of the first transcontinental railroad at the Golden Spike National Monument, Utah.*

a century after Rogers put the first on the rails in 1852. A few survive in industrial use in the remoter parts of the world even today. Numerous examples are preserved in museums and elsewhere all over North American, a few (a very few) perform on tourist railroads, while others are set aside for and occasionally star in western films.

Problem Class 2-2-2
Great Britain: London & North Western Railway (LNWR), 1862

Tractive effort: 9,827lb (4,458kg).
Axle load: 33,000lb (15t).
Cylinders: (2) 16 x 24in (406 x 610mm).
Driving wheels: 93in (2,324mm).
Heating surface: 1,097sq ft (102m²).
Superheater: None.
Steam pressure: 150psi (8.54kg/cm²).
Grate area: 15sq ft (1.39m²).
Fuel: 11,000lb (5t).
Water: 1,800 gall (2,160 US) (8m³).
Adhesive weight: 26,500lb (12t).
Total weight: 133,000lb (60.5t).
Length overall: 43ft 8in (13,310mm).

A working career on top main line expresses lasting more than 40 years is quite exceptional for any locomotive. John Ramsbottom's "Problem" or "Lady of the Lake" class singles, introduced on the LNWR in 1859 managed nearly 50, although a considerable element of luck entered into the achievement.

In the tradition of all the best steam locomotives from *Northumbrian* of 1830 to the Chinese "March Forward" class of 1980, the main characteristic of the "Problem" was simplicity. No one could call the Stirling singles described elsewhere complex, but the "Problem"'s were simpler still, having no bogies, the leading axle being carried in the frames like the others.

The first of the 60 built was turned out in 1859, the last in

Right: *A "Problem" class 2-2-2 at speed on the LNWR main line hauling an almost unbelievable 15-coach load.*

Stirling 8ft Single Class 4-2-2
Great Britain: Great Northern Railway (GNR), 1870

Tractive effort: 11,245lb (5,101kg).
Axle load: 34,000lb (15.5t).
Cylinders: (2) 18 x 28in (457 x 711mm).
Driving wheels: 97in (2,463mm).
Heating surface: 1,165sq ft (108m²).
Steam pressure: 140psi (9.8kg/cm²).
Grate area: 17.65sq ft (1.64m²).
Fuel: 7,500lb (3.5t).
Water: 2,900 gall (3,480 US) (13m³).
Adhesive weight: 34,600lb (15.5t).
Total weight: 145,500lb (66t).
Length overall: 50ft 2in (15,240mm).

Above right: *Preserved Stirling No.1 ready to take part in the Cavalcade celebrating 150 years of main-line railways, August 1975.*

Below: *Stirling 4-2-2 No.1 of the Great Northern Railway of England, showing the huge single pair of 8-foot diameter driving wheels. Note the domeless boiler and the* elegant brass safety valve cover and, on the tender, the gong which was connected to an early form of communication cord. No.1 is preserved in working order.

1865. The outside-cylinder inside-valve arrangement was extremely basic, and a further simplification occurred after the first ten had been built when the Giffard injector replaced tiresome pumps for feeding the boiler. A job for which the "Problem" locomotives were noted was the haulage of the Irish mail trains, known as the "Wild Irishmen", from Euston to Holyhead, changing engines at Stafford.

Francis Webb took over from John Ramsbottom in 1871 and he, like other locomotive engineers both before and after, made the mistake of thinking that complexity was the right path. The compound locomotives that resulted were not as reliable as they should have been and in time the LNWR operating department laid down that any express with a load greater than the equivalent of 17 six-wheel coaches

(about 270 tons) should be piloted. In this task the "Problem" locomotives, now 30 years old, found a niche and for it they were discreetly rebuilt in the 1890s. The dimensions given in the specifications refer to the final rebuilding, which involved a 25

Left: *"Problem" class No.610 Princess Royal before being fitted with a cab, but in LNWR's "blackberry black" livery.*

per cent increase in the total weight over the original. An earlier rebuild had provided the locomotives with cabs and no doubt little remained of the originals of 1859 by the end except their identities. The changes made, however, did little to obviate their worst fault which was the tendency to violent oscillation about a vertical axis at speed.

As regards these identities, a hallowed LNWR tradition was closely followed, with numbers and names chosen and allocated at random. Many of the names were evocative, for example, *Erebus, Harlequin, Atalanta, Lady of the Lake, Tornado, Pandora,* but others such as *Problem, Soult, Edith* and *Fortuna,* less so.

The "Stirling 8-foot single" is considered by many to be the epitome of the locomotive regarded as an art form. The graceful lines set off by lovely paint- and brass-work combine to produce a sight that has few rivals for beauty.

Patrick Stirling, Locomotive Superintendent of the Great Northern Railway had the first of them built in 1870 at the line's own Doncaster Locomotive Plant. As was the GNR custom, subsequent numbers were allotted at random, but the prototype was actually No.1 and as such enjoyed considerable fame. It was 23 years before the last and

47th of the class was completed.

The domeless boiler was very apparent to the onlooker; it was both unusual for the time as well as being a Stirling trademark. Mechanically the engine was as simple as can be, with outside cylinders but inside valve chests, the slide valves being driven direct by sets of Stephenson's link motion.

In those days, when trains were formed of six-wheel non-corridor coaches, these engines handled all the crack expresses of the line including the famous 10am Kings Cross to Edinburgh express, known then only unofficially as the "Flying Scotsman".

Many authentic recordings were made showing speeds around 75mph (120km/h) with surprisingly heavy loads being hauled by these locomotives, but the coming of such developments as eight- and twelve- wheeled bogie stock, corridor carriages and dining cars spelt their removal to lesser tasks. All had been withdrawn by 1916 except the legendary No.1 which survives at what was the boundary of her home territory at the National Railway Museum at York.

In 1938 Stirling's No.1 was taken out of the museum, restored and used for a publicity stunt in connection with some new rolling

stock for the "Flying Scotsman" express. Journalists were invited to Kings Cross for a preliminary run on the Flying Scotsman of 1888, before joining the new luxury train at Stevenage. The event caused a group of railway enthusiasts known as the Railway Correspondence and Travel Society to charter No.1 and its train of six-wheelers for an excursion from Kings Cross to Cambridge. It was the first occasion that a museum piece main-line steam locomotive was run to give steam enthusiasts pleasure, and was the precedent for such activities starting in earnest after World War II.

Class 121 2-4-2

France: Paris, Lyons & Mediterranean Railway (PLM), 1876

Tractive effort: 12,225lb (5,545kg).
Axle load: 31,000lb (14t).
Cylinders: (2) 19.7 x 23.7in (500 x 650mm).
Driving wheels: 82½in. (2,100mm).
Heating surface: 1,280sq ft (119m²).
Superheater: None.
Steam pressure: 129psi (9kg/cm²).
Grate area: 23sq ft (2.2m²).
Adhesive weight: 61,000lb (27.5t).
Total weight: 109,539lb (49.7t).
Length overall: 56ft 5¾in (1,7215mm).
(Tender details not available).

French steam locomotives always had great distinction and none more so than these enchanting creations which belonged to the famed *Route Imperiale*, otherwise known as the Paris, Lyons & Mediterranean Railway. Previous to their construction the PLM had relied on Crampton-type 4-2-0 locomotives. Finding they needed more power, in 1868 the company built 50 long-boiler 2-4-0s, both their Paris and Oullins shops sharing the work of construction.

Still more power was found to be necessary and in 1876 an enlarged version of these 2-4-0s was produced. It was necessary to go to the 2-4-2 wheel arrangement and, indeed, the earlier

Below: Paris, Lyon & Mediterranean Railway class "121" 2-4-2 No.90. Note the outside Gooch valve gear, the dome nearly as fat as the boiler, the spring-balance safety valves, the bell to provide communication and the flap to cover the chimney.

Above: PLM 2-4-2 locomotive No. 67. Four hundred of this class were built.

Class 79 4-4-0

Australia: New South Wales Government Railways (NSWGR), 1877

Tractive effort: 13,800lb (6,260kg).
Axle load: 32,000lb (14.5t).
Cylinders: (2) 18 x 24in (457 x 610mm).
Driving wheels: 67in (1,702mm).
Heating surface: 1,121sq ft (104m²).
Superheater: None.
Steam pressure: 140psi (9.8kg/cm²).
Grate area: 14.75sq ft (1.40m²).
Adhesive weight: 64,000lb (29t).
Total weight: 133,500lb (60.5t).
(Tender details not available).

An active working life of over 80 years says more for the qualities of these handsome locomotives than pages of print. One of them

which was later converted to a 4-4-2 tank locomotive in fact came close to working on its 100th birthday, for it was shunting at the NSWGR Clyde Workshops as late as mid-1972.

In spite of origins as an underground city railway locomotive, these 4-4-0s were intended for top-line express passenger trains. They were based on the layout of some famous and successful 4-4-0 tanks built by Beyer, Peacock of Manchester from 1864 onwards for London's Metropolitan Railway. The original Australian order was for 30, delivered between 1877 and 1879. Later 26 more were supplied by Dübs & Co. of Glasgow (later part of the North British Locomotive Co). A further four

came from Beyer, Peacock in 1881 and the final four were built in New South Wales by the Atlas Engineering Pty of Sydney, making 68 in all. It was a pleasant change from so much contemporary locomotive engineering, most of which was to NTA (No Two Alike) standards.

As we have seen and will see again many times throughout this narrative, simplicity was the steam locomotive's trump card and designers who thought to introduce complications, however promising they might seem, did so at their peril. Beyer, Peacock's classic design (the original is attributed to Sir John Fowler), repeated so many times for so many railways, came near the ultimate in this respect. One

feature which is hidden from sight is the Allen's straight-link motion which was fitted to these locomotives.

Originally the locomotives had no sides to the cab but later some shelter was provided. The resulting side-sheets had plain circular windows and this is a trade mark of these and other contemporary NSWGR locomotives. Another odd aesthetic feature of the "79"s is the sloping front to the smokebox door, inherited from their Metropolitan progenitors.

The New South Wales railways were notable for a large

Right: New South Wales Government class "79" 4-4-0 as restored and displayed at the NSW Railway Museum.

2-4-0s were soon rebuilt with the extra rear carrying axle. This extra pair of wheels gave increased stability when running. Interesting features included a Belpaire firebox, outside Gooch's valve gear (described in connection with Gooch's "Rover" class 4-2-2s) and, later on, big reservoirs on the boiler in connection with the PLM air brake system. Delicious rather than vital were various lesser features. The magnificent chimney, for example, is pure poetry, with that immense *capouchon* and lever-worked flap to close it shut. The sandbox too, whilst a plain rectangle in the side view, is exotically curved when seen from the front. The superb dome with spring-balance safety valves certainly is no anticlimax, while the shape of the cab (if that is the right word for

a slightly elaborate wind-shield) is distinctive seen from any direction.

Sixty of this sub-class (to which the dimensions etc given above refer) were built, numbered from 51 to 110, following the 50 earlier 2-4-0s converted to 2-4-2s.

So successful were these engines that between 1879 and 1883 their numbers were increased to 400, all except 40 of this huge fleet, being built "in house" by the PLM. These 40 were built by Sharp, Steward & Co of Manchester. They worked all kinds of passenger trains.

A further development took place in 1888, when yet more 2-4-2s were built. This final version of the design was a watershed of steam development in France. Although in overall weight they were a mere 10 per

cent greater than the originals, there were three features incorporated in the design, each of which meant a "Great Leap Forward" in French locomotive design: first, there was Walschaert's valve gear, later to become a world standard for steam locomotives; second the boiler was designed for an unprecedented pressure of 15kg/cm² (214psi), again typical of latter day steam engines the world over and representing a 65 per cent increase over the boiler pressure of the parent design. Thirdly, the design marked a change on the part of the greatest of French railway companies from simple locomotives to compound. This was eventually to lead, in France, to locomotives that beat the world by a big margin in thermal

efficiency; that is, in the amount of fuel burnt per unit of power produced.

Other very similar 2-4-2s were built from 1876 onwards for the neighbouring Paris-Orleans Railway. In fact, it seems likely that the PLM copied what they saw being done over the fence by one of the greatest of French locomotive engineers, Victor Fourquenot. In all 126 of the 2-4-2s were built for the P-O and some were even in use 70 years later. One has survived to be restored and displayed in the National Railway Museum at Mulhouse. Not only the PLM copied the P-O. Between 1882 and 1891, forty of the 2-4-2s were built for the Austro-Hungarian State Railway Co. The P-O is said to have had a financial interest in the Austro-Hungarian company.

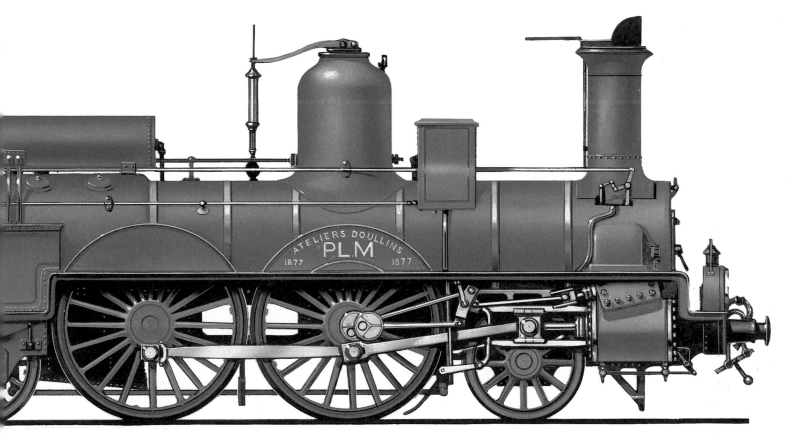

number of long lightly-laid branch lines serving the farming community. While the crops are growing traffic is minimal and so, long after the "79" class has been superseded on the crack trains of the system, there were the mail trains on these branches needing agile and light-footed locomotives. Hence one finds these 4-4-0s, now re-designated class "Z-12", (between 1885 and 1923 they were known as the "C" class) still at work in the 1960s, 85 years after the design was introduced. One notes, however, one interruption to this peaceful and prolonged old age when, one day in 1932, 7,000 tons of elderly locomotives placed buffer-to-buffer were used to test the Sydney Harbour Bridge.

Duke Class 4-4-0
Great Britain: Highland Railway (HR), 1874

Tractive effort: 12,338lb (5,597kg).
Axle load: 31,500lb (14.25t).
Cylinders: (2) 18 x 24in (457 x 610mm).
Driving wheels: 75½in (1,918mm).
Heating surface: 1,228sq ft (114m²).
Steam pressure: 140psi (9.84kg/cm²).
Grate area: 16.25sq ft (1.51m²).
Fuel: 9,000lb (4t).
Water: 1,800 gall (2,160 US) (8m³).
Adhesive weight: 59,500lb (27t).
Total weight: 161,500lb (73.5t).
Length overall: 51ft 3in (15,621mm.

Right: David Jones' "Duke" class 4-4-0, depicted in original livery. Later a more sombre green was adopted.

When they were introduced in 1874 the Highland Railway "Duke" class were the most powerful locomotives in Britain. Although a small concern with fewer than 60 locos on its books the HR needed strong engines to take its trains across the mountains. These ten 4-4-0s, built by Dübs of Glasgow and the first design of newly appointed Locomotive Superintendent David Jones, were the forerunners of several other very similar classes. These were the "Lochgorm Bogie" of 1876, the "Clyde Bogie" of 1886 and the "Strath" class of 1889. The celebrated "Skye Bogie" class of 1882 were also very closely related, but with considerably smaller driving wheels. In all, these engines added up to a very competent fleet of 30 locomotives, which profoundly improved speeds and loads on the Highland lines. That famous HR feature the louvred chimney, intended to throw the exhaust up clear of the cab as well as assist the draughting, appeared for the first time on this class, which also had the graceful double frame arrangement of previous HR locomotives. As befitted a line whose first locomotive chief was Alexander Allan, Allan's straight link valve gear was used.

Another interesting feature was Le Châtelier's counter-pressure brake, by means of which the cylinders could be used to provide the brake force as well as drive the train. The idea was to supplement hand-applied brake-blocks on the long down grades but the equipment never became standard. The principle was very similar to descending a long hill in a motor car by engaging a low gear. The later-fitted front vacuum brake pipe was arranged to fold down to permit the mounting of a wedge-type snowplough. Running numbers were 60 to 69.

Although a ride over the Highland main line was and is one of the finest railway journeys of the world, it has never been one of the fastest. In the early days of David Jones' locomotives the journey from Perth to Inverness 143 miles (230km) took 5¼ hours by the best train, and the continuation on the Wick, a further 162 miles

Gladstone Class 0-4-2
Great Britain: London, Brighton & South Coast Railway (LBSCR), 1882

Tractive effort: 13,211lb (5,993kg).
Axle load: 32,500lb (14.75t).
Cylinders: (2) 18¼ x 26in (464 x 660mm).
Driving wheels: 78in (1,980mm).
Heating surface: 1,492sq ft (139m²).
Superheater: None.
Steam pressure: 140psi (9.8kg/cm²).
Grate area: 20.3sq ft (1.88m²).
Fuel: 9,000lb (4t).
Water: 2,240 gall (2,700 US) (10.2m³).
Adhesive weight: 63,500lb (29t).
Total weight: 153,000lb (69.5t).
Length overall: 51ft 10in (15,800mm).

Ever since the days of Stephenson's first "Patentee" 2-2-2 it had been taken as a matter of course that express passenger locomotives needed guiding wheels ahead of their driving wheels. So when one of the most able of locomotive engineers introduced 0-4-2 type locomotives to haul the London, Brighton & South Coast Railway's principal expresses, his colleagues won-

Above: "Gladstone" class No.188 Allen Sarle at Oxted Surrey, in 1901. Note its spectacular cleanliness.

(260km), occupied another 8¼ hours. When this fleet of bogie engines had become established, improvements were made, the timings for the two sections of main line coming down to 4 hours and 6 hours respectively. This occurred in 1890.

One of the problems of the HR was that traffic was either a feast—during the beginning and end of the shooting season for example—or a famine. Foxwell (*Express Trains, English and Foreign,* 1895) records the Euston-Inverness mail train leaving Perth one August morning 1888 with two 4-4-0s and *36* carriages, including horseboxes and saloons from companies all over Britain. Not surprisingly and in spite of a banker being

provided for the 18 miles (29km) of 1 in 75 (1.3 per cent) from Blair Atholl to Druimachdar Summit, 22 minutes had been lost against the schedule by the time Kingussie was reached. These 4-4-0s stayed in charge of principal Highland expresses until Peter Drummond's bigger 4-4-0s and 4-6-0s arrived at the turn of the century.

David Jones' predecessor at Inverness was William Stroudley, who introduced to the HR his original, handsome and celebrated livery of yellow ochre, more famous for its use on the London, Brighton & South Coast Railway. The "Duke" class first appeared in this colouring although it was not long before David Jones's own green livery was adopted. The only Highland locomotive which is preserved, "Jones' Goods" 4-6-0 No103 of 1894, is (incorrectly) decked out in the yellow colour—this being as near as one can get to a preserved Highland 4-4-0. The

last "Duke" to survive was the one which gave the class its name. No.67, *The Duke,* later *Cromartie,* ceased work in 1923; the last of the associated classes (No.95 *Strathcarron*) was withdrawn as London, Midland & Scottish No14274 in 1928, well before the age of preservation.

Above: *"Duke" class No.82 Fife passing Welch's Cabin at Inverness en route to the south. The lines to the left lead into the departure platforms of the station. Arriving trains both then and now proceed straight on and back into the arrival platforms.*

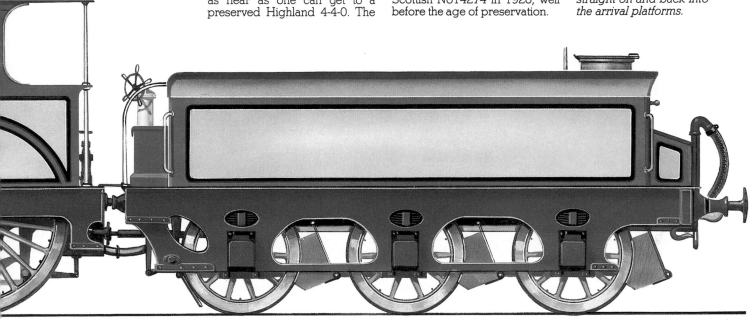

dered. But there was no need.

William Stroudley had been enticed away from the Highlands of Scotland by the LBSCR directors in 1871 in order to put the Company's then rather messy locomotive affairs in order. He was a man who believed that the best practice was also the most economical, and that good looks were important in locomotives. Stroudley belongs to that handful of locomotive men whose creations stayed in service for more than seventy years.

The last of his masterpieces was the express passenger locomotive class known as the "Gladstone", after the name bestowed on the prototype which first saw the light of day outside the company's own Brighton works in December 1882. Over the next eight years 35 more were built. In 1889 No189 *Edward Blount* crossed the channel and won a Gold Medal at the Paris Exhibition. Once the exhibition

was over No189 was tried out on the Paris, Lyons & Mediterranean Railway's Paris-Laroche section of the main line. The locomotive did very well, achieving 69½mph (111km/h) on level road with a heavy train, but, alas, William Stroudley caught a chill during the trials and died in Paris at the early of age of 56. But some of his locomotives (the famous "Terrier" class) were still in service with British Railways in the 1960s.

The success of the "Gladstone" locomotives lay, like that of most of the successful types described in this book, as much in their robustness and simplicity as in their sound design. For example, the slide-valves were placed under the cylinders, but the port faces were inclined when seen in elevation so that the Stephenson's valve gear would work them direct without the intervention of rocking levers. In the absence of guiding wheels in front, springing had special attention with leaf

springs on the leading axle and more flexible coil springs on the centre axle. One complication that was considered worthwhile was the installation of equipment to allow the exhaust steam to be condensed in the feed water, some of the waste heat being recovered thereby. Another was air-driven assistance—air was conveniently available from the Westinghouse air brake supply— for the screw reversing gear.

Whilst Stroudley was a man of his time and therefore a strict disciplinarian, the above was an example of his consideration for the men. He also insisted that the driver's name should be painted up in gold paint in the cab of the locomotive he drove; anyone visiting No.216 *Gladstone,* now on display in the National Railway Museum at York, should look for William Love's name. This practice led to a wonderfully high standard of service. Incidentally, *Gladstone* was almost certainly the first

main-line express locomotive to be preserved by a private group —in this case the Stephenson Locomotive Society, who bought her in 1927 from the Southern Railway, successor to the LBSCR. They were asked the princely sum of £140 and this included re-boilering and other work to restore the engine to near enough her original appearance. She was painted in that wonderful Stroudley yellow ochre livery and given a home in the London & North Eastern Railway's original museum at York.

As regards their work, the "Gladstone" class worked most of the principal LBSCR expresses including the London-Brighton Pullman trains, predecessors of the famed "Brighton Belle". They were capable of keeping a 60-minute timing with the Brighton Sunday Pullman train, introduced in 1898. The fastest timing today by express electric train is only five minutes less.

Vittorio Emanuele II 4-6-0

Italy:
Upper Italy Railroads (SFAI), 1884

Tractive effort: 15,335lb (6,958kg).
Axle load: 35,500lb (16t).
Cylinders: (2) 18½ x 24½in (470 x 620mm).
Driving wheels: 66in (1,675mm).
Heating surface: 1,720sq ft (124m²).
Superheater: None
Steam pressure: 142lb/sq in (10kg/cm²).
Grate area: 24sq ft (2.25m²).
Fuel: 7,700lb (3.5t).
Water: 2,200gall (2,630US) (10m³).
Adhesive weight: 106,000lb (48t).
Total weight: 184,475lb (83.7t).
Overall length: 54ft 1½in (16,500mm).

The old kingdom of Piedmont, home of Count Cavour, who with King Victor Emmanuel was responsible for ending the Austrian occupation in the north of Italy and going on to create a united Italy, had one of the first important mountain railways in Europe. It connected the capital, Turin, with the port of Genoa, via the Giovi Pass. The 103-mile line was opened throughout in 1853 after a nine-year construction period.

The problem was the crossing of the Apenines at 1,180ft. (360m) altitude, 14 miles (22.5km) from Genoa. The chosen grade up from the port involved an horrendous 1 in 28½ (3½ per cent). 0-4-0 and 0-6-0 saddle tank locomotives, working in pairs back-to-back with one crew,

were used by the Piedmont State Railroads with some success for working the incline.

In 1859 Italy was united and in 1865 the Giovi line became part of the Upper Italy Railroads (SFAI), which concern in 1872 set up the first railway locomotive design office in Italy. The last production of this establishment before the SFAI was absorbed into the Mediterranean System in 1885, was this absolutely remarkable machine, Europe's first 4-6-0,

No.1181 *Vittorio Emanuele II.*

It was proposed to use this class for working the new and more sensibly graded Giovi diversion line then under construction, on which (at some cost in extra mileage) the ruling grade would be reduced to 1 in 62 (1.6 per cent). It was opened in 1889, by which time many more 4-6-0s had been completed. By 1896 the class numbered 55. Ansaldo of Genoa, Miani & Silvestri of Milan and Maffei of Munich,

Class X2 4-4-0

Great Britain:
London & South Western Railway (L&SWR), 1891

Tractive effort: 16,426lb (7,453kg).
Axle load: 33,500lb (15.5t).
Cylinders: (2) 19 x 26in (483 x 660mm).
Driving wheels: 7ft 1in (2,160mm)..
Heating surface: 1,350sq ft (126.3m²).
Superheater: None.
Steam pressure: 175psi (12.3kg/cm²).
Grate area: 18.2sq ft (1.7m²).
Fuel: 8,000lb (3.5t).
Water: 3,300gall (4,000 US) (15m³).
Adhesive weight: 65,000lb (29.5t).
Total weight: 182,000lb (82.5t).
Length overall: 53ft 8in (16,383mm).

These lovely engines were the brain-children of William Adams, who, having served his time as a machine engineer and spent a period in charge of the loco-motive affairs of the North London Railway, became Mechanical Engineer of the London &

South Western Railway in 1878. His masterpiece was a group of 60 express passenger 4-4-0s for the London to Bournemouth and London to Exeter services of the company, constructed over the years 1891 to 1896. In the usual tradition of the day, a few small dimensional differences divided the group into four classes known as "X2", "T3", "T6" and "X6". The main difference lay in the 7ft 1in (2,160mm) driving wheels fitted to the X2s and T6s and the 6ft 7in (2,008mm) ones fitted to the others. All four classes, however, were uniform in giving first class performances. Speeds over 80mph (128km/h) were recorded on many occasions, a reflection on the excellent riding qualities of the Adams own celebrated design of bogie, which gave the drivers confidence to run at these speeds.

The outside cylinders originally had the unusual and spectacular feature of naked tail-rods—that is, the piston rods were extended to pass through glands in the

front covers of each cylinder, so the rod could be seen plunging out and in when the engine was in motion. These were removed after Adams had retired in 1895; Adams' elegant store-pipe chimneys were also replaced. The inside slide valves were worked by Stephenson link motion. Running numbers were:— "X2"—577 to 596; "T3"—557 to 576; "T6"—677 to 686; "X6"—657 to 666; there was no change when the L&SWR was absorbed into the Southern Railway.

The coming of corridor coaches and restaurant cars in the early years of the century meant that the Adams 4-4-0s were soon displaced by larger locomotives from normal top-line express work, but in their last years these handsome engines could occasionally be seen on such fast prestige trains as the three- and four-car pullman specials from Southampton to London in connection with Imperial Airways' Empire flying-boat services. Of course, like

everything that had wheels in the south of England, the war-time survivors were pressed into moving heavy troop trains at the time of the evacuation from Dunkirk. No.657 starred in the absurd but famous and still shown film "Oh, Mr. Porter", which was shot on the long-closed Basingstoke to Alton line.

Withdrawals began in 1930 and by the outbreak of war in 1939 the Adams 4-4-0s had almost vanished, only a dozen or so examples being left. Most of these were reprieved for the duration but by 1946 all had gone, except No.563 which in 1948 was restored for an ex-hibition held at Waterloo Station, London, in connection with its centenary. In due time No.563 became part of the national collection and can be seen in the museum at York.

Right: *London & South Western Railway class "X2" 4-4-0 No.563, designed by William Adams, as now restored.*

Bavaria, shared in the construction.

The locomotives had several unusual features including Gooch's valve gear outside the wheels. The working of this gear is explained in connection with Gooch's "Rover" class 4-2-2s, but here its workings are displayed in full view. The gear is actuated by two eccentrics mounted on a return crank, which in turn has its pivot set in line with the centre of the driving axle. It

can be seen that when the reversing rod leading from the cab is moved, the valve rod is raised or lowered, rather than the eccentric rods and link, as in the Stephenson's gear.

The rearward position of the cylinders and the forward position of the short-wheel base bogie and smoke-box will be noted. The designers were concerned that the boiler-tubes would be too long to allow the fire to be drawn properly and to obviate

this they recessed the firebox tubeplate into the boiler. This reduced the length of the tubes and increased the firebox volume, thereby forming one of the first-ever applications of a very modern feature known as a combustion chamber. The steam pressure was later raised to 156lb/sq in (11kg/cm²).

These engines were very successful and could climb the new Giovi line with 130 tons at a steady speed of 25mph

(40km/h). The maximum permitted speed, of course, was double that.

These 4-6-0s had another record—the unenviable one of being the first main-line steam locomotives to be displaced from the work for which they were built by a more modern form of traction. The old Giovi line went over to three-phase electric traction at 3,300 volts, 15 cycles (Hz) in 1910 and the diversion line followed in 1914.

Below: *The "Vittorio Emanuele II" 4-6-0 as built for the Upper Italy Railroads in 1884. These locomotives worked the famous Giovi incline near Genoa.*

Teutonic Class 2-2-2-0

Great Britain: London & North Western Railway (LNWR), 1889

Axle load: 35,000lb (16t).
Cylinders, HP: (2) 14 x 24in (356 x 610mm).
Cylinders, LP: (1) 30 x 24in (762 x 610mm).
Driving wheels: 85in (2,159mm).
Heating surface: 1,402sq ft (130m²).
Superheater: None.
Steam pressure: 175psi (12.3kg/cm²).
Grate area: 20.5sq ft (1.9m²).
Fuel: 11,000lb (5t).
Water: 1,800gall (2,160 US) (8m³).
Adhesive weight: 69,500lb (31.5t).
Total weight: 158,000lb (72t).
Length overall: 51ft 0¼in (15,552mm).

The story of Francis Webb, the London & North Western Railway and the compound locomotive is one of the saddest episodes in the whole of locomotive history. Both the man and the railway were of gigantic stature and with good reason. Not for nothing was the LNWR known as "the Premier Line, the largest joint stock corporation in the World", whilst Webb himself made Crewe Works into a manufacturing unit without a rival in its ability to make everything needed by a great railway, starting with raw material. His superb non-compound 2-4-0s (on which his first three batches of compounds were based) included *Hardwicke* which still survives and runs. This locomotive showed what Webb locomotives were capable of when on 22 August 1895, the last night of the famous Race to Aberdeen, she ran the 141 miles (226km) of hilly road from Crewe to Carlisle at an average speed of 67¼mph (107.5km/h) and with a maximum of 88 (141).

In the late 1870s the idea of compounding was in the air and Webb made up his mind that this was a world that he was going to conquer. He first had a Trevithick 2-2-2 *Medusa* converted to a two-cylinder compound 2-4-0 and then in 1882 came his first three-cylinder compound 2-2-2-0 No.

66 *Experiment*. The system Webb adopted was to have two outside high pressure cylinders, 11½in (292mm) diameter driving the rear driving wheels and a great dustbin of a low pressure cylinder 26in (660mm) diameter to drive the front driving axle. There were no coupling rods. Three sets of Joy's valve gear were provided.

Apart from the mechanism of compounding and the three cylinders, the rest of the locomotive was basically a standard LNWR 2-4-0 of which a large number were in use. *Experiment* needed modifications and the first production batch of 29, built in 1883-84, had 13½in (343mm) diameter high pressure cylinders in place of 11½ (292). They were not specially economical and were bad starters—men with pinch bars were needed to give the engines an initial starting movement before they would go. One of the problems was that Webb was an autocrat and any-

one who suggested that his beloved compounds were less than perfect was regarded as questioning his superior officer's judgment and hence offering his resignation. So no one told Webb how awful they were even when, inevitably, another 40, the "Dreadnought" class only slightly modified, appeared 1884-88. The only thing his hard-pressed staff could do was to "repair"—actually to *renew* in more powerful form —the fleet of simple express passenger 2-4-0s. By this means 256 new non-compound locomotives were turned out under the Chief's nose between 1887 and 1901.

In 1889 came the best of the Webb compounds, the ten "Teutonic" class; they are the basis of the drawing on this page and their particulars are listed above. The further modification in this case concerned the valve gear of the inside low pressure cylinder. Its Joy's valve gear was replaced by a "slip eccentric", a gear more

Above: *A 2-4-0 Webb compound being given an initial starting movement, manually with a pinch bar. Note the single central large low-pressure cylinder.*

familiar to manufacturers of steam toys than to full-size builders. In this arrangement a single eccentric is mounted loose on the driving axle. A pin attached to this eccentric and a stepped collar on the axle is arranged to drive it in one position relative to the crank for forward motion, and in another one for going backwards. The cut-off point of steam admission to the high pressure cylinders could be adjusted in the normal way, using the unusual inverted outside arrangement of Joy's valve gear visible in the drawing above. The arrangement worked well except

Below: *L&NWR Webb compound 2-4-0* Jeanie Deans *of the "Teutonic" class.*

Rover Class 4-2-2

for one problem; this typically occurred when a locomotive, having first backed on to its train, tried to start. The slip eccentric gear naturally still would be in reverse, but when the driver opened the throttle, the idea was that the two high-pressure cylinders would taken in the steam and move the train. By the time it had moved forward half-a-revolution of the driving wheels the inside slip eccentrics would have moved round into the forward position; therefore, when the first puff of steam exhausted from a high pressure cylinder into the low, off she would go. Alas, should the engine slip or spin its rear high pressure driving wheels when starting (which, as on all the 2-2-2-0 compounds were not coupled to the front low pressure ones), the low pressure cylinders would still have their valve gear in reverse when they received steam. The result was a stationary locomotive with its two pairs of driving wheels revolving in opposite directions!

Even so, the "Teutonic" locomotives were good once they got going—No.1304 *Jeanie Deans* was famous for regularly working and keeping time on the 2 p.m. Scottish Express from Euston to Crewe during the whole of 1890s. No.1309 *Adriatic* even starred in that legendary final night of racing in 1895, although her run from Euston to Crewe at an average speed of 63.1mph (102km/h) was not quite as great as achievement as that of her simple equivalent *Hardwicke* on the next stage; still it was certainly a very respectable effort. These ten "Teutonic" class which almost managed to approach simple performance, were the pinnacle of Webb's achievement with his compounds. It says little for the management structure of the old LNWR that no one could stop him building a further 140 compound express locomotives before he retired in 1903, none of which approached even the modest abilities of the "Teutonic", and all of which were an embarassment to the operating authorities of the Premier Line.

Tractive effort: 9,639lb (4,370kg).
Axle load: 35,800lb (16.3t).
Cylinders: (2) 18 x 24in (457 x 610mm).
Driving wheels: 96in (2,438mm).
Heating surface: 2,085sq ft (193.7m²).
Superheater: None.
Steam pressure: 140psi (9.8kg/cm²).
Grate area: 24sq ft (22.7m²).
Fuel: 7,000lb (3t).
Water: 3,000gall (3,600 US) (13.5m³).
Adhesive weight: 36,000lb (16t).
Total weight: 160,000lb (73t).
Length overall: 47ft 6in (14,478mm).

As the leaders of the Great Western's broad gauge express fleet, these legendary locomotives were the direct successors to the "Fire Fly" class 2-2-2s, the passenger version of Gooch's famous standard locomotives. The prototype *Great Western* of 1846 was basically a stretched version of the 2-2-2 with the grate area dimension enhanced by 68 per cent and the nominal tractive effort by 36 per cent. The penalty was a 21 per cent increase in weight, the price being paid when *Great Western* broke her leading axle at speed near Shrivenham soon after completion. Alteration to a 4-2-2 followed, but the leading pairs of wheels were held in the frames rather than mounted in a pivoted separate bogie.

Even before this had been done, on 13 June 1846, *Great Western* hauled a 100-ton train from Paddington to Swindon in 78 minutes for the 77½ miles (124km). The design was so sound that it was repeated again

and again, each time with slight enlargement and modernisation until the final batch which is the subject of this description appeared in 1888, over 40 years after the prototype was built and only 4 years before the broad gauge was finally abolished. Typically about 24 were in service at any one time, 54 being built altogether.

In order to provide for the expansive use of steam the gab valve gear originally fitted to the standard locomotives was replaced by Gooch's own valve gear, probably devised to get round the Stephenson patent to which the gear related closely. Both valve gears have a pair of eccentrics, one set for forward running and the other for reverse; the little ends of the eccentric rods are connected by a curved link. The curve of the Gooch link, however, faces the opposite way, being concave towards the cylinders instead of convex. The gear is adjusted by lifting or lowering the valve rod and die block, rather than by moving the link and eccentric rod assembly as in the Stephenson gear.

Apart from general sound construction the reasons for the success and longevity of these locomotives lay very much in the broad gauge itself. Most British locomotives of the day carried their cylinders and motion as well as their fire-beds between the frames, which themselves had to be between the wheels; it is therefore not surprising that an extra width of 27¾ inches (705mm) which there was to play with—the difference between the 7ft 0¼in (2,140mm) and 4ft 8½in (1,435mm) gauges—could be used to advantage by designers. For example, the wide firebox, which was later to come as a rightly extolled development at the expense of some complication

Above: *Great Western Railway broad-gauge "Rover" class 4-2-2 locomotive* Tornado. *Engines of this basic design ruled the broad gauge lines from 1846 until their demise in 1892 and were renowned for their speed and power. Daniel Gooch was the designer.*

on standard gauge, had come automatically many years before on the broad. Ample-sized valve chests could be placed between ample-sized cylinders and there was also plenty of room to get at the very sturdy and simple layout that resulted.

For 46 years, then, the Gooch 4-2-2s ruled the Great Western. The "Flying Dutchman" express from Paddington to Newton Abbot was entrusted to one of them in 1892 just as it was in 1848 when it was the fastest train in the world. Later versions naturally had much modification in respect of details and fittings; there were even such mollycoddling devices as exiguous cabs for the enginemen! Right up to the end also, no numbers were carried, only names; and what names, too—*Rover, Swallow, Balaklava, Hirondelle, Timour, Iron Duke, Tartar, Sultan, Warlock, Lightning, Amazon, Crimea, Eupatoria, Inkerman, Courier, Bulkely, Dragon, Great Britain, Emperor, Sebastopol, Alma, Prometheus, Great Western, Tornado. Tornado* was the last broad gauge engine built in July 1888.

E.L. Ahrons, that distinguished observer of late-Victorian train working, described how, in the last years of the broad gauge, he timed *Lightning* running down Wellington bank just west of Taunton at just over 81mph (130 km/h). It was, he said, "his highest speed, not only on the broad gauge but also on any railway until many years afterwards".

Johnson Midland Single 4-2-2
Great Britain: Midland Railway (MR), 1887

Tractive effort: 14,506lb (6,582kg).
Axle load: 39,500lb (18t).
Cylinders: (2) 19 x 26in (483 x 660mm).
Driving wheels: 93½in (2,375mm).
Heating surface: 1,237sq ft (115m²).
Superheater: None.
Steam pressure: 170psi (12kg/cm²).
Grate area: 19.6sq ft (1.82m²).
Fuel: 8,800lb (4t).
Water: 3,500gall (4,200 US) (16m³).
Adhesive weight: 39,500lb (18t).
Total weight: 181,500lb (82.5t).
Length overall: 52ft 7½in (16,038mm).

The Midland Railway of England was noted for having trains which were fast, frequent and, consequently, light. One reason was

certainly the fact that at only one town on the system — Kettering in Northamptonshire — did the company not have to face competition. One result was that the Midland was the last railway in Britain to have a fleet of single-driver locomotives and the only one to build them on into the twentieth century.

The first of the single-wheelers of S.W. Johnson, known colloquially as "Spinners", was constructed at the Company's Derby Works in 1887, after an interval of 21 years during which only coupled engines were made. By 1900, there were 95 locomotives in the class, made up of successive batches which differed slightly in main dimensions. Standardisation was then something the Midland left to newer and brasher railways! The dimensions given above refer to the "115" batch of 1897, considered to be the best.

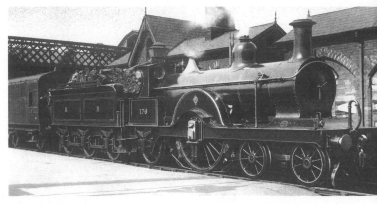

Their elegance was enhanced by a noble crimson lake livery — which was kept unbelievably clean. In fact, it is said that it was the practice for MR shed foreman to feel behind the *backs* of the wheels with white gloves to find if the engines had been sufficiently groomed to be allowed out in

Above: *Midland Railway 4-2-2 No.176 at Bedford station circa 1900. Note the horse-box as the leading vehicle of the train.*

traffic. Trays were placed under the engines when on shed in order to collect any oil drips which might sully the clean floor

Class 17 4-4-0
Belgium: Belgian State Railways (SNCB), 1902

Tractive effort: 20,261lb (9,193kg).
Axle load: 40,000lb (18t).
Cylinders: (2) 19 x 26in (482 x 660mm).
Driving wheels: 78¾in (1,980mm).
Heating surface: 1,370sq ft (128m²).
Superheater: See Text.
Steam pressure: 200psi (14kg/cm²).
Grate area: 22.5sq ft (2.1m²).
Fuel: 9,900lb (4.5t).
Water: 4,125gall (4,950 US) (18.5m³).
Adhesive weight: 80,500lb (36.5t).
Total weight: 219,500lb (99.5t).
Length overall: 57ft 4in (17,475mm).

Late in the nineteenth century, the railways of Belgium were specially notable for originality in locomotive design. Some strange-looking 2-4-2s whose appearance was made the stuff of nightmares by the use of *square* chimneys, were to the fore on prime passenger workings; also, of course, the names Alfred Belpaire and Egide Walschaerts are those of two Belgian locomotive engineers whose inventions were used world-wide on the steam locomotive.

So it is rather strange that just before the turn of the century this oldest of nationalised railway systems went overseas to a foreign builder for a foreign design; moreover, one that was among

the most simple and conventional and which included among its features neither a Belpaire firebox nor sets of Walschaerts valve gear.

Locomotive engineer J.F. McIntosh of the Caledonian Railway had produced his famous "Dunalaistair" 4-4-0s in 1897 and for many years these engines were the mainstay of express passenger operations on the line in question. Most of those built survived after 1923 into London Midland & Scottish Railway days and some even into the British Railways era after 1948. There were four "marks" (known as Dunalaistair I to Dunalaistair IV) and before 1914 they were bedecked in the superb Caledonian

blue livery. All were built at the company's St. Rollox works in Glasgow.

The Caledonian Railway was so proud of their new locomotive giant that they sent her to be displayed at the Brussels exhibition of 1897, from whence the engine returned with a gold medal. An unexpected result was an order from the Belgian State Railways for 5 duplicate locomotives, to be built by Nielson Reid & Co. (a predecessor of the North British Locomotive company), also of Glasgow. Following this, 40 more were built by Belgian firms in 1899 and 1900; all the locomotives were known as Belgian class "17". Subsequently, an enlarged version,

of a Midland loco depot! In such circumstances it is hardly surprising that the quality of maintenance was very high and this was also a factor in enabling low-powered locomotives to handle the traffic satisfactorily. It was also a factor in permitting all the mechanism—two sets of main motion plus two sets of Stephenson's valve gear—to be tucked away out of sight, but not out of mind so far as the fitters and drivers were concerned.

Another reason for the return of the single-wheeler was the invention of the steam sanding gear, which blew sand under the driving wheels just that bit more reliably than the gravity sanding previously used. Air sanding would have been just that bit more reliable still but, alas, the Midland showed a preference for the vacuum rather than the air brake and so compressed air

Above: *The restored Midland Railway "Johnson Single" 4-2-2 No.673 as it appeared during the crowd-pulling "Rocket 150" celebrations in 1975.*

Below: *Midland Railway "Johnson Single" 4-2-2 in all the glory of its superb crimson lake livery.*

was not available on MR locomotives. Good sanding gear was absolutely essential for a single-driver locomotive with limited adhesive weight.

Express trains of seven or eight bogie carriages weighing between 200 and 250 tons were just right for these celebrated locomotives. In dry calm weather

heavier loads could be managed and there are records of trains up to 350 tons being handled and time being kept. They were also certainly very speedy, with maxima of around 90mph (144 km/h) having been recorded. Another role for these beautiful locomotives was that of acting as pilots to the equally celebrated Midland 4-4-0s.

Before a logical system was adopted, numbers were allocated at random, but after 1907 the "Spinners" class occupied Nos. 600 to 694. Naming, like standardisation in those days, was not a Midland thing but, quite exceptionally, one of the last and twentieth-century batch—the ones with the big bogie tenders heavier than the locomotive—was given the name *Princess of Wales*.

One Midland single has survived; No.118 of the batch built in 1897 was set aside in Derby Works after withdrawal in 1928. Beautifully restored and with a fake wooden chimney now replaced by a proper one, she ran in steam at the Rocket 150 Cavalcade in June 1980.

class "18", was constructed, bringing the total to 185 locomotives by 1905. There was also a 4-4-2 tank engine version, constructed to the tune of 115 examples, which never existed on the Caledonian Railway.

Such continental features as bogie tenders and air brakes were already part of the design and the only obvious modification specified concerned the exiguous cabs of the original Scottish locomotives. These were altered to provide greater protection for the enginemen by the addition of side windows.

Left: *Belgian State Railway class 18 4-4-0 as restored and preserved today.*

Class S3 4-4-0

Germany:
Royal Prussian Union Railway (KPEV), 1893

Axleload: 35,000lb (15.6t).
Cylinders, HP: (1) 18.9 x 23.6in (480 x 600mm).
Cylinders, LP: (1) 26.6 x 23.6in (680 x 600mm).
Driving wheels: 78in (1,980mm).
Heating surface: 1,267sq ft (117.7m²).
Superheater: See descriptive text.
Steam pressure: 171psi (12kg/cm²).
Grate area: 25.0sq ft (2.3m²).
Fuel: 11,000lb (5.0t).
Water: 4,730gall (5,680US) (21.5m³).
Adhesive weight: 69,000lb (30.9t).
Total weight*: 112,000lb (50.5t).
Length overall: 57ft 7in (17,560mm).

(*engine only)

The passenger engines built by the Royal Prussian Union Railway in the 1880s were 2-4-0s with outside cylinders, but towards the end of the decade the desire for higher speeds and great comfort (and thus greater weight) brought a need for larger locomotives. At that time August von Borries, well known for the system of compounding which bears his name, was locomotive superintendent at Hanover, and the Minister of Public Works sent him on a tour of England and America to study locomotive developments in those countries. Von Borries reported that to carry the larger boiler which would be needed, the engines would need an extra axle, and that the best arrangement would be the American type of 4-4-0. This would give better riding at speed than the existing 2-4-0s with their long front overhang.

In 1890 Henschel built a pair of two-cylinder compound 4-4-0 locomotives to von Borries' design, and in the following year the same firm built four more engines of the same wheel arrangement to the designs of Lochner, the locomotive superintendent at Erfurt, two compound and two with simple expansion. A total of 150 engines were later built to the Erfurt simple-expansion design, but experience with these engines convinced the management of the superiority of von Borries' compounds, and in 1892 he produced an improved version of his design. This was the "S3", the "S" denoting "schnellzuglokomotiv", or express engine, and the digit being the serial number of the type from the introduction of this method of classification. The "S3" was highly successful, and in the period from 1892 to 1904 a total

of 1,027 engines of this design were built for the Prussian railways, as well as 46 for other German state railways. The engines eventually worked most of the express trains in Prussia. In addition to the "S3"s, a further 424 locomotives were built to the same design, but with smaller driving wheels, and classified "P4".

The bogie was placed symmetrically under the cylinders and smokebox, and with the leading coupled axle set well back to give as long a connecting rod as possible, the layout showed clearly the influence of von Borries' American visit. Outside Walschaert's (Heusinger) valve gear drove slide valves set at an angle above the cylinders. The engines were rated to haul 320 tonnes at 47mph (75km/h) on the level, and 150 tonnes at 31mph (50km/h) on a gradient

Above: *A Prussian class "S3" 4-4-0, the 5,000th locomotive built by the engineering firm of Borsig for the Prussian Railways.*

of 1 in 100 (1 per cent), and they established a reputation for economy in coal consumption and for smooth riding.

By its sheer size the "S3" class earns a notable place in locomotive history, but it is also important as being the first class to which steam superheating was applied. The need for superheating comes from a physical phenomenon—that water evaporates to steam at a definite temperature dependent on the prevailing pressure; thus at the working pressure of the "S3", 171psi (12kg/cm²), the temperature is 376°F (197°C). With water present in the boiler, the steam temperature cannot exceed that of the water. When

Below: *The class "S3" 4-4-0 was one of the most successful passenger locomotives to run in Germany. Over 1,000 were built around the turn of the century.*

The class was notable as being the first major application of superheating to steam traction; this offered a major improvement in efficiency at little cost.

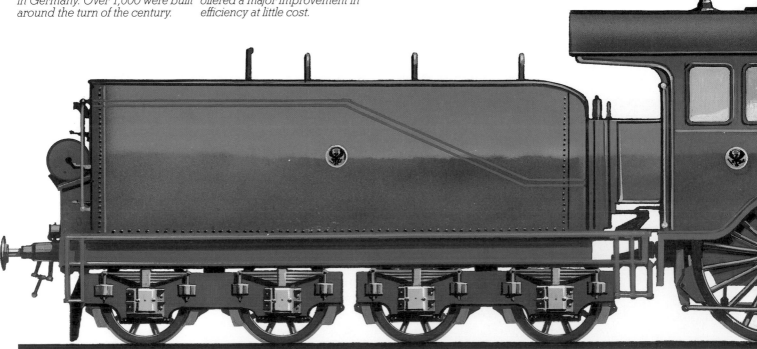

steam is drawn from the boiler it carries some particles of water with it, and when the steam comes into contact with the comparatively cool metal of the valves and cylinders, it loses that, and further particles of water form by condensation. Much of the work done on the piston is by the steam expanding after the valve has closed. Water has no capacity for expanding, and its presence in the cylinder is therefore a loss; it has been heated to the temperature in the boiler to no effect.

If the steam can be heated after it has left the boiler, and is no longer in contact with the mass of water there, the particles of moisture in the steam can be evaporated, making the steam dry. Still further application of heat causes the temperature of the steam to rise, and it becomes superheated. The main advantage of superheated steam is that if it is cooled slightly on making contact with the cool cylinder walls, no condensation occurs until all the superheat has been removed. Superheating is thus a means of eliminating condensation in the cylinder, and thereby making better use of the heat in the steam.

The attractions of superheating had been known to engineers for many years, but it was not until the 1890s that practicable designs of superheater were produced, by far the most important being those designed by Dr Wilhelm Schmidt of Kassel. The various schemes produced had in common that, after leaving the boiler, the steam flow was divided between a number of small tubes, known as "elements", by a distribution box or "header". After being heated in the elements, the steam was collected in another

header, and passed through the main steam pipes to the cylinders. In Schmidt's first design, known as the flame tube superheater, a number of the boiler tubes were replaced by a large tube 17.5in (445mm) in diameter, and the elements were inserted into this tube. It was intended that the tube should be sufficiently large for flames to reach the elements (flames from the firebox die out quickly on entering a small tube).

Schmidt found an enthusiastic supporter of his ideas in Robert Garbe, who was chief engineer of the Berlin division of the Prussian railways. With Garbe's support the flame tube superheater was fitted to two 4-4-0 locomotives, an "S3" and a "P4". The "S3" was completed in April 1898, and made its first trial trip on the thirteenth of that month, a notable date in locomotive history. Although the results were encouraging, trouble was experienced with distortion of the large flame tube. Schmidt therefore produced two more designs, in one of which the bundle of elements was housd in

the smokebox, and in the other of which a number of the boiler tubes were replaced by tubes slightly larger, and each element made a return loop in one of these tubes.

In 1899 two new "S3" locomotives were fitted with the smokebox superheater, and they were also given piston valves in place of slide valves. With the combination of superheater and well-proportioned piston valves, these engines contained the essential ingredients of the final phase of development of the steam locomotive.

One of these two engines was exhibited at the Paris Exhibition of 1900, and attracted considerable attention. In service a reduction in coal consumption of 12 per cent was achieved compared with a standard "S3", but it was recognised that the temperature of the gases in the

Below: *The predecessors of the "S3" class were these "S1" class 2-4-0s, of which 242 were built between 1877 and 1885 for the Prussian railway system.*

smokebox was too low for a very high degree of superheat to be attained, and that the scope for further development lay in the design with the elements in smoke tubes. However, increasing the temperature of the steam brought the need for improved lubricating oils, and whilst the problems of lubrication were being solved, many engines of class "S3" were fitted with smokebox superheaters.

The intensive development work needed to perfect superheating was largely due to the genius of Schmidt, and in little more than ten years after the first application of the smokebox superheater, the smoke tube design was virtually a standard fitting for large new locomotives; it was first applied to a Belgian Class 35 Caledonian type 4-6-0 in 1903. For a modest outlay, and with little increase in weight, an improvement in coal consumption of up to 20 per cent was obtained, and, equally important in some countries, a similar economy in water. For many engineers the superheater was an alternative to compounding, as it gave a fuel economy similar to that obtained by compounding, but without the mechanical complications of the compound. Others regarded superheating as an extra advantage to be added to that of compounding. Over a period of years after the fitting of the first superheater, both these points of view were apparent on the Prussian railways, and after a succession of superheated simple engines, a four-cylinder compound 4-6-0 was built.

A total of 34 of the "S3" locomotives survived to be incorporated in the stock of German State Railway in 1924.

No. 999 4-4-0
United States:
New York Central & Hudson River RR (NYC & HRRR), 1893

Below: *The famous record-breaking 4-4-0 No.999 of the New York Central & Hudson River Railroad.*

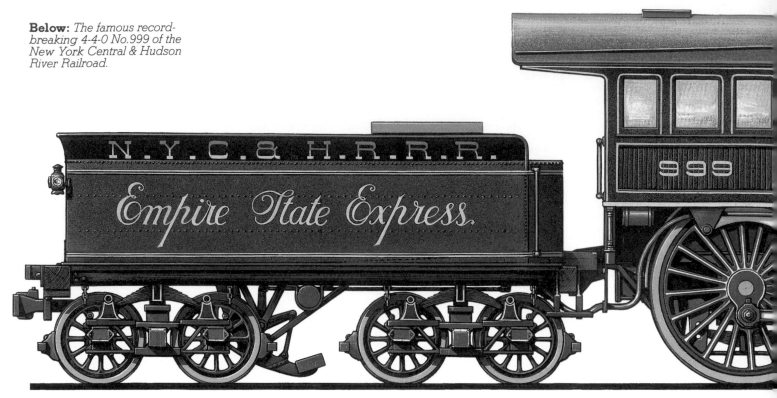

Tractive effort: 16,270lb (7,382kg).
Axle load: 42,000lb (19t).
Cylinders: (2) 19 x 24in (483 x 610mm).
Driving wheels: 86in (2,184mm).
Heating surface: 1,927sq ft (179m²).
Superheater: None
Steam pressure: 190psi (12.6kg/cm²).
Grate area: 30.7sq ft (2.85m²).
Fuel: 15,400lb (7t).
Water: 2,950gall (3,500US) (13.5m³).
Adhesive weight: 84,000lb (38t).
Total weight: 204,000lb (92.5t).
Overall length: 57ft 10in (17,630mm).

When on 10 May 1893 New York Central & Hudson River Railroad No.999 hauled the Empire State Express at 112.5mph (180km/h) down a 1 in 350 (0.28 per cent) grade near Batavia, New York State, it was not only a world record for steam railways but for any kind of transport. The only problem is that it is not a question of "when" but of "if".

The conductor timed the train (presumably with his service watch) to travel between two marks a mile apart. With four heavy Wagner cars weighing 50-55 tons each, about 2,000 cylinder horse-power would be needed and this would seem to be just a little too much to expect; not so much as regards steam production at a corresponding rate, but in getting that steam in and out of the cylinders in such quantities. A speed of 102.8mph (166km/h) over 5 miles, timed the previous night, is a little more credible, but both must, alas, be regarded as "not proven".

The man responsible for this locomotive's existence was no great railroad tycoon, but an irrepressible patent medicine salesman called Daniels, taken on as the line's passenger agent in New York. He persuaded the management to run this exclusive Empire State Express between New York and Chicago during the period of the Colombian Exposition; the time of 20 hours for the 960 miles (1,536km) was an unprecedented average speed for any journey of similar length.

This combination of speed and luxury was shortly to result in one of the most famous trains of the world, the legendary year-round "Twentieth Century Limited", running daily from New York to Chicago.

No.999 was specially built for the job and the train name was even painted on the tender. The NYC&HRR shops at West Albany turned out this single big-wheeled version of the road's standard 4-4-0s, themselves typical of the US locomotive of their day, with slide-valves, Stephenson's valve gear and more normal 78in (1,981mm) diameter driving wheels.

On account of the record exploit, No.999's fame is world-wide; the locomotive even figured on a US two-cent stamp in 1900. Today, much rebuilt and with those high-and-mighty drivers replaced by modest workaday ones, No.999 is on display at the Chicago Museum of Science and Industry.

Right: *No.999 as preserved for posterity. Although painted in the style of the original as built, the big 86in (2,184mm) diameter driving wheels have been replaced by less distinctive 79in (2,006mm) ones.*

Class 6 4-4-0
Austria:
Imperial and Royal State Railways (KKStB), 1893

Axle load: 32,000lb (14.5t).
Cylinders HP: (1) 19¾ x 26¾in (500 x 680mm).
Cylinders LP: (1) 29 x 26¾in (740 x 680mm).
Driving wheels: 82½in (2,190mm).
Heating surface: 1,507sq ft (140m²).
Superheater: None.
Steam pressure: 185psi (13kg/cm²).
Grate area: 31sq ft (2.9m²).
Fuel: 16,000lb (7.25t).
Water: 3,650gall (4,400 US) (16.5m³).
Adhesive weight: 63,000lb (28t).
Total weight: 207,000lb (94t).
Length overall: 54ft 1in (16,480mm).

Karl Gölsdorf, head of the locomotive department of the Imperial and Royal Austrian State Railways was an original thinker as well as a first rate engineer and, whilst his ideas never became part of the main stem of development, they not only worked but suited local conditions extremely well.

These little 4-4-0s built at Floridsdorf (a suburb of Vienna) illustrated this very vividly. They were compound locomotives but with only two cylinders, thereby avoiding one of the chief drawbacks of compounding, that is, the complexity that normally results. Of course, with a two-cylinder compound it is absolutely vital to be able to admit high-pressure steam to the low-pressure cylinder when starting,

otherwise the locomotive would often never move at all. Even so, the means to do this result in making the engine more difficult to drive, another drawback normally associated with compounding.

Gölsdorf got over this problem by giving the locomotive low pressure cylinder starting ports which were only uncovered by the valves when the valve gear—Walschaert's in this case—was in full gear, as at starting from rest. Once the train was moving, the driver would reduce the cut-off and compound working would commence. In this way the method of driving differed little from that of handling a normal simple locomotive. The permitted axle load on the Austrian railways

was very low and these relatively heavy locomotives could only be accommodated by means of another piece of originality. The wheelbase on these engines as in others, was set far back, so that the leading wheel was almost in line with the chimney. By this means the bogie would carry more of the weight than it would if placed in the more usual position, and the maximum axle load was reduced in relation to the total weight.

In service, this class proved itself to be not only powerful but speedy, with a maximum permitted speed of 81mph (130km/h). It was possible to reduce the scheduled time of the best expresses from Vienna to Karlsbad (now known as Karlovy Vary)

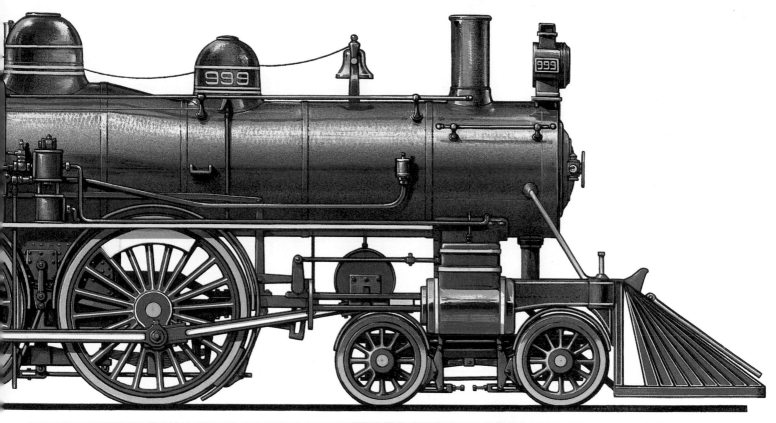

from 12 hours to 8. It is no credit to the politicians of Europe that the fastest time between the same two cities today nearly 90 years later is 11 hours 29 minutes.

A striking feature in the appearance of some Gölsdorf locomotives, including these class "6" 4-4-0s, was the pipe connecting the two domes. Technically, this is not so remarkable since in most steam locomotives a main steam pipe runs forward from the point at which steam is collected although it is customary—except in Russia and China—to have it inside the boiler.

Right: *KKStB class "6" 4-4-0. Note the external steam pipe connecting steam dome to throttle*

I-1 Class 4-6-0

United States:
Lake Shore & Michigan Southern Railroad (LS&MSRR), 1900

Tractive effort: 23,800lb (10,800kg).
Axle load: 45,000lb (20.5t)..
Cylinders: (2) 20 x 28in (508 x 711mm).
Driving wheels: 80in (2,032mm).
Heating surface: 2,917sq ft (271m²).
Superheater: None.
Steam pressure: 200psi (14.1kg/cm²).
Grate area: 33.6sq ft (3.1m²).
Fuel: 17,500lb (8t).
Water: 6,000gall (7,200 US) (27.2m³).
Adhesive weight: 135,000lb (61t).
Total weight: 300,000lb (136t).
Length overall: 62ft 3in (18,914mm)..

As has been described, the "American Standard" 4-4-0 hauled most USA passenger express trains from the 1850s

Class D16sb 4-4-0

United States:
Pennsylvania Railroad (PRR), 1895

Tractive effort: 23,900lb (10,850kg)
Axleload: 52,000lb (23.5t).
Cylinders: (2) 20½ x 26in (521 x 660mm).
Driving wheels: 68in (1727mm).
Heating surface: 1400sq ft (130.1m²).
Superheater: 253sq ft (23.5m²).
Steam pressure: 175psi (12.3kg/cm²).
Grate area: 33.2sq ft (3.1m²).
Fuel: 26,000lb (11.8t).
Water: 4,660gall (5,600US) (21.2m³).
Adhesive weight: 98,500lb (44.7t).
Total weight: 281,000lb (127.4t).
Length overall: 67ft 0in (20,422mm).

By the end of the 19th century the Pennsylvania Railroad had established a reputation for large locomotives, mostly built in own Altoona shops, and characterized outwardly by the Belpaire fire-box, a rarity in North America. Its 4-4-0 locomotives were no exception, and the high water mark of the type was reached with the "D16" class, introduced in 1895. With cylinders 18½ x 26in (470 x 660mm) and 185psi (13.0 kg/cm²) boilers, they were large engines for their day, and their appearance was the more impressive because the firebox was placed above the frames, making the boiler higher than was usual at this period.

Two varieties were built initially, one with 80 in (2,032mm) driving wheels for the more level divisions ("D16a"), and the other with 68 in (1,727mm) wheels for the hillier parts of the road ("D16"). The "D16a" engines soon established a reputation for high speed, as they were used in competition with the Atlantic City Railroad on the 58½ mile (94km) "racetrack" between Camden and Atlantic

until the 1880s. However, there came a time when loads began to outstep the capacity of locomotives with only two driven axles.

The obvious development was simply to add a third coupled axle, and this is what was done. Some of the best features of the 4-4-0 were retained in the 4-6-0 such as the bogie or leading truck to guide the locomotive, but in other ways problems arose. The ashpan was liable to get mixed up with the rear axle, for example, and the gap between the leading driving wheels and the cylinders, which on the 4-4-0 made the motion so easy to get at, became filled up. Even so, there was a period at the end of

Left: Lake Shore & Michigan Central Railroad "I-1" class 4-6-0 No.604 heads the "Twentieth Century Limited".

the 1800s when the 4-6-0 ruled the express passenger scene in the USA. About 16,000 examples went into service there all told, most between 1880 and 1910.

The high-wheeled example chosen to illustrate this famous type was built by the Brooks Locomotive Works of Dunkirk, New York State in 1900 for the Lake Shore & Michigan Southern Railroad. They were intended to take charge of the prime varnish trains of the Western part of the New York to Chicago main line belonging to what was soon to become the New York Central Railroad.

Kipling wrote of these great days in that evocative short story called "007" (collected in *The Day's Work*) but in fact they were to be brief. Wide fireboxes, piston valves and superheaters were shortly to replace narrow fireboxes, slide valves and the

use of saturated steam, so changing the world of steam for ever. In fact, the paint was hardly dry on these locomotives before the LS&MS ordered some 2-6-2s with wide fireboxes over the trailing pony trucks. However, the propensity of the flanges of the wheels of the leading single-axle pony truck of the 2-6-2s to ride up over the head of the rails at high speeds put these 4-6-0s back in charge of the legendary Twentieth Century Limited service running between New York and Chicago shortly after it was introduced on 15 June 1902.

The timing over the 960 miles (1,536km) between New York's Grand Central Terminal and La Salle Street station in Chicago was 20 hours, an average speed of 48mph (77km/h). This included several stops for servicing and changing locomotives and much slow running in such places

as Syracuse, where the main line in those days ran along the main street. Overall the schedule was one of the hardest in the world.

The train originally consisted of a buffet-library car, dining car and three sleeping cars, the last of which had an observation saloon complete with brass-railed open platform. The comforts offered were the equivalent of the highest grade of hotel.

One factor in all this comfort and luxury was the great weight of these 80ft (24.3m) Pullman cars even though there were only five of them. So soon enough it was necessary to increase the amount of accommodation provided and accordingly these 4-6-0s had to be replaced. But even if their days of glory were few, these locomotives with their 80-inch (2,032mm) drivers did wonders with what was then one of the hardest schedules in the world.

City. On this service one famous driver was credited with covering an eight-mile stretch at 102mph (164km/h). On another occasion the same driver worked a Presidential special over the 90 miles (145km) from Philadelphia to Jersey City at an average of 72mph (116km/h).

The mechanical quality of the design was well demonstrated by engine No.816, which distinguished itself by covering 300,000 miles (483,000km) on the middle division of the PRR in three years and four months, without shopping or other heavy

Left: On the Strasburg Railroad, preserved Pennsylvania RR class "D16" 4-4-0 No.1223 calls at Groff's Drove in July 1970.

Below: The superb quality of the restoration work done by the Strasburg Tourist RR is demonstrated by their D16 4-4-0.

repair. This was a notable feat for its day.

A total of 426 engines were built in five sub-classes of "D16" between 1895 and 1910. Apart from the two driving wheel sizes, their main dimensions were identical as built. With the introduction of Atlantics and then Pacifics in the new century, the "D16"'s were displaced from the best trains, but the class was given a new lease of life from 1914 onwards when nearly half of them were modernised in line with the later engines. Slightly larger cylinders with piston valves

were fitted, still with the inside Stephenson's valve gear, and the boiler was given a Schmidt's superheater, with the pressure reduced slightly. Most of the rebuilds were the smaller-wheeled engines, and these became "D16sb" (see the dimensions at the head of this article). In this form they settled down to working numerous branch lines,

and three of them were still engaged in this work early in World War II. One of these three, No.1223 built in 1905, was preserved on the Strasburg Rail Road in its native state.

Below: A head-on view of preserved "D16" class 4-4-0 No.1223 at Strasburg, Pennsylvania, USA.

Class Q1 4-4-0
Great Britain:
North Eastern Railway (NER), 1896

Tractive effort: 16,953lb (7,690kg).
Axle load: 42,000lb (19t).
Cylinders: (2) 20 x 26in (508 x 660mm).
Driving wheels: 91¼in (2,315mm).
Heating surface: 1,216sq ft (113m²).
Superheater: None.
Steam pressure: 175psi (12.3kg/cm²).
Grate area: 20.75sq ft (1.93m²).
Fuel: Coal, 11,200lb (5t).
Water: 4,000 gall (4,800 US) (18m³).
Adhesive weight: 77,000lb (35t).
Total weight: 206,000lb (93.5t).
Length overall: 56ft 3in (17,145mm).

Right: North Eastern Railway "Q1" class 4-4-0 built in 1896 for the railway races.

A racing locomotive! Not just a fast-running locomotive that sometimes went very fast, but one that was specially and uniquely built for the competitive racing of public trains. The intention was to get a trainload of passengers from London to Scotland before a rival one running on a competing line. The East Coast and the West Coast companies had raced each other day after day in 1888 from London (Kings Cross and Euston) to Edinburgh and night after night in 1895 from London to Aberdeen. During the racing the regular timing of about 12 hours was reduced to 8hrs32min from Euston and 8hrs40min from Kings Cross. To put these figures in perspective, the present night trains from Kings Cross take just short of 10 hours for the 525 miles (840km). On the whole in 1895 the West Coast had just the best of it and so their rivals were determined to obtain revenge. How seriously that matter was taken is illustrated by the fact that the North Eastern Railway, otherwise the staidest of companies and which ran the racing trains over (mostly) straight and level tracks from York to Edinburgh, ordered some specially-designed inside-cylinder 4-4-0s to be ready for a resumption of hostilities in 1896. In the event, a derailment at Preston on the West Coast route which, although not connected with the racing, was attributed to high speed, made the competitors lose their taste for the fast running and accordingly only two of the five (Nos. 1869 and 1870) ordered were ever completed. They were known as the Q1 class.

Wilson Worsdell's approach to the problem was to connect quite conventional boiler, cylinders and motion to very large driving wheels which at 7ft 7¼in (2,315mm) were some of the largest ever provided on a coupled engine. Huge wheels might well have meant a very bizarre appearance but the proportions were worked out in such a way as to produce one of the most

Camelback Class 4-4-2
United States:
Atlantic City Railroad (ACR), 1896

Tractive effort: 22,906lb (10,390kg).
Axle load: 40,000lb (18t).
Cylinders: (4) see text.
Driving wheels: 84in (2,134mm).
Heating surface: 1,835sq ft (170m²).
Superheater: none.
Steam pressure: 200psi (14kg/cm²).
Grate area: 76sq ft (7m²).
Water: 3,300 gall (4,000 US) (15m³).
Adhesive weight: 79,000lb (36t).
Total weight: 218,000lb (99t).

The unusual appearance of these strange-looking but path-finding locomotives belied a capability well ahead of their time. The Atlantic City Railroad (ACR) ran them on fast trains which took people from the metropolis of Philadelphia to resorts on the New Jersey coast. It was a 55½ mile (90km) run from Camden (across the river from Philadelphia) to Atlantic City and there was intense competition from the mighty Pennsylvania Railroad which had direct access into the big city. In July and August, for example, it was noted that the booked time of 50 minutes was kept or improved upon each day. On one day the run is reported to have been made in 46½ minutes start-to-stop, an average speed of 71.6mph (115km/h). This certainly implies steady running speed of 90mph (145km/h) or more, but reports of 100mph (160km/h) (and more) speeds with these trains should be regarded as conjecture. The "Atlantic City Flier" was certainly the fastest scheduled train in the world at that time.

Apart from broad-gauge locomotives, here is the first appearance amongst the locomotives in this book of a feature which was in the future to become an integral part of most steam passenger express locomotives—the

beautiful designs ever to run on the rails of the world. Unusually for the time, a large and comfortable cab with side windows and clerestory roof was provided for the comfort of their crews. The slide valves were placed on top of the cylinders and were driven by rocking shafts and Stephenson valve gear. The usual NER Westinghouse air brakes were fitted.

When it was apparent their exceptional services were not going to be needed, the two racers joined their normal-wheeled sisters of Class Q on normal top express passenger work. This continued until the coming of Atlantics in 1903 displaced them on the heaviest

trains. A favourite turn was the Newcastle-Sheffield express, which had a remarkable scheduled start-to-stop timing of 43 minutes for the 44¼ miles (71km) from Darlington to York, at 61.7 mph (98km/h) the fastest in the world at that time. Speeds in excess of 80mph (128km/h) were needed to keep time.

In spite of being non-standard, both survived until 1930, long enough to become London & North Eastern class D18 after the amalgamation of 1923; they kept their original numbers although the green livery and polished metalwork had been replaced by plain black long before.

Left: *North Eastern Railway class "Q" 4-4-0. These engines were similar to the racing "Q1" class with normal-size wheels.*

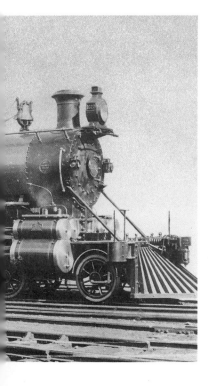

wide deep firebox, for which the 4-4-2 wheel arrangement is wholly appropriate. In this case it was adopted in order to allow anthracite coal to be burnt satisfactorily, but later it was realised that a large grate was also an advantage with bituminous coal and even with oil.

Two other features of these locomotives are fascinating but to some extent freakish. As can be seen they had pairs of compound cylinders on each side, driving through a common crosshead. The arrangement was named after Samuel Vauclain head of the Baldwin Locomotive

Left: *Atlantic City Railroad "Camelback" class 4-4-2 locomotive No.1027, built in 1896. Note the high- and low-pressure cylinders mounted one above the other, the separate cab for the driver (engineer) on top of the boiler and the ornate decoration on the sides of the tender.*

Works, and his object was to attain the advantages of compounding without its complexities. In this case the high-pressure cylinders, 13in bore by 26in stroke (330 x 660mm), were mounted on top and the low-pressure ones 22in bore x 26in stroke (559 x 660mm) below. A single set of valve gear and a single connecting rod served both cylinders of each compound pair. Alas, Vauclain compounds soon went out of fashion; as so often occurred, the work done by the HP and by the LP cylinders did not balance, and in the case of this arrangement it meant an offset thrust on the crosshead and consequent problems with maintenance.

The other oddity was the "Camelback" or "Mother Hubbard" cab on top of the boiler for the driver. The fireman, of course, had to remain in the normal position and for him a second and very exiguous shelter was also provided. The object was to

improve visibility at the expense of separating the two members of the crew. The Philadelphia & Reading Railroad (later known simply as the Reading RR) which took over the ACR at this time went on to build many "Camelbacks" and the idea spread to other railroads in the area. But it was a practice which never became widely used.

Strangely enough, the name "Atlantic", which even today refers the world over to the 4-4-2 type, did not originate with these remarkable machines. Instead, it was first given to some rather prosaic 4-4-2s (without wide fireboxes) built in 1893 for the Atlantic Coast Line, a railroad which ran southwards towards Florida. Even if the ACR 4-4-2s did not give the type name to the world, the mighty Pennsy took note of the beating its competing trains received at their hands and adopted the principle involved with results described later in this narrative.

Class 500 4-6-0
Italy:
Adriatic System (RA), 1900

Axle load: 32,500lb (14t). (14.5t).
Cylinders, HP: (2) 14¾in x 25in (370 x 650mm).
Cylinders, LP: (2) 23 x 25in (580 x 650mm).
Driving wheels: 75½in (1,920mm).
Heating surface: 1,793sq ft (166.6m²).
Superheater: fitted later.
Steam pressure: 200psi (14kg/cm²).
Grate area: 32sq ft (3m²).
Fuel: 9,000lb (4t).
Water: 3,300 gall (4,000 US) (15m³).
Adhesive weight: 98,000lb (44.5t).
Total weight: 221,000lb (100t).
Length overall: 79ft 2in (24,135mm).

Even as early as 1825, at the time the Stockton & Darlington Railway was opened, the direction in which a locomotive went and the position from which it was driven had been established. The chim-ney of *Locomotion,* the S&D's original locomotive, came first in front, while the driver and fireman did their work at the other end of the boiler, that is, to the rear, where the controls and firehole door were situated. Behind them again came the tender which carried supplies of coal and water. Almost all steam loco-motives built since then have followed this arrangement.

Questioning what almost seems a natural law is a hard thing to do, but there were some original minds who did so. One was

Above: *Italian "500" class back-to-front express engine.*

Giuseppe Zara, locomotive en-gineer of the Italian Adriatic System (Rete Adriatica or RA), in charge of the design office at Florence. He decided that it

Class E3sd 4-4-2
United States:
Pennsylvania Railroad (PRR), 1901

Tractive effort: 27,400lb (12,400kg).
Axleload: 64,500lb (29.3t).
Cylinders: (2) 22 x 26in (559 x 660mm).
Driving wheels: 80in (2,032mm).
Heating surface: 2,041sq ft (190m²).
Superheater: 412sq ft (38m²).
Steam pressure: 205psi (14.4kg/cm²).
Grate area: 55.5sq ft (5.2m²).
Fuel: 34,200lb (15.5t).
Water: 5,660gall (6,800US) (25.7m³).
Adhesive weight: 127,500lb (58t).
Total weight: 363,500lb (165t).
Length overall: 71ft 6in (21,640mm).

In the 19th Century the standard American passenger engine was the 4-4-0, but towards the end of the century the type was reaching the limit of size which was possible on eight wheels, and train loads were still increasing. A move to ten wheels was inevitable, and there were two attractive alternatives, the 4-6-0 and the 4-4-2 or Atlantic. The former could have a greater adhesive weight, but the grate was restricted by the need to fit between the rear coupled wheels. The Atlantic had more restricted adhesive weight, but could have a very large grate. For the Pennsylvania Railroad the Atlantic was the obvious choice. The road was already laying excep-tionally heavy rails, which could accept a very high axle load, whilst the locomotives had to be able to burn coal of moderate quality in great quantities.

In 1899 Altoona works pro-duced its first two Atlantics, and they exploited the wheel arrange-ment to the full, with an adhesive weight of 101,600lb (46.1t) and a grate area of 68sq ft (6.3m²), more than twice that of the largest PRR 4-4-0. However, a third engine had a more modest grate of 55.5sq ft (5.2m²), and it was this size which became standard for all subsequent Atlan-tics, as well as for many other engines of the same period. With

this engine the pattern was set for the construction of 576 more Atlantics, all having the same wheel diameter, boiler pressure and grate area.

Although the basic dimen-sions were common to all the engines, successive improve-ments were made. The three prototypes had Belpaire tops to the fireboxes, in accordance with established Pennsylvania prac-

Above: *a Pennsylvania Railroad class "E2" 4-4-2 at speed with a New York-Chicago express.*

tice, but the next two batches, totalling 96 engines, had the more usual round-topped fire-box. Thereafter the Belpaire box reappeared, and was used on all subsequent engines. The two batches mentioned above differed only in their cylinder diameter,

would be best to have the driver in front and to that end produced a 4-6-0 with the boiler and cylinders reversed on the frames. Coal was carried in a bunker on one side of the firebox, which itself was above the bogie rather than between the driving wheels. The tender trailed behind the chimney and of course carried water only.

The advantages claimed were, first, that the lookout was excellent, as good as that of any electric or diesel locomotive today. Second, the exhaust was discharged some distance behind the cab and this reduced the smoke menace in tunnels, so far as the crew were concerned.

There were four compound cylinders with an unusual arrangement. The two high-pressure cylinders were on one side, set at 180 degrees to one another; while the low-pressure pair were similarly arranged on the other. Each pair was set at 90 degrees to the pair on the other side, as in a normal locomotive. A single valve and valve chest each side, driven by sets of outside Walschaert's valve gear, controlled the admission of steam into each pair of cylinders. A number of locomotives in Italy had this arrangement of compounding, known as the Plancher system after its inventor. One drawback was that it was difficult to equalise the work done between the high-pressure and the low-pressure cylinders. The result was that a sideways swinging motion was liable to occur.

The prototype was exhibited at a meeting of the International Railway Congress held in Paris. A detail that impressed R.M. Deeley of the Midland Railway was the arrangement whereby a small opening of the regulator admitted live steam to the low-pressure cylinders, essential for starting. When the regulator was opened a little further, the locomotive changed over automatically to compound working. Deeley adopted this arrangement in his successful Midland compounds, but Zara did not use it for his remaining 42 "cab-forward" locomotives, preferring an independently worked valve instead. One reason might have been that it was desirable to use this valve to equalise the work done between the high—and low—pressure cylinders. Normally this would be a pious hope, but in the case of a Plancher compound it would coincide with making the ride more comfortable, since the high—and low—pressure cylinders were on opposite sides of the locomotive. There was therefore some prospect of drivers actually bothering to make this adjustment.

Whilst in France, tests were run with the prototype and 78 mph (126km/h) was reached with a 130-ton train. Back at home these strange locomotivs, which had become Italian State Railways 670.001 to 670.043 after the railways were nationalised in 1905, successfully worked express trains in the Po Valley for many years. They finally ceased work in the early 1940s. Most were later superheated, becoming class 671 when this was done.

Below: *This strange back-to-front steam locomotive was designed for the Italian Adriatic system at the turn of the century, Guiseppe Zara was the engineer responsible.*

class "E2" having 20.5in (521mm) cylinders, and class "E3" 22in (559mm), the intention being to use the "E3"s on heavier work. All these engines had slide valves, but in the next series, starting in 1903, piston valves were used, at first with Stephenson's valve gear, but from 1906 with Walschaert's.

By 1913 a total of 493 engines had been built, all having a boiler with a maximum diameter of 65.5in (1,664mm). By that time the Pacific was well established on the railway, and it seemed that the heyday of the Atlantic had passed. However, Axel Vogt, the Chief Mechanical Engineer, was still averse to incurring the expense of six-coupled wheels if four would suffice, and in 1910 he built a further Atlantic with another type of boiler, having the same grate area as the earlier Atlantics, but a maximum diameter of 76.75in (1,949mm), almost as large as the Pacifics, and with a combustion chamber at the front. The new engine, classified "E6", developed a higher power than the existing Pacifics at speeds above 40mph (64km/h). Two more "E6"s were then built, but with superheaters, and this made the performance even more impressive, and it was possible to increase the cylinder diameter to 23.5in (597mm).

After four years of intensive development work, a production batch of eighty "E6"s were built, having a number of changes from the prototypes, including longer boiler tubes. These engines were built at great speed between February and August 1914, that is, in the same year that the first of the famous "K4s" Pacifics was built. These engines took over the principal express workings on all the less hilly parts of the system, and during World War I they achieved prodigious feats of haulage for four-coupled engines. When large numbers of production "K4s" Pacifics appeared after the war, the "E6s" engines settled down to work on the less busy routes, mainly in New Jersey.

The smaller Atlantic soon established a reputation for high speed, but their full potential was realised in 1905 when the Pennsylvania Special was accelerated to an 18-hour schedule from Jersey City to Chicago, giving an overall average speed of 50.2mph (80.1km/h), with an average of 57.8mph (92.9km/h) over the 189 miles (304km) from Jersey City to Harrisburg. It was on the first westbound run to this schedule that "E2" No.7002 was credited with exceeding 120mph (193 km/h), but the claim was based on dubious evidence. On this service the "E2" and "E3" engines kept time with up to eight wooden coaches, totalling about 360 (short) tons, but with the introduction of the heavier steel stock, double heading became common.

The "E6s" engines were able to handle trains of 800-900 tons on the New York-Philadelphia-Washington trains, but it was on lighter trains that they produced their most spectacular performances. Their greatest distinction was to haul the Detroit Arrow between Fort Wayne and Chicago, for in 1933 this was the world's fastest train, with a start to stop average of 75.5mph (121.4 km/h) over the 64.1 miles (103km) from Plymouth to Fort Wayne and 75.3mph (121.1km/h) over 123 miles (198km) from Fort Wayne to Gary. On this service they hauled five or six steel coaches, weighing 300 to 350 tonnes.

Over the years many of the earlier Atlantics were modernised with superheaters and piston valves, making them into modern engines for light duties. Five of them survived until 1947, and one of them, by now classified "E2sd", was preserved. It was renumbered to 7002, thus purporting to be the engine of the 1905 record. The "E6s" engines survived well into the 1950s, and one of them, No.460, has been preserved. This engine had achieved fame by hauling a two-coach special from Washington to New York carrying news films of the return of the Atlantic flyer Lindbergh. The train averaged 74mph (119km/h); the films were developed en route and shown in New York cinemas before those carried by air.

Claud Hamilton Class 4-4-0

Great Britain:
Great Eastern Railway, 1900

Tractive effort: 17,100lb (7,757kg).
Axle load: 41,000lb (18.5t).
Cylinders: (2) 19 x 26in (483 x 660mm).
Driving wheels: 84in (2,134mm).
Heating surface: 1,631sq ft (151m²).
Superheater: none.
Steam pressure: 180psi (12.7kg/cm²).
Grate area: 21.3sq ft (2m²).
Fuel (oil): 715gall (860 US) (3.25m³).
Water: 3,450gall (4,150 US) (16m³).
Adhesive weight: 82,000lb (37.5t).
Total weight: 213,000lb (97t).
Length overall: 53ft 4¾in (16,276mm).

Below: *The glorious royal blue, brass and copper livery of the "Claud Hamilton"*

4-4-0s of the Great Eastern Railway of England was one of the finest ever used.

A new century was not yet three months old on the day when a really superb 4-4-0 locomotive, named *Claud Hamilton* after the chairman of the company and appropriately numbered 1900, emerged from the Great Eastern Railway's Stratford Works. Although its inside-cylinder layout was typical of the century that had gone, the large cab with four big side windows and many other features were way ahead of their time. Some of them, such as the power-operated reversing gear and water scoop, were still waiting to be adopted generally when the last steam locomotive for Britain was built 60 years later. Even energy conservation was considered, because the first "Claud"'s burned waste oil residues instead of coal; these were available from the company's oil-gas plant. Other equipment very up to date for the day included an exhaust steam injector and a blast-pipe with variable orifice. Two sets of Stephenson's valve-gear filled such space as was left after two sets of main motion had been accommodated between the frames. Before 1914, the livery of polished metal and royal blue was as magnificent as any applied to any steam locomotive anywhere at anytime.

The "Claud Hamilton" class has a complicated history. Eventually 121 of these engines were built between 1900 and 1923. Up-to-date features such as enlarged boilers, superheaters and piston—instead of slide—valves were gradually introduced on successive batches, culminating in the ten "Super-Claud"s of 1923. As these improvements were introduced on new construction, most earlier locomotives of the class were rebuilt to conform. The original "Claud"'s suffered several rebuildings and in due time most of them emerged as one or other of the last two sub-classes of "Super Claud". The latest of these varieties of rebuilding, done under the auspices of the London & North Eastern Railway, reverted to the round-topped firebox of the original No.1900, while intermediate construction and re-construction provided for a Belpaire firebox.

Using the LNER classification

Grosse C Class 4-4-0

France:
Paris, Lyons and Mediterranean Railway (PLM), 1898

Axle load: 38,600lb (17.5t).
Cylinders, HP: (2) 13.4 x 24.4in (340 x 620mm).
Cylinders, LP: (2) 21.3 x 24.4in (540 x 620mm).
Driving wheels: 78.7in (2,000mm).
Heating surface: 2,040sq ft (190m²).
Superheater: None.
Steam pressure: 213psi (15kg/cm²).
Grate area: 26.7sq ft (2.5m²).
Fuel: 11,000lb (5t).
Water: 4,400gall (5,280 US) (20m³).
Adhesive weight: 76,000lb (34.4t).
Total weight: 223,500lb (101.5t).
Length overall: 63ft 0in (19,200mm).

France produced insufficient coal to meet the needs of its railways, and any means of saving fuel was therefore important to French locomotive engineers. In the 19th century the most important fuel-saving development was the introduction of compounding. In a compound engine the steam passes through two sets of cylinders in series. By this means a greater overall expansion ratio is possible than in a "simple" engine, and more work is thus extracted from each cylinder-full of steam. One of the problems facing the designer of a compound locomotive was to even out the stresses in the moving parts of the engine, it was generally agreed that the work done in the high-pressure and in the low-pressure cylinders should be as nearly equal as possible. The ratio of the work done in the cylinders depended partly on the sizes of the cylinders, but also on the "cut-off", that is, the point in the piston stroke at which the admission of steam is shut off. In a full-blooded compound the driver could vary the cut-off in each set of cylinders at will by means of two reversing wheels, but to get the full benefit of this flexibility the driver needed to be very skilled. This was the method used by the Northern. An alternative was the driver having only one reversing wheel to operate.

The first PLM compound was an adaptation of an existing

Above: *Partial encasement of the engine is evident in this PLM 4-4-0 "Coupe-Vent" ("Windcutter") No.220C91.*

LNER class	Description	Number built new	Number of rebuilds	Length of service
D14	Original "Claud Hamilton" as described above	41	0	1900-1931
D15	Belpaire fireboxes introduced	66	9	1903-1933
D15/1	Superheaters introduced	4	70	1911-1935
D15/2	Extended smokebox	0	80	1914-1952
D16/1	Larger boilers ("Super-Claud")	10	5	1923-1934
D16/2	ditto	0	40	1926-1952
D16/3	Coupling-rod splashers removed. Round top boilers again	0	104	1933-1958

system, the details are given in the accompanying table.

During their days as the prime express locomotives of the GER, the original "Claud"s could handle a 14-car "Norfolk Coast Express" non-stop from the Liverpool Street terminus in London to North Walsham. The schedule provided for hauling loads up to 430 tons and running the 130 miles (208km) in 159 minutes, quite an amazing feat for so small a locomotive.

The coming of 4-6-0s in 1913 meant that the top timetable trains of East Anglia were no longer handled by these famous engines. The top assignment of all, however, remained with them for many years, for no heavier locomotives were permitted to run on the line serving Wolferton, the station for Sandringham House, a favourite Royal residence. The frequent Royal Trains from London to Sandringham were handled by either of two specially painted "Royal Claud"s. In the 1930s these superbly-kept engines were a reminder—even if green rather than blue—of the days when Great Eastern engines were indeed a sight for sore eyes.

On railway nationalisation day, 1st January 1948, there were 13 "D15/2"s, 16 "D16/2"s and 88 "D16/3"s. The class just failed to achieve a 60-year working life and also by a sad chance just failed to be represented in preservation. One was so set aside at Stratford works but, alas, was only marked on one side to be spared the torch. Inevitably the foreman of the cutting up gang approached the line of locomotives from the other side. So, alas these famous engines are now but a memory in the minds of their admirers.

design of 2-4-2 locomotive, of which the company possessed 290 examples. The four cylinders were in line, with the inside high-pressure cylinders driving the leading axle and the outside low-pressure cylinders driving the second axle. The valve gears were controlled by a single reversing wheel, on the second system mentioned above. The boiler pressure was 213psi (15kg/cm²), which was the highest in the world. Two locomotives were built to this design, numbered C1 and C2. They were successful, and a new design was therefore prepared, with the firebox between the coupled axles. This produced a more stable engine. The first of the new design, C3, was a 2-4-0, but two more were built with leading bogies, numbered C11 and C12. These also were successful, and a further refinement of the design was produced in 1894.

Forty engines, numbered C21 and C60 were built to this design between 1894 and 1896. The most conspicuous change from the three earlier engines was a partial encasing of the engine to reduce wind resistance. A pointed casing connected the front of the chimney and the smokebox door to the footplating, and the cab front was vee-shaped. As built, the engines had the inside and outside valve gears connected, as in the previous engines, but after a series of tests to determine the most favourable combination of cut-offs for maximum power output, it was decided that there was little benefit in ajdusting the low-pressure cut-off, which was therefore fixed at 63 per cent. The driver's reversing wheel then controlled only the high-pressure cut-off. A valve allowed the driver to admit some live steam to the low-pressure cylinders to assist at starting, but even this refinement was eliminated from some of the engines by giving the high-pressure cylinders the unusually long maximum cut-off of 88 per cent, which was considered to overcome starting difficulties.

These locomotives took over all the principal work on the less steeply-graded sections of the PLM, but train loads were increasing, and when more locomotives were required, a larger boiler was fitted, although the cylinder sizes remained the same. The 120 engines, numbered C61 to C180, were built to this design between 1898 and 1901. The boiler was slightly longer than in the earlier engines, so that the "point" or "beak" of the front of the casing was blunted, but a further casing was fitted between the chimney and the dome. The two classes had the nicknames compound à bec (beaked compounds) or coupe-vent (wind-cutter), and they were distinguished from one another by the class names "le petit C" and "le grosse C".

The "grosse C" became the standard PLM express engine until the introdution of Atlantics in 1906. They handled the fastest expresses on the ligne impériale from Paris to Lyons and Marseilles, including the famous "Côte d'Azur Rapide". With 220 tons they could maintain 53mph (85 km/h) on the 1 in 125 climb to Blaisy Bas, and the overall journey from Paris to Marseilles was covered at a running average of 54mph (87km/h). On test they reached 87 to 93mph (140 to 150km/h) with light trains. This capacity for high speed was credited to the coupe-vent casing, but in the light of later work on compound locomotives it is likely that it was as much due to the generous size of steam pipes and ports. No.C145 is preserved.

de Glehn Atlantic 4-4-2
France: Northern Railway, 1910

Axle load: 39,231lb (17.8t).
Cylinders, HP: (2) 13½ x 25¼in (340 x 640mm).
Cylinders, LP: (2) 22 x 25¼in (560 x 640mm).
Driving wheels: 80¼in (2,040mm).
Heating surface: 1,485sq ft (138m²).
Superheater: 420sq ft (39m²).
Steam pressure: 228psi (16kg/cm²).
Grate area: 33.4sq ft (2.75m²).
Fuel: 15,000lb (7t).
Water: 5,070gall (6,080 US) (23m³).
Adhesive weight: 78,500lb (35.6t).
Total weight: 264,500lb (120t).
Overall length: 59ft 10½in (18,247mm).

In spite of his name—partly French and partly German—Alfred de Glehn was born an Englishman, yet he rose to be Director of Engineering of the Société Alsacienne de Constructions Mécaniques at Mulhouse in the 1870s while still under 30. Together with Gaston du Bousquet of the Northern Railway of France he developed a system of compounding for steam locomotives which stood the test of time. In France a majority of twentieth-century express passenger locomotives were de Glehn compounds.

One major factor in its success was the fact that French locomotive drivers were not promoted from firemen but instead were trained as mechanics. In fact, the actual word used was *mechanicien*. This meant that the man in charge on the footplate could be expected to know the reasons for the complexities of a compound's controls and act accordingly to get the best results.

The de Glehn system was certainly complicated from the driver's point of view—there were *two* throttles and *two* sets of

reversing gear, as well as intercepting valves, to control the working. The locomotives could be set to work in five modes as shown in table 1.

In the A position of the intercepting valve, the exhaust from the HP cylinders was delivered to the receiver and steam chest of the LP cylinders. A safety valve set to blow off at 85lb/sq in (6kg/cm²) in this vessel limited the pressure applied on the LP side.

In the B position, this connection was closed and the HP exhaust sent direct to the blast pipe. Settings IV and V were used only to move the engine under light load, or in an emergency if some problem developed in the LP or HP engines respectively. Setting III could boost the pressure on the LP side up to the 85lb/sq in (6kg/cm²) to which the receiver safety valve was set.

Of course in addition to choosing the correct setting, it was necessary to select the correct combination of cut-offs by adjusting the two independent reversing gears. With all these alternatives to think of, the move from running a simple engine to

driving a compound could be likened to moving up from strumming a piano to conducting a whole orchestra!

Du Bousquet and de Glehn began their co-operation in connection with some very successful compound 4-4-0s produced during the 1890s, but their lasting place in the hall of fame was assured when Northern Railway Atlantic No.2.641 was exhibited at the Paris Exhibition of 1900. Outside bearings on the leading bogie and inside ones on

Above: Northern Railway of France de Glehn 4-4-2 No. 2.674. These four-cylinder compounds were outstanding.

the trailing wheels gave an unusual look, but the 4-4-2 was certainly a good-looking example of the locomotive builders' art and the engine was the first of a class of 32 built for the Northern Railway.

The inside LP cylinders were in line with the front bogie wheels and drove the leading coupled

Table 1 Mode	Purpose	Nominal tractive effort developed	
I	Normal	16,171lb	(7,337kg)
II	Starting	24,069lb	(10,921kg)
III	Boost	19,194lb	(8,709kg)
IV	LP Isolated	11,125lb	(5,048kg)
V	HP Isolated	12,944lb	(5,873gk)

Table II Mode	HP Throttle	LP Throttle	Intercepting Valves
I	Open	Shut	A
II	Open	Open	B
III	Open	Open	A
V	Shut	Open	B

NORD   2.643

Table III Country	Railway	Number ordered
France:	Eastern Railway	2
"	Paris-Orleans	14
"	Midi Railway	34
"	French State Railway	9
Britain:	Great Western Railway	3
Prussia:	Royal Union Railway	79
USA:	Pennsylvania BR	1
Egypt:	State Railways	10

axle whereas the outside HP pair were in the familiar position above the rear bogie wheels and drove the rear pair of coupled wheels. The arrangement had a slight objection in that the both sets of cylinders were attached to the frames at a point where the frames were weakened by a circular cut-out to clear the bogie wheels, but otherwise the only difficulty was the servicing and repair of two complete sets of mechanism in the limited space between the frames. Both bogie and six-wheel tenders were used.

In spite of these drawbacks (which could be lived with) the performances of the Atlantics, on such trains as the boat trains between Paris and Calais on some of the hardest schedules in the world, were remarkable. The economy in coal consumption was considerable and the money so saved was welcome, but this was not the only advantage. The

Atlantic had begun to approach the point where the performance was limited not by the capacity of the locomotive, but by the capacity of the man who shovels in the coal. It follows that a locomotive which had better thermal efficiency could also produce more power. And so it proved; trains of 270 tons weight hauled by a 4-4-2 were expected, say, to climb the 1 in 200 (0.5per cent) incline 13 miles long between St. Denis and Survilliers at an average speed above 100km/h (62.5mph).

Orders followed for similar machines, not only from all over France but also from many foreign countries. The tally was as shown in table III.

Some of these were of a slightly enlarged design and others differed quite markedly in details of layout, but all followed the same basic principles. The French railway systems went on to build many classes of 4-6-0, 2-8-2, 4-6-2, 4-8-2 and other types to this basic compound design, while the Great Western Railway of England based all their future express passenger designs on the same mechanical layout, but with four simple cylinders.

As elsewhere in the world, all-steel carriages and more spacious accommodation raised train weights to a point where a minimum of six coupled wheels were required, so the de Glehn 4-4-2s vanished between the wars. Northern Railway No.2.670 has survived and is displayed superbly restored in the National Railway Museum at its own city of origin, Mulhouse in Alsace.

Left: *Nord de Glehn 4-4-2 No.2.670 as restored for the National Railway Museum at Mulhouse, France.*

Below: *De Glehn four-cylinder compound 4-4-2 of the Northern Railway of France complete with more modern bogie tender.*

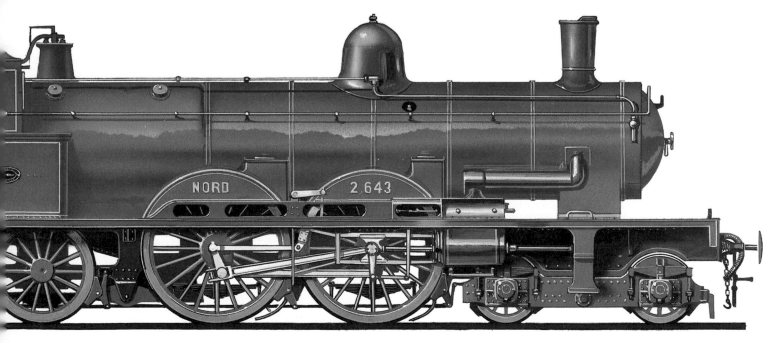

Class Q 4-6-2
New Zealand:
New Zealand Government Railways (NZGR), 1901

Tractive effort: 19,540lb (8,863kg).
Axle load: 23,500lb (10.5t).
Cylinders: (2) 16 x 22in (406 x 559mm).
Driving wheels: 49in (1,245mm).
Heating surface: 1,673sq ft (155m²).
Superheater: None.
Steam pressure: 200psi (14kg/cm²).
Grate area: 40sq ft (3.72m²).
Fuel: 11,000lb (5t).
Water: 1,700 gall (2,000 US) (7.7m³).
Adhesive weight: 69,500lb (31.5t).
Total weight: 165,000lb (75t).
Length overall: 55ft 4½in (16,872mm).

The year 1901 was marked by the construction of the first of a famous type—arguably *the* most famous type—of express passenger locomotive, which was to go on being built until the end of

steam. And it was not one of the great railway nations which was responsible for conceiving the idea (and to whose order it was built) but tiny New Zealand. A.W. Beattie, Chief Mechanical Engineer of the Government Railways, wanted a locomotive with a big firebox capable of burning poor quality lignite coal from South Island mines at Otago.

American manufacturer Baldwin suggested a "camelback" 4-6-0 with a wide firebox above the rear coupled wheels, but the New Zealander proposed a 4-6-0 with the big firebox carried by a two-wheel pony truck, making a 4-6-2. The 13 engines were quickly completed and despatched across the Pacific Ocean; and in this way a name was given to thousands of locomotives yet to be built. In due time the word "Pacific" entered that dialect of the English language used for describing railways.

Below: *NZGR class "Q"—she was the world's first class of Pacific locomotive when built in USA in 1901.*

Above: *Class "Q" No.343 on the southernmost passenger railway in the world between Invercargill and Bluff, Southland.*

Class F15 4-6-2
USA:
Chesapeake & Ohio Railway (C&O), 1902

Tractive effort: 32,400lb (14,696kg).
Axle load: 52,500lb (24t).
Cylinders: (2) 23½ x 28in (597 x 711mm).
Driving wheels: 72in (1,829mm).
Heating surface: 2,938sq ft (273m²).
Superheater: None.
Steam pressure: 180psi (12.7kg/cm²).
Grate area: 47sq ft (4.4m²).
Fuel: 30,000lb (13.5t).
Water: 7,500 gall (9,000 US). (34m³).
Adhesive weight: 157,000lb (71.5t).
Total weight: 408,000lb (185t).
Length overall: 74ft 0in (22,555mm).

The Chesapeake & Ohio Railroad (C&O) can trace its corporate history back to 1785 when the James River Company received a charter. The first President was George Washington in person! Railroad operations did not begin until 1836 when the Louisa Railroad in Virginia was opened.

Only a few weeks after the Missouri Pacific RR got the first of their 4-6-2s, this historic company took delivery from the American Locomotive Company of the prototype of their famous "F15" class Pacifics. This time there was no ambiguity—the standard North American express passenger locomotive of the twentieth century had finally arrived. This path-finding C&O No.147 was also fitted with piston valves, but it still had Stephenson's

A feature which was also to appear on most of the world's steam locomotives built after this time was the type of valve gear used on these engines. Of 105 locomotives yet to be described in this book, 86 have Walschaert's valve gear. The invention was not new—a Belgian engineer called Egide Walschaert had devised it back in 1844 and a German called Heusinger had reinvented it since—but this application marked its entry into general use outside continental Europe. The gear gave good steam distribution, but the main advantage lay in its simplicity, as well as in the fact that it could conveniently be fitted outside the frames in the position most accessible for maintenance. In this case the gear was arranged to work outside-admission piston valves, which piston valves themselves were in the forefront of steam technology at the beginning of the century.

It should be said that this class of engine came closer than ever before to the final form of the steam locomotive. Only two fundamental improvements were still to be applied generally—inside-admission piston valves in place of outside, and superheating.

After some minor modification the "Q" class gave long and faithful service, the last of them not ceasing work until 1957. During their prime, in addition to working the principal trains on the South Island main line, some came to the North Island for use on the Rotorua Express, running between Auckland and the famous hot springs of the same name.

Right: *The splendid New Zealand Government class "Q" 4-6-2 No.343 as running in 1956 when nearing the end of more than 50 years service to this 3ft 6in gauge railway system which had adopted US practice for its locomotives.*

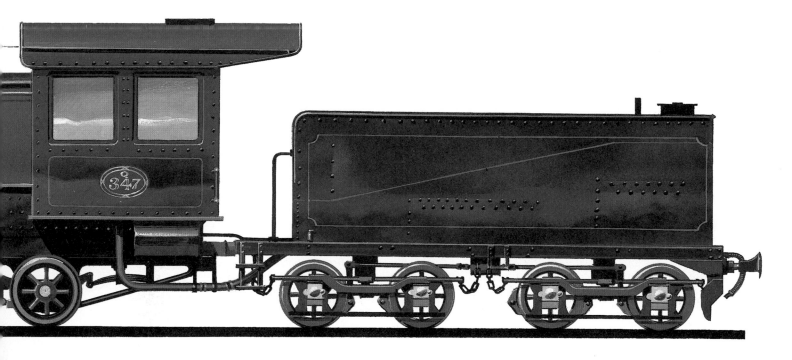

link valve motion between the frames. Naturally no superheater, but her size and power set a new standard. A further 26 followed during the years 1903-11. Most survived until the C&O turned to diesels in the early 1950s and, in a country that was not then given to hanging on to old machinery, that said a great deal for the qualities of the "F15" class. Of course, as the years went by, top-line express work was passed on to their successors, yet there

Left: *A latter-day Chesapeake & Ohio 4-6-2 of class "F16", introduced in 1937 and built by Baldwins of Philadelphia. Note that special C&O trademark, the mounting of two duplex air pumps on the front of the smokebox of No.174.*

were routes whose weak bridges meant that these comparatively light engines continued being used on prime trains nearly to the end. During the 1920s all the "F15" locomotives were modernised with Walschaert's valve gear, superheaters, larger tenders, different cabs, mechanical stokers, new cylinders and, in some cases, even new frames; in fact, just in the manner of the legendary Irishman's hammer—"a hundred years old, only two new heads and three new handles".

In addition to setting the style for nearly 7,000 USA 4-6-2s to follow, the "F15" founded a dynasty on their own road. The "F16" 4-6-2s of 1913 represented a 34 per cent increase in tractive effort and a 28 per cent increase of grate area, while for the "F17"

of 1914 these increases were 45 per cent and 71 per cent respectively, in each case for a penalty of a 27 per cent increase in axle load. After World War I, classes "F18" and "F19" appeared, notable for 18,000 gallon 12-wheel tenders. These 61 4-6-2s handled all C&O's express passenger assignments until the coming of 4-6-4s in 1941.

It will be noted that these 4-6-2s showed something else. During the age of steam no major system outside North America ever had track strong enough to carry an axle load greater than 22½ tons, so these locomotives were as good an indicator as any that the USA, having come up from well behind, was now starting to go far into the lead in industrial might.

Large Atlantic Class 4-4-2
Great Britain:
Great Northern Railway (GNR), 1902

Tractive effort: 17,340lb (7,865kg).
Axle load: 45,000lb (20.5t).
Cylinders: (2) 20 x 24in (508 x 610mm).
Driving wheels: 80in (2,032mm).
Heating surface: 1,965sq ft (182.5m²).
Superheater: 568sq ft (52.8m²).
Steam pressure: 170psi (12.0kg/cm²).
Grate area: 31sq ft (2.88m²).
Fuel: 14,500lb (6½t).
Water: 3,500 gall (4,200 US). (16m³).
Adhesive weight: 90,000lb (41t).
Total weight: 252,500lb (115t).
Length overall: 57ft 10¼in (17,634mm).

These famous engines introduced the big boiler with wide firebox to Britain; 94 were built between 1902 and 1910. Until the arrival of 4-6-2s in 1921, they ruled the Great Northern Railway's portion of the East Coast main line from London to Scotland, that is, between Kings Cross and York. Even after this, the light formation of the de-luxe all-Pullman expresses introduced in the 1920s was just right for these Atlantics.

By the mid-1930s, new streamlined Pacifics made the older 4-6-2s available for the Pullmans, but the thirty year old warriors found a new and skittish lease of life on the famous high speed light-weight "Beer Trains" between Kings Cross and Cambridge. They also stood by as

pilots at places like Peterborough, Grantham and Doncaster, demonstrating on various occasions that in favourable circumstances with a crew willing to 'have a go' they could keep "Pacific" timings with the streamliners as well as 17-coach expresses.

The coming of the "Green Arrow" class 2-6-2s which could stand in on any main line train and, in addition, the war-time lack of light fast trains, was the end for the 4-4-2s. The first one (GN No.1459, LNER No.4459) ceased work in 1943 and the last (GN No.294, LNER Nos.3294 and 2822, British Railways No. 62822) in November 1950. She reached 75mph (121km/h) on her last run. To the British public of 70 years ago they epitomised

the romance of the railway; their owners liked them too—at an original price of £3,400 each they could hardly be described as a bad investment. Their crews also liked the ease with which they could be driven and fired, even if the exiguous cabs gave little shelter from the elements.

Like most of the world's greatest steam locomotives they were starkly simple, but yet up-to-date. Cylinders were outside, valves and valve gear (Stephenson's) inside. The first 81 came out unsuperheated, with balanced slide valves. The last ten, built in 1910, had piston-valves and superheaters. In time all were fitted with the latter and most were converted from slide to piston valve. There were also

three experimental four-cylinder compounds, but none of them prospered against the standard version. All the 4-4-2s except one of the compounds were built at the company's own Doncaster Plant, to the design of Henry Ivatt.

One starkly simple feature, wholly unusual in the twentieth century for an express passenger locomotive, was the lever or Johnson bar reverse; this was more usually applied to shunting locomotives which ran slowly but needed to change direction frequently. It was difficult to alter the cut-off at speed with the lever—the combined strength of both driver and fireman were needed sometimes. There was certainly no chance of making

Midland Compound 4-4-0
Great Britain:
Midland Railway (MR), 1902

Axle load: 44,500lb (20.5t).
Cylinders, HP: (1) 19 x 26in (483 x 660mm).
Cylinders, LP: (2) 21 x 26in (533 x 660mm).
Driving wheels: 84in (2,134mm).
Heating surface: 1,317sq ft (122.5m²).
Superheater: 272 sq ft (25.3m²).
Steam pressure: 200psi (14.1kg/cm²).
Grate area: 28.4sq ft (2.63m²).
Fuel: 12,500lb (5.75t).
Water: 3,500 gall (4,200 US). (16m³).
Adhesive weight: 89,000lb (40.5t).
Total weight: 234,000lb (106t).
Length overall: 56ft 7½in (17,260mm).

The "Midland Compound" locomotives have a place in any locomotive hall of fame. S.W. Johnson introduced them in 1902; later they were developed by his successor R.M. Deeley, substantially rebuilt (in which form they are portrayed) by Henry (later Sir Henry) Fowler in 1914. They were the only long-term success-

ful application of the compound principle in Britain; and when the Midland Railway was amalgamated with others in 1923 to form the London Midland & Scottish Railway, the "Midland Compound" was chosen (just a little surprisingly) as the standard express locomotive for the new organisation. Eventually 240 of them were built. Their numbers ran from 900 to 939 and 1000 to 1199 in MR and LMS days and most survived to become British Railways' Nos.40900 to 41199.

The LMS examples had wheels 3in (76mm) less in diameter. The last of them ceased work in 1961 only seven years before the "final" finish of steam on BR. Midland No.1000 has been preserved in working order at the York National Railway Museum. Most were built at the Midland's Derby Works but a number of orders went to outside manufacturers in early LMS days.

Unlike the Webb compounds, these locomotives had a *single* high-pressure cylinder and *two* low-pressure ones. The high-pressure cylinder was between the frames and the two low pressure ones were outside. Also between the frames were *three*

sets of Stephenson's valve gear as well as the inside cylinder's motion. When the throttle was in the partly open position, live steam was admitted to the low-pressure cylinders, resulting in "simple" working. This was necessary for starting. At full throttle, the port which allowed this "simple" operation closed and proper "compound" working ensued.

This resulted in an anomaly that confused many drivers from non-Midland depots to which the engines were allocated in LMS days—that is that more steam was used when the throttle was partly closed than when it was fully open. Even so, the long-lived "Midland Compound" locomotives were considered to be reliable and useful machines. For the fast, frequent but short trains of their parent Midland Railway, the "Crimson Ramblers" were found to be adequate and economical.

Right: *"Midland Compound" No.1000 piloting enthusiasts' special at Settle Junction, Yorkshire, in May 1950. The second locomotive is LNER No.4771* Green Arrow.

Above left: *"Large Atlantic" No.4458 at the head of a Pullman Express in pre-World War II days.*

Above: *"Large Atlantic" No.251 as restored to the original Great Northern Railway livery. This locomotive is preserved in the National Railway Museum.*

the fine adjustments *en route* which were behind the lower coal consumption of certain contemporary types. But coal was a cheap part of the cost equation and if the the GN Atlantics did burn a bit more, their overall economics were quite beyond suspicion.

The first of the Ivatt large Atlantics, GN No.251, LNER No.3251 (later renumbered as LNER No.2800) has survived to find an honoured place in the National Railway Museum at York. Whilst stored in the paint shop at Doncaster waiting for a vacancy, it was taken out and in company with preserved "small" Atlantic *Henry Oakley*, was set to run a special train from Kings Cross to Doncaster to celebrate the centenary of the GN loco works. The use of these two locomotives on this "Plant Centenarian" special train of 20 September 1953 was important as it maintained the precedent so far as British Railways is concerned, for the running of museum pieces for entertainment purposes. The veterans did the 156 mile (250km) run in a respectable 192 minutes running time.

City Class 4-4-0

Great Britain:
Great Western Railway (GWR), 1903

Tractive effort: 17,790lb (8,070kg).
Axle load: 41,000lb (18.5t).
Cylinders: (2) 18 x 26in (457 x 660mm).
Driving wheels: 80½in (2,045mm).
Heating surface: 1,351sq ft (126m²).
Superheater: 216sq ft (20.1m²).
Steam pressure: 200psi (14.1kg/cm²).
Grate area: 20.56sq ft (1.91m²).
Fuel: 11,000lb (5t).
Water: 3,000 gall (3,600 US). (13.6m³).
Adhesive weight: 81,000lb (36.75t).
Total weight: 207,000lb (94t).
Length overall: 56ft 2¼in (17,126mm).

The Great Western "City" class 4-4-0s owe their fame to an occasion in May 1905 when a special mail train from Plymouth to Paddington descended the winding alignment of the Wellington incline, just west of Taunton, at a very high speed. That famous train-timer and journalist Charles Rous-Marten, had been invited and he recorded 102.3mph (164 km/h) then a world record for steam in respect of an authentically and independently recorded occasion.

A careful analysis of the timings at successive quarter-mile posts has since suggested that Rous-Marten mistook some other object for one of them and that the actual speed was a little less. Even so, the incident led to the preservation of its heroine No. 3717 *City of Truro*. The series was numbered originally from 3433 to 3442 then renumbered 3710-3719.

There were only ten "City" class proper, all built at the GWR works at Swindon, but a further 27 were created by rebuilding locomotives of the related "Bad-minton" and "Atbara" classes. They represented something of stop-gap, while the old GWR was making a huge and sudden leap forward from a locomotive fleet that was old-fashioned for the nineteenth century to one that was far ahead of its time for the twentieth. In the meantime this series of locomotives, with inside-cylinders and outside-cranks, as well as both outside- and inside-frames, but with up-to-date boilers, was turned out.

The mechanical layout, superficially at least, was very close to that very earliest 4-4-0 of all, Campbell's 4-4-0 of 1837 for the Philadelphia & Norristown Railroad in the USA. Few others, least of all those in the inventor's native land had built any similar locomotives, but many had been constructed in the last decade of the century for the GWR. There were 60 "Duke" class, 156 "Bulldog" class, 20 "Flower" class, and 40 "Stella" class in addition to "City" and conversions mentioned. The outside-framed 4-4-0 was very much a trademark of the turn of the century GWR passenger locomotive fleet.

In consequence of being stop-gaps, the "City" class had only a short reign on top express work, but even apart from the record had a reputation for fast running. The last of them ceased work in 1931, although *City of Truro* went back into traffic for a short time after World War II so that it would be available for enthusiasts' specials. She now resides in the Great Western Museum at Swindon.

Below: *Great Western No.3717 City of Truro as preserved, on a train near Hullavington, Wiltshire. This locomotive held the world speed record of 102.3mph (164km/h) for many years and is now preserved in the Great Western Railway Museum at Swindon, Wilts, England.*

Saint Class 4-6-0
Great Britain:
Great Western Railway (GWR), 1902

Tractive effort: 24,395lb (11,066kg).
Axle load: 41,500lb (19t).
Cylinders: (2) 18½ x 30in (470 x 762mm).
Driving wheels: 80½in (2,045mm).
Heating surface: 1,841sq ft (171m²).
Superheater: 263sq ft (24.4m²).
Steam pressure: 225psi (15.8kg/cm²).
Grate area: 27.1sq ft (2.52m²).
Fuel: 13,500lb (6t).
Water: 3,500 gall (4,200 US). (16m³).
Adhesive weight: 125,000lb (56t).
Total weight: 251,000lb (114t).
Length overall: 63ft 0¼in (19,209mm).

When, shortly before the turn of the century, a not-so-young man called George Jackson Churchward found himself apparent heir to William Dean, Chief Locomotive Engineer of the Great Western Railway, he (Churchward) had already decided that there would have to be very great changes when he took over Corridor trains and dining cars, as well as the demand for faster schedules meant a whole new express passenger locomotive fleet, for even by nineteenth century standards the then current GWR locomotives were both heterogenous and unsatisfactory. Whilst Churchward was number two under an ageing chief at the Swindon Factory, he was able to test his ideas by causing to be built a number of very strange designs indeed. Because so many peculiar oddments already existed—such as 4-4-0s converted from standard gauge 0-4-4s(!), themselves converted from the broad gauge on its abolition in 1892—they attracted little attention.

But 1902 was the year when a big outside-cylinder 4-6-0 No.100 (later 2900), tactfully named *Dean* (later *William Dean*), saw the

light of day. By the standards of the locomotive aesthetics of the period it was one of the strangest looking locomotives of all, though to those few who knew about the design and appearance of the typical North American Ten-wheeler, No.100 was totally familiar, despite being disguised by ornate Victorian brass and paint work. This reflected Churchward's friendship with A.W. Gibbs, Master Mechanic (Lines East) of the Pennsylvania Railroad.

The layout of the American Ten-wheeler prototype was followed exactly. Both cylinders and valve chests were mounted outside the frames in the most accessible possible position; the Stephenson's valve gear inside the frames drove the inside-admission valves via transverse shafts and pendulum cranks. With some refinement the arrangement was used by Churchward and his successors on some 2,000 locomotives. The frame arrangement for Churchward's standard locomotives was

a compromise between USA and British practice. Plate frames were used for the main portion in which the driving wheels were held, but the cylinders were in true Yankee style, each together with one half of the smokebox saddle, the front of the locomotive being carried on a short length of bar frame. The domeless boiler had less of the USA and more of Churchward than the engine part about it (but very little previous GWR practice); however, some time was to elapse before the design of this component became fully developed.

At this time Churchward was about to take full charge, not only (as on most British railways) of the building and repairing of locomotives, but also of their running. He would sit round a drawing board together with its incumbent, the incumbent's boss and the Chief Draughtsman and they would discuss the job in question. If doubts arose over manufacture, an expert from the works—the foundry foreman, maybe—would be sent for. If it

Above: *"Saint" class No.2937 Clevedon Court. The "Courts" were the last batch of the "Saints" built in 1911.*

was a point about the locomotive in service, then the running superintendent would come over. Perhaps Churchward would ask what others did about the problem, in which case the Record Office would quickly produce a book or periodical tabbed to indicate the relevant page. The result was that before long the GWR possessed a locomotive fleet that in many ways had few rivals the world over.

It was a far cry from the ways of some of the autocratic, self-important and "know-all" characters who occupied the chief's chair on a number of other British lines in those days. Churchward did it all, not by cleverness, but simply by listening to others and then applying that rarest of qualities, common sense. Churchward took some time to make up his mind whether to have as his best express power the 77 two-

cylinder "Saint" class 4-6-0s, derived from *William Dean;* or whether the four-cylinder contemporary "Star" class 4-6-0s of similar speed and power, of which there were 60 before Churchward retired in 1921, would be the better. He finally decided on the latter and it does seem to this writer at least that this is one of the very few times when the judgment of one of our greatest locomotive engineers could be seen to be at fault.

The jump from the first-line express power of 1892, the graceful 4-2-2 "Dean Single" to *William Dean* of 1902 involved the following increases in the various measures of power; tractive effort—20 per cent; cylinder stroke—25 per cent (the bore was the same); heating surface—35 per cent; steam pressure—12 per cent; grate area—30 per cent; adhesive weight—204 per cent. In addition to these shocks, there was that arising from the full side nudity of exposing wheels, cylinders and motion.

Although the locomotives came to be known as the "Saint" class, 32 had been built before the first Saint name appeared, No.2911 *Saint Agatha* in 1907. Following on *William Dean,* in 1903 there came a second prototype (No.98, later 2998 *Ernest Cunard*) and then in the same year another (No.171, later 2971, *Albion*). No. 171 was turned out temporarily as a 4-4-2 in order to make direct comparison with a French de Glehn compound 4-4-2 No.102 *La France,* which had been imported as an experiment. The first production batch of 19 (Nos. 172-190, later 2972-90) appeared in 1905, and some of these also had a short period as 4-4-2s; they were named after characters in Sir Walter Scott's Waverley novels. In May 1906 Nos.2901-10 were built, later named after Ladies. No.2901 well named *Lady Superior* was the first British locomotive to have a modern superheater, in this case of the

Schmidt pattern and all had been given superheaters (now of Swindon design) by 1912.

In the 20 genuine Saints which followed in 1907, the austere staight lines of the running boards were mitigated by providing the curved drop-ends so much a characteristic of most GWR locomotives built since that time. Finally in 1911 came 25 Courts, all superheated from the outset and with further improvements. Cylinder diameter was increased by ½in and, more obviously, the very characteristic "top-feed" fittings either side of the safety valves on the domeless boiler were added. These came to be very much a GWR trademark.

Churchward's boilers were his greatest triumph and the best among them was this No.1, which was not only fitted to the 77 Saints but also to 74 "Star" 4-6-0s, the 3 "Frenchmen" 4-4-2s,

Above: *Going and coming. Two views of "Saints" at work. The upper photograph shows that they were far from neglected even in British Rail days. As these views show, most of the "Saints' were altered to have the curved foot-plating of the later batches of these path-finding locomotives.*

330 "Hall" 4-6-0s, 80 "Grange" 4-6-0s and 150 "28XX" 2-8-0s.

Amongst the No.1 boiler features were measures to avoid the damage to boiler plates etc. caused by delivering relatively cold feed water straight into the hot boiler water, as was normal before his day. By placing the non-return feed valves (clack valve is the technical term) on top of the boiler and directing the delivery forward, the feed water flowed to the front of the barrel via a series of trays which collec-

ted impurities deposited as the water gathered heat. There, now fairly hot, the feed water mixed with that already in the boiler without detriment.

In due time the whole "Saint" class (except the prototype) was brought up to the standards of the last ones to be built. In building these latter, Churchward finally decided on the two-cylinder versus the four-cylinder question because at the last minute he cancelled the final five Courts, yet continued to build four-cylinder "Star" locomotives. Further development of the GWR express passenger locomotive was all based on the "Star" layout; yet the "Saint" was a remarkable engine and able to match anything in the way of performance which its complex four-cylinder sisters could produce.

In 1925 No.2925 *Saint Martin* was fitted with 72in (1,828mm) diameter wheels in place of 80½in (2,045mm). Tractive effort was increased in proportion and maximum speed was very little affected. In this form and described as the "Hall" class, a further 330 "Saint"s were built, most of which went on until dieselisation.

A particularly pleasing feature was the exceptional precision with which all these later engines were built and repaired. This was the main contribution of Churchward's successors, who saw to it that Swindon had the kit—the Zeiss optical setting out apparatus was one item—to achieve dimensional accuracy higher than was normal practice elsewhere. The story that British Railways' standards of fits and tolerances for a locomotive when it was new corresponded to Swindon's standards when they considered it was worn out, was not entirely apochryphal.

No.2920 *Saint David* was the final surivior of the Saints proper when withdrawn in 1953.

Below: *No.2902* Lady of the Lake *as depicted here retains the straight foot-plating of the original members of the class.*

Class P 4-4-2
Denmark:
Danish State Railways (DSB), 1907

Axle load: 40,000lb (18t).
Cylinders,HP: (2) 14¼ x 23½in (360 x 600mm).
Cylinders, LP: (2) 23½ x 23½in (600 x 600mm).
Driving wheels: 78in (1,980mm).
Heating surface: 2,072sq ft (192.5m²).
Superheater: None
Steam pressure: 785psi (13kg/cm²).
Grate area: 34.5sq ft (3.20m²).
Fuel: 13,500lb (6t).
Water: 4,650gall (5,550 US) (21m³).
Adhesive weight: 80,000lb (36t).
Total weight: 262,500lb (119t).
Length overall: 60ft 9in (18,515mm).

It could be argued that flat Denmark was uninteresting locomotive country. Nevertheless, Danish steam engines were both distinctive and handsome—and none more so than the "P" class Atlantics, introduced in 1907. Nineteen came from the Hannoversche Maschinenbau AG of Hanover, Germany (Hanomag) and in 1910 a further 14 from Schwartzkopff of Berlin. The second batch was designated "P-2" and had larger cylinders (14½ and 23½ x 25¼in—360 and 600 x 640mm) and higher boiler pressure (213lb/sq in—15kg/cm²).

They were four-cylinder compounds, with the low-pressure cylinders outside the frames and with a single piston-valve spindle serving both high and low pressure valves on each side. Heusinger's (Walschaert's) valve-gear was used, but out of sight inside the frames instead of in the usual position outside. All cylinders drove on the rear coupled axle; the inside ones were raised and their axis sloped downwards towards the rear so that the inside connecting rods would clear the leading coupled axle. Maximum permitted speed was 62mph (100km/h).

Visually the Danish 4-4-2s were very striking; the chimney was adorned with the Danish national colours—red, yellow, red—and there were such details as that near-complete circle described by the injector pipe on the side of the boiler before homing on to the clack valve.

Above and below: *Danish State Railways class "P" 4-4-2. These striking machines were the mainstay of Danish passenger services from 1910 to 1935.*

Class 640 2-6-0
Italy:
State Railways (FS), 1907

Tractive effort: 24,810lb (11,256kg)
Axle load: 33,000lb (15t).
Cylinders: (2) 21¼ x 27½in (540 x 700mm).
Driving wheels: 72¾in (1,850mm).
Heating surface: 1,163sq ft (108m²).
Superheater: 361sq ft (33.5m²).
Steam pressure: 171psi (12kg/cm²).
Grate area: 26sq ft (2.42m²).
Fuel: 13,300lb (6t).
Water: 3,300gall (3,940US) (15m³).
Adhesive weight: 98,000lb (44.5t).
Total weight: 197,970lb (89.8t).
Overall length: 54ft 2⅜in (16,530mm).

When the Italian State Railways was formed in 1905, one of the first tasks undertaken by the Chief Mechanical Engineer of the new organisation, Guiseppe Zara, was the design of a standard range of locomotives. He was a man of both ability and an original turn of mind—certainly his smaller express passenger locomotive was full of unusual and interesting features, but in spite of that some are still in use 75 years after the first one took the rails.

The class "640" 2-6-0 appeared in 1907 and the first batch was built by Schwartzkopff of Berlin. Production continued until 1930 and 188 in all were built. The majority were constructed by Italian builders. The class also included 15 rebuilt from class "630" two-cylinder compounds. Class "630" was originally intended as the standard class, but the advent of superheating meant that they were superseded by the "640" almost as soon as they came into service.

It was fairly original to choose the 2-6-0 or Mogul wheel arrangement at all for express passenger work—but combine it with large wheels, *inside* cylinders and *outside* steam chests and valve gear and you really have something that is worth a detour to see.

The reason why 2-6-0s have not often hauled the world's great trains is that the two-wheel leading pony trucks have been suspect for a fast running locomotive. Most express engines have four wheel bogies, yet a 2-6-0, say, has a higher proportion of adhesive weight in relation to total weight, an important advantage in a mountainous country such as Italy. However, Zara had a card up his sleeve—his Zara truck, called in Italy the Italian bogie. The leading coupled wheels are allowed about ¾in (20mm) of side-play in their axle-boxes, spherical journals and bushes are provided on the crank pins and coupling rods so that the coupling of the wheels will still work properly when the wheels are not in line. The leading pony wheels are mounted in a truck which also carries the leading axle, in such a way that both the pony wheels and the leading driving wheels play a

Denmark was a pioneer in the adoption of diesel-electric traction and the first diesel-electric express trains went into service as long ago as 1935. They were known as the "Lyntog" Lightning trains and, whilst there was no threat to steam haulage of heavy expresses, the Atlantics found that their duties on fast light trains were affected. For this reason between 1943 and 1955 a number were converted to rather close-coupled 4-6-2s at DSB's Copenhagen shops. The boiler was lengthened by adding an additional ring, while the original wide firebox was replaced by a narrow one the same size as that belonging to the class "R" 4-6-0s. The original cylinders and motion were retained but new wheels of lesser diameter (68in—1,727mm) were provided. The new engines were redesignated class "PR".

The forty-year long process of replacing Danish steam with diesel power came to fruition in the end, but a little before this time the last 4-4-2 was withdrawn. This was No.912 in 1968. Denmark is full of steam-lovers and their enthusiasm is recognised by the preservation of two of these superb 4-4-2s (Nos.917

Above: *Pre-war view of a Danish State Railways' class "P" 4-4-2, showing the clean lines before air brakes.*

and 931 — the latter is displayed in the museum at Odense) and one (No.908) as rebuilt into a Pacific.

part in guiding the locomotive round a curve. The device has been very successful and 2-6-0s and 2-6-2s have dominated steam express passenger operations in Italy ever since.

Main line electrification began in Italy before No.640.001 took the rails, so it is not surprising that no further new designs for express passenger work appeared after 1928. But electrification was also a factor in the survival of engines like the "640" — obsolescence would have overtaken them long before if the new engines built had been steam.

Left: *Italian State Railways' class "640" 2-6-0 No.640.004 at Allessandria Locomotive Depot in June 1972.*

BESA Class 4-6-0

India:
Indian Railways, 1905

Tractive effort: 22,590lb (10,250kg).
Axle load: 39,500lb (18t).
Cylinders: (2) 20½ x 26in (521 x 660mm).
Driving wheels: 74in (1,880mm).
Heating surface: 1,476sq ft (137m²).
Superheater: 352sq ft (32.7m²).
Steam pressure: 180lb/sq in (12.7kg/cm²).
Grate area: 32sq ft (3.0m²).
Fuel: 16,800lb (7½t).
Water: 4,000gall (4,800 US) (18m³).
Adhesive weight: 118,000lb (54t).
Total weight: 273,000lb (124t).
Length overall: 62ft 3¼in (18,980mm).

(These dimensions refer to later examples with Walschaert's valve gear, outside valves and superheater).

More British than anything that ran in Britain, this archetypal Mail Engine gave over 75 years of service and is still actively in use. This is the British Engineering Standards Association "Heavy Passenger" 4-6-0, introduced in 1905, of which a number (but not one of the originals) are still in passenger service in India at the time of writing.

The railways of India were developed mainly by private enterprise under a concession system whereby the then British Government of India guaranteed a modest return on investment in return for a measure of control, as well as eventual ownership. The government felt that one of their perquisites was to set standards and, having made rather a mess of the gauge question, made up for it with an excellent job of setting out a range of standard designs for locomotives.

The decision to do this was the result of representations made by the British locomotive manufacturers. At a time when there was an explosion of demand for steam locomotives, they found it difficult to cope efficiently with orders for small batches of similar locomotives which differed only in minor detail.

For the broad (5ft 6in — 1676mm) gauge there was a "Standard Passenger" 4-4-0, a "Standard Goods" 0-6-0, a "Heavy Goods" 2-8-0 and, finally, a "Heavy Passenger" 4-6-0, all of which were successful enough to be still in use 75 years after the designs were conceived. The "Heavy Passenger" 4-6-0s were still being *supplied* in 1950, well after independence, while the 4-4-0s operate still in Pakistan.

State-owned railways such as the North Western obeyed without question, but some of the others were slower to abrogate their independence in such a sensitive matter as locomotive design. However, the qualities of the standard product in due time spoke for themselves. Of course,

Above: *Indian Railways BESA 4-6-0 No.24256 now allocated to the Eastern Region, was built by the Vulcan Foundry in 1949.*

it was still possible to specify alternatives in the way of accessories, even if one had to accept the fundamental features of the design.

Below: *4-6-0 No.24328 of the Western Railway, this is a 1923 product of William Beardmore & Co. of Glasgow.*

The first BESA 4-6-0s were solid hunks of sound engineering, bigger when introduced than almost anything that ran in the same country. Their closest relations at home seem to have been some 4-6-0s built in 1903 for the Glasgow & South Western Railway by the North British Locomotive Co. of Glasgow. NBL were to supply the first standard 4-6-0s to India.

Down the years many more were built there and at the Vulcan Foundry at Newton-le-Willows as well as by Robert Stephenson & Co. A few came from Kitson of Leeds and, shortly after World War I, some were made by William Beardmore of Glasgow, better known for marine engineering than for locomotives. Early examples were non-superheated with outside cylinders, inside slide-valves and Stephenson's valve gear but, early on, outside Walschaert's gear, outside piston valves and superheaters were adopted. The boilers had Belpaire pattern fireboxes. Between the wars a few small batches were turned out with poppet valves. Some later examples had bogie tenders instead of six-wheeled.

When the all-India locomotive numbering system was adopted in 1957 there were 387 broad-gauge 4-6-0s still running in India. More existed in Pakistan, both East (now Bangladesh) and West. All but a very few were either built to the BESA design or close to it. The new running numbers ran from 24,000 to 24,470; the few gaps were for some 4-4-2s and a few non-standard 4-6-2s and 4-6-0s.

The BESA 4-6-0s stayed in top-line work even after their successors, the India Railway Standard (IRS), XA and XB 4-6-2s had arrived in the mid-1920s, because of unsatisfactory qualities amongst the new arrivals. The great success of the BESA designs seems to lie in the fact that they were taken from British practice as it existed, with the difference that both average and maximum speeds in India were 25 per cent lower than at home while loads were about the same. This more than compensated for rougher working conditions; one notes, for example, that in dusty areas, locomotives ran hot so frequently that pipes were provided to trickle cold water on to vulnerable bearings! One factor in the good performance offered by the older engines lay in the extra 9½in (240mm) of space available for the firegrate

Below: *The condition of 4-6-0 No.24280, supplied by the North British Loco Co. in 1915, belies its age, approaching 70 years.*

Above: *Some of the Indian Railways' surviving "BESA" 4-6-0s have bogie tenders instead of the six-wheel variety originally provided.*

between the wheels compared with similar engines in Britain, because of the broad gauge track.

Even so, the coming of the post-war 4-6-2s as well as diesels and electrics did spell out the beginning of the end for the BESA 4-6-0s. By 1980 the number in use had fallen to about 100, but they could still be found at work on passenger trains. And if the importance of trains can be measured by the amount of humanity packed into or clinging on to them, then those in question are important indeed. However, they are a far cry from the days when the "Imperial Indian Mail", hauled by one of these locomotives, provided luxury accommodation for 32 persons only—and their bearers (servants), of course—for the 1,230 mile (1,968km) journey from Bombay to Calcutta.

Class P8 4-6-0

Germany:
Royal Prussian Union Railway (KPEV), 1906

Tractive effort: 26,760lb
(12,140kg).
Axle load: 39,000lb (17.75t).
Cylinders: (2) 22.6in x 24.8in
(575 x 630mm).
Driving wheels: 68.9in
(1,750mm).
Heating surface: 1,542sq ft
(143.3m²).
Superheater: 634sq ft
(58.9m²).
Steam pressure: 170.6psi
(12kg/cm²).
Grate area: 27.8sq ft (2.58m²).
Fuel: 11,000lb (5.0t).
Water: 4,700gall (5,700 US)
(21.5m³).
Adhesive weight: 114,000lb
(52t).
Total weight: 172,500lb
(78.5t).
Length overall: 61ft 0in
(18,592mm).

At the beginning of the century the Prussian state railways were faced with a problem which other railways were to meet in the next ten years—was the newly invented superheater an alternative to, or an adjunct to, compounding? Since 1884 the railway had built both simple and compound locomotives, compounds predominating for express passenger work and simples for secondary passenger work. Construction of non-superheated compounds continued until 1911, but in the meantime some other new types had been introduced with superheaters and simple expansion. One of these was a mixed-traffic 2-6-0, Class "P6", of which 272 were built between 1903 and 1910. However, the 63in (1,600mm) driving wheels of these engines were found to be too small for the speeds that had been intended, and there were difficulties with weight distribution.

In 1906 an enlarged design, a 4-6-0 with wheels of 69in (1,750 mm) was introduced. It was originally envisaged that this new engine would have a permissible speed of 68mph (110km/h), and that it could undertake express passenger work on the hilly parts of the system. Unfortunately the first engines of the type proved to be unreliable and unpopular, and suffered many failures in service.

The solution to the problems included a reduction in the cylinder diameter and adjustments to the weight distribution between the axles, but it was also decided that the motion and valve gear was unsuitable for speeds in excess of 62mph (100km/h), and the engines were rated as secondary passenger and mixed-traffic engines, with the classification "P8". Thus a locomotive which originally had been intended for express passenger work on a limited part of the Prussian system became the most widely-used and popular mixed-traffic

engine ever built, serving eventually over much of Europe.

Like many of the most successful and popular steam engines, the "P8" was simple in layout, and initially at least, elegant in outline. The round-topped boiler, with a long narrow firebox, was well proportioned, and although at least two variants of boiler were fitted in due course, the basic shape was not changed. In addition to Dr Schmidt's superheater, the engines also had long-travel piston valves, which he recommended as an adjunct to his superheater. The combination of superheater and piston valves, with a well-proportioned Walschaert's valve gear, gave the engines an efficiency which approached the highest that was ever to be attained with simple expansion. Their load rating was 700 tonnes on the level at 50mph (80km/h) and 300 tonnes on 1 in 100 (1 per cent) at 31mph (50km/h).

Once the intitial snags had

Above: *Class "38" 4-6-0 No. 38.3635 at the head of a German Federal Railways local train at Lippstadt.*

been cleared from the "P8", it was built in large numbers, its axle load permitting its use over much of the Prussian system. It was also built in small numbers for the state railways of Oldenburg, Mecklenburg and Baden as well as for export. Although nominally a secondary passenger engine, it took a full share in express passenger work on which speed was limited to 62mph (100km/h).

At the end of World War I, by which time 2,350 "P8"s had been built for the KPEV, Germany was required to hand over large numbers of locomotives as reparations, and 628 "P8"s were allocated to other countries. The Belgian railways had been particularly badly affected, and they received 2,000 locomotives, of which 168 were "P8"s. These

Below: *In due time the "P8" class 4-6-0s of the Prussian railways became class "38" of The German State (now Federal) Railways whose smart red-and-black colours are depicted here.*

engines survived a second invasion by the Germans, and, adorned with an elegant lipped chimney, they lasted until the end of steam in that country in 1966.

The loss of "P8"'s was partly made good by building more of them, the last being completed in 1928. On the German State Railway the engines became class 38. Under the German State ownership and later there was much reboilering of the engines, but the alterations which affected their appearance were the fitting of full-depth smoke deflectors, feedwater heaters and other external fittings.

World War II saw the "P8"'s spreading into Eastern Europe as the Germans moved east, and this resulted in an even wider distribution than before. They worked in Czechoslovakia, Greece, Jugoslavia, Poland, Roumania and Russia, and many of them remained in those countries. In several countries they were modified externally in accordance with national practice, but the basic design was rarely altered. Eventually a total of 3,438 "P8"'s were built in Germany, and about 500 in other countries. In addition the Polish railways, which acquired a large number of genuine "P8"'s, built 190 engines in which a larger boiler, with wide firebox, was mounted on a "P8" chassis.

After World War II a nominal total of 2,803 "P8"'s remained in Germany, but many of them were unservicable. On the formation of the DB and DR (in West and East Germany respectively) the engines were divided between the two systems. On both railways the full-depth smoke deflectors were mostly replaced by the post-war variety. Although difficulties with steaming had never been a weakness of the "P8" class, some of the DR engines were fitted with Giesl exhausts.

Two of the DB engines were converted to quasi tank engines by coupling them to four-wheeled tenders by a coupling which was designed to permit running in both directions. In addition a number of engines were equipped for push-and-pull working with the original tenders. However, the spread of dieselization made rapid inroads into the "P8" class, and by 1968 the total was down to 73, mostly working south of Stuttgart. The rate of withdrawal then slowed, and the last engine survived until January 1975, three years after the last of them on DR had been withdrawn. However, engines of the class remained at work in other countries, and several were still at work in Poland and Roumania in 1979, 73 years after the introduction of the class. Eight are preserved at various sites in Germany.

It is interesting to note that, although the "P8" was built to the Continental loading gauge, the general layout and dimensions were very similar to some 1,500 British 4-6-0s, although the ancestry of the British engines was independent of that of the German ones. The valve events of the "P8" were almost identical with those of the LMS Class 5 Stanier 4-6-0 "Black Fives".

Above: *Royal Prussian Union Railway "P8" class 4-6-0 in its latter days as class "38" on the German Federal Railways.*

Below: *"P8" class 4-6-0 of Prussian design but hauling behind it a train belonging to the Roumanian State Railways.*

Cardean Class 4-6-0
Great Britain:
Caledonian Railway (CR), 1906

Tractive effort: 22,667lb (10,282kg).
Axle load: 41,500lb (19t).
Cylinders: (2) 20¾in x 26in (527 x 660mm).
Driving wheels: 78in (1,981mm).
Heating surface: 1,814sq ft (168.5m²).
Superheater: 516sq ft (48m²).
Steam pressure: 200psi (14.1kg/cm²).
Grate area: 26sq ft (2.4m²).
Fuel: 11,000lb (5t).
Water: 5,000gall (6,000 US) (22.7m³).
Adhesive weight: 123,000lb (56t).
Total weight: 294,000lb (133.5t).
Length overall: 65ft 6in (19,964mm).

No engines ever built have a better claim to be regarded as the epitome of the Golden Age of Steam than *Cardean* and her sisters. The complex and beautifully polished Caledonian Railway blue livery as depicted in the illustration speaks for itself, but in many other ways the running of

these engines seems now to be like some dream. For example, *Cardean* was allocated to one train and one driver at a time. The legendary David Gibson (described as being "temperamental as a film star") had her from 1911 to 1916. Every weekday she ran the famous "Corridor"—the 2pm from Glasgow to Euston—as far as Carlisle, returning in the evening on the corresponding train from Euston.

There is no doubt that Gibson regarded *Cardean* as his personal property and lavished on his locomotive a concern and a care that nowadays only a very few men give even to their own motor cars. The result was a degree of reliability that is far out of reach of any railway administration today. There were of course occasional happenings and one such took place in April 1909 when a crank axle broke at speed. One of the driving wheels became detached and bowled away down the bank. Although the train parted from the engine, became derailed and was brought quickly to a stand by the

automatic Westinghouse brake, the locomotive (now a 4-5-0!) went merrily on but quite amazingly stayed on the rails. This happened during the reign of James Currie, Gibson's predecessor.

Gibson is today remembered almost as well as John Farquharson McIntosh, the designer of

Above: Cardean's *lesser cousins. A class "908" mixed traffic 4-6-0. There were 10 engines of this class, all built at St. Rollox works in 1906.*

Class A 4-6-0
Australia:
Victorian Government Railways (VGR), 1907

Tractive effort: 27,480lb (12,464kg).
Axle load: 39,500lb (18t).
Cylinders: (2) 22 x 26in (559 x 660mm).
Driving wheels: 73in (1,854mm).
Heating surface: 2,048sq ft (190.6m²).
Superheater: 375sq ft (35m²).
Steam pressure: 185psi (13kg/cm²).
Grate area: 29sq ft (2.7m²).
Adhesive weight: 118,000lb (54t).
Total weight: 263,500lb (119.5t).
(Tender details not available).

The first of these "A" class 4-6-0s, which all followed this now well-established tradition of self-help in locomotive building, was delivered in 1905 from the Victorian Government Railways own Newport Workshops. They were large

these fine engines. The five members of the class were built at the Caledonian Railway's own St. Rollox shops in 1906 and were very conservative in design. Inside cylinders and motion, with Stephenson's valve gear driving slide valves situated on top of the cylinders via rocking levers, was an entirely nineteenth-century arrangement. McIntosh believed that the better riding and aesthetics given with the cylinders and motion inside the frames more than balanced the handicap of inaccessibility, as well as the extra costs involved in making a crank axle. Superheaters were added in 1911-12. Later, vacuum-brake equipment was fitted to enable vacuum-braked trains of other companies to be worked, for the Caledonian Railway was an air-brake line.

A steam servo-mechanism for the reversing gear was a help and large bogie tenders were provided for non-stop runs over such distances as the 150¾ miles (243km) from Carlisle to Perth. Rather oddly, only one of the class was named and it also seems strange that the one chosen should be that of the house in which the Deputy Chairman of the company lived. So all except No.903 *Cardean* had to be content with numbers which ran from 904 to 907.

No.907 perished in Britain's worst-ever railway disaster at Quintinshill near Carlisle on 22 May 1915. The other four survived through the railway grouping of 1923. The last survivor was *Cardean* herself, withdrawn as London Midland & Scottish No. 14752 in 1930. Only one Caledonian feature was adopted by the LMS, and that a few years later, when William Stanier specified the CR's deep-toned "hooter" style whistle for his locomotives.

Below: *Caledonian Railway 4-6-0 No.903* Cardean *in all her glory as running between Glasgow and Carlisle prior to 1914.*

Above: *The sole preserved Caledonian Railway locomotive, 4-2-2 No.123 of 1886, currently on display in Glasgow.*

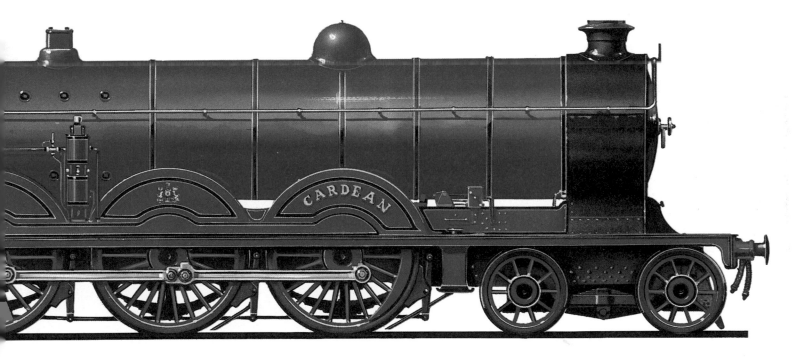

Left: *A Victorian Railways' class "A" 4-6-0. These were the principal express passenger locomotives for many years.*

handsome engines, typical of British practice of the day and seven years later there were 125 of them, all with outside cylinders, and inside slide-valves actuated by Stephenson link motion and bogie tenders. Originally, none had superheaters but these were added gradually over the years, the last being converted in 1949. In 1923, non-superheated engines became class "A-1", superheated ones class "A-2". All the "As" then took the running numbers 816-839.

Some 4-6-0s for freight traffic had arrived from Baldwin of Philadelphia as early as 1879. The famous "DD" class 4-6-0 for mixed traffic was built locally from 1902 onwards and they formed the progenitors of the most numerous and long-lasting express passenger locomotives of the state of Victoria.

There were a few modifications such as the conversion of 57 to oil-firing during the late 1940s and, earlier, the addition of smoke deflectors. A group of 5 were extensively modernised with new front-ends and "Boxpok" disc wheels, which considerably changed their appearance.

Between 1915 and 1922 sixty more "A2" class engines (Nos. 940 to 999) were delivered and these had Walschaert's valve gear and outside valves. There was no difference in classification between the "Walschaert A2s" and the "Stephenson A2s" and together the 185 locomotives were the mainstay of Victoria's passenger services until after World War II. There were a few modifications such as the fitting of smoke deflectors, conversions to oil firing and a group of five with Boxpok disc wheels. When one considers that there were only some 640 locomotives on the whole Victoria 5ft 3in (1,600mm) gauge railway system, it can be seen that the position the "A2" 4-6-0s occupied was an important one. It was if the London, Midland, Scottish Railway had 2,300 "Royal Scot" 4-6-0s instead of 70.

In 1950 some "R" class 4-6-4s were delivered from Britain and these made numerous class "A1" and "A2" 4-6-0s redundant. Even so, the class lasted until 1963 in normal service. Three have been preserved, No.995 at the Australian Railway Historical Society museum at Newport, No.964 at Edwardes Lakes and No.996 in the public park at Echucha. So ended an era in the history of the state.

4500 Class 4-6-2 France:
Paris-Orleans Railway (P-O), 1907

Axle load: 39,000lb (17.5t).
Cylinders, HP (2) 16.5 x 25.6in (420 x 650mm).
Cylinders, LP (2) 25.2 x 25.6in (640 x 650mm).
Driving wheels: 74¾in (1,900mm).
Heating surface: 2,100sq ft (195m²).
Superheater: 684sq ft (63.5m²).
Steam pressure: 232psi (16kg/cm²).
Grate area: 46sq ft (4.27m²).
Fuel: 13,500lb (6t).
Water: 4,400gall (5,280US) (20m³).
Adhesive weight: 117,000lb (53t).
Total weight: 301,000lb (136.5t).
Overall length: 68ft 2½in (20,790mm).

(These dimensions refer to the superheated version of the class before rebuilding by Chapelon.)

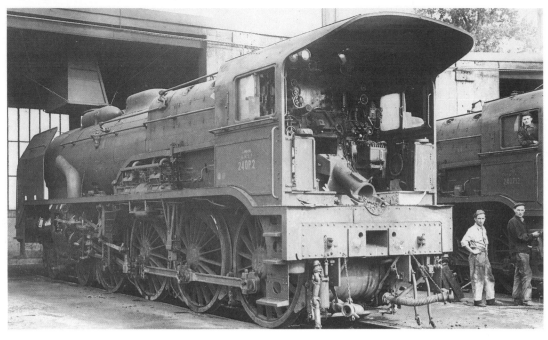

If the number of express passenger locomotives to be included in this book was reduced to a single one then this locomotive might well be the choice. It was by a short head the first Pacific to *run* in Europe (not the first to be built—some were built in Britain for Malaya earlier the same year) and later became not only the most powerful but also the most efficient 4-6-2 ever to run in Europe. It was also certainly the most technically advanced Pacific but also, of course, somewhat complex.

One hundred "4500" Pacifics were built between 1907 and 1910 mostly by French builders but rather strangely including a batch of 30 (Nos.4541-70) by the American Locomotive Co of Schenectady, USA. There were also another 90 of class "3500" which were identical except for wheels 4in (100mm) smaller in diameter. The "3500"s were constructed between 1909 and 1918.

All these Paris-Orleans 4-6-2s were four-cylinder de Glehn compounds. An interesting feature was the trapezoidal grate which was wide at the back in the usual manner of Pacific grates. At the front, however, it was narrow and sat between the frames. Later, examples were delivered with superheaters and some had them fitted later. The high-pressure cylinders had piston valves while the low-pressure ones had balanced slide valves. They were competent but not specially remarkable machines in those days, capable of cylinder horsepowers of around 2000.

In the 1920s the replacement of wooden carriages by steel began to show up the inadequacies of the Pacifics, yet a commitment to electrification absorbed totally any resources there might have been for new construction.

A young man called André Chapelon, who had an appointment as development engineer

on the Paris-Orleans Railway, proposed a drastic rebuilding and in 1926, persuaded his superiors—against their better judgement—to put the work in hand in accordance with his ideas. Changes in the administration meant further patient persuasion but eventually in 1929 the transformed No.3566 took the road. A new era in steam traction had begun; there was a 25 per cent increase in power production for the same amount of steam, while the boiler improvements which made more steam available took the possible cylinder horsepower up to 3,700, an 85 per cent increase over the originals.

Chapelon achieved this apparent miracle after a careful analysis of the shortcomings of the original design. He considered the whole process of producing steam power from cold water to exhaust steam and took the following measures to improve it:

(a) Pre-heating the feed-water with waste heat from the exhaust.

(b) Provision of extra heating surface in the firebox, using flattened vertical ducts known as thermic syphons.

(c) Provision of a superheater 24 per cent larger in size and of a more efficient (but also more complicated) design.

(d) Much larger steam pipes to improve steam flow.

(f) Poppet valves to give quicker and larger openings to steam and exhaust, replacing the existing high-pressure piston-valves and low-pressure slide-valves.

(f) An improved exhaust system giving greater draught with less back pressure. This took the form of a double chimney.

The existing Walschaert's valve gears were retained to work the oscillating camshafts of the poppet valves.

The P-O announced that No.3566 had hauled 567 tons

Above: *A Paris—Orleans 4-6-2 rebuilt into a 4-8-0 (No.240P2) for the Paris-Lyons Mediterranean main line in 1940.*

Below: *French National Railways 4-6-2 No.231E23, as rebuilt by Chapelon from the original 1907 Paris-Orleans Railway design.*

from Poitiers to Angoulême, 70.1 miles (113km), start-to stop at an average speed of 67.3mph (107.7km/h); a 1 in 200 (0.5 per cent) gradient was climbed at 77.5mph (124km/h). This was a performance unprecedented in France and caused a sensation in the world of locomotive engineering.

To cover requirements on the P-O, thirty-one further "3500" 4-6-2s were rebuilt. As electrification proceeded, some of the originals became surplus, and other railways in France could not wait to get their hands on these miracle locomotives. Twenty were rebuilt for the Northern Railway and later 23 for the Eastern. Later on a further 20 were built new for the Northern.

In 1932, sixteen further locomotives of the "3500" series were given a rather less drastic rebuilding, in which poppet valves were not provided, but instead a form of twin piston valve head was used. This gave double the amount of port opening for a given amount of movement and was known as the Willoteaux valve after its inventor, an assistant of Chapelon's.

During the same year one of the remaining unsuperheated "4500" class 4-6-2s was rebuilt into a 4-8-0 at Tours. The intention was to provide a locomotive with one-third more adhesive weight, more suitable for the gradients of the line to Toulouse, altogether steeper than those en route to Bordeaux. A different boiler was needed, having a narrow firebox to fit between the rear driving wheels and one based on those carried by the Northern 4-6-2s was used.

Otherwise the recipe was as before, except that some improvement in detail enabled 4,000 cylinder hp to be developed. Eleven more were rebuilt in 1934 and in 1940 a further twenty-five "4500" were rebuilt for the PLM (now South-Eastern Region SNCF) main line, designated class "240P". This time a mechanical stoker was fitted.

Dimensions etc. of these engines which differed substantially from the originals were as follows:

Axle load: 44,000lb (20t).
Cylinders LP: (2) 25.2 x 27.2in (650 x 690mm).
Heating surface: 2,290sq ft (213m²).
Superheater: 733sq ft (68m²).
Steam pressure: 290psi (20.4kg/cm²).
Grate area: 40sq ft (3.75m³).
Fuel: 26,500lb (12t).
Water: 7,500gall (9,000US) (34m³).
Adhesive weight: 177,500lb (80.5t).

The sort of achievement that these 4-8-0s were capable of included the surmounting of Blaisy-Bas summit between Paris and Dijon with 787 tonnes at 59mph (94½km/h) minimum after

Below: *Paris-Orleans Railway 4-6-2 No.4546 shown as restored to original condition for display at the French National Railway Museum at Mulhouse, Alsace.*

several miles at 1 in 125 (0.8 per cent). During the war the "240P" had to manage 28 coaches and could reach 53mph (85km/h) on the level with this load. Alas, after the Paris-Lyons line was electrified in 1952, proposals to use these engines elsewhere in France foundered, for reasons which have never been adequately explained.

In the 1960s the remaining Pacifics of Paris-Orleans design had become concentrated—much to the delight of their many British admirers—at Calais. Their effortless performances with heavy boat trains up, say, the 1 in 125 (0.8 per cent) climb to Caffiers between Calais and Boulogne will long remain in the memory.

In 1956 some tests were made of the behaviour of electric locomotive pantograph current collectors at high speeds, and 110.6mph (177km/h) was reached by 231E19 pushing an equivalent of 220 tons. This was the highest speed achieved by these engines.

Against this was the sad fact that, economical as the Chapelons were in respect of coal consumption, in overall terms they were more expensive to run than the fleet of simple rugged 2-8-2s— the 141R class—supplied from North America at the end of World War II. These could also

Above: *Calais Maritime Station. Chapelon 4-6-2 No.231E39 has just arrived from Paris with the "Golden Arrow" express. The connecting steamer is on the right*

manage, say, 850 tons on a 1 in 125 (0.8 per cent) gradient at over 52mph (84km/h), even if you would not describe the performance as effortless. So in the end at Calais as elsewhere in France, simple engines out-lasted even these superb compounds. No.231E22 is displayed at the Mulhouse Museum and No.231E41 is being restored at St Pierre-les-Corps. Unrebuilt Paris-Orleans No.4546 is also preserved.

Class S 3/6 4-6-2
Germany:
Royal Bavarian State Railway (KBStB), 1908

Axleload: 39,500lb (18t).
Cylinders, HP: (2) 16.7 x 24.0in (425 x 610mm).
Cylinders, LP: (2) 25.6 x 26.4in (650 x 670mm).
Driving wheels: 73.6in (1,870mm).
Heating surface: 2,125sq ft (197.4m²).
Superheater: 798sq ft (74.2m²).
Steam pressure: 228psi (16kg/cm²).
Grate area: 48.8sq ft (4.5m²).
Fuel: 18,800lb (8.5t).
Water: 6,030gall (7,240US) (27.4m³).
Adhesive weight: 116,000lb (53t).
Total weight: 328,500lb (149t).
Length overall: 69ft 11in (21,317mm).
(Dimensions refer to the 1923 series)

Above: *A class "S3/6" 4-6-2 at speed. Note right-hand running.*

Top: *The luxurious interior of one of the saloon cars of the Rheingold Express.*

The locomotives of Bavaria were as different from those of Prussia as were the Bavarian Alps from the stark North German plain. The reason for this was simple: most of the Bavarian engines were designed by A G Maffei, and in the present century that firm's chief designer, Heinrich Leppla, had a flair for locomotive lineaments which was quite lacking in the centrally-controlled designs of Prussia. The supreme achievement of Maffei was the family of Pacifics which originated in 1908, and were supplied over a period of 23 years to the railways of Bavaria and Baden and to the German State Railway.

From 1895 all the passenger engines bought by the Bavarian Railway were four-cylinder compounds, and these included two Atlantics acquired in 1901 from Baldwin of Philadelphia. Contact with these engines seemed to influence Maffei, for it became the first European locomotive builder to adopt the bar frame as standard. Associated with this was the American practice of casting the cylinders in massive blocks which incorporated the smokebox saddle. All four cylinders drove the same axle, which in the Pacifics was the middle one. The inside high-pressure cylinders were steeply inclined to allow the connecting rod to clear the leading coupled axle, and their valves were level with, but outside, the cylinders, which placed them conveniently alongside the outside valves, which were above their cylinders. A simple vertical rocker enabled the outside valve gear to drive the inside valves also, and all steam pipes were contained within the cylinder block.

The first engines to this design were supplied in 1908 to the Baden Railway; Bavaria took delivery of its first batch in the following year. By 1911 twenty-three had been built, with driving wheels 73.6in (1,870mm) in diameter and a boiler pressure of 213psi (15kg/cm²). Then came 18 engines with 78.7 in (2,000mm) wheels, and between 1913 and 1924 a further 78 with the smaller wheels. Succeeding batches incorporated detail changes, including the addition of feedwater heaters, an increase in axle load, and an increase in boiler pressure to 228psi (16kg/cm²). All were classified S3/6, which indicated an express locomotive (schnellzuglok) with three driving axles in a total of six. Of these engines 16 went to France and 3 to Belgium as reparations after World War I.

In 1925 the first German State Railway standard Pacifics were built, but these engines had a 20 tonne axleload, and pending the introduction of a smaller version of the class there was a need for more Pacifics with an axle load of 18 tonnes. So impressed were the DR authorities with the power output of the Maffei engines that they ordered a further 40, which were delivered between 1927 and 1931. These were the only engines ordered by DR to a design which originated on a state railway other than the Prussian. The class was then numbered from 18.401 to 18.548, with 8 blanks.

With these extra engines the class spread from its native haunts, and until the introduction of the standard "03" Pacific with 18 tonnes axle load they worked from sheds as far afield as Osnabrück and Berlin Anhalt. But even the "03"s did not

Class 10 4-6-2

Tractive effort: 43,800lb (19,800kg).
Axleload: 43,200lb (19.6t).
Cylinders: (4) 19.7 x 26.0in (500 x 660mm).
Driving wheels: 78in (1,980mm).
Heating surface: 2,500sq ft (232m²).
Superheater: 816sq ft (76m²).
Steam pressure: 199psi (14kg/cm²).
Grate area: 49.2sq ft (4.6m²).
Fuel: 15,400lb (7t).
Water: 5,280gall (6,340US) (24m³).
Adhesive weight: 130,000lb (59t).
Total weight: 352,640lb (160t).
Length overall: 70ft 3in (21,404mm).

displace them from the Rhine Valley main line, and it was Bavarian Pacifics which worked the prestigious Rheingold express both before and after World War II. So successful were they on this service that 30 of the final batch of 40 engines were given new welded boilers with combustion chambers between 1953 and 1956, as part of the German Federal Railway reboilering programme. These engines were renumbered 18.601-30. When displaced from the Rhine Valley by electrification they retired to Bavaria, and their last duties were the expresses between Munich and Lindau on Lake Constance. The last of them were withdrawn from Lindau shed in 1966.

One engine passed into the hands of the new German State Railway in East Germany, and this also was given a new boiler, and used for high-speed testing. It is scheduled to be amongst the 13 locomotives of the family which are preserved in various places. Amongst them is Bavarian No.3634 of 1912, which is in the Germany Museum in Munich restored to its original livery.

In side view the Bavarian Pacifics had a slender appearance, with "daylight" showing under the boiler and through the bar frames, but head-on the massive cylinder block gave a blunt impression. In DR days small smoke deflectors were fitted, and these helped to mask the bluntness of the cylinder block. At first stovepipe chimneys were fitted, but late chimneys were of a graceful flared shape, which was almost British. Usually modifications made to German designs worsened their appearance, but the Bavarian Pacifics became gradually better looking, although they suffered by losing their original holly green livery with yellow lines and black bands.

Below: *A German State Railway class "S 3/6" 4-6-2 poses with a set of Rheingold Express cars.*

Locomotive enthusiasts arriving for their first visit to Belgium might well have suspected a delayed attack of *mal de mer* when they saw a Pacific carrying a boiler apparently intended for an Atlantic. They were indeed seeing one of the most remarkable looking locomotives in Europe, but it was a 2-10-0 rather than an Atlantic which accounted for the shortness of the boiler.

At the beginning of the century the Belgian State Railway was passing through an interesting phase, in which a number of classes of inside cylinder locomotive were built with a close resemblance to the MacIntosh locomotives of the Caledonian Railway of Scotland, but in 1904 a new era of locomotive construction was instituted under the direction of J B Flamme. French compound locomotives were attracting much attention, and one of these was acquired on loan. It showed such an improvement over existing Belgian engines that 12 similar locomotives were built, followed by 57 compound 4-6-0s. The next move was the construction of four 4-6-0s of a new design to compare the application of superheating to simple and compound

locomotives. As a result of these tests, Flamme decided that he could revert to the simplicity of the non-compound, but for the largest classes it would be desirable to use four cylinders, to give the improved balancing which had been demonstrated by the four-cylinder compounds.

The outcome of this decision was the introduction of two classes of very large locomotives, a Pacific for express work and a 2-10-0 for freight work. Apart from a small difference in the firebox dimensions, the boilers of the two types were identical, and its length was determined by the weight limitations on the 2-10-0. This boiler would have looked short on any Pacific, but as Flamme arranged his inside cylinders to drive on the leading axle, with a generous length of connecting rod, the effect was accentuated. Even the outside cylinders were ahead of the smokebox, and there was a platform over the inside cylinders and motion protruding far ahead of the smokebox. The boiler itself was unusual for Europe of that time, as it had a very large grate to suit low-grade coal, and to accommodate this without excessive weight, the boiler tapered steeply outwards just ahead of the firebox, giving the outline of boiler known in the United States as "wagon top". Walschaert's valve gear was fitted to the outside valves, with rocking shafts to drive the inside valves.

Twenty-eight of these engines were built between 1910 and 1912, followed by a further 30 in the succeeding two years; the second batch had a slightly smaller grate and shorter rear end, which reduced the weight from 102 to 98 tonnes. These engines, which became Class 10 under a later classification, took over the principal express work on the routes from Brussels to Liège and Luxembourg, and proved very successful.

Under a programme of rehabilitation of the Belgian loco-

motive stock after World War I, the superheaters of the Pacifics were enlarged, double chimneys were fitted, designed by the then Chief Mechanical Engineer, Legein, the frames were strengthened at the front, and many smaller improvements were made. The process of improvement continued over the years. Smoke deflectors were added and ACFI feed water heaters, so that with the addition of extra fittings the weight gradually crept up. One locomotive was fitted with a mechanical stoker, and another had further shortening of the firebox and rear end to reduce the weight again. Neither of these alterations was repeated. The original six-wheeled tenders were replaced by bogie tenders from Prussian reparations engines.

From 1938 more major improvements were instituted, influenced by Chapelon's work in France. These included larger steam pipes, a still larger superheater, and the replacement of the Legein exhaust by the Kylchap pattern. With the massive chimney of the Kylchap exhaust, and the various extra fittings on the boiler, the engines now had a truly formidable appearance, but the alterations produced the intended improvement in performance. With successive improvements their loading on the heavily-graded Luxembourg line had been increased from 350 to 500 tonnes. They continued to haul the expresses on that route until electrificaton, and on 30 September 1956 one of them hauled the last steam-worked passenger train on that line. The last of the second series was withdrawn from service in 1956, but the last of the first series remained in service until 1959, 49 years after the introduction of the class.

Below: *The strange-looking front end of Belgian class "10" 4-6-2 No.10045, one of a very successful series.*

The Paris-Orleans Pacifics (see page 78)

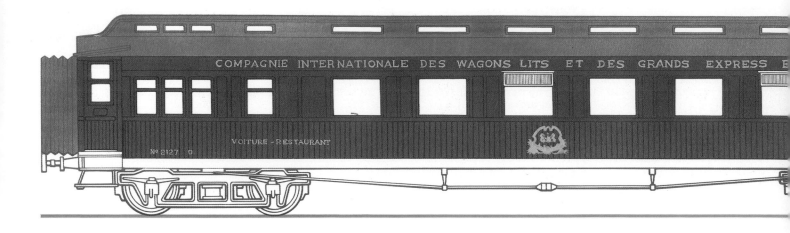

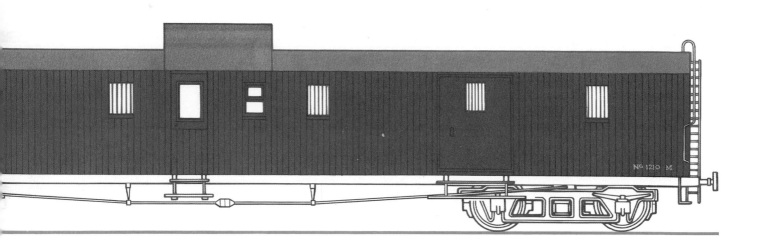

The artwork depicts the famous Sud-Express of the Paris-Orleans railway, as running before 1914. The locomotive is the Paris-Orleans 4501-class 4-6-2, the first pacific to run in Europe. They were four-cylinder de Glehn compounds and for their day were excellent if not remarkable machines. Later they were to be transformed by the magic wand of André Chapelon into some of the most capable and efficient steam locomotives ever to be seen on rails. The Sud-Express left Paris in the morning and reached the Spanish frontier at Hendaye by evening. Passengers could then change into a Spanish broad-gauge train for an overnight ride to Madrid or Lisbon. The legendary International Sleeping Car Company provided both the sleeping cars for the Spanish portion of the journey and also a day-time deluxe train in France. The types of vehicle which formed this French train are depicted above; dining car, saloon car (of which a varying number would be used according to demand) and a baggage car or fourgon. The cars were built of teak, finished with varnish and furnished with handsome brass lettering and insignia as shown.

The Bavarian Maffei Pacifics (see page 80)

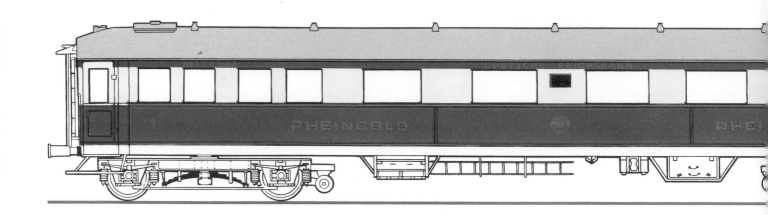

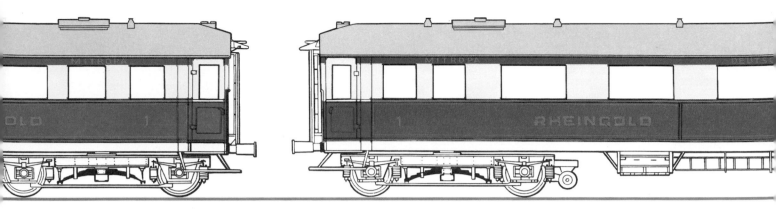

Above and right: *The three magnificent saloon cars in cream-and-violet livery were built for the pre-World War II Rheingold Express which ran from Hook of Holland and Amsterdam to Basle and Lucerne via Cologne and Mannheim. The service was provided by the German Mitropa Company, standing for Mitteleuropäische*

Speisewagen und Schlafwagen Aktien Gesellschaft, *whose name appears on the cars in company with that of the Deutsche Reichsbahn, who ran the train. Apart from the baggage car (shown right), the train consisted exclusively of these deluxe vehicles, both first and second class. Certain of the cars included kitchens, and*

meals were served to all passengers at their seats. A few cars survived the war and are at present in the hands of a preservationist group who occasionally run excursions with them. Over the southern section of the route in Germany, the Bavarian 4-6-2s (one of which is shown below) were used on this train.

ET DES GRANDS EXPRESS EUROPEENS

SALOON CAR

N° 1677 E

N° 1210 M

P.O

4021

ENS

COMPAGNIE INTERNATIONALE DES WAGONS LITS

AR   N° 2127 D

N° 1677 E   VOITURE - SALON

REICHSBAHN   MITROPA

RHEINGOLD   1

MITROPA

2

S ³⁄₆

K.Bay.Sts.B

MAFFEI
MÜNCHEN

Below: *One of the Royal Bavarian
State Railway's four-cylinder class
S3/6 compound 4-6-2s built by
Maffei of Munich from 1910 onwards,
shown in the original green colours.
After World War I the equally smart
standard German State Railway livery
of black with red wheels was applied.*

K. BAY. STS. B.

1501 Class 4-6-2
Argentina: Buenos Aires and Pacific Railway (BAP), 1910

Tractive effort: 26,472lb (12,011kg).
Axle load: 40,000lb (18t).
Cylinders: (2) 21 x 26in (533 x 660mm).
Wheels: 67in (1,701mm).
Heating surface: 1,597sq ft (148m²).
Superheater: 435sq ft (40.5m²).
Steam pressure: 150psi (10.5kg/cm²).
Grate area: 27sq ft (2.5m²).
Fuel (oil): 1,960gall (2,350 US) (8.9m³).
Water: 5,500 gall (6,600 US) (25m³).
Adhesive weight: 118,000lb (53.5t).
Total weight: 361,000lb (164t).
Overall length: 70ft 2¼in (21,392mm).

The four main British-owned railways of Argentina fanned out from the capital, Buenos Aires, across the pampas towards the west. The 5ft 6in (1,676mm) gauge main line of the Buenos Aires & Pacific was the one that went *due* west and at least partly earned its name by reaching Mendoza at the foot of the Andes from where the Transandine railway led across to Santiago on Chile's Pacific coast. The nature of the country served is indicated by the fact that there was a 205-mile (328km) length of straight track en route.

In 1909, the company ordered from the North British Locomotive Company of Glasgow some Pacifics of very distinctive appearance. They were of advanced design for their day and in fact they were the first locomotives supplied by NBL to have

superheaters. It is clear that they only barely needed that extra pair of carrying wheels at the rear end. On the broad gauge, of course, the narrow firebox is not so narrow and, furthermore, at less of a disadvantage anyway with oil firing. The hinged buffers were an Argentine specialty, cattle thrown aside by the cowcatcher might get caught on fixed ones; equally unconventional were the decorative shape of the hinges on the smokebox door, and the unusual aspect of the cab.

British-built locomotives of the day, for India say, could easily be confused with those for home use, but these imposing engines had an ambience all their own. Fourteen (Nos.1511-24) were supplied during 1910-11 and these were the last express passenger locomotives ordered for the company before nationalisation in 1948. This was a reflection of the parlous economic situation of the foreign-owned railways in Argentina during that period.

After nationalisation, the Buenos Aires and Pacific Railway became known as the General San Martin National Railroad, but the 4-6-2s soldiered on. They were still in use in the mid-1970s, giving good service on stopping passenger trains after more than sixty years at work.

Right: *After more than sixty years of service, 4-6-2 No.1515 of the General San Martin National Railway, stands at the head of a local train. Note the hinged buffers of European pattern in the folded position above the cowcatcher.*

Class A3/5 4-6-0
Switzerland: Swiss Federal Railways (SBB), 1913

Axle load: 18,000lb (16t).
Cylinders, HP: (2) 14¼ x 26in (360 x 660mm).
Cylinders, LP: (2) 22½ x 26in (570 x 660mm).
Driving wheels: 70in (1,780mm).
Heating surface: 1,389sq ft (129m²).
Superheater: 497sq ft (46.2m²).
Steam pressure: 220psi (15.5kg/cm²).
Grate area: 28sq ft (2.6m²).
Fuel: 15,500lb (7t).
Water: 3,900gall (4,700 US) (17.8m³).
Adhesive weight: 106,000lb (48t).
Total weight: 243,000lb (110t).
Overall length: 61ft 2in (18,640mm).

As inhabitants of a small country with two great locomotive designing cultures on their doorstep, the Swiss took basic locomotive principles from neighbouring France and Germany. The Jura-Simplon Railway, which led to the French border, used de Glehn compounds; while the

Class 3700 4-6-0

Netherlands:
State Railway (SS), 1910

Tractive effort: 25,647lb (11,633kg).
Axle load: 37,000lb (17t).
Cylinders: (4) 15¾ x 26in (400 x 660mm).
Driving wheels: 72¾in (1,850mm).
Heating surface: 1,566sq ft (145.5m²).
Superheater: 441sq ft (41m²).
Steam pressure: 171psi (12kg/cm²).
Grate area: 30.3sq ft (2.8m²).
Fuel: 13,200lb (6t).
Water: 3,960 gall (4,750 US). (18m³).
Adhesive weight: 110,000lb (50t).
Total weight: 270,500lb (123t).
Length overall: 60ft 8in (18,480mm).

To British eyes the steam locomotives which ran on the continent of Europe were certainly not things of beauty — except in Holland, where the principal express locomotives had a totally familiar style. The only thing that was strange about them was their enormous height; this was partly illusion because they were normally observed from platforms at ground level rather than three feet above the rails and partly because they really were a lot taller — almost 2ft (600mm), in fact. But there they all were — tall, stylish 4-6-0s, with low running boards, splashers, copper-capped chimneys, brass domes and apple green paint. The only un-British things about them were some big elegant oil lamps and an absence of names.

The first batch came from Beyer, Peacock of Manchester in 1910 and 120 were built between then and 1930. Some were built by Werkspoor, the native locomotive builders and others in Germany. Later versions had widened eight-wheel tenders instead of six-wheel ones. There were four cylinders in line, all driving on the leading coupled axle. Two sets of Walschaert's valve gear worked the valves of the outside cylinders direct and the inside ones via rocking levers. Knorr's feed-water heaters and pumps were fitted. In the 1920s two locomotives were the subject of experiments in the use of low-grade pulversided coal, but the results were not successful enough to be perpetuated.

In 1929 a 4-6-4 tank version of the class was built, ten in number, but time was running out for steam in Holland. Electrification proceeded apace during the next few years and, after the war, was resumed with greater urgency. Steam operations came to an end in 1958, but happily the railway administration set aside a 4-6-0 which is now displayed in the Railway Museum at Utrecht; This No.3737 is in running order and has worked steam specials in recent years.

Below: *Netherlands State Railways class "3700" 4-6-0 No.3737. This locomotive has been restored to near its original condition and is on display in the National Railway Museum at Utrecht.*

Gotthard Railway which pointed towards Germany, on the whole favoured the compounding system of Maffei of Munich.

When it came to building the engines, though, the famous Swiss Locomotive Works (SLM) of Winterthur did very nearly all of it. Of their express passenger 4-6-0s, only four out of 200 were not SLM products. To be sure, the Swiss had no 4-6-0s in one sense, because they used their own system of classification — what the Anglo-Saxon world called a 4-6-0 the Swiss would know as an A3/5; that is to say, a locomotive with maximum speed above 75km/h (47mph) and three coupled axles out of five.

It may appear strange that 4-6-0s were thought adequate for a mountainous country, but nearly all the main lines ran in the valleys and an exception the

Left: *Swiss Federal Railways' preserved "A3/5" class 4-6-0. This locomotive is currently in use for hauling special trains provided for the enjoyment of steam locomotive enthusiasts.*

Loetschberg Railway was built as an electric railway. So that left the Gotthard line and here it was convenient to employ 4-6-0s in pairs or a 4-6-0 piloted by a 2-10-0 to haul express passenger trains up the long 1 in 38½ (2.6 per cent) approach ramps to the Gotthard tunnel.

The dimensions given refer to the most common group of Swiss 4-6-0s, of which 109 (Nos. 701-809) were built for the Jura-Simplon and Swiss Federal railways between 1902 and 1909. The superheaters were added between 1913 and 1933.

The Gotthard Railway (GB) began using 4-6-0s in 1894 and by 1905 had 30 de Glehn compounds (GB Nos. 201-30, SBB Nos. 901-30) but the next orders were for Maffei compounds (SBB) Nos.931-38 and 601-49 of which 931-34 actually came from Maffei), distinguishable from de Glehn's by having the drive on to the leading pair of coupled wheels. 4-6-0 No.705 is preserved in running order — it is intended to be displayed in the Lucerne Transport Museum.

Fairlie 0-6-6-0

Mexico:
Mexican Railway (FCM), 1911

Tractive effort: 58,493lb
(26,533kg).
Axle load: 46,000lb (21t).
Cylinders: (4) 19 x 25in
(483 x 635mm).
Driving wheels: 48in (1,219mm).
Heating surface: 2,924sq ft
(272mm²).
Steam pressure: 183psi
(12.9kg/cm²).
Grate area: 47.7sq ft (4.43m²).
Fuel: 20,000lb (9t).
Water: 3,500 gall (4,200 US).
(16m³).
Adhesive weight: 276,000lb
(125t).
Total weight: 276,000lb (125t).
Length overall: 50ft 7¾in
(15,435).

Right: *A Mexican
Railways "Fairlie"
locomotive of the
batch supplied by
the Vulcan Foundry
in 1911.*

The Mexican Railway ran 264 miles (426km) from the port of Vera Cruz on the Atlantic Ocean to Mexico City, at an altitude of 7,349ft (2,240m). The summit of the route is at Acocotla, 8,320ft (2,536m), but in 108 miles (174 km) the line climbs to 8,050ft at Esperaza. The maximum gradient is a hideous 1 in 22 (4.5 per cent) and the sharpest curve is 325ft radius or 17½ degrees. Before electrification came in 1923, this superbly scenic but very difficult railway had not unexpectedly something rather special in the way of motive power.

The "Fairlie" articulated locomotive was invented by an English engineer called Robert Fairlie in 1864 and foreshadowed the majority of locomotives (other than steam) in service today by having a generator for the working fluid—steam in Fairlie's case, electricity in modern times—as part of the locomotive body; the body being carried on two power bogies which provided the traction. All the axles were therefore driven, so the total weight was available for adhesion, yet the whole vehicle remained extremely flexible. The arrangement made the locomotive an excellent proposition for sharply curved steeply graded mountain lines. Even so, "Fairlies" were never as popular as the "Garratt" or "Mallet" articulated locomotive types, and their application for this British-owned Mexican line was certainly their greatest both as regard size of individual locomotives and their success as haulage units.

The first "Fairlie" came to Mexico in 1871 and by 1911, a total of 49 had been delivered, of which 18 were still in service in 1923 when electrification made them finally redundant. The last and largest of them was a batch of three supplied by Vulcan Foundry in 1911, carrying running numbers 183 to 185. The advantage of the "Fairlie" is best summed up by comparison with

George the Fifth Class 4-4-0

Great Britain
London & North Western Railway (LNWR), 1910

Tractive effort: 20,066lb
(9,102kg).
Axle load: 43,680lb (19.5t).
Cylinders: (2) 20½ x 26in
(521 x 660mm).
Driving wheels: 81in
(2,057mm).
Heating surface: 1,547sq ft
(144m²).
Superheater: 303sq ft (28.1m²).
Steam pressure: 175psi
(12.3kg/cm²).
Grate area: 22.4sq ft 92.08m²).
Fuel: 13,440lb (6t).
Water: 3,000gall (3,600 US)
(13,640).
Adhesive weight: 85,680lb
(38.25t).
Total weight: 212,800lb (95t).
Length overall: 57ft 2¾in
(17,445mm).

In 1903 Francis Webb retired (somewhat reluctantly, so rumour has it) from the locomotive chieftainship of the London & North Western Railway. His compound locomotives, as well as the other

but outdated engines which had been kept on to bolster up the former's inadequate performance quickly followed. Webb's immediate successors, George Whale and W.J. Bowen-Cooke, restocked over the next ten years with 336 workmanlike 4-4-0s and 4-6-0 express locomotives, all built at Crewe Works. And when one says built at Crewe Works, that is exactly what is meant. Trainloads of coal, iron ore, limestone, copper ingots etc. would roll in at one end of Crewe Works and completed locomotives with evocative names decked out in that wonderful "blackberry black" livery would roll out at the other. For this capability, Francis Webb must take a good deal of the credit, even if he held on too long to funny ideas when it came to locomotive design.

Of the four types of express locomotive built at Crewe during those eventful years, outstanding

a typical British main-line locomotive of the day. Compare, for example, these Mexican Railway locomotives with a LNWR type. For a penalty of 29 per cent in weight and 5 per cent in axleload, one obtained an 114 per cent increase in grate area, 220 per cent more adhesive weight and 190 per cent more tractive effort. The "Fairlie"s were the most powerful locomotives built in Britain up to this time.

Although the speeds of trains on the Mexican Railway's inclines were severely restricted by traction limitations going up, and to 8mph (13km/h) for safety reasons coming down, the "Fairlie"s had

excellent riding and tracking qualities at high speeds. This was inadvertently discovered on one or two occasions when runaways occurred; speeds estimated at up to 70mph (113km/h) were achieved on sharp curves without derailment. The motion of these locomotives was quite conventional, with outside piston valve cylinders and Walschaert's valve gear. On the other hand the double boilers were very unusual indeed. The boiler barrels at both ends were nearly similar, but the firebox in the centre was common to both barrels. One big dome in the usual position for one half of the boiler (normally

the uphill end) collected the steam for all four cylinders.

The expense involved in this double boiler was almost certainly the main reason why the "double Fairlie" articulated locomotive was never widely used. It is true there were some problems with the flexible pipes and joints which fed the steam from the boiler to the powered bogies, but experience and the improvement of details would have solved them. In fact this is just what has happened on the one railway left in the world that has "double-Fairlie" steam locomotives still in use, the Festiniog Railway in North Wales. Their 40 ton 0-4-4-0

tanks, are, however, a far cry from the 123-ton Mexican monsters.

"Single Fairlie"s, however, went into quite extensive use. These locomotives had a normal boiler, a leading power bogie and a trailing un-powered bogie behind the firebox. An ability to negotiate absurdly sharp curves was the property that appealed and many (under various names, for Fairlie's patent was not recognised in the USA) were used on urban railways, particularly elevated lines which had to negotiate city street corners. But "single Fairlies" were only, as it were, half of what was a good idea.

was the later of the two classes of 4-4-0, the legendary "George the Fifth" locomotives which entered service in 1910. To the solid simplicity of the earlier design, the "Precursors" of 1903, were added piston valves and superheaters with results that today are hard to believe. Ninety "George the Fifths" were built, to which must be added a further 64 conversions from "Precursors" as well as another ten from a group of unsuperheated 4-4-0s known as "Queen Marys". These relatively small locomotives handled the great northbound expresses out of London's Euston station in a competent manner, handling trains of more than 400 tons in weight—shall we say 13 bogie coaches—on the Euston to Crewe schedules which involved average speeds of 55mph

Left: *A LNWR "George the Fifth" class 4-4-0 picks up water at speed.*

(88km/h) between stops and maxima of 75 (120) or so. When a "George" went roaring by hauling one of these long rakes of "plum and spilt milk" carriages, it was an exceedingly fine sight. There were very few railways in the world which at that time confided such exacting loads and timings to four-coupled power. North of Crewe towards Carlisle on steeper gradients the related 4-6-0 "Experiment" or "Prince of Wales" classes were at least in theory the usual motive power, but south of Crewe the most important workings were in the charge of these 4-4-0s.

The "Georges" had everything of the simplest; note the round top outer firebox wrapper instead of the more complex Belpaire pattern used elsewhere. The cylinders were inside, but the use of Joy valve gear, whose rods and slides were located in the same vertical plane as the connecting rods, meant that all the inside

motion was accessible for lubrication and maintenance. Some minor weaknesses marred their performance when in worn condition; for example, the Schmidt type piston valves would start to leak and increase steam and coal consumption by noticeable amounts. And having said that the Joy valve gear was very simple, the version fitted to the "George" was not quite as simple as it might have been. For some reason—one suspects it may have been in order to use the same gear as that fitted to the "Precursors" which had *outside* admission slide valves instead of inside admission piston valves— there was an extra rocking lever between the valve rod and the valve spindle. Wear here was also detrimental to steam consumption. Of course, LNWR locomotives were such that this only meant that as the time came nearer when a visit to Crewe Works was due, "Georges" just

needed to be thrashed a little harder than ever to get over the road "right time"; the "Georges" were certainly in the "North-West" tradition of being able to stand it.

In 1923, when the railways of Britain were merged into four groups, all the "Georges" came into the possession of the London Midland & Scottish Railway, ruled largely by Midland Railway men who thought little of any locomotives whose origin was LNWR. It was no surprise, then, that withdrawal of these splendid locomotives began in late 1935 and continued until the last one ceased work in May 1948. With the scrapping of superheated Precursor *Sirocco* in October 1949 the LNWR 4-4-0s (and, indeed, all the LNWR express passenger engines) disappeared. None of the 4-4-0s or the 4-6-0s was preserved, a surprising final piece of spite on the part of the 'Midlanders'.

Class S 2-6-2
Russia:
Ministry of Ways of Communication, 1911

Tractive effort: 30,092lb (13,653kg).
Axle load: see text.
Cylinders: (2) 22½ x 27½in (575 x 700mm).
Driving wheels: 72¾in (1,850mm).
Heating surface: 2,131sq ft (198m²).
Superheater: 958sq ft (89m²).
Steam pressure: 185psi (13kg/cm²).
Grate area: 51sq ft (4.72m²).
Fuel: 40,000lb (18t).
Water: 5,000gall (6,000 US) (23m²3).
Adhesive weight: see text
Total weight: 370,500lb (168t).
Overall length: 77ft 10½in (23,738mm).

This handsome design of express passenger locomotive either was just or was just not the most numerous in the world. Construction continued over a period of 40 years, usage over more than 60 and certainly its numbers were the largest in the hands of

Below: *The standard Russian passenger locomotive, the class "Su" 2-6-2.*

one administration. Compared with British locomotives, Russian ones can be four feet (1,200mm) higher and two feet (600mm) wider; in terms of weight, though, in steam days locomotive axles could be loaded at most with two tons less each. So there was no temptation towards (or even the possibility of) filling the huge space available with inaccessible ironmongery.

In both Czarist and Communist Russia, steam locomotive design was in the hands of university professors and they studied and tried out many fascinating theoretical possibilities—more thoroughly, perhaps, than elsewhere. But when it came to actual usage out on the road, then these learned gentlemen seemed always to reach the conclusion that Old Geordie (Stephenson) had got it right and the simplest answer was the best.

Another characteristic in which the old regime was far ahead of its time was standardisation; this continued as did locomotive classification, without even a wriggle, over that great watershed in human history the Russian Revolution. In 1955, Britain had, for example, some 20 classes of

express passenger locomotives ten or more strong, while the Soviet Union had a mere four; this out of a fleet intended for such traffic approximately the same in number. These class "S" (written "C" in Russian script) 2-6-2s were a standard design ordered by the Ministry of Ways of Communication for general usage amongst the many independent railways. The "S" stood for the Sormovo works at Nijni Novgorod where the class was built. About 900 were turned out before the Revolution.

Very little needs to be said of the design which took very early on the standard final form of the steam locomotive, having two cylinders, Walschaert's valve-gear, wide firebox, superheater and compensated springing. The fulcrum points of the latter could be altered to bring extra weight on to or off the driving wheels. For running on lines which had inadequate permanent way, the maximum axle-load could be quickly changed from 18 tonnes to 16 tonnes by a simple adjustment, at the cost of reducing the adhesive weight from 54 tonnes to 48 tonnes.

A modified and enlarged ver-

sion known as class "Su", was first produced at the Kolomna Works near Moscow in 1926. This sub-class, of which about 2,400 were built during the next 15 years, is the basis of the particulars and of art-work below. The "u" stood for *usilenny,* which means "strengthened"; in Russian script "Su" is written "Cy". The cylinders, wheelbase and boiler were enlarged but, interestingly, the boiler pressure was kept at the same modest level. The adoption of high boiler pressure was so often (like the substitution of diesel for steam 40 years later) a costly matter of "keeping up with the Jones'".

The extra cost of a high-pressure boiler is considerable, especially as regards maintenance, while even its theoretical

Right: *Class "Su" 2-6-2 No. 100-85 outside Sormovo works. This example is equipped for burning oil fuel.*

Class 685 2-6-2
Italy:
State Railways (FS), 1912

Tractive effort: 27,741lb (12,586kg).
Axle load: 35,500lb (16t).
Cylinders: (4) 16½ x 25½ (420 x 650mm).
Driving wheels: 72¾in (1,850mm).
Heating surface: 1,922sq ft (178.6m²).
Superheater: 516sq ft (48.5m²).
Steam pressure: 171psi (12kg/cm²).
Grate area: 38sq ft (3.5m²).
Fuel: 13,500lb (6t).
Water: 4,842gall (4,040 US) (22m³).
Adhesive weight: 103,500lb (47t).
Total weight: 265,362lb (120.4t).
Overall length: 67ft 6in (20,575mm).

The "685" class was developed from 1912 onwards as the standard Italian express locomotive. In total 390 eventually were produced, some by conversion from an earlier non-superheated compound design on the Plancher system (the "680" class) and others built new. The idea was to obtain almost the power of a "690" class 4-6-2, yet not suffer the restricted usage of the latter due to their 19 tons axle load. The "685"'s used superheated steam and had four cylinders, each pair using a common piston valve. The tortuous passageways intrinsic to that unusual arrange-

Right: *The Italian State Railways class "685" standard express locomotive of which 390 were made.*

advantages are dubious. Of course, some railways had to adopt high-pressures in order to obtain sufficient tractive effort with the largest cylinders that could be squeezed into a tight loading gauge, but Soviet Russia was not one of them. Those university owls again!

After World War II, production was restarted at Sormovo Works (whose location was by then known as Gorki) and continued until 1951, by which time some 3,750 "S" class had been built. Variations included some built in 1915 for the standard gauge Warsaw-Vienna line known as sub-class "Sv" (Cb). There was also a "Sum" (Cym) group, having a system for pre-heating the air used in combustion. A Scotsman named Thomas Urquhart introduced successful oil-burning locomotives to Russia in 1880, since when it became commonplace. Many "S" class used this form of firing.

ment did not assist the "685" class to become the world's most free running engines. A prominent but odd feature of all Italian steam locomotives including the "685" is the Salter's spring-balance safety valve required by law, provided in addition to two normal modern pop valves. The Zara truck described earlier was naturally also a feature.

Arturo Caprotti was of course an Italian and the patent poppet valve gear he devised (which might well have become a world standard if steam had continued) was later fitted to 123 of these engines. The usual problem of maintenance—which stemmed from the Caprotti cam-boxes being precision not blacksmith engineering—was overcome by a unit-replacement system.

Two other names associated with attempts to improve these and other Italian steam locomotives are Attilo Franco and Piero Crosti, whose Franco-Crosti boiler was designed to take the exhaust gases from a conventional locomotive and extract some of the heat from them in large drums, so pre-heating the feed-water. Aesthetically, the result is awful, but five "685" converted in 1940 showed an 18.93 per cent saving in fuel. Even so, those who devised the system had thrown away simplicity, steam's trump card; the remaining 385 were left alone.

Right: *An Italian State Railways class "685" 2-6-2 receives some attention to lubrication from its driver.*

Class 231C 4-6-2

France:
Paris, Lyons and Mediterranean Railway (PLM), 1912

Axleload: 40,500lb (18.5t).
Cylinders, hp: (2) 17.3 x 25.6in (440 x 650mm).
Cylinders, LP (2) 25.6 x 25.6in (650 x 650mm).
Driving wheels: 78.7in (2,000mm).
Heating surface: 2,185sq ft (203m²).
Superheater: 694sq ft (65m²).
Steam pressure: 228psi (16kg/cm²).
Grate area: 45.7sq ft (4.3m²).
Fuel: 11,000lb (5t).
Water: 6,160gall (7,400 US) (28m²).
Adhesive weight: 122,000lb (55t).
Total weight: 320,500lb (145.5t).
Length overall: 65ft 7in (20,000mm).

French engineers were early converts to the creed of compounding, and in no other country was compounding pursued more enthusiastically or successfully. Nevertheless, from time to time right up to the last steam designs, occasional doubts entered the minds of French engineers, and a batch of simple expansion locomotives appeared, but the outcome was always a strengthening of the orthodox doctrine.

The Pacifics of the PLM illustrated this process. Between 1890 and 1907 the railway ordered 845 locomotives, of which 835 were compounds, and in the period 1905 to 1907 construction of compound Atlantics and 4-6-0s was in full swing. But in 1907 the first European Pacific appeared, and in 1909 the PLM produced two prototype locomotives of that wheel arrangement, one simple and one compound. Apart from the recurrent desire to ensure that the mechanical complications of the compounds were really justified, there was a further reason for this particular digres-

sion into simple expansion. Compound expansion enables a higher proportion of the energy in the steam to be converted into work during expansion, but to get the full benefit of the greater expansion in the compound it is necessary to use a high steam pressure, and high steam pressure brings higher boiler maintenance costs. At this time there was a new attraction for engineers— the superheater—which offered the possibility of improving the thermal efficiency sufficiently for simple expansion to be acceptable, and with it the possibility of using a lower boiler pressure.

The two PLM Pacifics put this problem to the test, for the compound engine used saturated steam but the simple engine was superheated. The compound had the de Glehn layout of cylinders, with the outside high-pressure cylinders set well back over the rear bogie wheels, but the simple engine had the four cylinders in line, as in the PLM Atlantics and 4-6-0s. The in-line arrangement gave a much more

rigid assembly than the de Glehn arrangement. Apart from the differences in cylinders, motion and boiler already mentioned,

Above: *"The Flèche d'Or" (Golden Arrow) hauled by a long-serving, efficient ex-PLM "231C" 4-6-2.*

Above: *A Paris, Lyons and Mediterranean Railway compound 4-6-2, depicted in SNCF days, receives attention from its crew.*

Below: *The locomotive for the "Flèche d'Or" (Golden Arrow) express backs down from Calais depot to Calais Maritime station.*

the two engines were as far as possible identical, but the compound worked at 227psi (16kg/cm²) and the simple at 171psi (12kg/cm²).

In 1911 the two engines ran comparative trials, and the superheated engine developed higher powers and used 16 per cent less coal than the compound. A natural step would have been to try superheating *with* compounding, but at that time it was not found possible to build a superheated compound within the weight restrictions. Thus 70 more simples were ordered in 1911, but by the following year the design problems of the superheated compound had been overcome, and 20 were built, differing from the prototype in having all four cylinders in line, as in the simple engines. Uncertainty still prevailed, and 20 more simples were next built, but then in 1913 a careful comparison was made between the two varieties of superheated design, and the compound returned a 25 per cent lesser coal consumption and better performance. The issue was finally settled, and the PLM built no more simple Pacifics; the existing simple engines were in due course converted to compounds.

In 1921 a further 230 Pacifics were ordered, and in 1931 55 more, making a total of 462. Successive batches incorporated improvements, mainly to the exhaust arrangements and to the boiler proportions, but the basic layout remained unchanged. Improvements continued to be made, and later still Chapelon's ideas on steam passage and boiler proportions were incorporated in an engine which was rebuilt with a boiler having 284psi (20kg/cm²) pressure. A scheme to apply this boiler widely was initiated, but the incorporation of the PLM into the SNCF resulted in 30 engines only receiving this treatment, the last of them in 1948, but 284 engines received a more modest treatment on Chapelon lines. By this time the sub-divisions of the class were very complicated.

The PLM Pacifics had long and distinguished lives, and the quality of their performance responded directly to the improvements which were made to them, but they never achieved the levels of the Chapelon rebuilds of the Paris-Orleans Pacifics. As electrification displaced them from the PLM main line from 1952 onwards, they spread to other regions. Withdrawal began in the 1950s, but many of the boilers were not worn out, and there was thus a good supply of spare boilers, with which some of the engines were maintained in service until 1969.

Four engines were retained for preservation, including 231K22, a rebuild with partial Chapelon improvements, which is at Steamtown, Carnforth, Lancashire.

Class 310 2-6-4
Austria: Imperial and Royal State Railway (KKStB), 1908

Axleload: 32,200lb (14.6t).
Cylinders, HP (2) 15.4 x 28.3in (390 x 720mm)
Cylinders, LP: (2) 24.4 x 28.3in (620 x 720mm).
Driving wheels: 82.7in (2,100mm).
Heating surface: 2,077sq ft (193m²).
Superheater: 463sq ft (43m²).
Steam pressure: 213psi (15kg/cm²)
Grate area: 49.7sq ft (4.6m²)
Fuel: 19,000lb (8.5t).
Water: 4,620gall (5,550 US) (21m³).
Adhesive weight: 98,000lb (44t).
Total weight: 322,000lb (146t).
Length overall: 69ft 11in (21,318mm)

The railways of the Austrian empire were lightly constructed, and in places heavily graded. Locomotives were thus required to have a low axle load, but to be capable of developing high powers at moderate speeds when burning low-grade fuel. From 1897 to 1916 locomotive design in the empire was largely in the hands of Karl Gölsdorf, a designer of fertile imagination, who is credited with some 45 different designs, all branded clearly with his ideas.

After building two-cylinder compounds he reached the stage in 1908 when four cylinders became necessary, but as a means of reducing weight he used a single piston valve to serve the high-pressure and low-pressure cylinders on each side of the engine. This involved tortuous steam ports, which would have imposed a severe limit on power output at high piston speeds.

In that year Gölsdorf produced his masterpiece. When other European railways were just turning to the Pacific, Gölsdorf found that by reversing the Pacific into a 2-6-4, he could support the large firebox which the quality of coal required, and at the same time make the front of the engine lighter in weight than with a leading bogie. To mitigate the disadvantages of his valve arrangement, he used driving wheels 82.7in (2,100mm) in diameter, although the maximum speed was only 62 mph (100km/h). By this means piston speeds were kept low. Every possible device was used to keep the weight down, so that this large engine had a load on the coupled axles of only 32,200lb (14.6 tonnes), a remarkable achievement. At the speeds involved the leading pony truck proved to be no disadvantage.

The proportions of the cylinders, which are critical in a compound, proved to be less than ideal, and despite some

Below: *A class "210" 2-6-4 in Austrian Federal Railways' days when nearing the end of its life.*

Above: *Striking view of Gölsdorf 2-6-4 No.210.01 showing the original member of the class in as-built condition.*

modifications to the valves, the locomotives never achieved the power output which the size of boiler merited. Nevertheless they hauled the principal expresses on the easier main lines of old and new Austria until the appearance of 2-8-4 locomotives in 1928.

The first 2-6-4s were saturated and classified "210", but from 1911 superheaters were fitted. Austria had a total of 43 of these "310" class engines, and in addition seven were supplied to Prussia and three to Poland. The last of the Austrian engines was withdrawn in 1957.

Whatever their deficiencies in performance, the 2-6-4s were most imposing engines, and to build such a large locomotive for such a small weight was a masterpiece of design. One of them is preserved at the Vienna Technical Museum.

Remembrance Class 4-6-4 Tank

Great Britain:
London, Brighton & South Coast Railway (LBSCR), 1914

Tractive effort: 24,180lb (10,991kg).
Axle load: 44,000lb (20t).
Cylinders: (2) 22 x 28in (559 x 711mm).
Driving wheels: 81in (2,057mm).
Heating surface: 1,816sq ft (167.7m²).
Superheater: 383sq ft (35.6m²).
Steam pressure: 170psi (11.9kg/cm²).
Grate area: 26.7sq ft (2.48m²).
Fuel: 8,000lb (3½t).
Water: 2,700gall (3,250 US) (12m³).
Adhesive weight: 126,000lb (101t).
Total weight: 222,000lb (101t).
Length overall: 50ft 4¾in (15,361mm).

Those great trains of the world which were hauled throughout their journeys by tank locomotives were few and far between. One such was the immortal "Southern Belle", the all-Pullman express which ran non-stop several times a day over the 51 miles between London's Victoria Station and Brighton. Specially associated with this train was a group of seven 4-6-4 or "Baltic" tank locomotives, the most powerful motive power ever owned by the London Brighton and South Coast Company.

Previously, the express trains between London and the south coast had been hauled by a fleet of 4-4-0s, 4-4-2s, and 4-4-2Ts, supplemented by two 4-6-2Ts. The new 4-6-4s were to some extent a stretched version of the latter and were known as class L. Their designer Colonel L. B. Billinton was instructed to produce locomotives capable of running the "Belle" and other fast trains such as the "City Limited" to an accelerated timing of 45 or 50 minutes instead of the even hour. In fact, the 60 minute timing was never improved upon, even by the "Southern Belle's" successor, the electric "Brighton Belle" which replaced the steam train after 1933, but the addition of third-class Pullman cars to the previously all-first formation made the train an increasingly harder haulage proposition.

Conventional practice of the day was followed in most respects but the valve gear arrangement was interesting. Outside Walschaert's valve gear was used,

Below: 4-6-4T No.B333 (later 2333) Remembrance at Victoria Station, London in 1930. This was the Southern Railway's War Memorial locomotive and bore special plaques on the side tanks to that effect for many years.

Class F 4-6-2

Sweden:
Swedish State Railways (SJ), 1914

Axle load: 35,500lb (16t).
Cylinders, HP: (2) 16½ x 26in (420 x 660mm).
Cylinders, LP: (2) 24¾ x 26in (630 x 660mm).
Driving wheels: 74in (1,880mm).
Heating surface: 2,038sq ft (189m²).
Superheater: 732sq ft (68m²).
Steam pressure: 185psi (13kg/cm²).
Grate area: 38.5sq ft (3.6m²).
Fuel: 14,336lb (6.5t).
Water: 5,500gall (6,600 US) (25m³).
Adhesive weight: 105,000lb (48t).
Total weight: 322,000lb (146t).
Length overall: 69ft 9in (21,265mm).

Sweden is not a country associated in many people's minds with the building of steam locomotives, yet there was and is a locomotive-building industry there. Moreover, the country had its own style of locomotive engineering and this was even occasionally exported. It is a measure of the essential simplicity of the steam locomotive that very small countries (and railway companies) can build their own designs economically. More often, however, the Swedes took orders for other people's designs. Nydquist and Holm of Trollhättan had an order in the 1920s for some 0-10-0s for Russia. The locomotives were duly completed and the builders were instructed that a Soviet ship would call for them at the firm's own quay. They were loaded aboard, whereupon the captain promptly unloaded gold bars to their value on to the quayside.

Nydquist and Holm not only built but also designed Sweden's finest ever class of express locomotive, the class "F" 4-6-2s delivered to the Swedish State Railways in 1914. It will be seen that they were very distinctive and at the same time very handsome machines. The leading bo-

Above: Swedish State Railways' class "F" 4-6-2. All these engines were sold to Denmark when the Swedish Railways were electrified. This one was returned to Sweden for preservation.

gie had frames outside, partly no doubt for clearance reasons. This feature also facilitated the employment—it is thought for the first time ever—of roller bearings

Above: *"Remembrance" class No.329* Stephenson *is here depicted in its original LB&SCR umber livery. These famous tank locomotives handled the legendary "Southern Belle" all-Pullman express which ran several times a day between Victoria Station, London, and Brighton until in 1933 the steam train was superceded by the all-electric "Brighton Belle".*

actuating inside piston valves between the frames via rocking levers; all this in spite of having the cylinders themselves outside the frames. One reason for this unusual arrangement was the wish to have similar cylinders to

the 4-6-2Ts plus the need to provide a well tank between the frames under the boiler, which the existence of valve motion there would preclude. There had in fact been trouble including a derailment, whose cause had been attributed to the swishing of water in half-full tanks plus the high centre of gravity. This occurred soon after the prototype, No.321 *Charles C Macrae* first entered service in April 1914. The solution was on similar lines to the extra dummy funnels on some steamships of the day, that is, adopted so as not to spoil the appearance. It consisted of making all but the bottom 15 inches of the side tanks into dummies in

order to lower the centre of gravity of the locomotive. The modifications were successful and speeds as high as 75mph were quite frequently run without any further problems.

A second locomotive (No.328) was completed just before war broke out that autumn and five further examples (Nos.329-333) in 1921-22. Two more received names at that time—No.329 became *Stephenson*, while No.333 was chosen to be the War Memorial for the company's servants killed in the war and so was named *Remembrance*. The later examples of the class were never fitted with the feed-water heaters and steam-operated feed pumps

which, unusually in British practice, were fitted to the earlier ones for a time after they were new.

After electrification in 1933, the Southern Railway converted the 4-6-4 tanks into 4-6-0s known as class N15X in which guise they had a long and honourable career on the less exacting longer distance services of the bigger system, lasting well after 1948 into British Railways days. That this was considered worth-while doing demonstrates more than any words the excellent qualities of these extremely handsome locomotives. The last survivor (LB&SCR No.331, SR No.2331, BR No.32331) was withdrawn in July 1957.

(a Swedish speciality) for full-size locomotive axles.

The "F"s also used a system of compounding, of German origin, which attempted to get the advantages of a compound locomotive without the complications. The four cylinders all drove the centre coupled axle and were accordingly fairly steeply inclined at an angle of 6¼° to the horizontal. The two low-pressure cylinders were outside and the two high-pressure ones inside. Each pair was served by a single piston-valve spindle with multiple heads which controlled the admission of steam from the boiler to the high-pressure cylinders, the release of steam from the high-pressure cylinders, its admission to the low-pressure ones and finally the exhaust from the low pressure cylinders to atmosphere. The complicated feature of this arrangement was the labyrinth of passageways inside the cylinder castings, but at least these did not involve moving parts. A single set of Walschaert's valve gear was provided in full view on each side of the locomotive.

A "windcutter" cab was fitted, although the permitted speed was only 62mph (100km/h) reflecting, as did the very light axle load (16 tons) track conditions in Sweden at that time. The unusual "bath" shaped tender also made its contribution to the distinctiveness of the design. The

"F" class handled the principal expresses on the Stockholm-Gothenburg and Stockholm-Malmö main lines.

An absence of coal deposits combined with the presence of water power induced the Swedish railways to proceed with electrification and in 1936 these big

Left: *A Swedish "F" class 4-6-2 heads a passenger train near Nyboda in 1927. Note the electrification poles and wires, which were to spell the end of steam traction on the main line expresses of Sweden.*

4-6-2s were declared surplus to requirements. A customer was to hand just across the water and the class "F" 4-6-2s, Nos.1201-11 shortly became Danish Railways class "E" Nos.964 to 974. Their new owners took to their purchase readily, so much so that during and after World War II the Danish locomotive-building firm of Frichs built another 25 to the original drawings.

King Christian of Denmark was a lifelong railway enthusiast and he asked that his funeral train should be hauled by steam. Two "E"s did the duty, although by the time he died diesel traction had taken over generally. Two "E" class are preserved, No.974 (ex SJ 1211) of 1916 and No.999 of 1950. A further two locos (Nos.978 and 996) are also set aside for possible operation.

K4 Class 4-6-2

United States:
Pennsylvania Railroad (PRR), 1914

Tractive effort: 44,460lb (20,170kg).
Axle load: 72,000lb (33t).
Cylinders: (2) 27 x 28in (686 x 711mm)
Driving wheels: 80in (2,032mm).
Heating surface: 4,040sq ft (375m²).
Superheater: 943sq ft (88m²).
Boiler pressure: 205psi (14.4kg/cm²).
Grate area: 70sq ft (6.5m²).
Fuel: 36,000lb (16t).
Water: 10,000gall (12,000 US) (46m³).
Adhesive weight: 210,000lb (96t).
Total weight: 533,000lb (242t).
Overall length: 83ft 6in (25,451mm).

The Pennsylvania Railroad called itself the Standard Railroad of the World. This did not mean that the system was just average or typical, but rather that the railroad's status was one to which other lines might aspire, but a status that it was extremely unlikely that they would reach. The Pennsy's herald was a keystone, indicating the position the company felt it occupied in the economy of the USA. The famous "K4" 4-6-2s, introduced in 1914 and the mainstay of steam operations until after World War I, might well similarly be given the title Standard Express Locomotive of the World.

There were 425 of them, built over a period of 14 years, and they followed a series of classes of earlier 4-6-2s introduced previously. The Pennsy was normally exceedingly conservative in its locomotive engineering and its Pacific era was ushered in by a single prototype ordered from the American Locomotive Company in 1907, later designated class "K28". By 1910 the railroad felt it knew enough to start building some of its own and in a short time 239 "K2"s were put on the road. In 1912, quite late in the day really, superheating

was applied to these engines.

In 1913, the company went to Baldwin of Philadelphia for 30 "K3" 4-6-2s. These were interesting in that they were fitted with the earliest type of practical mechanical stoker, known as the "Crawford" after its inventor, D.F. Crawford, Superintendent of Motive Power (Lines West). This had been in use on the Pennsylvania Railroad since 1905 and by 1914 nearly 300 were in operation—but only 64 on 4-6-2s. Later designs of stoker used a screw feed, but the principle used in the Crawford was to bring forward the coal by means of a series of paddles or vanes, oscillated by steam cylinders, which were feathered on the return stroke like the oars of a rowing boat. The coal was fed into the firebox at grate level, unlike later types of stoker, which feed on to a platform at the rear, for distribution by steam jets.

In addition, there was a further Alco prototype supplied in 1911, larger than the "K28" and designated "K29". There was also the "K1" class, which was an "in house" project, designed but never built.

The prototype "K4" Pacific appeared in 1914; it was con-

siderably larger than the "K2" class, having 36 per cent more tractive effort and 26 per cent more grate area at a cost of a 9 per cent increase in axle loading. The design owed as much to that Apex of the Atlantics, the "E6" class 4-4-2 as to the earlier 4-6-2s.

Top: *Pennsylvania Railroad "K4" class 4-6-2 No.3749 built at Altoona.*

Above: *The "Broadway Limited" leaves Chicago in 1938. The streamline locomotive is "K4" class No.3768, styled by Raymond Loewy.*

The Pennsylvania Railroad was one of the very few North American lines to approach self-sufficiency in locomotive design and construction. It liked to build its own locomotives, designed by its own staff, in its own shops. One aid to this process was a locomotive testing plant at a place called Altoona — a hallowed name amongst the world's locomotive engineers. Altoona was then the only place in North America where a locomotive could be run up to full speed and power on rollers and where instrumentation could pick up exactly what was happening inside. In this way the designers' expectations could be checked under laboratory conditions and corrections applied.

The prototype "K4" was put to the question at Altoona soon after it was built, but few changes were needed as a result for the production version. The oil head-light and wooden pilot (cow-catcher) were not, however, repeated. By 1923, after more than 200 "K4"s had been built, power reverse replaced the hand-operated screw reversing gear of earlier engines. In due time the latter were converted, fore-shadowing a date (1937) when hand reversing gear would be illegal for locomotives with over 160,000lb (72.7t) adhesive weight. The same edict applied to the fitting of automatic stokers to locomotives of such size and many (but not all) "K4"s were fitted with them during the 1930s. Before then the power output had been severely limited by the amount of coal a man could shovel. The last five "K4"s had cast steel one-piece locomotive frames. Another interesting box of tricks that also became general in the 1930s, was the continuous cab signalling system. A receiver picked up coded current flowing in track circuits and translated this into the appropriate signal aspect on a miniature signal inside the cab.

One could see signs of Pennsy's conservatism, for example, even in the later "K4"s the ratio of evaporative heating surface to superheater size was as low as 4.3, instead of the 2.2 to 2.5, more typical of the passenger loco-motives which other North American railroads were using in the 1930s. There was also the modest boiler pressure, three-quarters or less of what was used elsewhere. It is not being sug-gested that such a policy was wrong, only that it was different. Low boiler pressures and modest degrees of superheat had a marked and favourable effect on the cost of maintenance and repair; perhaps the Pennsy, who could buy coal at pit-head prices, had done its sums in depth, trading some extra (cheap) coal for less (expensive) work in the shops.

Running numbers were allo-cated at random between 8 and 8378, although the last batches built during 1924-28 were num-bered in sequence from 5350 to

Above: *PRR "K4" class 4-6-2 No.5354, built between 1924 and 1928, takes water at a wayside station.*

5499. All were built at the PRR's Juanita shops at Altoona, Penn-sylvania except Nos.5400 to 5474 of 1927 which came from Baldwin.

There were a few "specials" amongst the "K4" fleet. Two engines (Nos.3847 and 5399) were fitted with poppet valve gear, thermic syphons in the firebox, and improved draughting; so equipped they could develop over 4000hp in the cylinders instead of the 3000hp typical of a standard "K4". A number of other engines (designated class "K4sa")had less drastic treatment with the same end in view; in this case the firebox and exhaust improvements were accom-panied by larger piston valves, 15in (381mm) diameter instead of 12in (305mm). One engine (No.3768) was fully streamlined

for a while; a number of others were partly streamlined and specially painted to match certain streamlined trains. Many types of tender were used, including a few which were so big they dwarfed the engine, but held 25 tons of coal and 23,500 US gallons (107m³) of water.

Until the coming of the Duplex locomotives after World War II, the "K4"s handled *all* Pennsy's express passenger trains outside the electrified area. During the winter of 1934 the *Detroit Arrow* was scheduled to cover the 64 miles (102km) from Plymouth to Fort Wayne, Indiana, in 51 minutes, an average speed of 75½mph (121km/h) and accord-ingly for a short time the fastest steam timing in the world. The cylinder limitations of the stan-dard "K4"s did, however, mean much double-heading in driving Pennsy's great "Limiteds" across these long level stretches of the Lines West. The fact that these legendary locomotives were so economical in other ways more than balanced such extrava-gances as the use of two on one train.

In crossing the Alleghany mountains, such heroic measures as three "K4"s (or even, it is said, sometimes *four*) at the head end were needed to take, say, an unlimited section of the "Broad-way Limited" up the 1 in 58 (1.72 per cent) of the Horseshoe Curve. Nowadays such things are only a memory, but a single "K4", presented to the City of Altoona, stands in a little park inside the famous semi-circle curve in re-membrance of the monumental labours of one of the world's greatest express locomotives. Another (more accessible) is under cover in the Strasburg Railway's excellent museum in the town of that name.

Below: *One of the famous "K4" class 4-6-2s of the Pennsylvania Railroad. Between 1914 and 1928 425 were built, mostly at the road's own Altoona shops.*

C53 Class 4-6-2
Dutch East Indies: State Railways (SS), 1917

Axle load: 28,000lb (12.5t).
Cylinders, LP: (2) 13.4 x 22.8in (340 x 580mm).
Cylinders, HP: (2) 20.5 x 22.8in (520 x 580mm).
Driving wheels: 63in (1,600mm).
Heating surface: 1,324sq ft (123m²).
Superheater: 463sq ft (43m²).
Steam pressure: 200psi (14kg/cm²).
Grate area: 29sq ft (2.7m²).
Fuel (oil): Not recorded
Water: Not recorded
Adhesive weight: 83,000lb (37.5t).
Total weight:* 147,000lb (66.5t).
Overall length: 68ft 6½in (20,889mm).
*(*Engine only—tender details not recorded).*

Java, the densely populated main island of Indonesia, was in pre-World War II days provided by its Dutch rulers with an excellent railway system. There were such things as 12-coupled freight locomotives, colour light signalling, flying junctions and even suburban electrification around Djakarta, then known as Batavia. There were also the fastest narrow gauge trains in the world—and they were steam.

This perhaps may seem a little strange, considering that Indonesians are hardly concerned with such handicaps to the enjoyment of life as worrying over time. But there was a reason; in colonial days it was not considered safe to run trains at night, not by reason of any possible sabotage, but because the natural hazards of tropical railroading in the dark were too much for the careful Dutch—mindful of their orderly native Holland—to contemplate.

Since Java is close to the equator, sunset occurs there sensibly at the same time throughout the year, so the timetable was not too complex; but it did also mean that trains between Batavia and Surabaya, the island's principal cities, could not complete their journeys of 512 miles (820km) between dawn and dusk unless they got a move on. For many years an overnight stop on the way was tolerated—possibly even enjoyed—but in the end measures were taken, including the purchase of new locomotive power, to improve matters.

These magnificent Pacifics were instrumental then in reducing the time for this journey from 29 hours to 12 hours 20 minutes. The overall average speed of 41.5mph (66.4km/h) included 12 stops and there were also intermediate start-to-stop speeds up to 47.4mph (75.8km/h) and maxima as high as 75mph (120km/h). In contrast, the present administration has inhibitions about running its diesels at these sort of speeds, but none about running them at night. So a more sedate 15-hour

Above: *Official works photograph of "C53" class 4-6-2 for Indonesia.*

journey is possible.

There were 20 of these 3ft 6in (1,067mm) gauge four-cylinder compounds, built by Werkspoor in Holland during 1917-21, running numbers 1001-20. During the Japanese régime of occupation they were designated class "C53" and numbered C5301-20. Three survived in use during the 1970s and one of these is reserved for the museum.

Right: *Indonesian Railways' "C53" class 4-6-2 in post-Colonial days.*

Class 231D 4-6-2
France: State Railway (Etat), 1914

Axle load: 40,500lb (18.5t).
Cylinders: HP (2) 16½ x 25½in (420 x 650mm).
Cylinders: LP (2) 25¼ x 25½in (640 x 650mm).
Driving wheels: 76½in (1,950mm).
Heating surface: 2,110sq ft (196m²).
Superheater: 861sq ft (80m²).
Steam pressure: 242psi (17kg/cm²).
Grate area: 46sq ft (4.27m²).
Fuel: 13,500lb (6t).
Water: 4,400gall (5,280 US) (20m³).
Adhesive weight: 121,500lb (55t).
Total weight: 300,000lb (136t).
Length overall: 75ft 4½in (22,974mm).

The Western Railway of France was for many years a by-word for inefficiency and things did not change very much for the better when it was taken over by the State in 1908. However, the one thing the new administration did which was sensible was to provide themselves, from 1914 onwards, with a stud of express passenger Pacific locomotives based on and very similar to those of the Paris-Orleans line. The principal difference lay in the use of a round-top firebox instead of the Belpaire type; this enabled adequate spectacles to be provided in the front of the cab, the top corners of which being heavily restricted by the tight loading gauge of this particular railway. During the first war, some locomotives were even supplied by North British of Glasgow, but after it was over the government adopted the design as a French standard and ordered 400 of them from French builders. Of these 280 went to the Etat lines. In the end the Alsace-Lorraine Railway—only recently back into the French fold—ended up with 100 of the remainder, although the Eastern, Northern and Paris-Orleans railway companies also had some for a time.

In 1928, the rather ramshackle state system began to mend its ways under the direction of Raoul Dautry. The administration took the sensible course of rebuilding on Chapelon principles no less than 269 of their now enormous fleet of 4-6-2s. All the engines got higher superheat, larger steam

Right: *Ex-Western Railway of France 4-6-2 No.231.D.722.*

passageways and double chimneys. Thirty only (Class "231G") had the full treatment with oscillating-cam poppet valves on both the high-pressure and the low-pressure sides. Then there were 134 (Class "231D") with poppet valves on the LP side only, while 23 (Class "231F") had Willoteaux double piston valves also only on the LP side. Finally, 85 (Class "231H") made do with some modest improvements to the geometry of their valve gears. The results were excellent and the engines were just as much at home on fast expresses as on 22-coach wartime trains carrying, say, 2,500 passengers, which were noted as running at up to 62mph (100kph) on level track.

A vivid impression of what it was like to drive and fire one of these fine machines can be gained from Jean Renoir's cinema film *La Bête Humaine.* A plot packed with blood and lust to an extent unheard of for the 1930s (it was based on Zola's 19th century novel) quite failed to steal the show from the chief star, an Etat Class "231D" Pacific.

No.231D596 is intended for the National Railway Museum at Mulhouse, while No.231G558 is preserved also.

Class A1 4-6-2
Great Britain:
Great Northern Railway (GNR), 1922

Tractive effort: 29,385lb
(13,333kg).
Axle load: 45,000 (20.5t).
Cylinders: (3) 20 x 26in
(508 x 660mm).
Driving wheels: 80in
(2,032mm).
Heating surface: 2,930sq ft
(272m²).
Superheater: 525sq ft (49m²).
Steam pressure: 180psi
(12.6kg/cm²).
Grate area: 41.25sq ft (3.8m²).
Fuel: 1,800lb (8t).
Water: 5,000gall (6,000 US)
(22.7m³).
Adhesive weight: 134,500lb
(61t).
Total weight: 332,000lb
(151t).
Length overall: 70ft 5in
(2,146mm).

The month of April 1922 was a milestone in the history of the railways of Great Britain for that was the month in which the first member of the first whole class of Pacific locomotive went into service. Few designs can match the record of these engines and their derivatives. Seventy-nine were to be built between 1921 and 1934 and they were originally class-designated with great appropriateness "A1".

The Great Northern Railway 4-6-2s were the work of a man called Nigel Gresley (later Sir Nigel Gresley) who became Locomotive Superintendent of the GNR in 1911. Gresley was very much what would now be called a "systems" engineer—by this one means that he was more a master of concepts than of detail.

The concept represented by these famous 4-6-2s was that, overall, a "big engine" (that is, one with ample capacity for the job in hand) was the most economical type. This in spite of the fact that it might cost more to build. The first ten "A1"s cost an average of £8,560 as against £6,840 for the first ten Great Western Railway "Castle" 4-6-0s. The thinking behind the design was also difficult to fault in that

Gresley recognised that simplicity was the steam locomotive's greatest asset. At the same time he realised the importance of having perfect balance of the reciprocating forces. The minimum number of cylinders to achieve this was three and, whilst this meant one cylinder and set of motion between the frames, Gresley adopted a "derived" valve gear which meant that there was no more mechanism to crowd out the limited space available there.

Gresley was also an artist and his locomotives were aesthetically very pleasing—and, as will be related, they went as well as they looked. He decked them out in a really attractive livery and gave them evocative names, most being taken from racehorses. They rightly hold their place of honour in any locomotive hall of fame.

In contrast, they were beset with bad details. A stiff "all-or-nothing" throttle combined with the absence of any compensating levers between the rear pony truck and the driving wheels made them liable to slipping their wheels at starting. Rails needed changing because of wheelburn every few weeks at places where Gresley's 4-6-2s habitually started heavy trains from rest! A tendency

for the large-ends of inside connecting rods to run hot seemed quite endemic—yet those of other companies' never gave more than occasional trouble. There were also such unforgiveable things as lubricator pipes which, if they broke, could only be replaced by lifting the boiler off the frames. Another problem was drifting steam obscuring the view of signals.

Certainly one cause of these shortcomings was that Gresley in 1923 became Chief Mechanical Engineer of the London & North Eastern Railway (LNER), an amalgamation of the Great Northern, Great Eastern, North Eastern, Great Central, North British and other smaller companies. He removed himself to London and became remote from locomotive development at Doncaster. Gresley has always been given the credit for certain changes to the Pacifics' valve gear made in 1926 which greatly improved their coal consumption at small cost. It has only recently come to light that Gresley was not only not responsible for initiating the changes but furthermore they were devised in the teeth of his opposition.

The situation arose in 1925

Above: *Preserved ex-London & North Eastern Railway class "A3" 4-6-2* Flying Scotsman *leaves York for the south with an enthusiasts' special.*

when an elegant but smaller and highly decorated 4-6-0 called *Pendennis Castle* from the rival Great Western Railway was tried out on the LNER. She did everything the big Pacifics could do with easy mastery and burned 10 per cent less coal, as well as creating a profound impression whilst doing it.

Why the "Castle" was so good was a bit of a puzzle to the LNER men, but suspicion rested on the detailed geometry of the Walschaert's valve gear. Some minor alterations to the Pacific's valve gear were tried but the results were inconclusive. After this, rather than lose face by asking for a set of drawings, a cloak-and-dagger operation was mounted while another "Castle" was on hand at Darlington after taking part in the Stockton & Darlington

Below: Flying Scotsman *as running before conversion from class "A1" to class "A3" but after the attachment of a corridor tender for long non-stop runs.*

FLYING SCOTSMAN

Railway Centenary celebrations later the same year. All the motion was secretly measured and through the enterprise of Bert Spencer, Gresley's Technical Assistant at Kings Cross, some new geometry was worked out and applied to No.2555 *Centenary*. The results were amazing—not the 10 per cent saving in coal which the "Castle" had achieved against the other Pacifics, but twice as much.

After a preliminary period of disbelief, Gresley took a ride on *Centenary*, expressed himself converted and issued instructions for all his Pacifics to be altered as they went through shops. The savings in coal amounted to around 1½ tons on a run from Kings Cross to Newcastle and in fact enabled runs of this length to be worked without engine change. About the same time, boilers designed for a higher working pressure of 225 psi (15.75 kg/cm²) were introduced, in some cases combined with a reduction of cylinder diameter. Engine weight rose by some six tons, axle load by two tons. Locomotives fitted with these boilers were designated class "A3" instead of "A1" and sometimes as "Super-Pacifics".

The longest non-stop journey in the world was run by these locomotives, over the 392¾ miles (632km) from London to Edinburgh each peacetime summer beginning in 1928. Special corridor tenders were built and attached to certain selected locomotives to enable crews to be changed en route. Pullman-type vestibule connections and automatic 'buck-eye' couplings to match those on standard LNER corridor carriages were provided at the rear of these tenders.

In 1935 No.2750 *Papyrus* made a high-speed run from London to Newcastle preparatory to the introduction of the "Silver Jubilee" express with a 240 minute schedule. The 268 miles (432km) were run off in an amazing net time of 230 minutes, an average of 69.9 mph (112.5km/h). Coming back, 108mph (174km/h) was touched at Essendine north of Peterborough, a speed believed to be still a world record for an unstreamlined steam locomotive. The streamlined version of the Gresley Pacific came into service to run this new high-speed train. This was the event that displaced the non-streamlined 4-6-2s from their prime position on the East Coast main line, but they had no problem in keeping time on the streamliners when called upon to do so in an emergency.

World War II brought 24-coach trains to the East Coast main line and the "A3" as well as the few remaining "A1"s performances on these and on freight trains were a vindication of their brilliance as a concept, although lower standards of maintenance emphasized their detail weaknesses.

After the war, during which Gresley had died, efforts were made to overcome these troubles. Some success was achieved but progress was somewhat hampered by the deaf ear which the main works were liable to turn towards suggestions from the running sheds, however sensible. The "A3"s appearance was slightly changed when the smoke problem was effortlessly solved (after 25 years of fiddling with it) by the fitting of German pattern smoke deflectors either side of the smokebox but even in the 1960s all were easily recognisable as running mates of the original "A1" class which first saw the light of day 40 years before.

The prototype itself had been rebuilt into what was virtually a new design and one other had been withdrawn in 1959. Otherwise the class remained intact until 1962, still on prime express passenger work, and performing better than ever with the double chimneys which had been fitted 1958-60. The last to go was British Railways No.60041 *Salmon Trout* in December 1965.

In 1934 the running numbers had been (in chronological order) 4470-81, 2543-99, 2743-97, 2500-08. The second of two post-war renumberings had left them as 102-112, 44-100, 35-43 (4470 no longer belonged to this class). In 1948 British Railways had added 60,000 to the numbers so that they became 60035 to 60112.

Happily, a certain Alan Pegler purchased the most famous locomotive in the class (and perhaps in the world), the immortal *Flying Scotsman*. After adventures which have included journeyings as far as the west coast of America, this grand engine is stationed at the Steamtown Museum, Carnforth, and performs with great regularity and panache on main-line steam-hauled special trains on British Railways lines.

Above: Flying Scotsman *wakes the echoes for a train-load of admirers. The colour change in the smoke from white to black indicates that a round of firing is in progress.*

Super-Pacific 4-6-2
France: Northern Railway (Nord), 1923

Axle load: 41,500lb (19t).
Cylinders, HP: (2) 17.6 x 26in (440 x 660mm)
Cylinders, LP: (2) 24.4 x 27.2in (620 x 690mm)
Driving wheels: 74.9in (1,900mm).
Heating surface: 2,680sq ft (249m²).
Superheater: 616sq ft (57m²).
Steam pressure: 227psi (16kg/cm²).
Grate area: 37.5sq ft (3.5m²).
Fuel: 15,500lb (7t).
Water: 7,000gall (8,500 US) (31.5m³).
Adhesive weight: 122,500lb (56t).
Total weight: 353,000lb (160t).
Length overall: 70ft 1in (21,350mm).

We have discussed how the Pacifics of the Paris-Orleans Railway were suddenly transformed by André Chapelon from run-of-the-mill locomotives into the most remarkable 4-6-2s ever to run. Another French company, the Nord, used the same methods and came nearly as far, but in easy stages. They began with two strange-looking 4-6-4s built in 1911—which perhaps showed what not to do rather than what should be done.

All except two of the Nord 4-6-2s were de Glehn compounds and a group of 40 quite standard for the day, based on some locomotives built for the Alsace-Lorraine Railway in 1908, was delivered in 1912-13. The war prevented any further development until 1923, when the first 40 "Super-Pacifics" were delivered from Blanc-Misseron of Lille. Improvements in the steam circuits and a modest increase in the steaming capacity of their boilers made them into remarkable engines, equally famous on both sides of the English Channel for their work on such legendary trains as the "Golden Arrow" and the "Calais-Mediterranean" expresses. It says enough that

Above: *A Nord "Super-Pacific" awaits departure from the Gare du Nord at Paris. These locomotives for many years ran the boat trains such as the "Golden Arrow" between Paris and the Channel Ports.*

Hornby, the British toy train makers, chose a "Super-Pacific"

Class P10 2-8-2
Germany: Royal Prussian Union Railway (KPEV), 1922

Tractive effort: 40,400lb (18,200kg).
Axle load: 43,000lb (19.5t).
Cylinders: (3) 20.5 x 26.0in (520 x 660mm).
Driving wheels: 68.9in (1,750mm).
Heating surface: 2,348sq ft (218.2m²).
Superheater: 883sq ft (82 m²).
Steam pressure: 200psi (14kg/cm²).
Grate area: 43.8sq ft (4.07m²).
Fuel: 15,430lb (7.0t).
Water: 6,930gall (8,320 US) (31.5m³).
Adhesive weight: 167,000lb (77t).
Total weight: 243,500lb (110.5t).
Length overall: 75ft 5in (22,980mm).

After World War I large numbers of Prussian locomotives, particularly "P8" 4-6-0s, were distributed throughout Europe as reparations, and in 1919, as part of a programme for making good the losses, design work began on a 2-8-2 locomotive, intended particularly for secondary passenger traffic on the more hilly routes of the country. Post-war difficulties delayed work on the new class, which was designated "P10" and although it was designed as a Prussian engine, the German State Railway had been established by the time that the first one was completed in 1922 by Borsig.

Although much of the design reflected Prussian practice of the previous twenty years, one class had a particular influence on the "P10". This was the "G12" three-cylinder 2-10-0, which had been produced in 1917 to meet the urgent need for a powerful goods engine for lines of medium axle load. For speed of design, the "G12" was based on a locomotive designed by Henschel for the Ottoman Railway, and it introduced some striking novelties for a Prussian design, particularly bar frames and a Belpaire firebox having a trapezoidal-shaped grate set above the driving wheels.

The novel features of the "G12" were carried over to the "P10", which also had three cylinders. With larger driving wheels there was insufficient clearance to position the firebox above the driving wheels, so the grate was constructed in three portions. The front one was parallel and fitted between the rear driving wheels; there was then a taper outwards, and the rear section was parallel at the greater width. Compared with a normal wide firebox behind the driving wheels, the trapezoidal grate brought the firebox further forward, and gave a better weight distribution, with more weight on the driving wheels. The resultant shape of the firebox walls, with double curves in both vertical and horizontal directions, gave trouble with maintenance, and no more Belpaire fireboxes or trapezoidal grates were built for the German railways.

Above: *Class "39" (ex-Prussian Union class "P10") 2-8-2 No.39.001. These powerful locomotives were one of a number of Prussian classes adopted for the new system.*

The derived motion for driving the inside valve from the outside valves, which had been used on previous Prussian three-cylinder engines, was abandoned in favour of three separate valve gears, but there was a novelty in that the drive for the inside valve was taken from a second return crank attached to the return crank of the left-hand valve gear.

Another new feature were the large smoke deflectors, which became standard practice for all large German locomotives until the introduction of a smaller pattern in the 1950s.

Under the German State the "P10"s were classified as "39", and 260 of them were built between 1922 and 1927. They became popular throughout the country, although their sphere of operation was limited by their high axle load. With a maximum permissible speed of 68mph (110km/h) they were able to haul any German express passenger train until the general increase of speed in the 1930s. Although classified as secondary passenger engines, they were true mixed-traffic engines, and they continued to share their time between passenger and freight work until the

E1/D1 Class 4-4-0 Great Britain: South Eastern & Chatham Railway (SECR), 1919

plus some blue "Wagon-Lits" cars as the basis for their first train set which had any pretensions to realism. The "Super-Pacifics" had no difficulty in running the 184 miles (296km) from Calais to Paris with 550 tons—and sometimes more—in 184 minutes. This included the 1 in 250 (0.4 per cent) climb to Caffiers as well as other long inclines, yet kept within the legal speed limit of 75mph (120km/h). A handsome brown livery ensured that these magnificent engines looked as well as they ran.

More "Super-Pacifics" were built in 1925 (10) and 1931 (40) and these differed in detail, but all 90 were regarded as interchangeable. A narrow firebox 11ft 9in (3,580mm) long seemed to present no problems to the French *chauffeurs* and the boiler provided ample steam for the two high-pressure cylinders. Some of the early engines had balanced slide-valves for the low-pressure cylinders in place of piston-valves. Two others had poppet valves and two more were rebuilt as two-cylinder simples with Cossart valve gear. One (No.3.1280) was streamlined for a time and this locomotive can be seen in the National Railway Museum at Mulhouse. The others were all withdrawn by 1962.

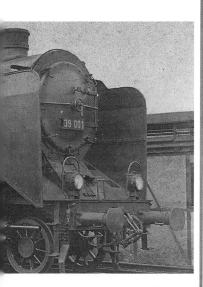

last was withdrawn in 1967.

After World War II the class was divided between the DB and DR (ie west and east Germany), and 85 of the engines on DR were rebuilt with new boilers, with round-topped fireboxes and wide grates. Their appearance was greatly altered by the fitting of the standard DR feedwater heater, with a trapezoidal tank ahead of the chimney.

The "P10"s were the high-water mark of Prussian design, but they were also important as marking the transition to the German State standard locomotives, experience with the "P10" class being available before the design of the standard locomotives was finally settled upon.

Tractive effort: 17,950lb (8,170kg).
Axle load: 38,000lb (17.5t).
Cylinders: (2) 19 x 26in (483 x 660mm).
Driving wheels: 78in (1,981mm).
Heating surface: 1,276sq ft (119m²).
Superheater: 228sq ft (21m²).
Steam pressure: 180psi (12.7kg/cm²).
Grate area: 24sq ft (2.2m²).
Fuel: 10,000lb (4.5t).
Water: 3,450gall (4,143 US) (15.7m³).
Adhesive weight: 75,000lb (34t).
Total weight: 204,000lb (93t).
Length overall: 55ft 2¾in (16,834mm).

On a journey from London to Paris there could be no greater contrast between the "Super-Pacifics" of the French Northern Railway, and the little 4-4-0s of the South-Eastern & Chatham Railway behind which a traveller of the early 1920s would begin his journey. One factor in their smallness was the difference in weight hauled per passenger—in first class de luxe a Pullman car on the SECR train might weigh 32 tons and carry 16 people, whereas the same passengers across the channel would use first class sleeping cars which might weigh 40 tons and carry

only twelve. Since the same variation also occurred in the less luxurious accommodation, a 300-ton boat train on the English side of the channel could become a 500-ton one on the French.

Even so, after the 1914 war was over, the SECR had a problem. Boat train traffic had been transferred from Charing Cross to Victoria but the ex-London Chatham & Dover Railway lines leading there had severe weight restrictions, which precluded the 'L' class 4-4-0s—the most powerful SECR passenger locomotives—from working the new route. Furthermore, plans were afoot to introduce luxurious corridor stock on these boat trains, which would make the problem even worse. At the time neither new locomotives—some 4-6-0s were mooted—or new bridges could be considered and Locomotive Superintendent Richard Maunsell decided to give what might now be called the "Chapelon treatment" to some aged but beautiful 4-4-0s of his predecessor Harry Wainwright.

The immediate result was handsome rather than beautiful. The first conversion was 'E' class 4-4-0 No.179, a new fire box with a 13 per cent bigger grate was added to the existing boiler barrel, and the boiler centre-line was pitched 7in (178mm) higher to give greater depth to the new

Above: *In British Rail days ex-Southern Railway 4-4-0 class "E1" No.31687 on a semi-fast train leaving Folkstone Junction for London.*

firebox. Piston valves (with long travel valve-gear which involved revised geometry) and larger superheaters, combined with the improved boilers to transform the performance of what even before were regarded as excellent engines. Success was such that 31 further 4-4-0s of the 'E' and the similar 'D' classes were rebuilt over the next few years, some by Beyer, Peacock and some by the company, and were designated 'E1' and 'D1' classes respectively.

Whilst Southern Railway 4-6-0s soon displaced these 4-4-0s from the principal boat trains, they continued to perform in brilliant style on other routes. They were to the fore on summer holiday extras and forces leave trains even as late as 1958. A swan-song in top-line work occurred when it was found that the London-Paris sleeping car train, introduced in 1938, containing as it did several steel sleeping cars weighing 45 tons-plus apiece, was too much for the a "Lord Nelson" to handle. The solution was to haul this Southern Railway flag train with two 4-4-0s in double harness—a thrilling sight indeed!

Castle Class 4-6-0

Great Britain:
Great Western Railway (GWR), 1923

Tractive effort: 31,625lb (14,182kg).
Axle load: 44,500lb (20.25t).
Cylinders: (4) 16 x 26in (406 x 660mm).
Driving wheels: 80½in (2,045mm).
Heating surface: 2,049sq ft (190 m²).
Superheater: 263sq ft (24.4 m²).
Steam pressure: 225psi (15.8 kg/cm²).
Grate area: 30.3sq ft (2.81 m²).
Fuel: 13,500lb (6t).
Water: 4,000gall (4,800 US) (18m³).
Adhesive weight: 133,500lb (60t).
Total weight: 283,500lb (129t).
Length overall: 65ft 2in (19,863mm).

When Churchward of the GWR produced his first "Saint" largely based on rugged American practice, he also obtained from France a four-cylinder de Glehn compound, later named *La France*. This elegant French lady was put through her paces and compared with the two-cylinder design. Whilst there was not sufficient advantage to justify the complication of compounding, it did seem that the easier running of the compounds' sophisticated mechanical layout was something worth examining further. Hence the building in 1906 of a four-cylinder simple 4-4-2, with the same "No.1" boiler as the "Saint" class, to make direct comparison between a two-cylinder and a four-cylinder mechanism. This 4-4-2 was No.40 (later 4-6-0 No.4000) *North Star*.

The advantages of four-cylinders were, first, that the reciprocating parts could in principle be arranged to be perfectly in balance, whereas the balancing of a two-cylinder locomotive was always a compromise. Second, the forces in the various rods and

guides which transmitted the piston force to the wheels would only be half those in the two-cylinder machine. The disadvantages, of course, were the extra costs involved in making nearly twice as much mechanism and also that the moving parts inside the frames would be difficult to reach.

This was compounded in the case of Churchward because, having decided very sensibly to use the same set of Walschaert's valve gear for both the cylinders on one side of the locomotive, he displayed a strange reluctance to expose this gear to the vulgar gaze. Hence the mechanism between the frames became very complex indeed. *North Star* herself in fact had a peculiar "scissors" valve gear, whereby the drive on each side was taken from the cylinder crosshead on the other. This slightly mitigated the complexity between the

frames, but there was a problem with R M Deeley of the Midland Railway over patent rights.

Two more French compounds had to be obtained before the simple versus compound issue was finally determined, but construction of "Star" locomotives proceeded to the quantity of eleven in 1907. A batch of ten called Knights followed in 1908, ten Kings (not to be confused with the "King" class of 1927) in 1909 and ten Queens in 1910 and 1911. The year 1913 brought five Princes, 1914 fifteen Princesses and finally there came twelve Abbeys in 1922-23. But all were known generally by the class name of "Star".

By now Churchward had retired and his successor as Chief Mechanical Engineer, Charles Collett ordered his staff to work out the details of a "Star" enlarged to take advantage of an increase in the permitted axle load from

Above: *The Great Western Railway honoured its builder with this "Castle" class locomotive in 1935 livery.*

18½ to 20 tons. It had been hoped that the Swindon No.7 boiler, recently introduced for the big "47xx" class mixed traffic 2-8-0s, would suit but the design incorporating it became too heavy. In the end a new No.8 boiler was designed especially for the "Castle" class, with very happy results indeed. The rest of the locomotive was pure "Star" with an extra inch on the diameter of the cylinders; visually, the slightly larger (but still exiguous) cab with its side windows made

Below: *"Castle" class 4-6-0 No. 5094* Tretower Castle *at speed with a Bristol to Paddington express. These superb locomotives were the mainstay of GWR express services.*

an impact on those who worshipped each separate Great Western rivet. The first "Castle", No.4073 *Caerphilly Castle* appeared in August 1923 numbered consecutively after the last "Star" No.4072 *Tresco Abbey*.

The second "Castle" No.4074 *Caldicot Castle,* was put through a series of coal consumption tests. Afterwards Collett presented a paper to the World Power Conference in which he announced that the result was an overall figure of 2.83lb of coal per drawbar-horsepower-hour. This was received with a certain scepticism by other locomotive engineers who had been apt to give themselves a pat on the back if they got down anywhere near 4lb. Certainly the GWR was then far ahead of its rivals; a major factor was the design of the valves and valve gear, which enabled very short cut-offs to be used; hence expansive use of steam gave most of the advantages of compounding without the complications.

The tenth "Castle" No.4082 *Windsor Castle,* was new when King George V and Queen Mary visited the Swindon Factory in 1924; no doubt the name was held back until then. His Majesty personally drove the engine from the station to the works and a brass plaque was added to the cab side commemorating the fact. No.4082 carried this for many years but not all her days for by an unhappy chance she was under repair when King George V died in 1952. The insignia of No.4082 were quickly transferred to No.7013 *Bristol Castle,* which assumed the identity of this Royal engine for the funeral train. It was perhaps a trifle naïve of the authorities to think they would not be found out, but the row which GWR fans raised in the national press — the differences were easily spotted — was a major embarassment to

the then infant (and hated) British Railways.

This time the successive batches kept to the same generic name for the class — fortunately the stormy past of Great Western territory meant that there was an adequate supply of fortified houses therein. Even so, there were a few exceptions such as the 15 converted "Star"s (actually two Stars, one Knight, two Queens and ten Abbeys) and there was a group named after noble Earls, the result of complaints from some aristocratic gentlemen that their names had been given to some rather small and old-fashioned engines. In World War II twelve were given names of famous aircraft and three gentlemen by the names of *Isambard Kingdom Brunel, Sir Daniel Gooch* and *G.J. Churchward* amongst others also were remembered.

At the time of its introduction the "Castle" class was the most powerful locomotive design in the country, although far from being the largest. Those sceptical of this claim were convinced during exchange trials in 1925 and 1926 during which a "Castle" was proved to have an economical mastery — with something to

Above: *Preserved Castle class No.7029* Clun Castle. *This locomotive is kept at the Birmingham Railway Museum and is used on mainline enthusiast specials.*

spare — over the hardest schedules the LNER or LMS had to offer, whereas those companies were unable to field a candidate which could do the same on the GWR. The "Castle" class handled the "Cheltenham Flyer" which for some years was the fastest train in the world with a 65 minute schedule for the 77¼ miles (124km) from Swindon to Paddington Station, London. A run with this train on 6 June 1932 with *Tregenna Castle* in 56¾ minutes, an average speed to start-to-stop of 81.7 (131.5km/h), was also a world record for some time after it was accomplished.

The "Castle" class was capable of handling heavy trains. The famous "Cornish Riviera Limited" could load up to 15 of the GWR's 70ft carriages on the by no means easy road from Paddington to Plymouth on a schedule which averaged 55 mph (88 km/h) for the 225.7 miles. For many years this was the longest non-stop run in the country. It is

true that carriages were slipped at three points en route but on the last stretch gradients of up to 1 in 37 (2.7 per cent) were encountered.

The last and 171st "Castle" No.7037 *Swindon* appeared in 1950, by which time a few of the earliest had already been withdrawn. The 171 included those fifteen which were converted from "Star" and one (No.111 *Viscount Churchill*) which had originally been that odd-man-out amongst GWR locomotives, Churchward's 4-6-2 *The Great Bear.* These older "Castles" were the first to go.

During the years 1957 to 1960, some time after the GWR had become part of British Railways in 1948, a number of the "Castle" class were modernised with larger superheaters and double chimneys. The results were excellent, but the dieselisation which immediately followed prevented the improvements having any beneficial effect on train working.

Withdrawal began in earnest in 1962 and the last "Castle" ceased running in normal service in July 1965. But this was not to be the end of their history, and it is a measure of the esteem and affection in which they were held that seven have been preserved. The Science Museum had room for one only modern steam engine to illustrate the best in British locomotive engineering and they chose No.4073 *Caerphilly Castle.* This steam locomotive is also the only modern one to appear on a British postage stamp.

Three preserved "Castles" are currently in working order, No. 7029 *Clun Castle* at the Birmingham Railway Museum, No.5051 *Drysllwyn Castle* at the Great Western Society's Didcot Steam Centre, and, so far away and in such a remote part of Australia that its best address is latitude 20°45'S longitude 116°10'E, is No.4079 *Pendennis Castle.*

Class 424 4-8-0
Hungary:
Hungarian State Railways (MAV), 1924

Tractive effort: 39,280lb
(17,822kg).
Axle load: 32,000lb (14.5t).
Cylinders: (2) 23.6 x 26in
(600 x 660mm).
Driving wheels: 63¼in
(1,606mm).
Heating surface: 2,230sq ft
(207m²).
Superheater: 624sq ft (58m²).
Steam pressure: 200psi
(14kg/cm²).
Grate area: 48sq ft (4.45m²).
Fuel: 20,000lb (9t).
Water: 4,620gall (5,550 US)
(21m³).
Adhesive weight: 129,000lb
(58.5t).
Total weight: 315,000lb (143t).
Length overall: 68ft 10¾in
(17,334mm).

It speaks volumes for the qualities of these excellent locomotives that they continued to be built over a period of 32 years and their period of service has now spanned 58 years. As so often, their success stems largely from their being simple and rugged machines in the Stephenson mould. The most unusual feature is the wheel arrangement; by reason of the leading bogie for guidance plus the high proportion of adhesive weight to engine weight, the 4-8-0 type (in North America known as "Mastodon") would seem to be well suited to heavy express trains, yet cases of its use are rare. In this instance the high structure gauge of the

Hungarian railway system permitted a deep wide firebox and ashpan to be mounted above the rear coupled wheels, which were given side play of one inch (25mm) either side of centre to ease the running on sharp curves.

They were maids-of-all-work on the MAV, handling top expresses, suburban locals and freight trains with equal facility. Those employed on suburban service could work "push-and-pull"—that is, they were fitted with equipment actuated by compressed air which enabled them to be controlled from a driver's cab at the other end of the train.

The design was developed from an unbuilt 2-8-0 of 1915, without the Brotan boiler of that predecessor, and 27 were built initially by the State Works in Budapest. During the war years a further 218 were built and finally in 1955-6 there were another 120. Numbers ran from 424,001 to 424,365, but not all of these ran in Hungary at the same time. The design has been exported to Slovakia (during World War II when Czechoslovakia was partitioned), and to North Korea. Some were taken over by the Jugoslav State Railways in 1945, and from the same date a few ran in Russia for a time, pending return to Hungary.

Right: *Hungarian State Railways class "424" 4-8-0 No.424.075 on a local passenger train.*

241A Class 4-8-2
France:
Eastern Railway (Est), 1925

Axle load: 42,000lb (19t)..
Cylinders HP: (2) 17¾ x 28½in
(450 x 720mm).
Cylinders LP: (2) 26 x 28½in
(660 x 720mm)..
Driving wheels: 76¾in
(1,950mm).
Heating surface: 2,335sq ft
(21.8m²).
Superheater: 996sq ft (92.6m²).
Steam pressure: 228psi
(16kg/cm²).
Grate area: 47.7sq ft (4.4m²).
Adhesive weight: 165,000lb
(75t).
Length overall: 86ft 2½in
(26,275mm).
(Tender details not available).

The de Glehn system of compounding was capable of expansion not only to the 4-6-2 but also to the 4-8-2. The first de Glehn 4-8-2 entered service in 1925; this was No.41001 of the Eastern Railway of France, a line which connected Paris with cities such as Chalons-sur-Marne, Nancy, Belfort and Strasbourg. The loco was built at the company's works at Epernay and, after a four year period of testing and some modification, 41 more were built as the top express locomotive fleet of the line. Soon afterwards, a further 49 were constructed for the State (ex-Western Railway)

Railways, but after nationalisation of all the railways in France in 1938, they joined their 41 sisters on the Est lines.

In the meantime, during 1933, some very severe trials were held

Below: *Two views of Eastern Railway of France class "241A" 4-8-2s. That on the left shows No.241A.68 in French National Railways livery. The other shows 241-008 as running in Est days.*

on the Northern Railway. One test was to haul the Golden Arrow express between Paris and Calais made up with extra carriages to 650 tons. Both the Eastern and the PLM companies supplied 4-8-2s while the Paris-Orleans-Midi line sent one of their famous rebuilt 4-6-2s. The Eastern engines suffered damage to the frames and also showed a higher fuel consumption than the P-O 4-6-2. So far as the Eastern

4300 Class 4-8-2

United States:
Southern Pacific Railroad (SP), 1923

Tractive effort: 57,100lb (25,907kg).
Axle load: 61,500lb (28t).
Cylinders: (2) 28 x 30in (711 x 762mm).
Driving wheels: 73½in (1,867mm).
Heating surface: 4,552sq ft (423m²).
Superheater: 1,162sq ft (108m²).
Steam pressure: 210psi (14.8kg/cm²).
Grate area: 75sq ft (7m²).
Fuel (oil): 4,000gall (4,700 US) (18m³).
Water: 13,300gall (10,000 US) (60m³).
Adhesive weight: 246,000lb (112t).
Total weight: 611,000lb (277.5t).
Length overall: 97ft 9in (29,794mm).

The 4-8-2 or "Mountain" type was appropriately named; its origins are a nice illustration of the difference between tractive effort and power. Locomotives with a high tractive effort are often described as powerful, but this is misleading. The 4-8-2 was developed from the 4-6-2 but, whilst the extra pair of drivers meant that a higher tractive effort could be exerted, the power output—which depends on the size of the fire—had to remain limited because there was still only one pair of wheels to carry the firebox.

For climbing mountains a high

Above: Southern Pacific Railroad "4300" class 4-8-2 No.4330. The number "51", carried near the smokestack is the number of the train which the locomotive is hauling.

tractive effort is essential, but high *power* output only desirable. These things were relevant to the Southern Pacific Railroad, for their trains leaving Sacramento for the east had the notorious climb over the Sierras to face, from near sea level to 6,885ft (2,099m) in 80 miles (128km).

So in 1923 SP went to the American Locomotive Co. of Schenectady for the first batch of 4-8-2 locomotives. The design was based on standard US practice, the one feature of note being the cylindrical so-called Vanderbilt tender. A booster engine was fitted, driving on the rear carrying wheels, and this could give an extra 10,000lb (4,537kg) of tractive effort, provided the steam supply held out.

SP impressed their personality on the "4300"s by having them oil-burning and by their trade mark, the headlight mounted *below* centre on the silver-grey front of the smoke box. The 77 engines of the class were very successful, all the later ones being built in SP's own shops at Sacramento. Some of the earlier batches had 8-wheel tenders of lower capacity, instead of 12-wheel ones. None of the class has been preserved.

---

was concerned, the result of these very searching tests was that some rebuilt P-O 4-6-2s were acquired and, moreover, the rebuilding of the 4-8-2s on Chapelon lines was put in hand with some success. At a cost of only 6 tons extra weight, the converted engines could produce 3,700hp in the cylinders, a 40 per cent increase. At the same time coal consumption fell by some 15 per cent.

An interesting feature was a six-jet blast-pipe; the amount of draught produced by this could be controlled from the cab. This was one further control to add to the two throttles, two reversing gears and the intercepting valve of the de Glehn system!

The prototype of the class, originally No.41.001 but latterly No.241A1, superbly restored, is displayed in the National Railway Museum at Mulhouse.

Class 01 4-6-2

Germany:
German State Railway (DR), 1926

Tractive effort: 35,610lb (16,160kg).
Axle load: 44,500lb (20.25t).
Cylinders: (2) 23.6 x 26.0in (600 x 660mm).
Driving wheels: 78.7in (2,000m).
Heating surface: 2,661sq ft (247.3m²).
Superheater: 915sq ft (85.0m²).
Steam pressure: 228psi (16kg/cm²).
Grate area: 47.5sq ft (4.41m²).
Fuel: 22,000lb (10.0t).
Water: 7,500gall (9,000 US) (34m³).
Adhesive weight: 130,500lb (59.2t).
Total weight: 240,000lb (109t) *(without tender).*
Length overall: 78ft 6in (23,940mm).
(These dimensions etc. refer to engines with copper fireboxes, other than the first 10).

Above: *A German Federal Railways class "01" 4-6-2 makes a fine show crossing a wide-span girder bridge.*

Below: *German "01" class 4-6-2 No.012204-4. The final figure is a check digit for use with a computer system.*

In 1922, when the German railways were under Government control, a Central Locomotive Design Section was set up under Dr R P Wagner, an engineer trained on the KPEV, but having a wide knowledge of railways in other countries. After the establishment of the German State Railway in 1922, Wagner's team prepared a scheme for standard locomotives, much influenced by Prussian practice, but taking into account that, in some parts of the country, the engines would have to burn coal of a lower quality than that to which the Prussian engines were accustomed, and that they would have to work in more mountainous country than the North German plain, which dominated the KPEV locomotive designs.

The standard classes therefore had larger grates than their Prussian predecessors, and in the engines with trailing carrying wheels, there was a clear space under the firebox for the entry of air and the removal of ashes, as had been provided, largely under the influence of Maffei of Munich,

in the modern passenger engines of the southern German states.

Until this time the maximum axle loading permitted in Germany had been 18 tonnes, but a programme of upgrading of track and bridges to take 20-tonne axle loads had been put in hand, and the first of the new locomotives to be built were two classes of Pacific designed to this increased axle load, and designated "01" and "02". The specification required the engines to haul 800 tonnes at 62mph (100km/h) on the level, and 500 tonnes at 31mph (50km/h) on a 1 in 100 (1 per cent) gradient; the maximum speed was to be 74.6mph (120 km/h).

Of the 139 Pacifics which DR inherited from the railways of the southern states, all but 10 were four-cylinder compounds. It was originally intended that the standard locomotives should all have two cylinders, but in deference to the representatives of the states other than Prussia on the central design committee, the new Pacific was produced in two versions, Class "01" with two cylinders and Class "02" with four compound cylinders. Ten engines of each type were built, and were divided between three locomotive depots for comparison. Trials of the two classes showed a small advantage in fuel consumption to the compounds, but the advantage was considered to be offset by the increased costs of maintaining the latter, and the "01" was adopted as standard for future construction. The use of two cylinders only in the largest passenger class was a clear break with former German practice.

Although the basic layout of the "01" was simple, much of the detailed work was complicated, and there was a full range of auxiliary equipment, including a feedwater heater, with a distinctive heat exchanger buried in the smokebox ahead of the chimney. The use of a round-topped firebox

was a reversion from recent Prussian practice, and, at a time when engineers in many countries were building boilers with a forward extension of the firebox (the so-called "combustion chamber"), Wagner made the front of his firebox almost straight, as he considered that the extra maintenance cost of the combustion chamber was not justified. It was also unusual for a boiler of this size to have a parallel barrel.

The general appearance of the engines owed much to Prussian practice, but with various parts attached to the outside of the boiler for accessibility, there was a distinct North American touch. Of the three apparent domes, the first housed the feedwater inlet, the second was the sand box, and the third housed the regulator. Like the final Prussian designs the engines had bar frames. The long gap between the trailing coupled axle and the trailing carrying axle resulted in the carrying axle having a slightly greater axle load than any of the coupled axles.

The detailed design of the engines was undertaken by Borsig of Berlin, and the first engines were built by that firm and by AEG. Slow progress with upgrading lines for 20-tonne axle loads inhibited the rapid construction of "01"s, but by 1938 a total of 231 had been built, to which were added a further 10 by the rebuilding of the "02" compounds.

Experience with the first engines resulted in later engines having the cylinder diameter increased from 25.6in (650mm) to 26.0in (660mm). The boiler tubes were lengthened, with a corresponding shortening of the smokebox, and later still steel fireboxes were used in place of copper. Improved braking and larger bogie wheels were introduced as part of a programme for increasing the maximum speed of the class to 80.8mph (130km/h).

In the meantime, in 1930, a slightly smaller version of the "01", designated "03", was introduced for lines still limited to an 18-tonne axle load, and 298 of these were built up to 1937.

Until 1937 the speed limit of most lines in Germany was 62mph (100km/h), so it was not until the general raising of the maximum speed to 120km/h in 1937 that the "01" and "03" had full scope as express engines. However, by 1937 there were already 58 runs daily in Germany booked at start-to-stop speeds of 60mph (97km/h) or more, and the majority of these were worked by the "01" or "03".

When further express engines were built from 1939 onwards, the continued acceleration of

Below: *A German Federal Railways' class "01" 4-6-2, used for handling the principal steam express trains in Germany.*

Above: *This picture shows one of the smaller German class "03" 4-6-2s, No.032180-2. Note the small post-war "Witte" pattern smoke deflectors and, again, the computer check digit.*

passenger trains made it necessary for them to have a maximum speed of 93mph (150km/h), and following experience with the "05" 4-6-4 locomotives, the new engines were given full streamlining and three cylinders. These engines were classed "01¹⁰" and "03¹⁰", and 55 of the former and 60 of the latter were built between 1939 and 1941; but for the war, the totals would have been 250 and 140 respectively. Apart from two experimental Pacifics made in West Germany in 1957 these were the last new steam express locomotives to be built in Germany.

After the partition of Germany 171 locomotives of class "01"

came into the stock of DB in West Germany and 70 into the stock DR in East Germany. Of these 55 of the DB locomotives and 35 of the DR locomotives were rebuilt. The remaining locomotives on DB received the post-war "Witte" smoke deflectors, in place of the full-depth deflectors. Another alteration which affected the appearance of many of the engines was the removal of the sloping plates which connected the side running plates to the buffer beam. The unrebuilt engines on DR retained their original appearance. The last of the DB engines was withdrawn in 1973, but several of the DR engines were still at work in 1981, after being returned to regular service because of the shortage of oil. With their rebuilt sisters they were the last express steam engines at work in Europe.

There was one other German Pacific to be mentioned, which had an unusual history. As part of the experimental work on high-speed steam trains, a streamlined three-cylinder 4-6-6 tank was built in 1939. Like the Class "05" 4-6-4 it had driving wheels 90½in (2,300mm) in diameter, and was designed for a maximum speed of 108mph (175km/h); it was used between Berlin and Dresden. This engine came into DR ownership, and in 1960 parts of it, together with some parts of an experimental high-pressure 2-10-2 locomotive, were used to produce a high-speed Pacific for testing new rolling stock and making brake tests. The all-welded boiler was identical to that used in rebuilding the former Prussian Class "P10" locomotives, DR Class "39". The engine was partially enclosed in a streamlined casing of distinctive shape, with a shapely chimney. The designed speed of the engine was 100mph (160km/h), but it was operated well above this speed into the 1970s, being the last steam engine in the world to exceed the magic speed of 100 miles per hour.

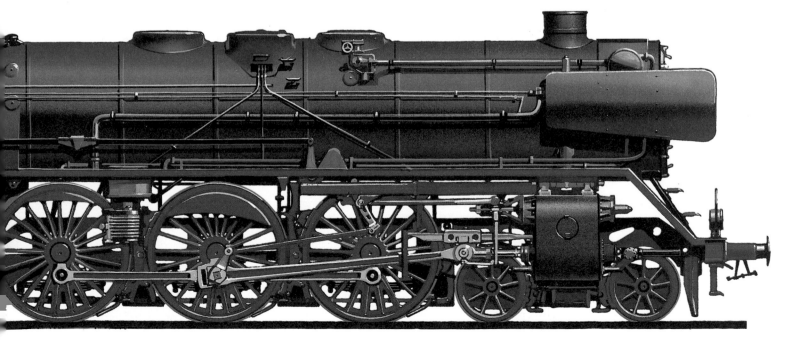

King Arthur Class 4-6-0
Great Britain: Southern Railway (SR), 1925

Tractive effort: 25,320lb (11,485kg).
Axle load: 45,000lb (20.5t).
Cylinders: (2) 20½ x 28in (521 x 711mm).
Driving wheels: 79in (2,007mm).
Heating surface: 1,878sq ft (174.5m²).
Superheater: 337sq ft (31.3m²).
Steam pressure: 200psi (14.1kg/cm²).
Grate area: 30sq ft (2.8m²).
Fuel: 11,000lb (5t).
Water: 5,000gall (6,000 US) (22.7m³).
Adhesive weight: 134,500lb (6t).
Total weight: 310,500lb (141t).
Length overall: 66ft 5in (20,244mm).

These Knights of the Turntable got their romantic names from the Arthurian legends and this veiled an extreme ordinariness.

No doubt the same applied to King Arthur's knights themselves, but in both cases this was no detriment to—indeed it would enhance—the service they gave.

In 1923 Richard Maunsell was made Chief Mechanical Engineer of the Southern Railway newly formed by amalgamating the London & South Western, London, Brighton & South Coast and South Eastern & Chatham

Above: *In British Rail days, ex-Southern Railway "King Arthur" No.30804 Sir Cador of Cornwall leaves Bromley, Kent, with a London to Ramsgate train.*

Lord Nelson Class 4-6-0
Great Britain: Southern Railway (SR), 1926

Tractive effort: 33,500lb (15,196kg).
Axle load: 46,000lb (21t).
Cylinders: (4) 16½ x 24in (419 x 610mm).
Driving wheels: 79in (2,007mm).
Heating surface: 1,989sq ft (18.5m²).
Superheater: 376sq ft (35m²).
Steam pressure: 220psi (15.5kg/cm²).
Grate area: 33sq ft (3.1m²).
Fuel: 11,000lb (5t).
Water: 5,000gall (6,000 US) (22.7m³).
Adhesive weight: 139,000lb (63t).
Total weight: 314,000lb (142.5t).
Length overall: 69ft 9¾in (21,279mm).

When Southern Railway No.850 *Lord Nelson* was new in 1926, she was pronounced the most powerful locomotive in the country—on the slightly spurious basis of tractive effort. So Britain's

smallest railway had the strongest locomotive, as well as a publicity department which made the most of it. *Lord Nelson* was the prototype of a class of 16 noble locomotives, named after great seamen of bygone days. Of the other locomotives, seven appeared in 1928 and eight in 1929. Running numbers were 850 to 865. So when latter-day explorers set off to travel to, say, Moscow, Istanbul, Bombay, Athens, Monte Carlo or even Le Touquet, up front at Victoria Station was *Sir Francis Drake* or perhaps *Sir Walter Raleigh,* to speed them on their way.

The "Lord Nelson" class was born out of a need for a more powerful locomotive than the "King Arthur" class in order to handle the heavy holiday expresses, a locomotive with a little more in hand to cover out-of-course delays. The Southern Railway's Civil Engineer was persuaded to allow a ¾-ton increase in axle load on certain principal

main lines because of the better balancing implicit in a multi-cylinder locomotive. The result was a magnificent but rather complex four-cylinder 4-6-0, with a Belpaire firebox and a large grate.

An interesting feature of the design was the setting of the cranks successively at 135 degrees to one another, instead of the more usual 90 degrees. The effect of this was to double the number of puffs or beats from four to eight for each revolution of the wheels; the object was to give a more even torque, which would be a help in avoiding slipping the wheels at starting. One adverse effect of the consequent smoothness of running was that coal in the long bogie tenders failed to feed itself forward—as it did when shaken by a rough and rugged "King Arthur"; so "Lord Nelson" firemen who had shovelled all day had to perform near the end of their stints the additional chore of

bringing coal forward in the tender.

The "Lord Nelson's" one defect was that they were hard to fire. The even slope of a "King Arthur" grate presented little difficulty, but the "Lord Nelson" one was not only larger (10ft 6in—3,200 mm instead of 9ft—2,743mm) but had a level section at the rear. In consequence, shovelfuls had to be placed very accurately and the front end had to fed with coal thrown all the way, instead of being placed further back to work itself forward. The whole picture was that of a locomotive that needed very skillful firing if it was to steam properly. If that skill was present, the "Lord Nelson" class ran superbly; if not, then time was lost in running and maybe the final disgrace for an engine crew would occur—an out-of-course stop to raise steam. The problem was compounded by the fact that, with only 16 of the class in existence, many crews unfortunately encountered a

Railways. His own SECR locomotive affairs were getting into good shape, but he understandably had doubts about the foreigners. The LSWR ran long-distance expresses to the west country and the front runners in its fleet were twenty 4-6-0s called the "N15" class. Simplicity was the theme of their design with two big 22in x 28in (559 x 711mm) cylinders, outside valves and valve gear, and a parallel boiler with a round-top firebox. Since the LSWR did not have water troughs, big bogie tenders were attached. They ran well but by SECR standards not brilliantly, and Maunsell set about making some improvements to be incorporated in a further batch.

Cylinders on the new locomotives had valves and valve gear which gave events of the kind that had made the "E1" class 4-4-0s such a success on the

SECR. More direct steam passages and larger superheaters were used and the ashpan redesigned to improve combustion. A young man called John Elliot, in charge of Public Relations on the SR—a post in which at that time there was plenty of scope—suggested the names and in February 1925 No.453 *King Arthur* left the ex-LSWR works at Eastleigh, to be followed in March by *Queen Guinevere*, *Sir Lancelot* and eight other knights. Associated names like *Excalibur*, *Camelot* and *Morgan le Fay* were given to the 20 older locomotives, which also had some of the new technical features applied to them.

At the same time 30 more were ordered from the North British Locomotive Co. of Glasgow while the following year a final 14 were built at Eastleigh. These latter were intended for the Central

(ex-LBSCR) section of the SR and had smaller 3,500 gallon six-wheel tenders. So there were now, all told, 74 of the "King Arthur" class and they handled most of the principal SR express passenger assignments until Maunsell's first "Lord Nelson" class arrived in 1927.

The line on which *King Arthur* and his knights rode most often and most nobly into battle was the switchback road beyond Salisbury to Exeter. No.768 *Sir Balin*, travelling eastwards one day in 1934 was observed to regain 6 minutes on a 96-minute schedule with 420 tons, 65 tons more than the maximum laid down for the timing. On this day the maximum speed reached was 86½mph (139km/h) at Axminster but speeds of 90mph (145km/h) and over were not uncommon.

Perhaps the most remarkable run with one of these engines occurred in 1936 when No.777 *Sir Lamiel* regained 17½ minutes in covering the 83¾ miles (134km)

from Salisbury to Waterloo in 72¾ minutes an average speed start-to-stop of 69.2mph (111 km/h) with a load of 345 tons.

It is thus appropriate that the "King Arthur" allocated to the National Railway Museum and currently being restored to running order was this same No.777. The "King Arthur" class started to be withdrawn well before steam locomotive preservation became a mania, so none were preserved privately. The saying "happy is the land that has no history" applied to the class, since apart from playing general post with types of tenders, their owners found the "King Arthur" locomotives good enough to remain virtually as they were built, right to the end.

Below: *"King Arthur" class No. 772* Sir Percivale *depicted in the livery adopted by the Southern Railway in 1938, when a brighter green was substituted for the olive green of the 1920s.*

"Lord Nelson" very infrequently.

Eventually, in the late 1930s the problem was solved by improving the air-flow through the firegrate by fitting a multiple-jet blast pipe arrangement known as the Lemaître. Double chimneys were tried at first on two of the locomotives but did not find favour. The tenders were altered so that they were self-trimming, even when attached behind a smooth-running "Lord Nelson" and also, of course, as time went on, expertise needed to make these shy steamers go became more widespread amongst the firemen. In other respects the designers certainly knew their business in that the complex and not too accessible mechanism with two sets of cylinders, motion and the Walschaert's valve gear between the frames, gave little trouble and was not as costly to maintain as might have been expected.

A test with No.850 intended to simulate an enlarged "Atlantic

Above: *No. 850* Lord Nelson, *as preserved and restored to Southern Railway colours, with an enthusiasts' steam Special in 1980.*

Coast Express", which carried through portions to *six* Devon and Cornwall resorts, and loaded up to 16 coaches, was run on 10 April 1927. It was necessary to

schedule the test for a quiet Sunday because the train stretched so far out of busy Waterloo Station that several other platforms would be blocked. Even so, normal schedule time was kept to Exeter, the 171¾ miles (275km) being run in 197 minutes, including a four minute stop at Salisbury and a shorter one at Sidmouth Junction. There were also delays due to weekend engineering works—the leopard had plenty of spots even in those high and far off times. In the end, though, so few "Lord Nelson's" were built that it was not possible to schedule these long trains on a regular basis.

Lord Nelson has survived to be taken into the National Railway Museum collection and is currently doing great things on various special main line excursions. Once or twice, though, it has shown a trace of the old unforgiving spirit towards firemen who thought they were the masters.

Class XC 4-6-2
India:
Indian Railways Standard (IRS), 1927

Tractive effort: 30,625lb (13,895kg).
Axle load: 43,500lb (19.75t).
Cylinders: (2) 23 x 28in (584 x 711mm).
Driving wheels: 74in (1,880mm).
Heating surface: 2,429sq ft (226m²).
Superheater: 636sq ft (59m²).
Steam pressure: 180psi (12.7kg/cm²).
Grate area: 51sq ft (4.75m²).
Fuel: 31,500lb (14.3t).
Water: 6,000gall (7,200 US) (27.25m³).
Adhesive weight: 130,000lb (59.5t).
Total weight: 392,500lb (178t).
Length overall: 76ft 1½in (23,203mm).

The story of the Indian Railways Standard (IRS) 4-6-2 locomotives has not been a happy one. After World War I, a desire to make use of cheaper coal of lower quality than that used formerly led to a specification for locomotives for India provided with wide fireboxes. The passenger engines were the "XA", "XB", and "XC" classes, i.e. light, medium and heavy 4-6-2s. They had maximum axle loads of 13, 17 and 19½ tons respectively. British practice was followed; most were built by the Vulcan Foundry of Newton-le-Willows, Lancashire.

With ample evidence to hand of the first-class qualities of the "BESA" 4-6-0s previously described, the arrival of the first of these locomotives from Britain was awaited with pleasurable anticipation. Alas, they were not satisfactory, being poor steamers, and bad riders to the point not of discomfort but of danger. The valve events were good on paper, but for some reason gave sluggish performance; while the engines were also prone to cracks in the boiler and fractures of the motion and frames.

Although none of the problems were fundamental, nothing was done until in 1937 an "XB" derailed at Bihta on the East Indian Railway, this time with the loss of many lives; this at last got things moving. After an investigation had been made by engineers from France and Britain some of the quite modest modifications required to put the faults right were done. If only the inertia of bureaucracy had not prevented these corrections being made earlier before 284 locomotives had been built and 11 years had elapsed since construction began!

When British India was partitioned in 1947, about 60 "IRS" 4-6-2s went to East and West Pakistan, leaving 76 "XA"s, 81 "XB"s and 50 "XC"s in India proper. In 1957 they were renumbered in the all India list Indian Railways' ("XA" 22001-76; "XB" 22101-81; "XC" 22201-50) although by then occupied on rather menial passenger duties. a few (a very few) survived into the 1980s, the last being withdrawn in 1981.

Right: *Indian Railways class "XB" 4-6-2 No.22104. This was the medium size of the three IRS Pacific designs.*

Class S 4-6-2
Australia:
Victorian Government Railways (VGR), 1928

Tractive effort: 41,100lb (18,643kg).
Axle load: 53,000lb (24t).
Cylinders: (3) 20½ x 28in (521 x 711mm).
Driving wheels: 73in (1,854mm).
Heating surface: 3,121sq ft (290m²).
Superheater: 631sq ft (59m²).
Steam pressure: 200psi (14kg/cm²).
Grate area: 50sq ft (4.7m²).
Fuel: 18,500lbs (8.5t).
Water: 13,000gall (15,500 US) (59m³).
Adhesive weight: 158,000lb (72t).
Total weight: 497,500lb (226t).
Length overall: 85ft 6in (26,060mm).

These big 4-6-2s were built by the Victorian Railways in 1928 for the principal trains between Melbourne and the New South Wales border at Albury, on the way to Sydney. Their heavy axle load precluded running elsewhere on the VGR and the four constructed were adequate for the needs of the one line on which they were permitted to work.

They were one of the very few classes of steam locomotives in Australia to have three cylinders. The valves of the outside cylinders were actuated by Walschaert's valve gear, while the inside valve was driven via a set of Holcroft-Gresley two-to-one derived gear, as used on the British London & North Eastern Railway. Indeed, with their round-topped boilers and double side-windows, the

Australian engines had a definite resemblence to the LNER 4-6-2s. Out of sight, however, were a set of totally un-British cast-steel bar frames. Streamline shrouds were added in 1937; in combination with a blue livery the addition matched a set of new all-steel coaches for the "Spirit of Progress" express. The big 12-wheel tenders dated from this time and enabled the 192

Above: *Victorian Government Railways "S" class 4-6-2 No. S300 before streamlining.*

mainly level miles (307km) from Melbourne to Albury to be run non-stop in 220 minutes, an average speed of 52mph (83 km/h). Fairly modest as this might seem, diesel traction today has only meant 8 minutes less journey time. Names of people

Class Hv2 4-6-0

Finland:
State Railways (VR), 1922

Tractive effort: 20,373lb (9,244kg).
Axle load: 29,000lb (13t).
Cylinders: (2) 20¼ x 23½in (510 x 600mm).
Driving wheels: 68¾in (1,750mm).
Heating surface: 1,185sq ft (110m²).
Superheater: 333sq ft (31m²).
Steam pressure: 171psi (12kg/cm²).
Grate area: 20.2sq ft (2m²).
Fuel: 11,000lb (5t).
Water: 3,150gall (3,780 US) (14.3m³).
Adhesive weight: 85,000lb (38.5t).
Total weight: 192,000lb (87t).
Length overall: 51ft 10½in (15,814mm).

Finland's steam locomotives were very tall, very handsome, very distinctive and very few. Many were fired by birch logs and sported spark-arresting smoke stacks in the best traditions of an American Western film. Many were also built at home.

These 4-6-0s of classes "Hv2" and "Hv3" were built in the 1920s and 1930s. Until 4-6-2s arrived in 1937 they were the principal express passenger engines, as indicated by their class

Below: *Finnish State Railways class "Hv3" 4-6-0 No.782 heads a local train. Note the spark arrester formed of wire mesh at the top of the chimney.*

Above: *Finnish State Railways "Hv" class 4-6-0 No.758 at Oulu, Finland. Note spark-arresting smoke-stack.*

letter "H". The second letter is an indication of the axle-load and it is indicative of Finnish conditions that "v" stands for an axle load between 11 and 14 tons and, moreover, that it is not the lowest classification. Some lines of this 5ft (1,524mm) gauge system needed more light-footed locomotives than that!

Interesting features of these engines included by-pass valves —visible as a bump on the side of each cylinder—as an elegant way of avoiding pumping action when coasting. The class held on to cylinder tail-rods long after they ceased to be fashionable elsewhere. A neat air-operated bell was carried in front of the cab and Stephensonian simplicity was not carried so far that the blessings of electric light were not available on board. The "Hv3" class differed only in that they had bogie tenders of higher water capacity instead of six-wheel.

The first native-built "Hv2"s appeared in 1922 from Lokomo of Tampere but a preliminary batch of 15 had been supplied by Schwartzkopff of Germany three years earlier. One (No.680 supplied by Lokomo in 1940) is preserved in the Helsinki Technical Museum.

important in the history of Victoria were given later to these engines, which then became S300 *Matthew Flinders*, S301 *Sir Thomas Mitchell*, S302 *Edward Henty* and S303 *C.J. Latrobe*. They were early victims of dieselisation, being displaced from the "Spirit

Above: *"S" class 4-6-2 No. S302* Edward Henty *heads the air-conditioned "Spirit of Progress" on the Melbourne-Albury run.*

of Progress" train in 1952; all had been withdrawn by 1954.

Royal Scot Class 4-6-0

Great Britain:
London Midland & Scottish (LMS), 1927

Tractive effort: 33,150lb (15,037kg).
Axle load: 46,000lb (21t).
Cylinders: (3) 18 x 26in (457 x 660mm).
Driving wheels: 81in (2,057mm).
Heating surface: 1,851sq ft (172m²).
Superheater: 367sq ft (34.1m²).
Steam pressure: 250psi (17.6kg/cm²).
Grate area: 31.25sq ft (2.90m²).
Fuel: 20,000lb (9t).
Water: 4,000gall (4,800 US) (18m³).
Adhesive weight: 137,000lb (62t).
Total weight: 312,500lb (142t).
Length overall: 64ft 11in (19,787mm).

The "Royal Scot"'s were another notable class of locomotive that managed more than thirty years on top express work, although a rebuilding which left little of the originals intact halfway through their lives perhaps detracts a little from this achievement. In the mid-1920s the then rather new LMS Railway had to face the fact that there was no locomotive capable singly of hauling the principal train, the 10a.m. Scottish Express from London to Edinburgh and Glasgow, shortly to be known as the "Royal Scot". An ex-LNWR 4-6-0 and 4-4-0 combination would take the train from Euston to Carnforth, while two Midland 4-4-0s would take it on over the hills from there.

A Great Western "Castle" class 4-6-0 was borrowed and demonstrated very effectively in October 1926 that better things were possible. It is said that the LMS made enquiry for 25 "Castles" to be built for the summer service of 1927 but, more practically, the biggest locomotive factory in Britain was given a design-and-build contract for 50 large 4-6-0 express locomotives. The contract

with the North British Locomotive Co. (NBL) of Glasgow was not signed until February 1927 and, whilst the first locomotive did not quite go into service in time to help with the summer trains that year, all the "Royal Scot" class were in service by the end of November.

Three cylinders were provided, each with its own set of Walschaert's valve gear and a parallel-barrel boiler with a Belpaire firebox as big as the loading gauge would allow. The locomotives had no technical innovations but were representative of the best practice of the day. In consequence they took to the job they were designed for with the minimum of trouble—and at the same time became much admired by both professionals and the enthusiasts.

Of the 50 locomotives, 25 were given names of regiments and 25 the names of early locomotives. Subsequently, though, all the locomotives were named after

regiments of the British Army.

A few minor problems had to be overcome; one was that the piston valves leaked when worn, to an extent that increased steam consumption by nearly half before repairs became due. An accident at Leighton Buzzard in 1931 was attributed to smoke beating down and obscuring the driver's view of signals—this led to the rapid fitting of large smoke deflector plates at the front end, using the pattern developed on the Southern Railway. During the previous year a further 20 "Royal Scot" class had been built, at the old Midland Railway works at Derby; this time the names included a few non-Army titles such as *The Royal Air Force*, *The Girl Guide* and *The Boy Scout*.

The period was notable for experiments aimed at improving the thermal efficiency of the steam locomotive by increasing the pressure and hence the temperature of the steam. Although it is by no means the only factor

Above: *Preserved Royal Scot No.6115 Scots Guardsman approaching Chinley with an enthusiast special in November 1978.*

involved, steamships and steam power stations use much higher steam temperatures and produce much higher efficiencies, so the prospects were there.

The LMS therefore commissioned from NBL a further "Royal Scot"-like 4-6-0, but with a Schmidt-pattern boiler which generated steam at 1,800psi (and at 325 degrees C) and used that steam to generate more steam (at 900psi) in a separate circuit (steam pressure 126 and 63 kg/cm²). This new steam was fed to three compound cylinders (one high-pressure, two low-pressure) that were fairly conventionally arranged, except that the feed to the two low-pressure cylinders was supplemented by a steam supply at 250psi (17.5 kg/cm²) from yet another com-

partment in the complex steam generating system.

The locomotive was No.6399 and named *Fury*. Steam at 325 degrees C is very nasty stuff indeed, and when a fire tube burst while *Fury* was on test at Carstairs in February 1930, one man was killed and another seriously injured. After this accident the locomotive was laid aside.

In 1933 the LMS sent a "Royal Scot" locomotive — which changed names with *Royal Scot* for the occasion — to North America, complete with rolling stock, for exhibition at the Chicago World Fair. The train was also exhibited at many places, including Montreal, Denver, San Francisco and Vancouver, on an 11,000-mile (17,700km) tour which followed.

By this time a new locomotive chief had arrived on the LMS scene. William Stanier came from the Great Western Railway, the reputation of which line as the leader in British locomotive practice was then at its zenith. Four things that he did directly affected the "Royal Scot" class. First, he finally eliminated axlebox troubles by initiating a new design of bearing based on GWR practice, which reduced the incidence of "Royal Scot" hot boxes from some 80 to seven annually. Second, he had all the class fitted with new and larger tenders with high curved sidesheets, as used on the other types of locomotive being introduced on the LMS. Third, he took the carcase of *Fury* and rebuilt it into a new locomotive called *British Legion*. The rebuild differed from the others in having a taper-barrel boiler, thereby foreshadowing the shape of things to come. The fourth item was the advent of the Stanier 4-6-2s, which had the effect of displacing the "Royal Scot" class from the very highest assignments.

The effects of well over a decade of hard steaming now began to be felt and in the normal course of things new boilers would be needed, plus other repairs so extensive that the costs would approach that of renewal. The decision was taken to rebuild all the class with taper-barrel boilers of a new pattern, thereby bringing the "Royal Scot" class into line with all Stanier's designs. The rebuilding included new cylinders, in many cases new frames and even new wheel centres only the tenders, cabs and nameplates remained.

Above: *No.6129* The Scottish Horse *shown in the LMS post-war livery.*
Below: *No.46103* Royal Scots Fusilier *in British Rail colours sets out with the "Thames-Clyde Express". Note the horse box coupled next to the tender.*

The first rebuilt "Royal Scot" (No.6103 *Royal Scots Fusilier*) appeared in unlined black livery in 1942, while the last did not come out until 1955. One alteration, fairly insignificant as far as the locomotives were concerned but significant to their public, was the change from the high-pitched Midland Railway whistle to a low-pitched hooter of Caledonian Railway origin, which in Stanier's time was fitted to new LMS locomotives.

The rebuilding was a great success. The new engines stood up to all the abuse of high speed running, heavy loads and wartime neglect better than the originals, and then after the war covered themselves with glory. In the locomotive trials which took place in 1948, shortly after the nationalisation of the main line railways "Royal Scot" representatives performed particularly well.

Although these trials were mounted with great attention to detail by the mechanical side of the railway, there is much evidence in the voluminous report issued afterwards that the results were invalidated by lack of co-operation on the part of the operating authorities and the staff. For example, comparative coal-consumption figures based on a run from Carlisle to Euston of the "Royal Scot" express which included 27 signal checks and stops could be of little use. Such things happened on many of the test runs due to thoughtless controllers allowing a slower train to occupy the line in front.

One thing that did emerge, however, was that the "Royal Scot" 4-6-0s could handle any express train in Britain with something to spare, more economically and just as ably as the bigger and more costly 4-6-2s of nominally much greater power. This surprised many observers, but it is perhaps an indication of the point that these trials were never intended to be taken seriously, and that the one valid conclusion that could be drawn from them, that 4-6-2s could do no more when fired by hand than 4-6-0s, was totally ignored.

The 70 "Royal Scots" disappeared in a very short time once dieselisation was undertaken. The first withdrawal was BR No.46139 (ex-LMS No.6139), *The Welch Regiment* in October 1962. The last ceased work in January 1966, when BR No.46115 *Scots Guardsman* was set aside for preservation. A Mr. Bill acquired her and she is at present on show at the steam centre at Dinting, near Manchester; No.6115 had been out on the main line on various occasions including the Rocket 150 Cavalcade at Rainhill in May 1980. No.6100 *Royal Scot* is also preserved, and can be seen at Alan Bloom's steam centre at Bressingham.

Class A 4-8-4

Tractive effort: 61,600lb (27,950kg).
Axle load: 65,000lb (29.5t).
Cylinders (2) 28 x 30in (711 x 762mm).
Driving wheels: 73in (1,854mm).
Heating surface: 4,660sq ft (433m²).
Superheater: 1,992sq ft (185m²).
Steam pressure: 225psi (15.8kg/cm²).
Grate area: 115sq ft (10.7m²).
Fuel: 48,000lb (22t).
Water: 12,500gall (15,000 US) (58m³).
Adhesive weight: 260,000lb (118t).
Total weight: 739,000lb (335t).
Overall length: 105ft 4⅜in (32,125mm).

The King of wheel arrangements at last! It needed 96 years for the 0-2-2 to become a 4-8-4, because all at once in 1927 4-8-4s quickly appeared on several railroads. But by a photo-finish the Northern Pacific's class "A" 4-8-4 was the first and hence the type-name Northern was adopted. The Canadian National Railway, whose first 4-8-4 appeared in 1927 made an unsuccessful play for the name Confederation. Delaware, Lackawanna & Western put forward Pocono for their version. Other early members of the 4-8-4 Club—eventually to be over 40 strong in North America alone—were the Atchison, Topeka & Sante Fe and South Australia, the first foreign member.

The genesis of the 4-8-4 lay in the inbalance between possible tractive effort and grate area of its predecessor the 4-8-2. The Northern Pacific Railroad had a special problem in that its local coal supplies—known rather oddly as Rosebud coal—had a specially high ash content; hence the need for a big firebox and a four-wheel truck at the rear.

And when we say a big firebox, we mean a *really* big one—measuring 13½ x 8½ft (4 x 2½m)—exceeding that of any other line's 4-8-4s. Northern Pacific themselves found their first Northerns so satisfactory they never ordered another passenger locomotive with any other wheel arrangement, and indeed contented themselves with ordering modestly stretched and modernised versions of the originals—sub-classes "A-2", "A-3", "A-4" and "A-5"—right up to their last order for steam in 1943.

The originals were twelve in number and came from the American Locomotive Co of Schenectady. Apart from those enormous grates they were very much the standard US locomotive of the day, with the rugged features evolved after nearly a century of locomotive building on a vast scale. A booster fitted to the trailing truck gave a further 11,400lb (5,172kg) of tractive effort when required at low speeds.

The next 4-8-4 to operate on NP was another Alco product, built in 1930 to the order of the Timken Roller Bearing Co to demonstrate the advantages of having roller bearings on the axles of a steam locomotive. This "Four Aces" (No. 1111) locomotive worked on many railroads with some success as a salesman. The NP was particularly impressed—not only did they buy the engine in 1933 when its sales campaign was over but they also included Timken bearings in the specification when further orders for locomotives were placed. On NP No. 1111 was renumbered 2626 and designated "A-1".

Baldwin of Philadelphia delivered the rest of the Northern fleet. The ten "A-2"s of 1934 (Nos. 2650-59) had disc drivers and bath-tub tenders, and the eight "A-3"s of 1938 (Nos. 2660-67) were almost identical. The final two batches of eight and ten respectively were also very similar; these were the "A-4"s of 1941 (Nos. 2670-77) and the "A-5"s of 1943 (Nos. 2680-89). These last two groups may be distinguished by their 14-wheel Centipede or 4-10-0 tenders of the type originally supplied for Union Pacific.

Below: *Northern Pacific Railroad class "A-4" 4-8-4 No. 2670 was built by Baldwins of Philadelphia in 1941.*

Above: *Northern Pacific Railroad class "A-5" 4-8-4 No. 2680 built by Baldwin in 1943. Note the "centipede" fourteen-wheel tender.*

This final batch is the subject of the art-work above. The amount of stretching that was done may be judged from the following particulars . . .

Tractive effort: 69,800lb (31,660kg).
Axle load: 74,000lb (33.5t)
Driving wheels: 77in (1,956mm)
Steam pressure: 260psi (18.3kg/cm).
Fuel: 54,000lb (24.5t)
Water: 21,000gall (25,000 US) (95m³).
Adhesive weight: 295,000lb (134t).
Total weight: 952,000lb (432t).
Overall length: 112ft 10in (34,391mm).

Other particulars are sensibly the same as the "A" class.

Northern Pacific had begun well by receiving a charter from President Abraham Lincoln in 1864 to build the first trans-continental line to serve the wide north-western territories of the USA. Through communication with the Pacific coast was established in 1883. By the time the 4-8-4s began to arrive it had established itself under the slogan "Main Street of the North West", and connected the twin cities of St Paul and Minneapolis with both Seattle and Portland.

The flag train on this run was the North Coast Limited, and the 4-8-4s assigned to it, after taking over from Chicago Burlington & Quincy Railroad power at St Paul, ran the 999 miles to Livingston, Montana, without change of engine. This is believed to be a world record as regards through engine runs with coal-fired locomotives. No doubt it was made possible by using normal coal in a firebox whose ash capacity was designed for the massive residues of Rosebud lignite.

Right: *Front end of Northern Pacific Railroad 4-8-4 No.2650. Note the bell and headlight typical of US railroad practice.*

Class Ps-4 4-6-2
United States: Southern Railway (SR), 1926

Tractive effort: 47,500lb (21,546 kg).
Axle load: 61,000lb (27.25t).
Cylinders: (2) 27 x 28in (686 x 711mm).
Driving wheels: 73in (1,854mm).
Heating surface: 3,689sq ft (343m²).
Superheater: 993sq ft (92.3m²).
Steam pressure: 200psi (14.1kg/cm²).
Grate area: 70.5sq ft (6.55m²).
Fuel: 32,000lb (14.5t).
Water: 11,600gall (14,000 US) (53m³).
Adhesive weight: 182,000lb (81t).
Total weight: 562,000lb (255.0t).
Length overall: 91ft 11⅞in (28,038mm).

Hundreds of classes of Pacific locomotives ran in America; to illustrate them the first choice was the earliest proper 4-6-2, of the Chesapeake & Ohio. Second choice was the Pennsylvania RR class "K4", as the 4-6-2 design built in the largest numbers. This locomotive, our third choice, is without any doubt the most beautiful amongst the Pacifics of America.

The history of the Southern Railway's Pacifics began in World War I, when the United States Railroad Administration, which had taken over the railroads for the duration, set out to design a standard set of steam locomotives to cover all types of traffic. One of these was the so-called USRA "heavy" 4-6-2. Based on this design, the American Locomotive Company built the first batch of 36 Class "Ps-4" 4-6-2s in 1923.

In 1925 President (of Southern Railway) Fairfax Harrison, visited

King Class 4-6-0
Great Britain: Great Western Railway (GWR), 1927

Tractive effort: 40,300lb (18,285kg).
Axle load: 50,500lb (23t).
Cylinders: (4) 16¼ x 28in (413 x 711mm).
Driving wheels: 78in (1,981mm).
Heating surface: 2,201sq ft (204m²).
Superheater: 313sq ft (29.0m²).
Steam pressure: 250psi (17.6kg/cm²).
Grate area: 34.3sq ft (3.19m²).
Fuel: 13,500lb (6t).
Water: 4,000gall (4,800 US) (18m³).
Adhesive weight: 151,000lb (69t).
Total weight: 304,000lb (138t).
Length overall: 68ft 2in (20,777mm).

In 1926, the Great Western Railway decided that more powerful locomotives were needed—the "Castle" class 4-6-0s were stretched to their limits on some duties. At the same time a 20 year programme of strengthening bridges was nearing completion; furthermore, the report of an official body known as the Bridge Stress Committee, then recently published, had recommended that for locomotives which had low "hammer-blow" higher axle loads could be allowed. All of this added up to making it practical to build a four-cylinder 4-6-0 with a 22½ ton axle load; just as the "Castle" class had been a stretched "Star" class so the new locomotives were to be a stretched "Castle".

In enlarging the "Castle" class, the original principles were followed exactly. The domeless taper-barrel boiler, with Belpaire firebox was there, and so was the four-cylinder arrangement with the inside cylinders driving the leading coupled axle. Walschaert's valve gear, also inside the frames, drove the valves of the inside cylinders driving the those of the outside ones through rocking shafts. Problems with clearances at the front end of the locomotive led to a unique design of bogie with outside bearings to the leading wheels and normal inside bearings to the trailing ones—this rather striking feature was very much a trademark of the newly named "King" class.

Some slight subterfuges were indulged in so as to bring the tractive effort above 40,000lb. Cylinders designed to be 16in (406mm) diameter were bored out to 16¼ (413) whilst the driving wheel diameter was reduced from the hallowed GWR standard of 6ft 8½in (2,045mm) to 6ft 6in (1,981mm). With the increased boiler pressure the required target was reached and the GWR's capable publicity department could once again claim the possession of Britain's most powerful express passenger locomotive. Tractive effort is no measure of locomotive capability at speed but in the "King" class it was backed up by adequate steam-raising power, inlcuding a firebed 10ft 9in (3,277mm) long. But even without that, a high drawbar pull was an advantage on those steep South Devon inclines, of which the most notorious was the long stretch of 1 in 42 (2.4 per cent) at Hemerdon,

east of Plymouth. A "King" was rated to take 360 tons unaided up here, 45 tons more than a "Castle".

The prototype, No.6000 *King George V* which appeared from the works in June 1927, was sent off to the USA when only a few weeks old, to appear at the Baltimore & Ohio Railroad's centenary "Fair of the Iron Horse" held at Baltimore in August. No.6000 led the parade each day and attracted much attention with the famous green livery lined out with black and orange, and with brasswork, name and copper-capped chimney. It must be remembered that American locomotives of the day were much bigger but relatively drab.

Later, a train was worked between Baltimore and Philadelphia; with 544 tons (representing only seven American cars instead of 16 British ones) a speed of 74 mph (119km/h) was reached on level track and a gradient of 1 in 80 (1.25 per cent) was surmounted satisfactorily during the 272 miles (438km) return jour-

his line's namesake in England and was impressed with its green engines. He determined that his next batch of 4-6-2s would make an equal if not better showing. He naturally chose a style very similar to the English SR except that a much brighter green was used together with gold—the small extra cost paid off quickly in publicity. Coloured locomotives were then quite exceptional in North America. A little later the earlier batch of locomotives appeared in green and gold also.

The 1926 batch of 23 locomotives had the enormous 12-wheel tenders illustrated here, in place of the USRA standard

8-wheel tenders on the earlier engines, and a different and much more obvious type (the Elesco) of feed water heater involving the large transverse cylindrical vessel just in front of the smokestack. Some locomotives from each batch had the Walschaert's gear, others had Baker's. A final batch of 5 came from Baldwin in 1928. These had Walschaert's valve gear and 8-wheel tenders of large capacity. All were fitted with mechanical stokers.

Southern had what it called an "optional equipment policy" whereby drivers were allowed to adorn their locomotives in various

Left: One of the Southern Railway's superb "Ps-4" 4-6-2s in action. This particular loco is the one preserved in the Smithsonian Museum.

Below: The glorious green and gold beauty of the livery applied to the Southern Railway (of USA) "Ps-4" class Pacific is superbly depicted below.

ways, ways in fact that were similar to those of 70 years earlier. Eagles could be mounted above the headlights, themselves flanked by brass "candlesticks"; stars were fixed to cylinder heads, brass rings to smokestacks. Some locomotives were named after and by their regular drivers. A lot of this might be considered mere nonsense, but the end effect was that few steam engines anywhere were better maintained.

Of the 64 locomotives built, 44 were allocated to the Southern Railway proper, 12 to subsidiary Cincinnati, New Orleans & Texas Pacific and 8 to the Alabama Great Southern, although "Southern" appeared on the tenders of all. Running numbers were as follows:
SR proper—Nox.1366 to 1409.
CNO&TP—Nos.6471 to 6482.
AGS—Nos.6684 to 6691.

The CNO&TP engines had a device known as a Wimble smoke duct, by which the exhaust which otherwise would issue from the chimney could be led backwards to level with the sand dome and discharged there. The CNO&TP was a line with many timber-lined tunnels and a direct close-up vertical blast would have played havoc with the tunnel linings.

The "Ps-4" class was the last steam passenger locomotive type built for the Southern and they remained in top-line express work until displaced by diesels in the 1940s and 1950s. No.1401 is preserved and is superbly displayed in the Smithsonian Museum, Washington, D.C.

Alas, this involved erecting the display building around the locomotive, thereby preventing its use on special trains for railfans, a Southern speciality.

SOUTHERN

ney. *King George V* came back with medals, a large bell (still carried) and much honour.

Five more "King" class appeared during 1927, then 14 during 1928 and the last ten in 1930. As a result of early experience, including the derailment of a pair of leading wheels at Midgham near Newbury, modifications were made to the springing and other details affecting the riding. Once these things were corrected the "King" class performed in accordance with expectation and seven minutes were cut from the schedule of the *Cornish Riviera Limited* between London and Plymouth, the new 4 hour timing being attained with heavier loads.

One thing that seems to have been ignored was the fact that the capacity of the locomotive was increased but not that of the human link in its power cycle, that is the fireman who shovelled the coal. The "King" class boiler certainly had the potential of steaming at rates which corresponded to coal consumption

maybe 30 per cent greater than the 3,000lb (1,360kg) or so per hour a man could be expected to shovel. Even so, no attempt was made to fit mechanical stokers.

As an illustration of the potential that was available and after some modifications to increase the superheater heating surface by 56 per cent and also to improve

Left: Great Western Railway "King" class No.6010 King Charles I passing Corsham at speed on Brunel's original main line between Bath and Bristol.

the draughting, tests were made using two firemen. An enormous 25-coach load was hauled between Reading and Stoke Gifford near Bristol at an average speed of over 58 mph (93km/h). Later, further improvements were made which involved the fitting of double chimneys. It was with the first locomotive so equipped, No.6015 *King Richard III* that the highest ever speed with a "King" class was recorded, 108½mph (175km/h) near Patney with the down *Cornish Riviera Limited* on 29 September 1955. All the "King" class had double chimneys by the end of 1958.

Time, however, was running out for the "King" class. Their end began early in 1962 when No.6006 *King George I* was withdrawn. It was complete early in 1963, when the last was taken out of service.

Class J3a 4-6-4

United States:
New York Central Railroad (NYC), 1926

Tractive effort: 41,860lb (19,000kg).
Axleload: 67,500lb (30.5t).
Cylinders: (2) 22½ x 29in (572 x 737mm).
Driving wheels: 79in (2,007mm).
Heating surface: 4,187sq ft (389.0m²).
Superheater: 1,745sq ft (162.1m²).
Steam pressure: 265psi (18.6kg/cm²).
Grate area: 82sq ft (7.6m²).
Fuel: 92,000lb (41.7t).
Water: 15,000gall (18,000 US) (68.1m³).
Adhesive weight: 201,500lb (91.5t).
Total weight: 780,000lb (350t).
Length overall: 106ft 1in (32,342mm).

Some locomotive wheel arrangements had a particular association with one railway; such was the 4-6-4 and the New York Central. In 1926 the Central built its last Pacific, of Class "K5b," and the road's design staff, under the direction of Paul W Kiefer, Chief Engineer of Motive Power, began to plan a larger engine to meet future requirements. The main requirements were an increase in starting tractive effort, greater cylinder power at higher speeds, and weight distribution and balancing which would impose lower impact loads on the track than did the existing Pacifics. Clearly this would involve a larger firebox, and to meet the axle loading requirement the logical step was to use a four-wheeled truck under the cab, as was advocated by the Lima Locomotive Works, which had plugged engines with large fireboxes over trailing bogies under the trade name of Super Power. As the required tractive effort could be transmitted through three driving axles, the wheel arrangement came out as 4-6-4. Despite the Lima influence in the design, it was the American Locomotive Company of Schenectady which received the order for the first locomotive, although Lima did receive an order for ten of them

some years later. Subsequent designs of 4-6-4s took over the type-name Hudson applied to these engines by the NYC.

Classified "Jla" and numbered 5200, the new engine was handed over to the owners on 14 February 1927. By a narrow margin it was the first 4-6-4 in the United States, but others were already on the production line at Alco for other roads. Compared with the "K5b" it showed an increase in grate area from 67.8sq ft (6.3m²) to 81.5sq ft (7.6m²), and the maximum diameter of the boiler was increased from 84in (2,134mm) to 87⅝in (2,226mm). The cylinder and driving wheel sizes were unchanged, so the tractive effort went up on proportion to the increase in boiler pressure from 200psi (14.1 kg/cm²) to 225psi (15.8kg/cm²). The addition of an extra axle enabled the total weight on the coupled axles to be reduced from 185,000lb (83.9t) to 182,000lb (82.6t), despite an increase in the total engine weight of 41,000lb (22t). Improved balancing reduced the impact loading on the rails compared with the Pacific.

The engine had a striking appearance, the rear bogie giving it a more balanced rear end than a Pacific, with its single axle

under a large firebox. At the front the air compressors and boiler feed pump were housed under distinctive curved casings at either side of the base of the smokebox, with diagonal bracing bars. The boiler mountings ahead of the cab were clothed in an unusual curved casing.

No.5200 soon showed its paces, and further orders followed, mostly for the NYC itself, but 80 of them allocated to three of the wholly-owned subsidiaries, whose engines were numbered and lettered separately. The latter included 30 engines for the Boston and Albany, which, in deference to the heavier gradients on that line, had driving wheels three inches smaller than the remainder, a rather academic difference. The B&A engines were classified "J2a", "J2b" and "J2c", the suffixes denoting minor differences in successive batches. The main NYC series of 145 engines were numbered consecutively from 5200, and here again successive modifications produced sub-classes "Jla" to

Below: *Standard Hudson or 4-6-4 of class "J3" design. The Railroad had 275 engines of this type in passenger service and they monopolised the road's express trains for twenty years.*

Above: *"J1" 4-6-4 No.5280 hauling the Empire State Express at Dunkirk, New York State, in February 1950.*

"Jle". Amongst detail changes were the substitution of Baker's for Walschaert's valve gear; the Baker's gear has no sliding parts, and was found to require less maintenance. There were also changes in the valve setting.

From their first entry into service the Hudsons established a reputation for heavy haulage at high speeds. Their maximum drawbar horsepower was 38 per cent more than that of the Pacifics, and they attained this at a higher speed. They could haul 18 cars weighing 1,270 tonnes at an average speed of 55mph (88 km/h) on the generally level sections. One engine worked a 21-car train of 1,500 tonnes over the 639 miles (1,027km) from Windsor (Ontario) to Harmon, covering one section of 71 miles (114km) at an average speed of 62.5mph (100.5km/h).

The last of the "J1" and "J2" series were built in 1932, and there was then a pause in construction, although the design staff were already planning for an increase in power. In 1937 orders were placed for 50 more Hudsons, incorporating certain

NEW YORK CENTRAL

improvements and classified "J3". At the time of the introduction of the first Hudson, the NYC, like the German engineers of the time, were chary of combustion chambers in fireboxes because of constructional and maintenance problems, but by 1937 further experience had been gained, and the "J3" incorporated a combustion chamber 43 in (1,092mm) long. Other changes included a tapering of the boiler barrel to give a greater diameter at the front of the firebox, raising of the boiler pressure from 225 psi (15.9kg/cmm²) to 275psi (19.3km/cm²) (later reduced to 265psi), and a change in the cylinder size from 25 x 28in (635 x 711mm) to 22½ x 29in (572 x 737mm). The most conspicuous change was the use of disc driving wheels, half the engines having Boxpok wheels with oval openings, and the other half the Scullin type with circular openings.

The final ten engines were clothed in a streamlined casing designed by Henry Dreyfus. Of all the streamlined casings so far applied to American locomotives, this was the first to exploit the natural shape of the locomotive rather than to conceal it, and the working parts were left exposed. Many observers considered these to be the most handsome of all streamlined locomotives, especially when hauling a train in matching livery. Prior to the building of the streamlined "J3"s, a "J1" had been clothed in a casing devised at the Case School of Science in Cleveland, but it was much less attractive than Dreyfus' design, and the engine was rebuilt like the "J3"s; while two further "J3"s were given Dreyfus casings for special duties.

The "J3"s soon showed an improvement over the "J1"s both in power output and in efficiency. At 65mph (105km/h) they developed 20 per cent more power than a "J1". They could haul 1,130 tonnes trains over the 147 miles (236km) from Albany to Syracuse at scheduled speeds of 59mph (95km/h), and could

Above: *The prototype New York Central class "J1" No.5200 on test-train of 18 heavyweight cars at Albany in 1927.*

reach 60mph (96km/h) with a 1,640 tonne train. The crack train of the NYC was the celebrated 20th Century Limited. At the time of the building of the first Hudsons this train was allowed 20 hours from New York to Chicago. This was cut to 18 hours in 1932 on the introduction of the "J1e" series, and in 1936 there was a further cut to 16½ hours. Aided by the elimination of some severe service slacks, and by the "J3" engines, the schedule came down to 16 hours in 1938, which gave an end-to-end speed of 59.9mph (96.3km/h) with 900-tonne trains, and with seven intermediate stops totalling 26 minutes. On a run with a "J3" on the Century, with 940 tonnes, the 133 miles (214km) from Toledo to Elkhart were covered in a net time of 112½ minutes, and the succeeding 93.9 miles (151km) from Elkhart to Englewood in 79½ minutes, both giving averages of 70.9mph (114km/h). A speed of 85.3mph (137km/h) was maintained for 31 miles (50km), with a maximum of 94mph (151km/h). The engines worked through from Harmon to Toledo or Chicago, 693 and 925 miles (1,114 and 1,487km) respectively. For this purpose huge tenders were built carrying 41 tonnes of

coal, but as the NYC used water troughs to replenish the tanks on the move, the water capacity was by comparison modest at 18,000 US gallons (68.1m³).

Eventually the engines allocated to the subsidiaries were brought into the main series of numbers, and with the removal of the streamlined casings in post-war years, the NYC had 275 engines of similar appearance numbered from 5,200 to 5,474. It was the largest fleet of 4-6-4 locomotives on any railway, and constituted 63 per cent of the total engines of that wheel arrangement in the United States.

Although the Hudson had their share of troubles, they were generally reliable, and the "J3"s

Above: *The streamline version of the New York Central's famous Hudson. The designer was Henry Dreyfus.*

ran 185,000 to 200,000 miles (297,000 to 321,000km) between heavy repairs, at an annual rate of about 110,000 miles (177,000km).

After World War II the Niagara 4-8-4s displaced the Hudson from the heaviest workings, but as that class numbered only 25 engines, the Hudsons still worked many of the 150 trains daily on the NYC booked at more than 60mile/h (96km/h) start-to-stop. Despite rapid dieselisation the engines lasted until 1953-6, apart from an accident casualty.

Schools Class 4-4-0
Great Britain: Southern Railway (SR), 1933

Tractive effort: 25,133lb (11,400kg).
Axle load: 47,000lb (21t).
Cylinders: (3) 16½ x 26in (419 x 660mm).
Driving wheels: 79in (2,007mm).
Heating surface: 1,766sq ft (164m²).
Superheater: 283sq ft (26.3m²).
Steam pressure: 220psi (15.46kg/cm²).
Grate area: 28.3sq ft (2.63m²).
Fuel: 11,000lb (5t).
Water: 4,000gall (4,800 US) (18m³).
Adhesive weight: 94,000lb (42t).
Total weight: 245,500 (110t).
Length overall: 58ft 9¾in (17,926mm).

British locomotive engineers command respect for their mastery of the processes involved in producing and assembling the many components that go to make a steam express passenger locomotive. In some cases, though, one is more cautious when appraising their theoretical approach to design. This slight reluctance to do sums often produced surprises, usually unpleasant. But sometimes they were pleasant ones, as witness the excellent "Schools" class first put into service by the Southern Railway in 1930. The "Schools" locomotives were originally intended as small engines for lesser services but the engineering staff got a pleasant surprise when it

was found that in many ways their capability was on a level with the SR's bigger "King Arthur" class as well as with the much bigger but rather disappointing "Lord Nelson" class.

A shortened "King Arthur" boiler was the basis of the design and since it was the barrel rather than the firebox which was reduced in length, it was the big fire plus the hottest part of the heating surface that remained and so steam raising was hardly affected. The bigger ashpan possible because of the wide space between the coupled axles was also a help. Most 4-4-0s with outside cylinders were notorious for the "boxing" effect—i.e. oscillation about a vertical axis—

caused by the impossibility of counter-balancing all the reciprocating parts in a two-cylinder engine.

Three cylinders were chosen therefore for the new locomotives, all driving on the leading coupled axle. Each cylinder had its own set of Walschaert's valve gear, but access to the inside motion is much easier on a 4-4-0 than on a 4-6-0 or 4-6-2 as we have seen already in the case of the "American Standard" 4-4-0.

The design was a great success from the start and very few changes were needed over the years. A few locomotives were later fitted with multiple-jet blastpipes and large diameter chimneys, but otherwise the main

Class 500 4-8-4
Australia: South Australian Government Railways (SAR), 1928

Tractive effort: 51,000lb (23,133kg).
Axle load: 49,500lb (22.5t).
Cylinders: (2) 26 x 28in (660 x 711).
Driving wheels: 63in (1,600mm).
Heating surface: 3,648sq ft (339m²).
Superheater: 835sq ft (77.5m²).
Steam pressure: 200psi (14.1kg/cm²).
Grate area: 66.5sq ft (6.2m²).
Fuel: 2,4500lb (11t).
Water: 7,000gall (8,400 US) (32m³).
Adhesive weight: 196,500lb (89t).
Total weight: 498,000lb (226t).
Length overall: 83ft 1½in (25,641mm).

South Australia is by no means easy locomotive country. For example, when South Australian Railways' trains leave the capital, Adelaide, for Melbourne, they have to face a long 1 in 45 (2.2

per cent) climb into the Mount Lofty ranges. In spite of this their motive power sixty years ago was on the small side. In the early 1920s the latest and largest express passenger power was the class "S" 4-4-0 of 1894, with 12,700lb (5,762kg) of tractive effort and 17½sq ft (1.6m²) of grate area.

The State government was not happy about the state of its 5ft 3in (1,600mm) gauge railway system and so adopted the idea of inviting a senior executive from a USA railroad to be the Railway Commissioner. In due time a certain Mr. W.A. Webb, who hailed from the Missouri-Kansas-Texas Railroad—the famous "Katy"—arrived in Australia. His plans for SAR were to include some very large locomotives indeed.

The most notable of Webb's two passenger designs were the ten "500" class 4-8-2s, which had over four times the tractive effort

event was the addition of 30,000 to the numbers upon nationalisation in 1948.

The names of famous schools in SR territory were chosen for the locomotives, in spite of the drawback that many of them had the same names as SR stations and people occasionally confused the nameplate with the train's destination boards. No.900 *Eton* appeared in March 1930, the first of a batch of ten built at Eastleigh Works that year. Five more appeared in 1932, ten in 1933 (including a series commencing with No.919 *Harrow*, named after schools away from the SR), seven in 1934 and eight in 1935, making 40 in all.

One requirement was to permit running through the below-standard-size tunnels on the Tonbridge to Hastings line and to this end the sides of both cabs and tenders had an upper sloping portion. This certainly added to the neat and compact appearance.

Their greatest work was done on the Bournemouth line, on which they regularly hauled the crack *Bournemouth Limited* express, scheduled to run the 116 miles (186km) in 120 minutes non-stop. Cecil J. Allen noted an occasion when a 510-ton train was worked by No.932 *Blundells* from Waterloo to Southampton at an average speed of 61mph (98km/h) and another when with 305 tons No.931 *King's Wimbledon* ran from Waterloo to a signal stop outside Salisbury at an average of 66mph (106½ km/h), 90mph (145km/h) being just touched at one point. Neither of these feats would disgrace a Pacific.

The class was withdrawn in

1961 and 1962 but three examples have been preserved. No.925 *Cheltenham* belongs to the National Railway Museum and is currently in main-line running order. No.928 *Stowe* is with the Bluebell Railway and No.926 *Repton* is in the USA, currently at Steamtown, Bellows Falls, Vermont, although it is understood a move is pending.

Above: *"Schools" class No. 30934* St Lawrence *on an up troop special at Folkestone Warren, Kent, England.*

Below: *"Schools" Class loco No.919,* Harrow, *depicted in the Southern Railways' pre-war livery. A superb locomotive, it suprised even its designers with its efficiency and power.*

SOUTHERN

919

of the previous top-line passenger locomotives plus other attributes in proportion! Although typically American in design, these monsters were built in 1926 by the English armaments firm, Armstrong-Whitworth of Newcastle-upon-Tyne. In 1928 the locomotives, apparently still not regarded as sufficiently strong pullers, were further enhanced by a booster giving an additional 8,000lb (3,640kg) of tractive effort. This was accommodated in a four-wheel truck, thereby giving Australia the honour of having the world's first 4-8-4 outside North America; the pony truck had previously had an axle loading of over 22 tons.

Another later addition was a pair of elegant footplate valances

Left: *Two views of 4-8-4 No. 500 on a special farewell run from Adelaide to Victor Harbour, Victoria, in March 1962, just before withdrawal from service.*

bearing the "Overland" motif. This reflected the labours of these magnificent locomotives on "The Overland" express between Adelaide and Melbourne. The 1 in 45 of the Mount Lofty incline could be negotiated at 15mph with 550 tons—this with booster in action. It must have been worth listening to—but then so would be *three* of the "500"s 4-4-0 predecessors on the 350-ton Melbourne express of a few years earlier.

The "500"s and the other Webb classes were not multiplied, mainly because heavy axle-loadings precluded their use on all but the principal main lines. Diesel-electric locomotives appeared in South Australia from 1951 on and in 1955 the first "500" was withdrawn. By 1962 all had gone, except No.504, which is preserved at the Australian Railway Historical Society's museum at Mile End, near Melbourne.

KF Type 4-8-4
China:
Chinese Ministry of Railways, 1935

Tractive effort: 36,100lb (16,380kg).
Axle load: 38,000lb (17.5t).
Cylinders: (2) 21¼ x 29½in (540 x 750mm).
Driving wheels: 69in (1,750mm).
Heating surface: 2,988sq ft (278m²).
Superheater: 1,076sq ft (100m²).
Steam pressure: 220psi (15.5kg/cm²).
Grate area: 68.5sq ft (6.4m²).
Fuel: 26,500lb (12t).
Water: 6,600gall (8,000 US) (30m³).
Adhesive weight: 150,000lb (68t).
Total weight: 432,000lb (196t).
Length overall: 93ft 2½in (28,410mm).

Twenty-four of these magnificent locomotives were supplied by the Vulcan Foundry of Newton-le-Willows, Lancashire, to China in 1935-6. They were paid for out of funds set aside as reparations

Right: 4-8-4 locomotive (later class "KF") as built by the Vulcan Foundry for the Chinese Ministry of Railways in 1936.

for damage done in China to British property in the so-called Boxer riots of 1910. Although British built as well as designed by a Briton, Kenneth Cantlie, the practice followed was American—except in one respect, that is, the limitation of axle load to 16½ tons. Twice that would be more typical of United States locomotive.

The typical American locomotive was directly in line with the original simple Stephenson concept of a locomotive having just two outside cylinders, but it was very fully equipped in other ways. Hence these "KF" locomotives, destined for what was in those days and in material things a rather backward country had, for example, electric lights, while crews of the last word in passenger steam locomotives back in Britain had to make do with paraffin oil. British firemen had to use a shovel to put coal in the firebox, while Chinese ones had the benefit of automatic stokers.

Above: *Chinese class "KF" 4-8-4 locomotive awaiting departure from Nanjing station.*

Other equipment included a supply of superheated steam for

certain auxiliaries, and a cut-off control indicator to advise the driver on the best setting for the valve gear. In the case of some of the locomotives, the leading tender bogie was fitted with a

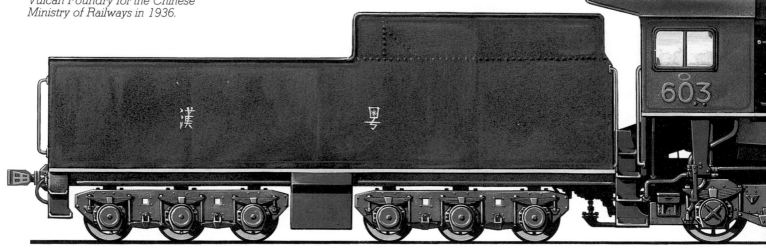

Class K 4-8-4
New Zealand:
New Zealand Government Railways (NZGR), 1932

Tractive effort: 32,740lb (14,852kg).
Axle load: 30,500lb (14t).
Cylinders: (2) 20 x 26in (508 x 660mm).
Driving wheels: 54in (1,372mm).
Heating surface: 1,931sq ft (179m²).
Superheater: 482sq ft (45m²).
Steam pressure: 200psi (14.1kg/cm²).
Grate area: 47.7sq ft (4.4m²).
Fuel: 17,500lb (8t).
Water: 5,000gall (6,000 US) (22.7m³).
Adhesive weight: 122,000lb (55t).
Total weight: 306,000lb (139t).
Length overall: 69ft 8in (21,233mm).

It is always a surprise to think that far-off and remote New Zealand should have one of the finest railway systems in the world. Furthermore, in steam days this sheep-raising country of a mere 1.6 million population produced

its own motive power not only in one but in both the main islands. Amongst many fine locomotives designed and built there, the "K" class 4-8-4s were outstanding.

Apart from the cab (which had to accommodate full size New Zealanders) the "K"s appeared as scaled-down versions of typical North American 4-8-4s, with their dimensions reduced in proportion to the narrower 3ft 6in (1,067mm) gauge standard in New Zealand. Even so, the designers certainly had all their buttons on to produce a locomotive of such power within the limitations of an 11ft 6in (3,480 mm) overall height and a 14-ton axleload.

In all 71 "K"s were built between 1932 and 1950, all in NZGR's own workshops. There were three sub-classes, "K", "Ka" and "Kb" numbering 30, 35 and 6 respectively. Running numbers were 900 to 970. The first group had roller bearings to the guiding and tender axles, while the re-

mainder had all axles so fitted. Class "Kb" were built at Hillside workshops, Dunedin, South Island, and the remainder at Hutt, near Wellington, North Island.

The "Kb"s, intended for a transverse line which crosses the mountain spine of the South Island, had boosters which gave an extra 8,000lb (3,640kg) of tractive effort. Originally the "Ka"s and "Kb"s had a boxed-in front end, looking for all the world like the front end of a modern "hood-unit" diesel locomotive, but these ugly attachments were removed immediately after World War II. Two "Ka"s Nos.958 and 959 had Baker's valve gear in place of Walschaert's.

Baker's valve gear was a patented USA arrangement, very much akin to Walschaert's, which did away with the curved link and die-block. In its place there was an ingenious arrangement of levers and simple pin-joints which produced the same effect. The

use of Baker's valve gear outside the USA was minimal but even on its home ground it never showed signs of superseding Walschaert's in any general sense. A number of applications are illustrated elsewhere in this book—the patent gear *did* have more of an advantage when it came to the long valve-travel associated with fast-running passenger locomotives.

In the late 1940s the "K"s and "Ka"s, all of which were built for and remained on the North Island lines, were converted to oil-burning, while the "Kb"s on the South Island remained coal fired. This seems to have been the only major modification which occurred—and of course it was one which was dictated by external circumstances rather than by any shortcomings of these

Right: *NZGR class "K" 4-8-4 crosses a temporary bridge of steel girder and timber trestle.*

booster engine; two axles of the six-wheel truck were coupled, so that the booster drive was on four wheels. The booster gave an additional 7,670lb (3,480kg) of tractive effort while in operation. These engines were allocated to the Canton-Hankow railway, while the others were divided between that line and the Shanghai-Nanking railway. One interesting feature was that the Walschaert's valve gear was arranged to give only half the amount of valve travel needed. A 2-to-1 multiplying lever was provided to give the correct amount. The piston valves were 12½in (320mm) in diameter, an exceptionally large size. Running numbers were 600 to 623.

When locomotive-building firms set out to build locomotives bigger than were used in their native land they were not always a success, but this case was an exception, and the class gave excellent service. During the war years exceptional efforts were made to keep these engines out

of the hands of the Japanese and to some extent the efforts were successful. It has been reported that 17 out of the 24 survived World War II, which for China lasted over ten years and was exceptionally devastating.

After the communists gained control, the class was designated "KF"—in Roman not Chinese

Above: *Class "KF" 4-8-4 No.7 at Shanghai in 1981 awaiting shipment back to England for the National Railway Museum.*

characters—and renumbered from 1 upwards. The letters KF seem to correspond with the English word Confederation; other class designations of what

are now non-standard Chinese types lend support to this supposition. The prime position given to these engines in the renumbering is some indication of the regard in which they were held.

Dieselisation of the Chinese Railways is proceeding slowly, priority being given to long distance passenger trains. Trains entrusted to these 4-8-4s were early targets for dieselisation and no 4-8-4 has been seen by Western visitors since 1966, although it is reported they were in use in the Shanghai area as late as 1974.

In 1978, the Chinese Minister of Railways, while on a visit to Britain promised one to the National Railway Museum at York, as a prime example of British exports to the world. This was to happen when a "KF" was taken out of use; accordingly in 1981 No.KF7 was shipped from Shanghai back to the country from whence it came.

wonderful engines. An exception was the replacement of feed-water heating equipment by exhaust steam injectors on the "Ka" and "Kb" batches.

For many years the whole class performed with great distinction on the principal passenger trains and speeds of up to 69mph (110km/h) have been recorded. As regards famous ascents such as the Raurimu spiral incline, they could maintain 20mph (32km/h) with 300 tons on the 1 in 50 (2 per cent) grade, uncompensated for curvature.

Proportionate to the population, New Zealanders have a passion for steam locomotives unmatched even in Britain; this is reflected in the preservation of five of these engines. No.900 is with the Pacific Steel Co. of Otahuhu, No.935 at Seaview, near Wellington and Nos.942 and 945 are at Paekikari, all in the North Island. No.968 is at the Ferrymead Museum of Science and Industry near Christchurch in the South Island.

Class P2 2-8-2
Great Britain:
London & North Eastern Railway (LNER), 1934

Tractive effort: 43,462lb (19,715kg).
Axle load: 44,800lb (20t).
Cylinders: (3) 21 x 26in (533 x 660mm).
Driving wheels: 74in (1,880mm).
Heating surface: 2,714sq ft (252m²).
Superheater: 777sq ft (72m²).
Steam pressure: 220psi (15.5kg/cm²).
Grate area: 50sq ft (4.6m²).
Fuel: 18,000lb (8t).
Water: 5,000gall (6,000 US) (23m³).
Adhesive weight: 177,000lb (80t).
Total weight: 370,000lb (168t).
Length overall: 74ft 5⅜in (22,692mm).

In thinking of the London & North Eastern Railway's East Coast main line from London to Scotland, one is liable to forget that it extends 130 miles (208km)

beyond Edinburgh to Aberdeen. This final section was much more severe than the rest of the line. The ruling gradient north of Edinburgh was 1 in 74½ (1.34 per cent), in place of 1 in 96 (1.05 per cent) on the line south of the Scottish capital.

The standard "A1" and "A3" class 4-6-2s were overtaxed by trains such as the "Aberdonian" sleeping car express and it was decided to build some locomotives with some 20 per cent more adhesion weight than the Pacifics. The result was the first (and only) class of eight-coupled express locomotives to run in Britain, of which the prototype was built in 1934, a handsome 2-8-2 called *Cock o' the North* and numbered 2001. To match the high adhesive weight, the tractive effort was the highest ever applied to an express passenger locomotive working in Britain.

Amongst many unusual fea-

Class V 4-4-0
Ireland:
Great Northern Railway (GNR (I)), 1932

Axle load: 47,000lb (21.5t).
Cylinders: (3) see text.
Driving wheels: 79in (2,007mm).
Heating surface: 1,251sq ft (116m²).
Superheater: 276sq ft (25.6m²).
Steam pressure: 250psi (17.6kg/cm²).
Grate area: 25sq ft (2.3m²).
Fuel: 13,200lb (6t).
Water: 3,500gall (4,200 US) (16m³).
Adhesive weight: 92,000lb (42t).
Total weight: 232,000lb (105t).
Length overall: 55ft 3½in (16,853mm).

Beginning in 1876, the Great Northern Railway of Ireland owned and operated the main line railway connecting Dublin to Belfast. For many years the steel viaduct over the Boyne River 32 miles north of Dublin presented a severe limitation on the size of

locomotives; but once it was stengthened in 1931, the way was clear for some really powerful express locomotives to use it, and the distinctive Irish Class Vs were among the first.

The five Class 'V' compound 4-4-0s were supplied by Beyer, Peacock of Manchester; the tenders were built by the company at their own Dundalk Works. They were three-cylinder compounds on the Smith principle — similar to those built for the

Midland Railway of England. The high-pressure inside cylinder was 17¼in (438mm) diameter, whereas the two outside low-pressure ones were 19in (483mm) diameter; all were 26in (660mm) stroke. Three sets of

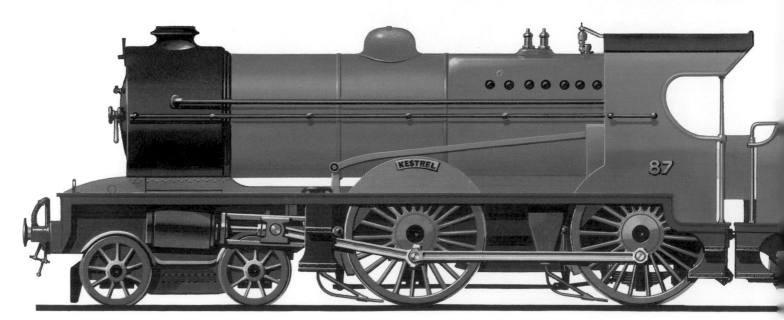

tures of this three-cylinder locomotive were the use of poppet valves actuated by a rotating camshaft and a specially-shaped front end, whose external contours were designed to lift smoke and steam clear of the cab in order to improve visibility. The internal contours of the front end, which included a double chimney, were also designed to obtain adequate draught for the fire with the minimum of back pressure. A second 2-8-2 (No.2002 *Earl Marischal*) was built with the normal (for the LNER) arrangement of piston valves driven by two sets of Walschaert's valve gear and the Gresley-Holcroft 2-to-1 motion. This standard arrangment was preferred for the final four members of the class,

Left: A handsome-looking class "P2" 2-8-2 No.2005 Wolf of Badenoch works an Aberdeen to Edinburgh train.

built in 1936, which externally looked more like the streamline "A4" class 4-6-2s of 1935.

Alas, despite the increase in the size of the P2 compared with the Pacifics, double-heading could not be entirely eliminated. Inadequate bearing surfaces and a lack of guiding force in the leading pony truck caused heavy wear on the sharp curves of the Edinburgh-Aberdeen line, and the engines proved to be heavy in maintenance costs. In 1943-44, therefore, the 2-8-2s were 'rebuilt' as 4-6-2s of class "A2/2", although the lack of continuity of LNER locomotive policy at that time meant these "P2" conversions also remained non-standard. So the objective of doing the conversion remained unattained, while a group of fine-looking locomotives were turned into some of the ugliest ones ever to run on a line renowned for the good looks of its motive power.

Stephenson's link motion filled what space remained between the frames. The LP cylinders originally had balanced slide valves but these were soon altered to piston valves as on the HP cylinder.

The new locomotives were used to provide faster train services, including a run over the 54¼ miles (138km) from Dublin to Dundalk in 54 minutes, the fastest anywhere in Ireland at that time. The timing for the 112½ miles (286km) between Dublin and Belfast was 148 minutes but this included five stops as well as customs examination at the border. In terms of net time this is still the fastest ever sched-

Left: Great Northern of Ireland class "VS" 4-4-0 built in 1948 by Beyer Peacock & Co. These locomotives differed from the original batch in having Walschaert's valve gear and being non-compound.

Below: One of the original class "V" 4-4-0s built by Beyer Peacock in 1932.

uled between the two cities; but it lasted only a short time, for the slump combined with a disastrous strike led in 1933 to drastic economies which included decelerations and, in the case of these locomotives, to a reduced boiler pressure.

The simple yet handsome lines of the five compounds were enhanced by the beautiful blue livery and the names *Eagle, Falcon, Merlin, Peregrine* and *Kestrel*. Running numbers were 83 to 87. *Merlin* is preserved and is at present being restored to running condition under the auspices of the Railway Preservation Society of Ireland.

A further five similar locomotives (Class 'VS') with three simple cylinders and Walschaert's valve gear were built in 1948. These were numbered 206 to 210 and were named *Liffey, Boyne, Lagarn, Foyle* and *Erne*, after Irish rivers.

The last "V" class 4-4-0 was withdrawn in 1961 and the last "VS" in 1965; both classes outlasted the GNR which was dismembered in 1958.

Turbomotive 4-6-2

Great Britain:
London, Midland & Scottish Railway (LMS), 1935

Tractive effort: 40,000lb (18,150kg).
Axle load: 54,000lb (24t).
Cylinders: None.
Driving wheels: 78in (1,981mm).
Heating surface: 2,314sq ft (215m²).
Superheater: 653sq ft (61m²).
Steam pressure: 250psi (17.6kg/cm²).
Grate area: 45sq ft (4.2m²).
Fuel: 20,000lb (9t).
Water: 4,000gall (4,800 US) (18m³).
Adhesive weight: 158,000lb (72t).
Total weight: 367,000lb (166.5t).
Length overall: 74ft 4¼in (22,663mm).

Turbines had been for many years the normal motive power for ships and electric generators so why not, reasoned so many engineers, try one on a locomotive. In 1932 William Stanier, then the newly appointed Chief Mechanical Engineer of the London Midland & Scottish Railway, saw a Swedish turbine freight locomotive at work and resolved to try a turbine loco himself. Turbine locomotives had already been tried on the LMS experimentally sometime before, but these were condensing locomotives of a very different concept. The Swedish design avoided the complications of a condenser and Stanier was particularly impressed with the simplicity achieved. Valves and valve gear were entirely eliminated and because there were no reciprocating parts perfect balance could easily be achieved. Three prototype 4-6-2s—the forerunners of the "Duchess" class—were in hand at Crewe and so promising did the idea seem that one of these was earmarked to become a guinea pig for an experiment in turbine propulsion, which came to fruition in 1935.

A multi-stage Metropolitan-Vickers turbine of about 2,000 horsepower was mounted more or less where the left-hand outside cylinder would have been. It drove the leading coupled axle

through a three-stage gear train totally enclosed in an oil bath; the reduction ratio was 34:1, so that at 70mph (113km/h) the turbine would be doing 10,000 rev/min. To control the locomotive, rather than throttle the steam which would effect the turbine's efficiency, any number of the six separate nozzles could be "switched in" by being given steam. It was all an exceedingly simple arrangement and on test this No.6202 proved to be more efficient than a conventional 4-6-2. A small turbine was provided on the right-hand side to move the locomotive in reverse at low speed, engaged through a dog-clutch and a fourth gear train. This feature was, sadly, not to prove entirely foolproof.

Unlike most steam locomotive experiments which had the temerity to challenge Stephenson's principles, the so-called "Turbomotive" gave good service—300,000 miles of it, in fact. Her regular turn was the "Liverpool Flyer" up to London in the morning and back in the afternoon, for several years the fastest train on the LMS. Inevitably there were problems but there was also promise; alas, the war came, then nationalisation.

People who were not concerned with the original experiment were in charge and, following a failure of the main turbine in 1947, the locomotive was set aside at Crewe. In 1951 it was rebuilt into a normal reciprocating 4-6-2 named *Princess Anne* but perished in the triple collision at Harrow a very short time after re-entering service.

So ended one of the most promising attempts to produce a turbine-powered express passenger locomotive. A similar story could be told about others such as the Zoelly turbine locomotives tried in Germany, or the enormous 6,000hp one made by Baldwin of Philadelphia for the Pennsylvania Railroad in the USA.

Below: The "Turbomotive", LMS No.6202, works its usual turn from Euston to Liverpool.

Andes Class 2-8-0
Peru:
Central Railway of Peru (FCC), 1935

Tractive effort: 36,600lb (16,600kg).
Axle load: 36,500lb (16.5t).
Cylinders: (2) 20 x 28in (508 x 711mm).
Driving wheels: 52in (1,321mm).
Heating surface: 1,717sq ft (160m²).
Superheater: 341sq ft (32m²).
Steam pressure: 200psi (14.1kg/cm²).
Grate area: 28sq ft (2.6m²).
Fuel: (oil) 1,465gall (1,760 US) (6.7m³).
Water: 2,650gall (3,180 US) (12m³).
Adhesive weight: 146,000lb (66t).
Total weight: 250,000lb (113t).
Length overall: 61ft 11¼in (18,879mm).

"Highest and Hardest" wrote Brian Fawcett in *Railways of the Andes*. He was describing the Central Railway of Peru—a line in whose service he spent much of his life—which climbed from sea level near Lima to 15,693ft (4,783m) altitude at the Galera Tunnel, a bare 99 miles (158km) from Lima, en route for the copper mines high up in the mountains. For many years it was said that the necessarily slow passenger service remained invulnerable to air competition, because none of the airlines operating on the Pacific coast had an aircraft which could go as high as the trains!

Most of the climbing, much of it at between 1 in 22 and 1 in 25 (4.5 and 4 per cent), is concentrated in the final 74 miles (118km) to the top; some of the most spectacular engineering in the world takes the trains via six 'Z' double-reversals up to the summit. Oxygen is provided for passengers, but curiously enough steam locomotives become more rather than less efficient as the atmospheric pressure drops. Even so, the task of lifting traffic up this railway staircase was an horrific one and it was only after many years of traumatic experience that a class 2-8-0 was evolved, combining rugged North American design features with the best

British Beyer, Peacock workmanship, which could do the job satisfactorily.

A short boiler was essential because of the heavy grades which meant quick alterations of slope relative to water at each zig-zag. On the other hand a narrow firebox between the wheels was no detriment with oil firing and on such gradients it was an advantage that as many as four out of the five pairs of wheels should be driven. The existence of ample water supplies over the mountain section meant that only a very small quantity

Class 5P5F 4-6-0
Great Britain:
London Midland & Scottish Railway (LMS), 1934

Tractive effort: 25,455lb (11,550kg).
Axle load: 40,700lb (18.5t).
Cylinders: (2) 18½ x 28in (470 x 711mm).
Driving wheels: 72in (1,829mm).
Heating surface: 1,938sq ft (180m²).
Superheater: 307sq ft (28.5m²).
Steam pressure: 225psi (15.8kg/cm²).
Grate area: 28.65sq ft (2.7m²).
Fuel: 20,200lb (9t).
Water: 4,000gall (4,800 US) (18m³).
Adhesive weight: 119,000lb (56t).
Total weight: 285,000lb (129t).
Length overall: 67ft 7¾in (20,618mm).

The Black Fives! Arguably the best buy ever made by any railway anywhere, in respect of engines capable of handling express passenger trains. These legendary locomotives formed not only the most numerous but also the most versatile such class ever to run in Britain.

In spite of being modestly dimensioned mixed-traffic loco-

motives, on many occasions they demonstrated that they could handle and keep time on any express passenger assignment ever scheduled on LMS or ex-LMS lines. In its first months of service during 1934, Cecil J. Allen reported the doings of the prototype on the LMS flag train "Royal Scot", loaded to 15 coaches and 495 tons gross. No.5020 was a last-minute deputy for a "Princess" 4-6-2 or "Royal Scot" 4-6-0, the greater complexities of which made them that much the more liable to fall sick, but the smaller engine kept the "Special Limit" timing to Crewe with the maximum allowed load. Excellent valve events and a well-tried boiler lay behind the surprising qualities of these famous locomotives.

In later years, with "Black Fives" on the route of the "Royal Scot" allocated to sheds at Camden, Willesden, Rugby, Crewe, Warrington, Wigan, Preston, Carnforth, Carlisle, Carstairs and Glasgow, it was a great comfort to the operators to know that so many understudies of similar abilities were waiting in the wings when the *prime donne*

need be carted up the mountain —hence the small tender.

The arrangements for sanding were vital because hideous gradients are usually combined with damp rails. Since both gravity and steam sanding gear had been found wanting, the "Andes" class were fitted with air sanding. The quantity of sand carried was also important and on later versions of the class a vast box on the boiler-top held supplies of this vital element in Andean railroading. It also incorporated the steam dome, thereby keeping the sand warm and dry.

By law, a "counter-pressure" brake had to be fitted, but was not normally used because of the damage that was caused to piston and valve rings when it was used. The double-pipe air braking system used avoids the necessity of releasing the brakes periodically during the descent to re-charge the reservoirs—something that might well lead to a runaway in Andean conditions.

As a locomotive that would need to be driven "wide-open" for hour after hour on the ascent, the "Andes" class was very robustly constructed indeed. That the class gave a satisfactory performance on the world's hardest railway is indicated by the fact that the company came back for more, eight times, no less, between 1935 and 1951. Finally there were 29, numbered 200 to 228. Neighbouring railways had some too—the Southern of Peru (under the same ownership) had 20 with slightly larger driving wheels, while the Cerro de Pasco Railroad (which connected with the Central) had a further five. These latter were the last "straight" steam locomotives to be built by the great firm of Beyer, Peacock.

Alas, no longer does steam rule the mountain section, but the 6-hour timing of the old days has not been improved upon. Maybe a 22mph (35km/h) average speed does not seem much but the ascent certainly justified the inclusion of the daily train over the mountain section amongst the Great Trains of the World. No.206 is preserved at Lima.

Below: *One of the world's hardest-working locos, a Central Railway of Peru "Andes" class 2-8-0 depicted in the company's handsome green livery.*

of the route showed signs of the temperament for which they were traditionally celebrated.

It is fair to say, though, that the LMS four-cylinder 4-6-2s did ride more smoothly at speed. At 90mph (145km/h) downhill it was fairly exciting in the dark (no headlight!) on a "Duchess", but on a "Black Five" it could be called a Total Experience. Another advantage of the bigger engines lay in the much larger ash-pan; whilst No.5020 mentioned above did as well as a 4-6-2 was normally expected to do from. Euston to Crewe, the 4-6-0 could hardly have continued to Glasgow without the fire becoming choked with the end-products of combustion. Of course, the 4-6-2 also had the *potential* of higher power output; but in order to realise the potential either a super-man or more than one fireman had to be carried, and this

Left: *A Stanier "Black Five" 4-6-0 leaves a wayside station in the Scottish Highlands with a local train in tow. North of Perth these versatile locomotives had a near-monopoly of service.*

was not normally the practice.

North of Perth on the Highland lines, "Black Fives" were the heaviest and largest locomotives permitted, and here they handled most trains of significance from the 550-ton "Royal Highlander" downwards. A pair of them, driven wide open, took such trains up the 20-mile ascent (32 km), mostly at 1 in 60 (1.66 per cent), from Inverness to the 1,300ft (400m) summit at Slochd. Steaming was usually rock-steady, the sound magnificent, and the firemen's task proportionately onerous as the tonnage moved over this and other neighbouring inclines.

William Stanier came to the LMS from rival Great Western in 1932. Under his direction, a design for this two-cylinder mixed-traffic 4-6-0 was produced in 1933 as a replacement for numerous ageing medium-sized 4-6-0s of the LMS constituent companies. The concept was derived directly from the "Hall" class of Stanier's native line, but really only the taper-boilers and the axleboxes of the new engine were based on those of the

GWR. Much of the rest seemed to reflect the choice of the best practice from amongst the various areas of the LMS; Lancashire and Yorkshire Railway cylinders, Walschaert's valve-gear and cab, for example; Midland boiler fittings; and Caledonian hooter-type whistle.

London & North Western thinking showed in the arrangements for repair and maintenance of the "Black Five" fleet, which was eventually to number 842 engines and which took eighteen years to build. LMS works at Crewe, Derby and Horwich all contributed with 231, 54 and 130 respectively. Under a pre-war Government scheme to provide work for depressed areas, two outside firms built the remainder; Vulcan Foundry of Newton-le-Willows produced 100 and Armstrong-Whitworth & Co of Newcastle-upon-Tyne 327. Running numbers went from 4758 to 5499, those below 5000 being newer than those above. One hundred more were built under British Railways, the class then being numbered 44658 to 45499. Few changes in design were

found necessary, but earlier engines had less superheat originally than the later ones.

On the last batches numerous experiments were tried, such as roller bearings, rocking grates, double chimneys, Caprotti poppet valves, even outside Stephenson's link motion on one engine; but the only major modification that "took" was the installation of renewable high-manganese steel liners to the axlebox guides. This was successful in increasing considerably the mileage between overhauls.

The "Black Fives" based on Preston were the last steam locomotives to haul timetabled express passenger trains on British Railways. It was as late in the day as January 1967, only 20 months before the end, that No.44917 achieved the highest-ever recorded speed for the class. This was 96mph (155km/h), reached north of Gobowen between Chester and Shrewsbury. Fifteen have been preserved and, of these, four can currently be seen from time to time, either individually or in pairs, on main-line steam specials.

Class A 4-4-2
Chicago, Milwaukee, St. Paul & Pacific Railroad (CMStP&P), 1935 (see fold-out, page 142)

Tractive effort: 30,685lb (13,920kg).
Axle load: 72,500lb (33t).
Cylinders: (2) 19 x 28in (483 x 711mm).
Driving wheels: 84in (2,134mm).
Heating surface: 3,245sq ft (301.5m²).
Superheater: 1,029sq ft (96m²).
Steam pressure: 300psi (21kg/cm²).
Grate area: 69sq ft (6.4m²).
Fuel (oil): 3,300galls (4,000 US) (15m³).
Water: 10,800gall (13,000 US) (49.5m³).
Adhesive weight: 144,500lb (66t).
Total weight: 537,000lb (244t).
Length overall: 88ft 8in (27,026mm).

Class F7 4-6-4
USA:
Chicago, Milwaukee, St. Paul & Pacific Railroad (CMStP&P), 1937

Tractive effort: 50,295lb (22,820kg).
Axle load: 72,250lb (33t).
Cylinders: (2) 23.5 x 30in (597 x 762mm).
Driving wheels: 84in (2,134mm).
Heating surface: 4,166sq ft (387m²).
Superheater: 1,695sq ft (157m²).
Steam pressure: 300psi (21kg/cm²).
Grate area: 96.5sq ft (9.0m²).
Fuel: 50,000lb (22½t).
Water: 16,700gall (20,000 US) (76m³).
Adhesive weight: 216,000lb (98t).
Total weight: 791,000lb (359t).
Length overall: 100ft 0in (30,480mm).

"Fleet of foot was Hiawatha" wrote Longfellow ... Intensive competition for the daytime traffic between Chicago and the Twin Cities of St. Paul and Minneapolis was the inspiration for the "Hiawatha" locomotives and trains, the fastest-ever to be run by steam. Three railroads were involved in the competition; first, there was the Chicago & North Western Railway; this line had a 408½ mile (657km) route which its "400" expresses traversed in 400 minutes. The "400"s were formed of conventional equipment of the day, but specially refurbished and maintained. The Chicago Burlington & Quincy Railroad pioneered some stainless steel lightweight diesel—propelled "Zephyr" trains—fairly noisy in spite of their name—over a route 19 miles (30km) longer than the North-Western one.

Lastly—and to us most importantly—there was the Chicago, Milwaukee, St. Paul and Pacific Railroad, whose management decided to enter the lists with special matching high-speed steam locomotives and trains designed to offer a 6½ hour timing for the 412-mile (663km) route. For the first time in the history of steam locomotion a railway ordered engines intended

Top: *Class "F7" 4-6-4 No.103 towards the end of its days; a forlorn sight after some use as a source of spares.*

Above: *With boiler lagging and driving wheels removed, a class "F7" 4-6-4 awaits the ungainly end.*

for daily operation at 100mph (160km/h) and over.

The American Locomotive Company of Schenectady, New York, responded with two superb oil-fired and brightly coloured streamlined 4-4-2s. They were known as class "A" and received running numbers 1 and 2. In service they earned this prime designation by demonstrating that as runners they had few peers. They could develop more than 3000 horsepower in the cylinders and achieve 110mph (177km/h) on the level. It says enough about that success of these locomotives that they were intended to haul six cars on a 6½-hour schedule, but soon found themselves handling nine cars satisfactorily on a 6¼-hour one. These schedules included five intermediate stops and 15 permanent speed restrictions below 50mph (80km/h).

The design was unusual rather

than unconventional; the tender with one six-wheel and one four-wheel truck, for instance, or the drive on to the leading axle instead of the rear one, were examples. Special efforts were made to ensure that the reciprocating parts were as light as possible—the high boiler pressure was chosen in order to reduce the size of the pistons—and particular care was taken to get the balancing as good as possible with a two-cylinder locomotive. Another class "A" (No.3) was delivered in 1936 and a fourth (No.4) in 1937.

Further high-speed locomotives were ordered in 1938 and this time the six 4-6-4s supplied were both usual *and* conventional. This time also the class designation "F7" and running numbers (100 to 105) were just run-of-the-mill. The 4-4-2s were superb with the streamliners but not at all suited to the haulage of heavy ordinary expresses. This restricted their utilisation; hence the 4-6-4s which combined heavy haulage powers with high-speed capability. The main concession to speed in the design were the big driving wheels, whilst the main concession to general usage was a change back to coal-burning, in line with most Mil-

waukee steam locomotives. This in its turn necessitated a high-speed coal hopper and shoots at New Lisbon station, which enabled an "F7" to be coaled during the 2-minute station stop of the "Hiawatha" expresses there. The "F7"s were also very successful engines, capable of 120 mph (193km/h) and more on

level track with these trains.

Test running showed that such speeds could be maintained with a load of 12 cars, a load of 550 tons, and this makes the feat an even more remarkable one. There are also reports of maximum speeds of 125mph (200km/h) and it is a great pity that these cannot be authenticated, since if true would be world records. One did occur in 1940: a speed-up and re-timing produced the historic fastest start-to-stop run *ever* scheduled with steam power—81¼mph (130km/h) for the 78½ miles (126km) from Sparta to Portage, Wisconsin. This was on the east-bound "Morning Hiawatha", for by now a second daily run in each direction was operated. Also in 1940 came the "Mid-West Hiawatha" from Chicago to Omaha and Sioux Falls and it was to this train that the 4-4-2s gravitated, although one was usually held in reserve against a 4-6-4 failure on the Twin Cities trains.

Dieselisation came gradually; diesel locomotives made their

Above: *In a cloud of coal smoke, and towards the end of its days, a Milwaukee Road class "F7" 4-8-4 sets forth.*

first appearance on the "Hiawatha" trains in 1941, while steam did not finally disappear from the "Twin Cities Hiawatha" until 1946. The 4-4-2s held on two years longer on the Mid-West train. The last of both types were withdrawn—after a period on lesser workings or set aside—in 1951. It is a matter of considerable regret that none of these record-breaking steam locomotives has been preserved, especially now that the whole Milwaukee Road from Chicago to the Pacific is following them into oblivion.

Even so, models and memories keep these wonderful locomotives alive in the minds of those who admired them in their prime.

Below: *A builder's view of the original "F7" class 4-8-4 supplied to the Chicago, Milwaukee, St. Paul & Pacific Railroad in 1938 for working the "Hiawatha" expresses.*

Class F-2a 4-4-4

Canada:
Canadian Pacific Railway (CPR), 1936

Tractive effort: 26,500lb (12,000kg).
Axle load: 61,000lb (28t).
Cylinders: (2) 17¼ x 28in (438 x 711mm).
Driving wheels: 80in (2,032mm).
Heating surface: 2,833sq ft (263m²).
Superheater: 1,100sq ft (102m²).
Steam pressure: 300psi (21kg/cm²).
Grate area: 55.6sq ft (5.2m²).
Fuel: 27,000lb (12t).
Water: 7,000galls (8,400 US) (32m³).
Adhesive weight: 121,000lb (55t).
Total weight: 461,000lb (209t).
Length overall: 81ft 2⅞in (24,762 mm).

In 1936 the Canadian Pacific Railway introduced four trains which were announced as a High-Speed Local Service. In each case the formation consisted of a mail/express (parcels) car, a baggage-buffet and two passenger cars. By North American standards they counted as light-weight, the weight being 200 tons for the four-coach train. Most American railroads would have found some hand-me-down locomotives discarded from first-line passenger service to work them, but that was not the CPR way. They ordered five new 4-4-4 steam locomotives, designated the "Jubilee" type, from the Montreal Locomotive Works to work these trains—although spoken of as streamlined, they are better described as having a few corners nicely rounded. Running numbers were 3000 to 3004.

The new services for which this equipment was ordered comprised the "Chinook" in the West

between Calgary and Edmonton (194 miles—310km—in 315 minutes including 22 stops) and the international "Royal York" between Toronto and Detroit (229 miles—366km—in 335 minutes with 19 stops) and two others between Montreal and Quebec. It was the sort of service for which a home-based British company might field a 100 ton 4-4-0 with perhaps 25sq ft (2.3m²) of grate area, but these "small" 4-4-4s weighed some 90 per cent more than this and had a fire-grate 120 per cent bigger.

Even if it was a case where the trans-Atlantic love of bigness might have been misplaced, the "F-2a"'s were certainly magnificent. They had such sophisticated features as mechanical stokers, feed-water heaters and roller bearings. One feature that was important for operation in Canada was an all-weather insulated cab, able to provide comfortable conditions for the crew in a country where the outside temperature could easily drop to minus 40°F (−40°C), 72 Fahrenheit degrees of frost.

A further series of similar and slightly smaller 4-4-4s, numbered from 2901 to 2929, were built in 1938, designated class "F-1a". The second series was easily recognisable by the drive on to the rear coupled axle, instead of on to the front axle as with the "F-2a". Nos.2928 and 2929 of this later series are preserved at the National Railway Museum at Delson, Quebec, and (currently but with future undecided) at Steamtown, Bellows Falls, Vermont, USA, respectively.

Below: *Class "F2a" 4-4-4 No. 3003 leaves Montreal with a "High-Speed Local Service".*

A4 Class 4-6-2

Great Britain:
London & North Eastern Railway (LNER), 1935 (see fold-out, page 138)

Tractive effort: 35,455lb (16,086kg).
Axle load: 49,500lb (22.5t).
Cylinders: (3) 18½ x 26in (470 x 660mm).
Driving wheels: 80in (2,032mm).
Heating surface: 2,576sq ft (240m²).
Superheater: 749sq ft (70m²).
Steam pressure: 250psi (17.5kg/cm²).
Grate area: 41sq ft (3.8m²).
Fuel: 18,000lb (8t).
Water: 5,000gall (6,000 US) (23m³).
Adhesive weight: 148,000lb (67t).
Total weight: 370,000lb (170t).
Length overall: 71ft 0in (21,647mm).

If British railway enthusiasts were to vote for one express passenger locomotive that they considered to be the best, there is little doubt that this one would be elected. For one thing, it would be difficult to ignore the claims of the all-time holder of the world's speed record for steam locomotives.

The Class "A4" streamlined 4-6-2 came in direct descent from the Class "A1" or "Flying Scotsman" 4-6-2s. The LNER management had taken note of a two-car German diesel train called the "Flying Hamburger" which in 1933 began running between Berlin and Hamburg at an average speed of 77.4mph (124km/h) for the 178 miles (285km). The makers were approached with the idea of having a similar train to run the 268 miles (429km) between London and Newcastle, but after an analysis had been done and the many speed restrictions taken into account the best that could be promised was 63mph (102km/h), that is, 4¼ hours. The train was surprisingly expensive for two cars, as well. On 5 March 1935, standard "A3 4-6-2 (No.2750 *Papyrus*) showed what steam could do by making the run with a six-coach train in 230 minutes, thus demonstrating that a four hour timing was practicable.

In this way was born the concept of a streamlined matching locomotive and train to be called "The Silver Jubilee". The LNER Board authorised the project on 28 March 1935 and the first of the four streamlined locomotives No.2509 *Silver Link* was put into steam on 5 September.

The new train, bristling with innovations, was shown to the press on 27 September. Unkind people might compare this with the recent gestation period of British Railways' celebrated High Speed Train, not dissimilar in appearance, concept and in degree to which it extended beyond the bounds of current performance. This was six *years* not six *months*.

On this press trip the British speed record was broken with a speed of 112½mph (180km/h) at Sandy. The locomotive rode superbly and 25 miles (40km) were

Above: *Preserved "A4" class 4-6-2 No.4498 Sir Nigel Gresley with an enthusiast's train.*

Right: *An "A4" class 4-6-2 bursts from Gas Works tunnel shortly after leaving Kings Cross station, London, for Scotland.*

covered at a speed above 100 mph (160km/h), those aboard being sublimely unconscious of the terror they were inspiring in the lively-sprung articulated carriages behind. Even so, three days later "The Silver Jubilee" went into public service, achieving an instant and remarkable success. In spite of a supplementary fare, the down run at 5.30 p.m. from Kings Cross, with a first stop at Darlington, 232½ miles (374km) in 198 minutes and due at Newcastle 9.30 p.m., was fully booked night after night.

The new locomotives did not bristle with innovations like the trains, but those they had were important. The internal streamlining and enlargement of the steam passages from the regulator valve to the blastpipe made them particularly free-running, while extra firebox volume in the form of a combustion chamber helped steam production. Evocative three-chime whistles gave distinction to the voice of the "A4"s.

The "A4"s were so good that 31 more were built between 1936 and 1938, not only for two more streamline trains ("Coronation" and "West Riding Limited") but also for general service. A few were fitted with double blastpipes and chimneys and it was with one of these (No.4468 *Mallard*) that on 4 July 1938, the world speed record for steam traction was broken with a sustained speed of 125mph (201 km/h), attained down the 1 in 200 (0.5 per cent) of Stoke bank north of Peterborough. Driver Duddington needed full throttle and 45 per cent cut-off and the dynamometer car record indicated that 126mph (203 km/h) was momentarily reached. Equally impressive was an occasion in 1940 when No.4901 *Capercaillie* ran 25 level miles (40km) north of York with 22

coaches (730 tons) at an average speed of 76mph (122km/h).

At first a distinction was made between the original "silver-painted" locomotives, and those in LNER green with bird names for general service, and those in garter blue livery with Empire names for the "Coronation". Also in blue were *Golden Fleece* and *Golden Shuttle* for the "West Riding Limited". By 1938, blue had become the standard colour and very nice it looked—not only on the streamlined trains but also with the varnished teak of ordinary stock.

After the war, during which the "A4"s had to cope with enormous loads and one (No. 4469 *Sir Ralph Wedgwood*) was destroyed in an air raid on York, they were renumbered 1 to 34, later becoming British Railways Nos.60001 to 60034. In the famous locomotive exchange trials of 1948, the "A4"s proved to be substantially the most efficient of all the express engines tested, but their proneness to failure also showed up on three occasions during the trials.

Although by no means the most recent LNER large express

Above: *Class "A4" No.2510 Quicksilver when new in 1935. Note the footplate valences which were later removed.*

passenger locomotives, they were never displaced from prime workings, such as the London to Edinburgh non-stop "Elizabethan", until the diesels came in the early 1960s. The reliability problem—one serious weakness was over-heating of the inside large-end—was resolutely tackled and to a great extent solved.

Since the last "A4" was withdrawn in 1966, six have been preserved—No.4498 *Sir Nigel Gresley*, No.60009 *Union of South Africa* and No.19 *Bittern* privately; No.4468 *Mallard* is in the National Railway Museum, No.60010 *Dominion of Canada* is in the Canadian Railway Museum at Delson, Quebec, and No.60008 *Dwight D. Eisenhower* is in the USA at the Green Bay Railroad Museum, Wisconsin. Nos.4498 and 60009 currently perform on special trains, thereby giving a new generation of rail fans just a hint of what these magnificent locomotives were like in their prime.

Below, left: *London & North Eastern Railway class "A4" 4-6-2* Empire of India *one of the batch built in 1937 to work the "Coronation" express.*

Below: *Class "A4" No.60024* Kingfisher. *The locomotives of this class built ostensibly for "general service" were named after birds.*

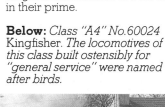

No.10000 4-6-4

Great Britain:
London & North Eastern Railway (LNER), 1930

Axle load: 47,000lb (21.5t).
Cylinders, HP: (2) 10 x 26in (254 x 660mm).
Cylinders, LP: (2) 20 x 26in (508 x 660mm).
Driving wheels: 80in (2,032mm).
Heating surface: 1,986sq ft (184m²).
Superheater: 140sq ft (13m²).
Steam pressure: 450psi (32kg/cm²).
Grate area: 35sq ft (3.25m²).
Fuel: 20,000lb (9t).
Water: 5,000gall (6,000 US) (23m³).
Adhesive weight: 140,000lb (63.5t).
Total weight: 372,000lb (169t).
Length overall: 74ft 5in (22,682mm).

The tale of LNER No.10000, the "hush-hush" locomotive, is the story of a promising experiment which failed. It was mounted in great secrecy—hence the name—and executed with considerable flair and ability but, like so many attempts before and some afterwards, the principles laid down by Stephenson in *Northumbrian* proved in the end to be the victor.

It is a fundamental law of physics that the efficiency of a heat engine is proportional to the ratio between the upper and lower temperatures reached by the "working fluid"—in this case steam—during its working cycle. The upper temperature depends on the working pressure as well as the amount of superheat; if the pressure could be substantially increased, then there would be a gain in efficiency.

Alas, the conventional locomotive-type boiler is not suitable for very high pressure—there are too many flat surfaces, for one thing. Ships and power stations can make steam at higher pressures in various types of boiler made entirely of tubes and drums and Nigel Gresley held discussions with Messrs. Yarrow of Glasgow to see if anything on these lines could be adopted.

A scheme for a four-cylinder compound was evolved, with a five-drum water-tube boiler pressed to double the normal pressure. There was a long steam drum at the top connected to two pairs of lower water drums, by 694 small-diameter water tubes. The two low-pressure outside cylinders and much of the outside motion was standard with the "A1" class 4-6-2s. Two high-pressure inside cylinders were close to the centre-line; their valves were driven by a rocking shaft from the outside Walschaert's gear sets. The rocking shafts had an arrangement designed so that the valve travel of the HP cylinders could be varied independently of the LP ones by a separate control. The locomotive was built at the Darlington shops of the company.

Once teething troubles had been overcome, No.10000 worked from Gateshead shed for several years. Alas, any fundamental saving in coal consumption there may have been was swamped by extra costs of maintenance and loss of heat through small faults in design. Hence it was no surprise when in 1937 the "hush-hush" engine was rebuilt on the lines of an "A4" class streamliner, remaining the sole member of Class "W1" and the only 4-6-4 tender engine to run in Britain.

Below: *The London & North Eastern Railways' "Hush-Hush" high-pressure compound 4-6-4 No.10000 on a test run hauling the company's dynamometer car.*

The A4 Pacifics (see page 136)

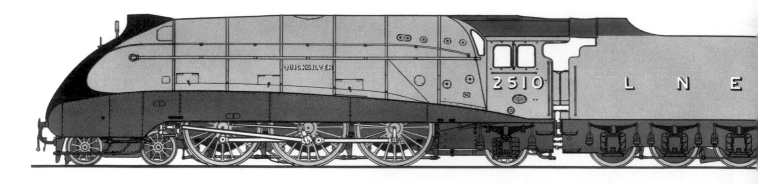

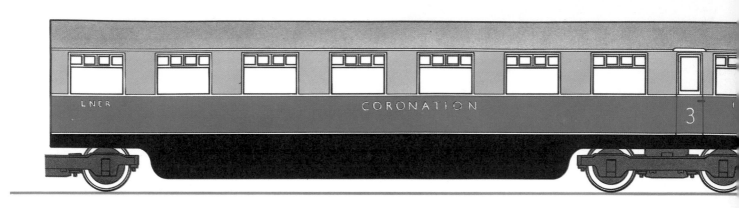

Right: *The A4 Class Dominion of Canada as built in 1937 for the "Coronation" express. Note the Canadian Pacific Railway whistle. A Canadian bell was fitted in 1938 in front of the chimney, but after an occasion when it rang throughout the journey it was made inoperative.*

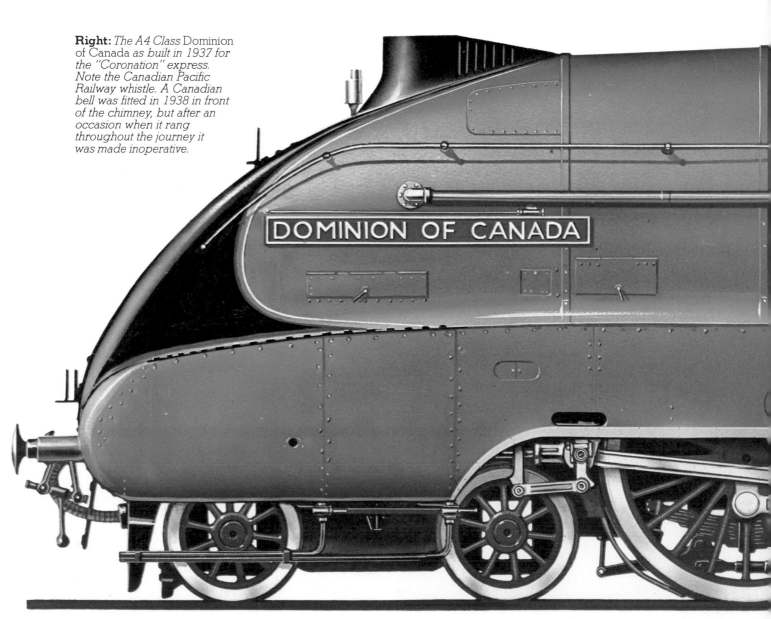

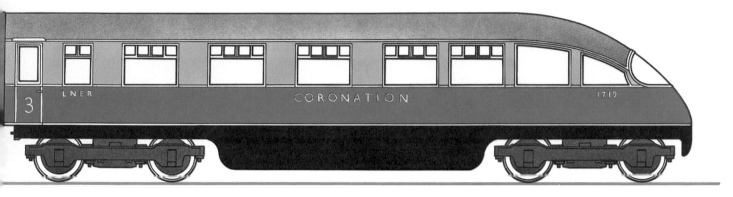

The Milwaukee Hiawathas (see page 134)

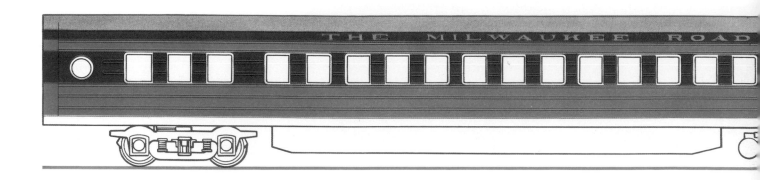

Below: *One of the original Hiawatha "A" Class 4-4-2 locomotives of the Chicago, Milwaukee, St. Paul & Pacific Railroad. These magnificent oil-fired Atlantics were built by the American Locomotive Company, of Schenectady, New York, in 1935 in order to power some matching streamlined high-speed trains between Chicago and the two cities of St. Paul and Minneapolis. The profile of the original cars exactly corresponded with the tender of the locomotive, having plain steel sides without stiffening ribs. The sets of cars with longitudinal ribs as depicted above came four years later, by which time other "Hiawatha" trains on several routes had been introduced. All of them are now just a memory.*

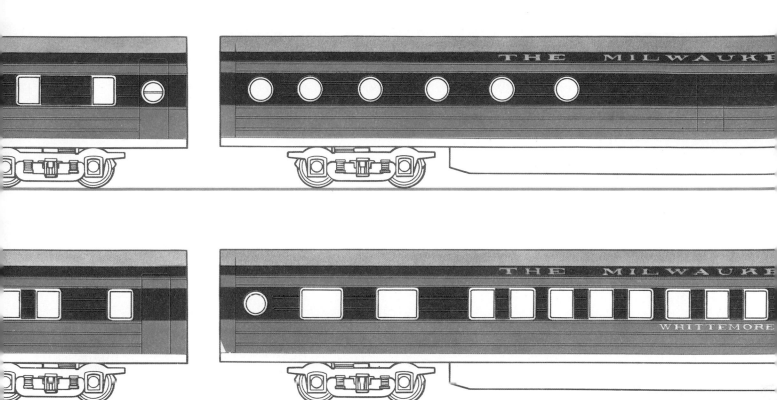

These drawings depict the famous streamlined A4 Class 4-6-2s designed by Sir Nigel Gresley for the London & North Eastern Railway in 1935. On the far left are shown the original silver-grey colours, matching the sets for the "Silver Jubilee" train between London and Newcastle introduced in that year. Near left is shown an example of a batch built in 1936 named after birds and intended for general service, and accordingly finished in the then-standard LNER light green livery. To the right is shown the class as painted medium green in British Railways' days. Below are coaches of the "Coronation" express depicted in the garter-blue colour introduced in 1937. The express ran between London and Edinburgh. A selection of the vehicles which made up the train are shown; the formation was normally as follows: articulated twin brake third class/kitchen third class; articulated twin first class; articulated twin third/kitchen third; articulated twin third/third brake; beavertail observation car.

GOLDEN EAGLE

4482

L N

LNER CORONATION 3 1716

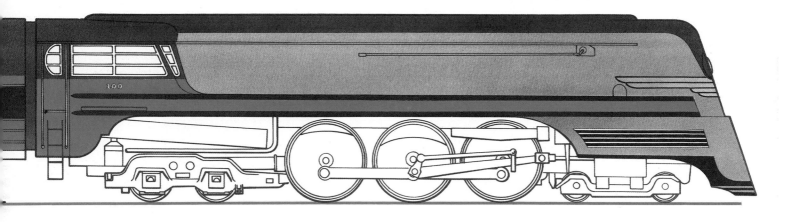

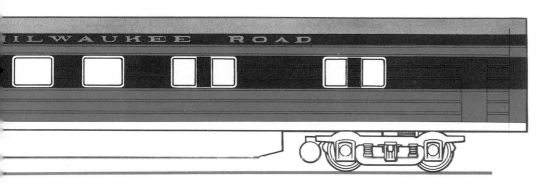

Above: The "Hiawatha" express as running in 1940. These expresses were the fastest scheduled steam trains ever to run, and the drawing shows one of the then-new streamlined "F7" Class 4-6-4s at the head of a typical consist. Next to the engine comes an express-tap car (called a parcels/bar car in Britain), then a day-coach (which would be present in multiple), the dining car, the pullman parlour car and the pullman parlour-observation car.

Class 05 4-6-4
Germany:
German State Railway (DR), 1935

Tractive effort: 32,776lb (14,870kg).
Axle load: 43,000lb (19.5t).
Cylinders: (3) 17¾ x 26in (450 x 660mm).
Driving wheels: 90½in (2,300mm).
Heating surface: 2,750sq ft (256m²).
Superheater: 976sq ft (90m²).
Steam pressure: 284psi (20kg/cm²).
Grate area: 51sq ft (4.71m²).
Fuel: 22,000lb (10t).
Water: 8,200gall (9,870 US) (37m³).
Adhesive weight: 127,000lb (56t).
Total weight: 475,064lb (213t).
Length overall: 86ft 2in (26,265mm).

In 1931 the general speed limit on the German railways was only 62 miles per hour (100km/hr) but in that year the first of the high-speed diesel railcars was introduced, with a maximum speed of 100 miles per hour (160km/hr), and suddenly Germany leapt from a backward position in world rail speed to be the world leader. However, the twin railcars had limited accom-

modation, and their immediate popularity was a challenge to the steam engineers to produce a locomotive which could attain similar speeds when hauling a longer train of conventional coaches. It was calculated that a steam locomotive and train having a seating capacity of 50 per cent more could be built for half

Above: *Class "05" locomotive No.05.001, as built in streamline form, depicted on a run in March 1935 when the speed record for steam was broken.*

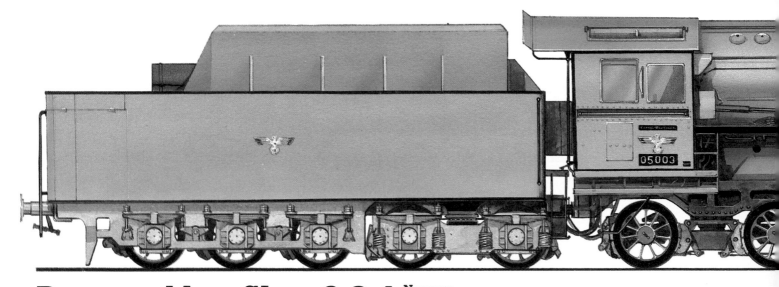

Dovregrubben Class 2-8-4
Norway:
Norwegian State Railways (NSB), 1935

Axle load: 34,000lb (15.5t).
Cylinders, HP: (2) 17½ x 25½in (440 x 650mm).
Cylinders, LP: (2) 25½ x 27½in (650 x 700mm).
Driving wheels: 6¼in (1,530mm).
Heating surface: 2,742sq ft (255m²).
Superheater: 1,092sq ft (101m²).
Steam pressure: 240psi (17kg/cm²).
Grate area: 55.55sq ft (5m²).
Fuel: 18,000lb (8t).
Water: 6,000gall (7,200 US) (27m³).
Adhesive weight: 138,000lb (62.5t).
Total weight: 334,000lb (151.5t).
Length overall: 72ft 2in (22,000mm).

The 2-8-4 was a very unusual wheel arrangement outside the USA but the railways of Norway, a surprisingly small country to be a builder of its own locomotives, made it one of their principal express locomotive types. Norway is a long thin mountainous country measuring 1,150 miles (1,850km) from north to south but only an average of 110 miles (177km) wide. The building of a trunk line up the spine of the country has been in progress for many years, the current terminus being Bodø, 797 miles (1,282km) from Oslo. The southern half of this line, the 345 miles (553km)

Right: *Norwegian State Railways "Dovregrubben" (Dovre Giant) class 2-8-4 locomotive depicted when new.*

the cost of a railcar set.

In 1932, therefore, in accordance with normal German practice, private locomotive builders were invited to submit proposals for a locomotive to haul 250 tons at 93mph (150km/h) in normal service, with the capacity to reach 108mph (175km/h) with this load if required. In the meantime wind tunnel work was conducted at the research establishment at Göttingen to determine the possible benefits of streamlining, and it was found that full streamlining of the engine could reduce by 20 per cent the power required to haul 250t at 93mph.

From the 22 proposals submitted, a scheme by Borsig of Berlin for a 3-cylinder 4-6-4 was selected. The detailed design, produced under the direction of Adolf Wolff, incorporated standard DRG features as far as possible, but the overall concept of a locomotive to develop very high speeds with limited loads called for a boiler larger than those of the existing Pacifics, but with the possibility of a smaller adhesive weight. The 4-6-4 wheel arrangement was chosen because a bogie at each end was

thought necessary for stability at high speed. Aids to high speed included large driving wheels 90½in (2,300mm) diameter, and very large valves and steam passages. For good balance at speed three cylinders were fitted. The boiler pressure of 284psi (20kg/cm²) was the highest so far used on a conventional German locomotive. Special attention was paid to braking, all axles being braked, with two blocks on all wheels except the leading bogie wheels. Tender was also of record size, with five axles and weighing 86 tons fully loaded. The casing enveloped the engine and tender almost down to rail level, and access to the motion was achieved through roller shutters.

Three engines were ordered, two arranged for conventional coal firing, but the third equipped for burning pulverised fuel, and arranged with the cab leading. The first two engines, 05001/2

Below: *Class "05" locomotive No.05.003, originally designed for the burning of pulverised fuel, in shop grey finish after rebuilding in normal form.*

appeared in March and May of 1935, and in their highly-finished red livery they made a great impression. For more than a year they were subjected to intensive testing, partly on the road and partly on the locomotive testing plant at Grunewald. In the most notable of the road tests, on 11th May, 1936, 05002 reached a speed of 124.5mph (199km/h) on the level with a load of 197 ton. On another test run with the 169 ton, a speed of 118mph (189km/h) was maintained for 26 miles (42km), requiring an indicated horsepower of 3409, an exceptional figure at that speed.

In October 1936, 05001/2, working from Hamburg Altona depot, entered regular service on trains FD 23/4 from Hamburg to Berlin and back. For the 178.1 miles (285km) from Hamburg to Berlin Lehrter the time allowed was 144 minutes on the outward journey and 145 on the return, giving average speeds of 74.2 and 73.7mph (118.7 and 117.9 km/h) the normal maximum running speed being 94 mph (150 km/h). These were then the highest speeds by steam in

Europe, although allowing for the gradients, the locomotive work required was no heavier than with the LNER "Silver Jubilee". The engines often demonstrated their ability to recover time lost by engineering works.

The war brought these high-speed schedules to an end, and after a period of use on ordinary trains, the engines were laid aside until 1950, when they were rebuilt by Krauss-Maffei of Munich into non-streamlined engines with new boilers. The experimental pulverised fuel firing on the third engine, 05003, was not successful, and it was rebuilt as a conventional engine in 1944/5, but it saw little service until it too was further rebuilt by Krauss-Maffei in 1950. In their rebuilt form the three engines worked for seven years on the fastest steam workings then in force on Deutsche Bundesbahn, but the tide of electrification then overtook them. 05002/3 were scrapped, but 05001 was restored to its original streamlined condition, and in 1961 it was placed in the German National Railway Museum in Nürnberg.

between Oslo and Trondheim is called the Dovre Railway and it was for this line that these "Dovregrubben" (Dovre Giants) were built.

Messrs. Thune of Oslo built three of these fine locomotives in 1935 and 1936; running numbers were 463 to 465. During the war two more (Nos.470 and 471) were supplied by Krupp of Essen in Germany and later a further two (Nos.472 and 473) were built. They were four cylinder compounds with low-pressure cylinders inside the frames, and high-pressure cylinders outside. A single set of Walschaert's valve

Right: *A Norwegian State Railways "Dovre Giant" 2-8-4 in action on an Oslo to Trondheim express in 1935.*

gear mounted outside each side served both HP and LP cylinders on that side, the higher valves being driven via rocking shafts.

There were a number of features unusual to Norwegian or European practice. Two regulators were provided, one in the dome and one in the "hot" header of the superheater. There were thermic syphons in the firebox and a "Zara" truck (so named after its Italian designer) which connected the front pony wheels and the leading coupled wheels. The cylindrical frameless tender with covered coal bunker alone would make these engines notable, but perhaps the most remarkable thing of all about them is the successful creation of such a powerful machine within so restricted an axle-loading.

Class I-5 4-6-4
United States:
New York, New Haven & Hartford (New Haven), 1937

Tractive effort: 44,000lb (19,960kg).
Axle load: 65,000lb (29.5t).
Cylinders: (2) 22 x 30in (559 x 762mm).
Driving wheels: 80in (2,032mm).
Heating surface: 3,815sq ft (354m²).
Superheater: 1,042sq ft (97m²).
Steam pressure: 285psi (20kg/cm²).
Grate area: 77sq ft (7.2m²).
Fuel: 32,000lb (14.5t).
Water: 15,000gall (18,000 US) (68m³).
Adhesive weight: 193,000lb (87.4t).
Total weight: 698,000lb (317t).
Length overall: 97ft 0¾in (29,585mm).

These handsome engines were the first streamlined 4-6-4s in the USA to be delivered. They were also very much an example to be followed in that firstly, the desire to streamline was not allowed to interfere with access to the machinery for maintenance and secondly, they followed in all essential respects the simple Stephenson concept.

The New Haven Railroad ran the main line from New York to Boston. This was electrified as far as New Haven, leaving 159 miles (256km) of steam railroad from there to the "home of the bean and the cod". Trains such as "The Colonial" or the all-Pullman parlor car express "The Merchants Limited" heavily overtaxed the capacity of the existing class "I-4" Pacifics and, in 1936, after a good deal of research and ex-

Class 16E 4-6-2
South Africa:
South African Railways (SAR), 1935

Tractive effort: 40,596lb (18,414kg).
Axle load: 47,000lb (21.3t).
Cylinders: (2) 24 x 28in (610 x 711mm).
Driving wheels: 72in (1,830mm).
Heating surface: 2,914sq ft (271m²).
Superheater: 592sq ft (55m²).
Steam pressure: 210psi (14.75kg/cm²).
Grate area: 63sq ft (5.8m²).
Fuel: 31,000lb (14t).
Water: 6,000gall (7,200 US) (27m³).
Adhesive weight: 134,000lb (61t).
Total weight: 375,000lb (170t).
Length overall: 71ft 8¼in (21,850mm).

High-speed locomotives are rare in most of Africa. Driving wheels as large as 60in (1,524mm) diameter were exceptional and larger ones were unknown except in the countries bordering the Mediterranean coast. Most of Africa is narrow-gauge country, it is true, but that is no reason for low speeds, provided the track is well aligned and maintained. During the 1930s South African Railways perceived this fact and,

with a view to accelerating such schedules as 30 hours for the 956 miles (1,530km) from Cape Town to Johannesburg (average speed 32mph—51km/h), they ordered five high speed locomotives from Henschel & Son of Kassel, Germany, to be known as class "16E"; running numbers were 854 to 859.

Driving wheel diameter was increased by 20 per cent compared with the "16 DA" class, which previously had handled such crack expresses as the famous "Blue Train". This involved a boiler centre line pitched very high (9ft 3in—2,820mm) above rail level—2.6 times the rail gauge of 3ft 6in (1,067mm). This in its turn made necessary a domeless boiler, steam being collected by pipes with their open end placed as high as possible in the boiler barrel. Aesthetically the effect was most imposing and it all worked well too.

The valve gear was interesting, being more akin to that usually found in motor cars than in steam locomotives. As in nearly all car engines, the "16E" class had poppet valves actuated by rotating cams on camshaft. Naturally there had to be a set of valves at

each end of each cylinder, steam locomotive cylinders being double acting; in addition, since steam engines have to go in both directions without a reversing gearbox, and in order to provide for expansive working, the cams were of some length and coned longitudinally. The camshaft could be moved laterally by the driver, so that the cam followers engaged different cam profiles, and thus caused the poppet valves to open for longer or shorter periods to vary the "cut-off" for expansive working, while a still greater

Above: *South African Railways' "16E" class 4-6-2 No.858 Millie on "Sunset Limited" at Kimberley*

lateral movement reversed the locomotive. The "RC" poppet valve gear gave wonderfully free running and, moreover, its complexities gave little trouble in SAR's competent hands.

On various special occasions (it can now be told) the "16E"'s have shown abilities to reach safely and easily—but illegally according to the SAR rule-book—what by African standards

Left: *During the late 1930s many USA railroads introduced streamlined trains. Here is the Lehigh Valley RR's "Black Diamond".*

periment, ten 4-6-4s were ordered from Baldwin of Philadelphia. Running numbers were 1400 to 1409.

This "I-5" class with disc driving wheels, roller bearings and Walschaert's valve gear went into service in 1937. They certainly met the promise of their designers in that they showed a 65 per cent saving in the cost of maintenance compared with the 4-6-2s they replaced and, moreover, could handle 16-car 1100-ton trains to the same schedules as the Pacific could barely manage with 12.

Another requirement was met in that they proved able to clear the 1 in 140 (0.7 per cent) climb out of Boston to Sharon Heights with a 12-car 840-ton train at 60mph (97km/h). But, alas, the "I-5"s were never able to develop their no doubt formidable high speed capability because of a rigidly enforced 70mph (113 km/h) speed limit. For this reason and because the line was infested

Above: *The New York, New Haven & Hartford Railroad class "I-5" 4-6-4, which was built for running fast trains from New Haven to Boston.*

with speed restrictions, the schedule of the "Merchants Limited" never fell below 171 minutes including two stops, representing an average of 55mph (89km/h). Forty years "progress" and a change from steam to diesel traction since the days of the "I-5"s has only succeeded in reducing this time to 170mins today.

were very high speeds indeed. Alas, these locomotives never had an opportunity to demonstrate their high-speed abilities in normal service. South African Railways—the only railway to *fly* into London's Heathrow Airport —has also operated the national airline since its inception and early on it seemed reasonable to encourage anyone in a hurry to travel by aeroplane. So the rail schedules remained unaccelerated and the five handsome "16E"s remained unduplicated.

Four of the five were withdrawn in the 1960s and 1970s, but one (No.858) named *Millie*, is kept on hand in order to work special trains for steam enthusiasts. These are very much a speciality of SAR and often last for ten days or so, the train being stabled each night while its occupants sleep on board. The run behind this beautiful engine, polished like a piece of jewellery and at speed up to about 70mph (110km/h) is always one of the high spots of the trip.

Right: *A pair of beautifully polished South African "16E" class 4-6-2s handle a special train for steam enthusiasts.*

231-132BT Class 4-6-2 + 2-6-4

Algeria:
Paris, Lyons & Mediterranean Co (PLM), 1937

Tractive effort: 65,960lb (29,920kg).
Axle load: 40,500lb (18.5t).
Cylinders: (4) 19¼ x 26in (490 x 660mm).
Driving wheels: 71in (1,800mm).
Heating surface: 2,794sq ft (260m²).
Superheater: 975sq ft (91m²).
Steam pressure: 284psi (20kg/cm²).
Grate area: 58sq ft (5.4m²).
Fuel: 24,000lb (11t).
Water: 6,600gall (7,900 US) (30m³).
Adhesive weight: 241,000lb (111t).
Total weight: 47,500lb (216t).
Length overall: 96ft 6⅞in (29,432mm).

Should there ever have been a requirement for a reciprocating steam locomotive to emulate the performance of Britain's new diesel-electric HST125 trains, this locomotive of British concept but French execution would be a reasonable starting point.

One day in 1907, an engineer by the name of H.W. Garratt visited a firm of locomotive manufacturers in Manchester called Beyer, Peacock. Garratt was then working as an inspector for goods manufactured in Britain for the New South Wales Government, but he came to discuss with them an idea which he had patented for articulated locomotives built to the same basic format as mobile rail-mounted guns. The main result in due time was some hardware in the form of two little 0-4-4-0 compound locomotives, hinged twice in the middle, for far-off Tasmania.

This Garratt layout consisted of taking two conventional locomotive chassis or engine units, of whatever wheel arrangement was preferred, and using them back-to-back as bogies a certain distance apart. A boiler cradle was then slung between them, tanks and fuel bunkers being mounted on the engine units.

The reason for the Garratt's success when compared with rival types of articulated locomotives such as the "Mallet", was mainly due to the elegance of its geometry. For example, when swinging fast round curves, the boiler and cab unit moved inwards like a bowstring in the bow of the curve, thereby countering an overturning effect of centrifugal force.

Another advantage of the Garratt arrangement was that there was no running gear (so vulnerable to grit) immediately under the fire-grate; just lots of room and plenty of the fresh air so necessary to ensure good combustion. More important, the absence of running gear beneath the boiler gave complete freedom in respect of the design of this important component. Although a Garratt gives the impression of great length and slenderness, in fact, the boiler can be relatively short and fat. For fundamental reasons short fat boilers are considerably lighter and cheaper than long thin ones, for a given steam raising capacity.

Although many were sold for freight and mixed traffic use, the excellent riding qualities of Beyer-Garratts were seldom exploited for express passenger work, until 1927 when a group of 2-6-2+2-6-2s—later altered to 4-6-2+2-6-4s—with 5ft 6in (1,676mm) diameter driving wheels, were built for the 5ft 3in (1,600mm) gauge Brazilian San Paulo Railway. With them 70mph (113km/h) was achieved, with excellent stability. In 1931 the Spanish Central Aragon Railway obtained six 4-6-2+2-6-4s with 5ft 9in (1,753mm) driving wheels, and these were equally satisfactory; these latter locomotives were built by Euskalduna of Bilbao under licence from Beyer, Peacock.

In 1932 the Paris, Lyons & Mediterranean Company ordered an experimental Garratt-type locomotive from the Franco-Belge Company of Raismes, France, for the Algerian lines. This 4-6-2+2-6-4 was successful,

Below: *The magnificent class 231-132BT Beyer-Garratt locomotives built in France for the Algerian railways.*

Class 142 2-8-4

Roumania:
Roumanian State Railways (CFR), 1935

Tractive effort: 44,050lb (19,980kg).
Axle load: 41,000lb (18.5t).
Cylinders: (2) 25.6 x 28.4in (650 x 720mm).
Driving wheels: 76½in (1,940mm).
Heating surface: 3,002sq ft (280m²).
Superheater: 774sq ft (72m²).
Steam pressure: 213psi (15kg/cm²).
Grate area: 51sq ft (4.72m²).
Fuel: see text.
Water: 6,500gall (7,800 US) (29.5m³).
Adhesive weight: 161,000lb (74t).
Total weight: 406,000lb (184t).
Length overall: 74ft 9in (22,784mm).

Another example of a small country building its own express-passenger locomotives, and 2-8-4s to boot, was Roumania. The firms Malaxa and Resita built 58 and 27 respectively between 1936 and 1949. They continued in use until the 1960s. In fact they were copies, built under licence, of the greatest of Austrian steam locomotives, the "214" class. In their home country the history of the class was overshadowed by events; 13 only were built and this unlucky number certainly justified its reputation. First came the German takeover which turned the proud Federal Austrian Railway into a mere division of the German State Railway. Then the war, Russian occupation and finally electrification. All of these traumatically affected the Vienna to Salzburg main line for which the 2-8-4s were built but their cousins in Roumania (called "142"s) flourished and multiplied.

Like so many large locomotives of the time, the genesis of the type lay in a desire to avoid the indignity of double-heading on their owners' principal expresses, in this case between Salzburg and Vienna. Loads had outstripped the haulage capacity of the excellent class "210" 2-6-4s.

A prototype was built in 1931, together with a three-cylinder version for comparative purposes. Poppet valves actuated by oscillating cams driven by Walschaert's valve gear were used, except for one which was fitted with Caprotti gear. The

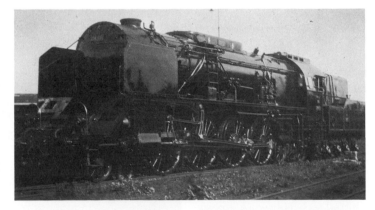

Above: *The Austrian "214" class 2-8-4 locomotives adopted as the standard express locomotive design by Roumania.*

Roumanian copies had the former arrangement, except for a batch which were built in 1939 with Caprotti and later altered to standard.

An unusual feature of these

both at fast running as well as at climbing over the mountains, to a point where further express Garratts of an improved design were ordered. When the PLM lines in Algeria had been amalgamated with the Algerian State Railways (CFAE) an initial order for 10 was later increased to 29 by Algerian Railways (CFA).

Amongst many interesting features of a design which kept wholly to the standard Garratt layout was the Cossart valve gear. This unusual gear drove cam-operated piston valves and enabled the locomotive to use very early cut-offs indeed, in the range of 5 per cent to 7 per cent. If normal valve gears such as Stephenson's or Walschaert's are arranged so they can be linked up to give cut-offs as early as this, it is impossible to arrange the geometry so that the exhaust ports would then open for an adequate fraction of the return stroke. Such a locomotive would experience a checking influence at speed—generally speaking 15 per cent or 17 per cent is the limit

with conventional gears, and any more fully expansive working is not possible. The valve gear was also interesting in that it was operated electrically.

Other equipment included duplicate controls at the rear of the cab for running hind end first, a feed water heater, and a turbofan for ventilating the cab. There were drench pipes to the ashpan and smokebox, a soot blower to clean the boiler tubes on the run, and a recording speedometer. A double chimney and double variable blast-pipe was provided; unusually the two orifices were placed side by side instead of end-on. A coal-pusher assisted in bringing coal forward ready to be fed to the fire. The tanks and bunker were arranged to correspond in shape with the boiler. The ends were streamlined and the result aesthetically most impressive.

On test on the Northern Railway between Calais and Paris, it was found that the engine rode steadily and could develop cylinder horse-power up to 3,000. In

service on the Algiers-Constantine main line, which included gradients as steep as 1 in 38½ (2.6 per cent), the running time for the 288 miles (464km) was reduced from 12½ hours to 8½. Between Algiers and Oran the new timing of 7 hours for the 262 miles (422km) represented an acceleration of 2 hours.

Until the war came to Algeria the express Garratts gave good service but, alas, the electrical valve gear did not stand up to the inevitable neglect when the fighting began. Soon after the war there was an opportunity to dieselise and by 1951 these 30 superb locomotives were out of use.

Perhaps the most interesting point is that, whilst conventional "straight" locomotives in express passenger service have certainly been stretched up to the limit as regards various critical dimensions, the Garratt had still some way to go. Larger wheels could easily be combined with a larger boiler of much greater power output. For example, that hypo-

thetical steam replacement for the HST 125 could have 7ft 6in (2,286mm) driving wheels combined with a 7ft 6in (2,286mm) diameter boiler, all inside the British loading gauge 9ft wide by 13ft high (2,740mm by 3,300mm). A grate-area of 80sq ft. (7.5m²) would make a steady output of 5,000 horsepower in the cylinders feasible. The large space vacant beneath the firebox would provide space for an adequate ashpan to contain the residue left behind when the considerable quantities of coal involved had been burnt. The Da Porta combustion system described in connection with the South Africa class "25" 4-8-4s would be a possibility. A turbo-generator could provide electric power for heating and air-conditioning the present carriages of the HST 125 trains, to which little or no modification would be needed. But, alas, such a magnificent means of locomotion must remain haulage power for the Dreamland Express, and hence live entirely in our imagination.

and other Roumanian locomotives is the coal-plus-oil firing system. The coal fire provides the base supply of steam, while the oil supplement covers periods of exceptional demand.

For many years these imposing locomotives covered their share of Roumania's top express passenger assignments. Very unusually for a small country, Roumania has its own diesel and electric locomotive industry; being dependent on modest production from this source, the change to new forms of motive power was sure rather than fast. Even so, the "142"s had ceased work by the end of the 1960s; No.142.008 is set aside at Bucharest's Grivita depot and 142.072 is displayed at the Resita Locomotive Museum.

Right: *A humble use in this pastoral Roumanian scene for a class "142" 2-8-4 locomotive of the state railway system.*

Duchess Class 4-6-2
Great Britain: London, Midland & Scottish Railway (LMS), 1939

Tractive effort: 40,000lb (18,144kg).
Axle load: 52,500lb (24t).
Cylinders: (4) 16½ x 28in (419 x 711mm).
Driving wheels: 81in (2,057mm).
Heating surface: 2,807sq ft (261m²).
Superheater: 856sq ft (79.5m²).
Steam pressure: 250psi (17.6kg/cm²).
Grate area: 50sq ft (4.6m²).
Fuel: 22,400lb (10t).
Water: 4,000gall (4,800 US) (18m³).
Adhesive weight: 147,500lb (68t).
Total weight: 362,000lb (164t).
Length overall: 73ft 10¼in (22,510mm).

The most powerful steam locomotive ever to run in Britain! This was demonstrated in February 1939, when No.6234 *Duchess of Abercorn* was put to haul a 20-coach 605-ton test train from Crewe to Glasgow and back. An authentic recording of an indicated horse-power of 3,330 was made and this power output from a steam locomotive has never been matched in Britain. It occurred coming south when climbing the 1 in 99 (1.01 per cent) of Beattock bank at a steady speed of 63mph (102 km/h). This feat was, however, a purely academic one, not because of any limitations on the part of the locomotive but because the power developed corresponded to a coal-shovelling rate well beyond the capacity of one man. Two firemen were carried on the occasion of the test run, which certinaly equalled anything achieved later with diesel traction before the recent arrival of the High Speed Train.

It remains a pity that none of the "Duchess" class 4-6-2s were tried with oil firing or mechanical stoking, not so much because a somewhat academic record might then have been pushed higher, but rather that the faster train services which followed diesel-

isation might have been achieved years earlier with steam.

Incidentally, the "Duchess" locomotives were fast runners as well as strong pullers and even held the British rail speed record for a short period, although it was not an occasion for any pride. This was because in order to obtain the 114mph (182km/h) maximum, steam was not shut off until the train was so close to Crewe that the crossovers leading into the platforms and good for only 20mph (32km/h) were taken at nearly 60 (96km/h). Minor damage was done to the track and much to the crockery in the kitchen car, but the train and the newsmen aboard survived. The practical features of the design which saved the day were a credit to the engineers concerned, but this was cancelled out by a typical disdain for theory, which could so easily have established the point at which steam should have been shut off and the brakes applied so that the safety of the train

should not have been endangered.

Completely unshaken by this incident, with the down train, the imperturbable Driver J.T. Clarke using the same locomotive then proceeded to take the party back to London in 119 minutes at an average speed of 79.5mph (127km/h) with several maxima over 90mph (144km/h) and the magic 100 (160) maintained for some distance near Castlethorpe.

Enough has been said to show that the "Duchess" class represented something close to the summit of British locomotive engineering. Simplicity was not the keynote of the design, but sound conventional engineering made these locomotives the success they were. The designer was William Stanier who had come to the LMS from the Great Western Railway in 1932; he was a worthy product of the Churchward tradition and at the age of 52 far from being a young man. He had one great advantage over his predecessors on the LMS—a

Above: *Ex-London Midland & Scottish Railway 4-6-2 No.46236* City of Bradford *on the down "Royal Scot" in the Lune Gorge near Tebay, Lancashire.*

direct line to Lord Stamp, President of the company, who had recruited him personally over lunch at the Athenaeum Club. Previous locomotive engineers had been dictated to even over such details as axleboxes by the operating department of the railway—and then blamed for the consequent failures.

So Stanier was able without interference to initiate design work on an excellent range of standard locomotives; the results took the LMS from a somewhat backward position into an enviable one so far as their locomotive stud was concerned. His first

Below: *No.46251* City of Nottingham *depicted in LMS-style British Railways livery, but with the streamline pattern tender originally attached.*

CITY OF NOTTINGHAM

4-6-2 was the *Princess Royal* which appeared in 1933; her cylinder layout was similar to the Great Western "King" class, except that two more independent sets of Walschaert's valve gear were fitted outside the wheels for the outside cylinders. At first the taper boiler did not steam as well as it should and several quite considerable successive internal alterations had to be made, which were applied new to later "Princess Royal" class locomotives as they came out and retrospectively to those already built. One of these locomotives was the "Turbomotive".

A decision to run a streamlined high-speed express from Euston to Glasgow in 1937 was the opportunity to apply all that had been learnt from the 12 locomotives of the "Princess Royal" class for these 4-6-2s were far larger than anything the LMS had had before. The train and the first of the five new locomotives built for it took the names *Coronation Scot* and *Coronation* respectively.

This time the cylinder layout was moved well away from that of the GWR. The centre lines were inclined upwards at a slope of 1½ degrees, while the outside cylinders were brought forward from the original position in line with the rear bogie wheel. The outside valve gears were made to work the valves of the inside cylinders as well as the outside by rocker arms just to the rear of the outside cylinders. A similar arrangement had been fitted to No.6205 *Princess Victoria*. Both wheel and cylinder diameters were slightly larger on the "Coronation" class than on the "Princess Royal" class. An interesting gadget in the tender was the steam coal-pusher which helped the fireman bring coal forward from the back of the tender when supplies at the front got used up. The boiler was notable for an 11 per cent larger fire grate area and a 133 per cent increase in superheater heating surface, compared with the original *Prin-*

cess Royal*—although subsequent "Princess Royal" class locomotives had bigger superheaters, none were as large as that. Not many people liked the sausage-shaped streamlined shroud that enveloped the locomotive, but the new blue and silver livery was lovely. The other four locomotives were named after members of the royal family —*Queen Elizabeth, Queen Mary, Princess Alice* and *Princess Alexandra*.

The 6½-hour schedule of the "Coronation Scot" from London to Glasgow with only a 270-ton load was not too demanding for these great locomotives but, quite aside from this, they were found to be excellent heavy artillery for general express passenger use on this West Coast main line. Accordingly, a further ten were ordered of which only the first five were streamlined. All ten were named after duchesses (in fact, the whole class is now usually referred to by that name) and it was No.6230 *Duchess of Buccleuch* that first demonstrated how extremely handsome these engines were when unclothed.

More streamlined engines of an order for 20 (named after cities) placed before the war were delivered gradually over the war years 1939-43. After 18 of them had been completed construction continued with non-streamlined examples, and in 1945 instructions were issued for the streamline casings to be

Above: *The second-from-last and considerably modified "Duchess" No.46256 was named* Sir William A Stanier FRS *in honour of her designer.*

Below: *In London Midland & Scottish Railway days and as originally built in streamline form, No.6225* Duchess of Gloucester *passes Rugby.*

removed from locomotives fitted with it. This was not completed until 1949 by which time the last and 38th "Duchess" (No.6257 *City of Salford*) had been complete for a twelve-month.

The success of the class is measured by the minimal number of changes that were made over their years of service from 1937, until electric and diesel locomotives took over in 1964. Nos.6256 and 6257 had some modification, but these were more in the nature of experiments than cures for recognised ills. In contrast, the number of livery changes were legion—blue and gold

streamline, standard LMS maroon, maroon and gold streamline, plain wartime black, lined post-war black, experimental gray, BR dark blue, BR medium blue, BR green and finally LMS maroon with BR insignia as shown in the painting below.

Three have been preserved— No.6229 *Duchess of Hamilton*, in charge of the National Railway Museum, and currently restored to main line running condition; No.6233 *Duchess of Sutherland* in Alan Bloom's collection at Bressingham, near Diss, and No. 6235 *City of Birmingham* in the Birmingham Science Museum.

Class GS-4 4-8-4
United States:
Southern Pacific Railroad (SP), 1941

Tractive effort: 71,173lb (32,285kg).
Axle load: 68,925lb (31.25t).
Cylinders: (2) 25½ x 32in (648 x 813mm).
Driving wheels: 80in (2,032mm).
Heating surface: 4,887sq ft (454m²).
Superheater: 2,086sq ft (194m²).
Steam pressure: 300psi (21.1kg/cm²).
Grate area: 90.4sq ft (8.4m²).
Fuel (oil): 4,900galls (5,900 US) (22.3m³).
Water: 19,600gall (23,500 US) (89mm³).
Adhesive weight: 276,000lb (125.5t).
Total weight: 883,000lb (400.5t).

Above: Southern Pacific's tough-haulage class "GS-4" 4-8-4 No. 4456 at San Francisco, California, in May 1952.

The "Daylight" express of the Southern Pacific Railroad was the third of three famous train services worked by matching streamlined express locomotives and coaches over a similar distance. The "Hiawatha" trains of the Milwaukee line between Chicago and the Twin Cities and the "Coronation" of the British London & North Eastern Railway between London and Edinburgh have been noticed elsewhere. Each of the three trains introduced new standards of speed, comfort and decor, and each train was spectacularly successful in attracting new traffic.

The 470-mile route between Los Angeles and San Francisco was much the hardest as well as the longest of the three. For example, there was nothing on either of the other lines to compare with the 1 in 45 (2.2 per cent) gradient of Santa Margarita Hill, north of San Luis Obispo. The "light-weight" 12-car "Daylight" express weighed 568 tonnes, nearly double the weight of the British train—though it must be said that as regards weight hauled per passenger carried, the latter came out at 15 per cent less than the former.

Because of the severe curvature of the line as well as the heavy gradients the 48.5mph (78km/h) average speed of the "Daylight" train was considerably less than that of the other two, although

the lessening of running times represented by all three of the new trains were roughly even. The gradients encountered by the "Daylight" nicely balanced out with the "Hiawatha" faster running, but certainly the "Daylight" was a far tougher haulage proposition than the British train. The motive power provided reflected this.

Eight-coupled wheels were needed and enabled the resulting "Daylight" 4-8-4 to have (with booster) 124 per cent more tractive effort than the LNER "A4" 4-6-2. As regards grate area, that is, the size of the fire, the increase was 119 per cent. The SP already had fourteen 4-8-4s (class "GS-1"), which came from Baldwin of Philadelphia in 1930. As with the LNER's but unlike the Milwaukee's, the SP's new locomotives (class "GS-2") were from a mechanical point of view based very closely on their immediate predecessors. Of course, the decor was something else again and it gave these four black, silver and gold monsters from the Lima Locomotive Works of Lima, Ohio, an appearance which could hardly be described as less than superb.

Like so many large North American locomotives of the time, the success of the "Daylight" type was due to the application of the excellent standard of US practice of the day. Amongst a

few special features worth recording was one that has almost no steam traction parallel elsewhere, that is the provision of electro-pneumatic brake equipment. With other forms of traction, the electro-pneumatic brake is commonplace today, especially for multiple-units. Application of the brakes on a normal air-brake system relies on a pressure change travelling down the brake pipe from the locomotive to switch on the brakes under each successive car. This involves a flow of air towards the driver's brake-valve and in consequence a delay of several seconds occurs before the brakes are applied to the wheels of the rear car. In contrast, with EP braking the signal to apply the brakes goes down the train with the speed of electric current. The thinking was that these few seconds—during which the train would travel several hundred feet—might in the case of a high-speed service be the difference between an incident and a disaster.

The curvature of the route was recognised by the provision of spring-controlled side-play on the leading coupled axle. In this way the wheels could "move-over" on a curve and allow the flange force to be shared between the two leading axles, with benefits to the wear of both rails and tyres. The hilliness of the line gave rise to a series of water

sprays to cool the tyres on engine and tender wheels during braking on the long descents. Air sanding gear was provided, fed from a tank under that boiler-top casing, which held a full *ton* of sand! With booster cut in, the "GS"s could manage the standard "Daylight" consist on the 1 in 45 grades (2.2 per cent); but if any extra cars were attached a helper was needed.

Although the "Daylight" type held to the simple and world-standard concept of a two-cylinder locomotive with outside valve gear, the host of equipment provided did add a certain complexity. There were three turbo-generators, for example, and a feed-water heater and pump as well as injectors. It must be said that virtually all of this complication was made up of items of proprietary equipment each of which, as it were, came in a box and could be bolted on. Such fittings were apt to work well because competition kept the suppliers

Below: One of the original batch (class "GS-2") of Southern Pacific's "Daylight" 4-8-4s as delivered from the Lima Locomotive Works, Ohio, in 1937.

on their toes; and if problems arose a replacement could be fitted quickly. Even so, an electro-magnetic gadget—inside the boiler!—which sensed foaming and opened the blow-down cocks automatically, did not last.

Like most SP steam locomotives, the "Daylight"'s were fired with oil—indeed, SP were the United States' pioneers in this area—economy being achieved with a device called a "locomotive valve pilot" which indicated to the engineer what cut-off he should set to suit any particular speed and conditions of working.

Streamlined trains, worked by further batches of these magnificently-equipped locomotives, spread to all parts of SP's system and thus served such far distant places as Portland in Oregon, Ogden in Utah and New Orleans. Details of the 60 locos were as shown in the table.

The War Production Board refused to sanction the "GS-6" batch, but on being told that "GS" now stood for "General Service" rather than "Golden State", they accepted the proposal. Of an order for 16, six went to Western Pacific Railroad.

The first "GS" to be withdrawn was No.4462 in 1954 and in October 1958 No.4460 (now displayed at the Museum of Transportation at St. Louis, Missouri) brought SP steam operations to a close with a special excursion from Oakland to Reno, Nevada. No.4449 also survived to haul the "Freedom Train" several thousands of miles across the USA in connection with the bi-centennial of independence in 1976. The locomotive is still able to run and has recently been restored to the original superb "Daylight" colours.

Designation	Date	Running Nos	Features
GS-2	1937	4410 to 4415	Driving wheels 73½in (1,867mm) dia instead of 80in (2,032mm)
GS-3	1937	4416 to 4429	
GS-4	1941-2	4430 to 4457	Fully enclosed cabs began with this batch
GS-5	1942	4458 to 4459	As GS-4 but with roller bearings
GS-6	1943	4460 to 4469	No streamlining—plain black

Top: *Southern Pacific's "Daylight" express from Los Angeles to Chicago being pulled at speed behind a class "GS" 4-8-4, which was originally built to haul this particular train.*

Above: *Southern Pacific unstreamlined class "GS-6" 4-8-4 at Dunsmuir, California, with the "Klamath" express in June 1952.*

Royal Hudson Class 4-6-4

Canada:
Canadian Pacific Railway (CPR), 1937

Tractive effort: 45,300lb (20,548kg).
Axle load: 65,000lb (29.5t).
Cylinders: (2) 22 x 30in (559 x 762mm).
Driving wheels: 75in (1,905mm).
Heating surface: 3,791sq ft (352m²).
Superheater: 1,542sq ft (143m²).
Steam pressure: 275psi (19.3kg/cm²).
Grate area: 81sq ft (7.5m²).
Fuel: 47,000lb (21t).
Water: 12,000gall (14,400 US) (54.6m³).
Adhesive weight: 194,000lb (88t).
Total weight: 659,000lb (299t)..
Length overall: 90ft 10in (27,686mm).

To be both Royal and North American is almost a contradiction in terms but, forty years ago, the Canadian Pacific Railway was as much British as it was Canadian. It had been incorporated by an Act of the British Parliament, and its east-most terminal was situated at Southampton, England. It was here in 1939 that King George VI and Queen Elizabeth set sail in the Canadian Pacific liner *Empress of Britain* for a tour of their largest Dominion. Once ashore, their home for much of the visit was a Royal train, at the head of which was a new 4-6-4, No.2850, specially turned out in royal blue and silver with stainless steel boiler cladding. The royal arms were painted on the tender and a replica crown was mounted on the running board skirt just ahead of the cylinders; later this crown was affixed to all 45 of CPR's famous 4-6-4s built between 1937 and 1945.

The genesis of these fine locomotives lay in a wish to improve upon the class "G-3" 4-6-2s which before 1931 had been the top-line power of the system, by increasing their steam-raising capacity a substantial amount. A fire-grate 23 per cent larger was possible if the 4-6-4 wheel arrangement was adopted and the boilers of the new locomotives were based on this. But in other

ways, such as tractive effort or adhesive weight, the new locomotives were little different to the old. Their class designation was H-1 and the running numbers were 2800 to 2819.

The boilers had large superheaters and combustion chambers (the latter an addition to the firebox volume, provided by recessing the firebox tubeplate into the barrel), as well as front-end throttles which worked on the hot side of the superheater. This enabled superheated steam to be fed to the various auxiliaries. There were arch tubes in the firebox and, necessary with a grate of this size, a mechanical stoker.

The first effect of the new locomotives was to reduce the

number of engine changes needed to cross Canada, from fourteen to nine. The longest stage was 820 miles (1,320km) from Fort William, Ontario, to Winnipeg, Manitoba; experimentally a 4-6-4 had run 1,252 miles (2,015km) between Fort William and Calgary, Alberta, without change.

For five hectic months in 1931 the afternoon CPR train from Toronto to Montreal, called the "Royal York" became the world's fastest scheduled train, by virtue of a timing of 108 minutes for the 124 miles (200km) from Smith's Falls to Montreal West, an average speed of 68.9mph (111km/h). The record was wrested from the Great Western Railway of England, whose "Cheltenham

Flyer" then had a timing of 70min for the 77¼ miles (124km), an average speed of 66.3mph. The 4-6-4s were normally assigned to this train. Subsequently the GWR dropped 3 minutes from their timing and took back the record.

An interesting feature, later provided on one of the "H-1"s, was a booster engine working on the trailing truck. One of the problems of a 4-6-4 was that only six out of 14 wheels were driven; this was no detriment while running at speed but starting was sometimes affected by the limited

Below: *Ex-Canadian Pacific "Royal Hudson" class No.2860 progresses gently along the shore of Howe Sound, B.C.*

adhesion. The extra 12,000lb (5,443kg) of tractive effort provided by the booster came in very handy; the mechanism cut out automatically at 20mph (32km/h).

The 1930s were the period when streamlining was in fashion but when the time came to order some more 4-6-4s, H.B. Bowen, the CPR Chief of Motive Power, decided to compromise. He came to the conclusion that the shrouds which enveloped many contemporary designs made the mechanism inaccessible to an extent which smothered any savings attributable to reduced air resistance. On the other hand, he accepted that the public liked their trains hauled by locomotives which were a little easier on the eye than was then customary.

The result in 1937 was another batch of 30 Hudson type, Nos. 2820 to 2849 designated "H-1c", (the earlier ones had been delivered in two batches of ten, "H-1a" and "H-1b") which had not only softer lines but also sported a superb coloured livery, as our artist has tried to show. Very few mechanical changes needed to be made—although there were certain improvements or changes such as power-operated reversing gear, domeless boilers and a one-piece cast locomotive frame, while boosters were fitted to five of the locomotives. A further ten 4-6-4s, designated "H-1d" were delivered in 1938, while the last batch of five ("H-1e"), Nos.2860 to 2864 of 1940, differed from the others in being oil burners. All the "H-1e"s and five of the "H-1d"s had boosters.

The last batch of 4-6-4s were intended to operate in the far west, between Vancouver and Revelstoke, British Columbia, where oil firing had been the rule for many years. After the war, when the big Canadian oil fields were being exploited, all the "H-1"s operating over the prairies were also converted. This was made easier by the fact that it was customary to allocate a particular locomotive to a particular depot

Above: *A head-on view of 4-6-4 No.2860 as preserved and now running on the British Columbia Railway.*

when they were built and they would then remain there for many years. This unusually stable approach to locomotive allocation also allowed the booster-fitted locomotives to be rostered for sections of line where their extra push was needed. For example, booster fitted "H-1c"s allocated to Toronto could take the 18-car 1,300-ton "Dominion" express up the Neys Hill incline on Lake Superior's north shore unassisted with booster in operation; otherwise a helper engine would have

been an obvious necessity.

Like other lines which had excellent steam power, well maintained and skilfully operated, the Canadian Pacific Railway was in no hurry to dieselise and, in fact, it was not until 1956 that the first 4-6-4 was scrapped. By mid-1960 all were out of service, but five have survived the scrap-men's torches. Standard Hudson No. 2816 is (at the time of writing) at Steamtown, Bellows Falls, Vermont, USA. Of the "Royal Hudson" types, No.2839 has recently been seen in operation in the USA on the Southern Railway, a line which regularly operates special steam trains for enthusiasts. No.2850 is in the Canadian

Railway Museum at Delson, Quebec, No.2858 is on display at the National Museum of Science and Technology at Ottawa and, most famous of all, No.2860 works regular tourist trains on the British Columbia Railway between Vancouver and Squamish. No.2860 has visited Eastern Canada as well as steaming south as far as Los Angeles, hauling a show train intended to publicise the beauties of British Columbia.

Below: *The beautiful red livery of preserved 4-6-4 No. 2860 was basically the same as used on these engines in Canadian Pacific Railway days.*

Class U-4 4-8-4 Canada: Canadian National Railways (CN), 1936

Tractive effort: 52,457lb (23,794kg).
Axle load: 59,500lb (27t).
Cylinders: (2) 24 x 30in (610 x 762mm).
Driving wheels: 77in (1,956mm).
Heating surface: 3,861sq ft (322.5m²).
Superheater: 1,530sq ft (142m²).
Steam pressure: 275psi (19.5kg/cm²).
Grate area: 73.7sq ft (6.8m²).
Fuel: 40,000lb (18t).
Water: 11,700gall (14,000 US) (35m³).
Adhesive weight: 236,000lb (107t).
Total weight: 660,000lb (300t).
Length overall: 95ft 1in (28,990mm).

During the steam age the longest railway in America was not located in the USA, for Canadian National Railways held the title. Around 60 years ago Canada suffered from the sort of railway problems that the United States is in the throes of now and the Govern-ment had perforce to take over 24,000 miles of bankrupt lines. The task ahead was formidable and one of the most remarkable railwaymen of all time was engaged to take charge. This was Sir Henry Thornton, who had learnt his trade on the Pennsylvania Railroad and its notorious subsidiary, the Long Island Railroad. In 1914 he was appointed general manager of the British Great Eastern Railway. During World War I he became a brigadier-general in charge of rail movement in France, and received a knighthood.

It was a far cry from 0-6-2 tanks on Thornton's famous jazz service which so much eased the lot of commuters homeward bound from London's Liverpool Street station, to the Trans-Canada Limited running 2,985 miles (4,776km) across a great continent, but he took it in his stride. Adequate tools for the job was very much a Thornton principle. It should, therefore, have been no surprise that CN was right in the vanguard of roads in ordering that ultimate of passenger types, the 4-8-4.

The Canadian Locomotive Company delivered No.6100—named *Confederation* to celebrate the 60th anniversary of the Canadian Confederation—just seven months after Northern Pacific received its 4-8-4s. By the end of the year, CN and its US subsidiary Grand Trunk Western, had a fleet totalling 52 of these great machines. This made CN by far the greatest 4-8-4 owner in the world, a position which was retained until the USSR took the lead in the mid-1950s. Running numbers were 6100-39 and 6300-11, classes "U2" and "U3", for CN and GTW respectively.

Further batches, generally similar, built in 1929 and 1936 brought the numbers up to 77 and then in 1936-38 a high-speed streamline version was built. This "U-4" class, the subject of the dimensions given on this page, had larger driving wheels and a less than typically ugly shroud, but was also very much the same locomotive basically. Running numbers were 6400-4 (CN) and 6405-11 (GTW).

Yet more standard 4-8-4s followed in 1940 and 1944 until finally the total reached 203. All the CN locomotives were built in Canada either by the Montreal Locomotive Works or by the Canadian Locomotive Company also of Montreal, while (no doubt because of import duties) those for GTW were built by US builders.

It is no disparagement to say that the CN engineers were not keen on innovation, and so the class was very much the standard North American product. CN's trade marks were the cylindrical Vanderbilt tenders and, on those built up to 1936, a prominent transverse feed-water heater placed just in front of the chimney. Naturally, such improvements as roller bearings and cast-steel locomotive frames were adopted as they became available.

One locomotive (No.6184) was

Right: *No.6218, a fine specimen of CN's class "U-2".*

Class U1-f 4-8-2 Canada: Canadian National Railways (CN), 1944

Tractive effort: 52,500lb (23,814kg).
Axle load: 59,500lb (27t).
Cylinders: (2) 24 x 30in (610 x 762mm).
Driving wheels: 73in (1,854mm).
Heating surface: 3,584sq ft (333m²).
Superheater: 1,570sq ft (146m²).
Steam pressure: 260psi (18.3kg/cm²).
Grate area: 70.2sq ft (6.6m²).
Fuel: 40,000lb (18t).
Water: 11,500gall (9,740 US) (53m³).
Adhesive weight: 237,000lb (107.5t).
Total weight: 638,000lb (290t).
Length overall: 93ft 3in (28,426mm).

It was in 1923, very soon after the formation of Canadian National Railways, that eight-coupled locomotives were first introduced into passenger service there. This was the original "U1-a" a batch consisting of 16 locos, built by the Canadian Locomotive Company. Then 1924 and 1925 brought the "U1-b" and "U1-c" batches of 21 and five from Canadian and from Baldwin respectively. The latter were for CN's Grand Trunk Western subsidiary in the USA. In 1929 and 1930 there followed five "U1-d" and 12 "U1-e" from Canadian and from the Montreal locomotive works.

Thus in seven years, fifty-nine 4-8-2s, numbered from 6000 to 6058, became available, although by now the class had become overshadowed by the 4-8-4s introduced in 1927, described on this page. There were also four 4-8-2s acquired by the Central Vermont

tried with poppet valves and in later years when Canada struck oil, many 4-8-4s changed over to that method of firing. Withdrawals began on a small scale in 1955 and grew slowly until the final holocaust of the last 159 took place in 1960. The sadness felt by Canadian railwaymen at the 4-8-4s departure from the scene is well expressed by Anthony Clegg and Ray Corley, in their excellent book *Canadian National Steam Power*, by quoting the following verse chalked on a withdrawn 4-8-4:

"In days gone by this junk pile now
Was a grand sight to behold
On threads of steel it dashed along
Like a Knight in armour bold...."

For a period Canadian National operated certain 4-8-4s in excursion service. This is now finished, but eight have survived; two, including streamliner No. 6400, are on display at Ottawa in the National Museum of Science and Technology.

Railway, another CN subsidiary but one which did not then number or classify its locos as part of the main CN fleet. It did use the CN method of classification, though, so these 4-8-2s were also Class "U1-a". In fact they were rather different in design, having been acquired from amongst a flood of 4-8-2s which the Florida East Coast Railroad had ordered but found itself unable to pay for.

The 6000s performed with *élan* on the then highly competitive express trains between Montreal and Toronto; speeds up to 82mph (131km/h) have been noted with 700 tons or so. Later, the same engines operated well in pool

Left: *Canadian National Railways class "U1-f" 4-8-2 No.6060 depicted in mint condition as delivered.*

service in conjunction with Canadian Pacific.

In 1944, a further twenty 4-8-2s were delivered from Montreal, of the "U1-f" batch illustrated here. They were brought up to date by having cast-steel locomotive frames, disc wheels and other improvements. Some were oil-burners and all had Vanderbilt cylindrical tenders and outside bearings on the leading bogies. Most significant was a major simplification consisting of the replacement of the boiler feed pump and feed-water heater, by a device called an exhaust steam injector. Injectors are usually tucked away tidily under the side of the cab but in this case the device was hung outside the driving wheels, the large pipe which supplied the exhaust steam adding to its conspicuousness.

Like other injectors but more

so, exhaust steam injectors are remarkable conjuring tricks in the application of natural laws. It is difficult to believe that exhaust steam at, say 10psi (0.7kg/cm²) could force water into a boiler containing steam and water almost 30 times that pressure. However, an arrangement of cones turns a high velocity jet of low pressure steam into a low velocity high-pressure flow of water, which has no difficulty in forcing its way past the non-return clack valves into the boiler.

With just a few exceptions, CN steam locomotives were totally utilitarian, but with these excellent engines, efforts were made to make them good looking too. Side valences, a flanged British-style smokestack, green and black livery, brass numbers and placing the dome and sand container in the same box all contributed to

the clean lines. The result is so good that one can almost forgive the designers that bullet nose to the smokebox!

Canadian National is amongst that superior class of railway administrations who offer steam for pleasure, as exampled by the fact that a total of six of these locomotives are preserved. No. 6060 of class "U1-f" does the honours and in addition No.6069 is displayed at Bayview Park, Sarnia and No.6077 at Capreol, Ontario. Of the elder CN Mountains, No.6015 is at the Museum at Delson, Quebec, No.6039 (Grand Trunk Western) was at Steamtown, Bellows Falls, Vermont, and No.6043 at Assinboine Park, Winnipeg.

Below: *Canadian National Railways class "U1-f" 4-8-2 as originally built in 1944.*

V2 Class 2-6-2
Great Britain:
London and North Eastern Railway (LNER), 1936

Tractive effort: 33,730lb (15,304kg).
Axle load: 49,500lb (22.5t).
Cylinders: (3) 18½ x 26in (470 x 660mm).
Driving wheels: 74in (1,880mm).
Heating surface: 2,431sq ft (225.8m²).
Superheater: 680sq ft (63.2m²).
Steam pressure: 220psi (15.5kg/cm²).
Grate area: 41.25sq ft (3.86m²).
Fuel: 17,000lb (8t).
Water: 4,200gall (5,040 US) (19m³).
Adhesive weight: 146,000lb (66t).
Total weight: 323,000lb (146.5t).
Length overall: 66ft 5in (20,244mm).

These remarkable locomotives were a sympton of the trend apparent during the 1930s for producing all-purpose locomotives. Because the diameter of the wheels had to be a compro-mise between those previously thought right for freight trains and those appropriate for pas-senger trains, at full speed they had to turn faster. A better understanding of the best way to balance the reciprocating parts, excellent valve gears to get the steam in and out of the cylinders quickly enough and (in this case) the use of more than two cylinders helped to make this feasible.

In June 1936 the first of Sir Nigel Gresley's (he was knighted that very year) famous "V2" 2-6-2s appeared from Doncaster Works. It was to be the master designer's last major class, for he died in 1941.

The locomotive was named *Green Arrow* after a system of registering freight consignments — from a single packing case to a train-load — just introduced at the time and it was finished in the apple-green passenger livery of the company. Before war broke out the class numbered 86; sub-sequent building brought the total up to 184. Only a few had names but (with reason) they came to be known (in LNER territory) as the "engines that won the war". In order of con-struction, their running numbers were 4771-4898, 3653-64, 4899, 3641-3654, 3665-3695. After the war they became (more sensibly) 800 to 983 and in BR days 60800-60983.

As one might have expected with a fire-grate sensibly the same in size, the V2s were vir-tually as good as the 4-6-2s when it came to express passenger work. A V2 was noted running at 93mph (149km/hr) on the "York-shire Pullman". Express fully-braked freight trains were the class's speciality and these en-gines could manage over 60mph on the level on such trains as the famous "Scotch Goods" (sic) with 600 tons. On occasion, they were pressed into service on the streamliners and no difficulty was found in keeping time, while wartime trains of up to 25 packed carriages were also well within their capabilities.

On the debit side was the fact that whilst the V2s were general-purpose locomotives in the sense that they could haul anything, they were by no means go-anywhere locomotives. An axle-load as heavy as 22 tons meant that only some 40 out of every 100 miles of the LNER system was open to them. Indeed two prototypes of a miniaturised ver-sion (class "V4") appeared in 1941 to fill this gap, but Gresley's successor had other ideas and no more were built.

Two other question marks hung over details of the class; the Gresley conjugated valve gear

Right: *Preserved ex-LNER "V2" class 2-6-2 No. 4771* Green Arrow *at the Birmingham Railway Museum depot.*

Below: *The apple green LNER "V2" or "Green Arrow" class 2-6-2, completed in 1936.*

Class E4 4-6-4
United States:
Chicago and North Western Railway (C&NW), 1938

Tractive effort: 55,000lb (24,798kg).
Axle load: 72,000lb (32.7t).
Cylinders: (2) 25 x 29in (635 x 737mm).
Driving wheels: 84in (2,134mm).
Heating surface: 3,958sq ft (368mm²).
Superheater: 1,884sq ft (175m²).
Steam pressure: 300psi (21kg/cm²).
Grate area: 90.7sq ft (8.4m²).
Fuel (oil): 5,000gall (6,000 US) (22.7m³).
Water: 16,500gall (20,000 US) (75.5m³).
Adhesive weight: 216,000lb (98t).
Total weight: 791,500lb (359t).
Length overall: 101ft 9¾in (31,033mm).

These handsome locomotives of advanced design have the un-happy distinction of being the first to be superseded by the diesel-electric locomotive from the job for which they were built. The Chicago & North Western Railway had its own way of doing things; not for nothing did its trains run on the left-hand track, whereas most North American trains take the right. When, in 1935, the gloves came off for the fight between the Milwaukee, Burlington and C&NW com-panies for the daytime traffic between Chicago and the twin cities of St Paul and Minneapolis, the last-named was first into the ring with the famous "400" trains —named because they ran (about) 400 miles in 400 minutes. The C&NW stole this march over their competitors by running

which worked the valves of the middle cylinder was one which has already been mentioned in connection with other LNER locomotives. The other query has also been referred to elsewhere; this was the usual one associated with the 2-6-2 wheel arrangement, viz the tracking qualities of the leading pony truck. All went well until 1946, when two derailments on wartime quality permanent way took place. After investigation the original swing-link self-centring suspension of the leading pony truck was replaced by a side control system which used transverse springing and no further trouble was experienced.

These matters apart, the V2s were superb engines and the last one was not withdrawn until late 1966 when the class was finally overtaken by dieselisation. Happily, the original *Green Arrow* has been preserved and is now restored to working order as part of the national collection.

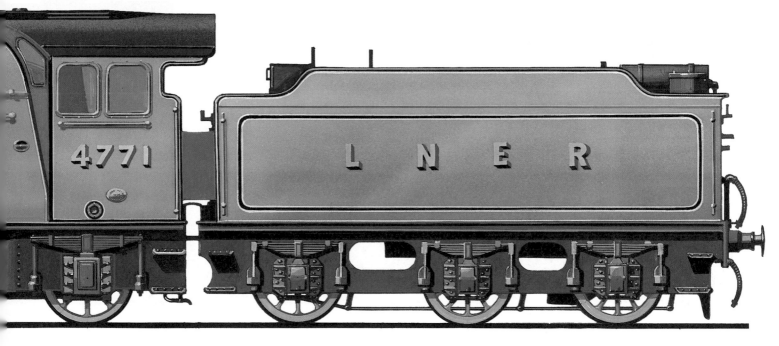

Left: *Gone, but not forgotten, the original class "E4" 4-6-4 No.4001 of Chicago and North Western Railway in action.*

refurbished standard rolling stock hauled by a modified existing steam locomotive, instead of trains brand new from end to end.

Soon enough, though, the C&NW had to follow their competitors' example. They chose to copy the style of the Milwaukee's "Hiawatha" rather than the Burlington's diesel "Zephyr" and accordingly the American Locomotive Company was asked to supply nine high-speed streamlined 4-6-4s.

The new locomotives, designated "E4" and numbered 4000 to 4008, were delivered in 1938, but in the meantime the C&NW

management decided it had backed the wrong horse and went to General Motors Electromotive Division for some of the first production-line diesel locomotives. These took over the new streamlined "400" trains, leaving the new 4-6-4s to work the transcontinental trains of the original Overland Route, which the C&NW hauled from Chicago to Omaha.

Because of the arithmetic of design the basic physical statistics of the "E4" were very close to the "Hiawatha" 4-6-4s, yet it is very clear that lesser differences between the two meant two separate designs. So we have two classes of six and nine locomotives respectively, intended for the same purpose, built by the same firm at the same time, which had few jigs or patterns in common. Such

was the world of steam railway engineering.

Amongst the advanced features of the "E4" may be mentioned Baker's valve-gear, oil firing, roller bearings throughout and, particularly interesting, a Barco low water alarm. Boiling dry such a large kettle as a locomotive boiler is a very serious matter indeed and on most steam locomotives there is no automatic guard against the crew forgetting to look at the water-level in the gauge glasses.

Brash styles of painting were not the C&NW's way, and thus it is particularly sad that, when the time came in the early 1950s for the "E4"s to go to the torch, none *of them was preserved. So, therefore, only in imagination is it possible to feast our eyes on their green and gilded elegance.*

Class 56 4-6-2
Malaysia:
Malayan Railway (PKTM), 1938

Tractive effort: 23,940lb (10,859kg).
Axle load: 28,560lb (12.9t).
Cylinders: (3) 13 x 24in (330 x 610mm).
Driving wheels: 54in (1,372mm).
Heating surface: 1,109sq ft (103m²).
Superheater: 218sq ft (20.25m²).
Steam pressure: 250psi (17.5kg/cm²).
Grate area: 27sq ft (2.5m²).
Fuel (coal): 22,000lb (10t).
Water: 3,500gall (4,200 US) (16m³).
Adhesive weight: 86,000lb (39t).
Total weight: 226,000lb (102.5t).
Length overall: 61ft 1⅜in (18,628mm).

These metre-gauge Pacific locomotives were one of the most elegant of all the British colonial designs and they worked on one of the best colonial systems. Before it turned to diesels, the Malayan Railway operated the majority of both its passenger and freight trains with this one class of 66 neat Pacific locomotives. The PKTM had long been a "railway of Pacifics", since the days when railways back home in Britain were still building 4-4-0s as top line express power. In fact, the first Malayan Pacific, the initial member of a run of 60 known as Class "H", was built for what was then the Federated Malay States Railways (FMSR) back in 1907 by Kitson of Leeds. Others were supplied by Nasmyth, Wilson of Manchester and Robert Stephenson of Darlington. Another 79 Pacifics of four more classes followed during the next 30 years.

In 1938 the North British Locomotive Co. of Glasgow supplied some remarkable Pacifics which were to be the ultimate in Malayan steam power. Before the war and Japanese occupation 28 were supplied, and 40 immediately afterwards. They were extremely neat and handsome little machines both in their looks and in their design. One feature was the excellent balance of the moving parts, and consequent absence of hammer blow to make them suitable for lightly laid track, obtained by the use of three cylinders, all driving the middle coupled axle. Another was the use of rotary-cam poppet valve gear; on other railways which tried this promising arrangement it failed to offer any savings, because of the better use of steam in the cylinders, to compensate for its extra cost and additional maintenance expenses. All credit, then, to the FMSR (and later the PKTM), which made enough of a success of this sophisticated system for it to become standard on the railway. No other railway administration in the world managed it—only this one, run by a combination of British, Chinese, Indian and Malay staff, succeeded.

Originally the class was designated "O" and the running numbers were 60 to 87. After the war they were redesignated class "56" and the various batches supplied were numbered 561.01 –11, 562.01–06, 563.01–11, 564,01–40. Of these 561.09 and 562.01 were scrapped after war damage and not replaced.

In the late 1950s there was a period when locomotives were painted and lined out in Great Western Railway colours, but before this as well as afterwards, a smart black livery was used. Malayan names were applied to all the motive power at this period—Malay script is used on one side of the locomotive, Roman on the other.

In 1955 there was a proposal to run faster trains in Malaya and two "56" class locos were tested up to 70mph (112km/h) a re-

800 Class 4-6-0
Ireland:
Great Southern Railways (GSR), 1939

Tractive effort: 33,000lb (14,970kg).
Axle load: 47,000lb (21t).
Cylinders: (3) 18½ x 28in (470 x 711mm).
Driving wheels: 79in (2,007mm).
Heating surface: 1,870sq ft (174m²).
Steam pressure: 225psi (15.8kg/cm²).
Grate area: 33½sq ft (3.10m²).
Fuel: 18,000lb (8t).
Water: 5,000gall (6,000 US) (23m³).
Adhesive weight: 141,000lbs (64t).
Total weight: 302,500lbs (137t).
Length overall: 67ft 6in (20,550mm).

The 450 or so broad-gauge (5ft 3in–1,600mm) locomotives of Ireland that existed between the wars were of amazing age and variety, divided as they were into over 80 classes. Some of the last single-wheelers to remain in service in the world were running between Waterford and Tramore as late as 1932. All the companies which did not cross the border into the six counties known as Northern Ireland, had been grouped into the Great Southern Railways in 1925. The economics of the GSR did not allow for any significant new construction of any type of locomotive, let alone new express passenger power.

Aside from a group of ten 4-6-0s inherited from the old Great Southern & Western Company, the GSR relied on 26 locomotives of South Eastern & Chatham Railway design, 2-6-0s put together from parts made at Woolwich Arsenal after World War I and obtained cheaply as surplus stores from the British government. Whilst the need was there for something better for the heavy Mail expresses on the hard road between Dublin and Cork, it seemed most unlikely that anything could be done.

As is well known, in Ireland the unlikely can always be relied upon to happen, but it was still a surprise when three large and handsome three-cylinder 4-6-0s, as up-to-date as any locomotive in Europe, emerged from the Inchicore Works of the Great Southern Railway. They had taper boiler-barrels, Belpaire fireboxes, three independent sets of Walschaert's valve gear and resembled very closely in appearance, size and layout the rebuilt "Royal Scot" class of the London Midland & Scottish Railway—at least they would have done if the rebuilt "Scot"'s had then existed. The running numbers were 800 to 802 and the locomotives received the names of the Irish queens *Maeve*, *Macha* and *Tailte*, complete with nameplates in Erse script. They were the only express passenger locomotives to be built in an independent Ireland, all subsequent ones having been imported.

This illustrates the nice thought that quite small and agricultural nations can set out to design and build steam locomotives of top quality with success and economy; and also the less nice thought that the diesel locomotives which superseded steam can only be built economically by large industrial nations.

The "800" class had just time to prove itself in service that summer of 1939. *Maeve* was timed by O.S. Nock on a journey from Cork to Dublin, when extra carriages added for passengers from a trans-Atlantic liner had swelled the usual load of about 300 tons to 450. A remarkable

markable speed for the metre gauge. The tests were completely satisfactory but nothing came of the proposal and the speed limit remained at 45mph (72½km/h) Malayan Railway's trains, in those days anyway, made up for speed with comfort. Luxury comparable to the "Night Scotsman" or to the "Blue Train" was a feature of the "Golden Blowpipe" express; this used to come as a pleasant surprise to people making their first trip up country after arriving from Europe.

During the same period all Malayan locomotives were converted to burn oil instead of the local coal for which their wide fireboxes were eminently suitable. But there were no problems with the new fuel and Malayan rail travel suddenly became much cleaner.

In 1957 the first diesels arrived and by 1972 only half the Class "56" 4-6-2s were still in service. In 1981 the only steam locomotives left are a pair (No.564.33 *Jelebu* and No.564.36 *Temerloh*) stationed at Kuala Lumpur—where the main works of the system is situated—and used mainly to haul charter trains for tourists plus an occasional service run in some emergency.

Left: *Malayan Railways preserved class "56" 4-6-2 No.564 36 Temerloh leaves Kuala Lumpur on a private excursion to Batu Caves in September 1979. This locomotive is one of two kept aside after the end of steam in Malaya. The Railway Administration can arrange special trains using one of these two steam locomotives at short notice and and at surprisingly modest cost.*

Below: *Malayan Railways class "0" 4-6-2 No.71 Kuala Lumpur (later class "56" No.56201) in pre-1941 livery.*

23mph (37km/h) was maintained with this big load on the severe 1 in 60 (1.66 per cent) gradient out of Cork. Later in the journey the ability to run fast was demonstrated with 79mph (126km/h) near Newbridge.

A chronic shortage of fuel persisted long after the war and there seemed little time in the short interregnum before diesel traction took over to see more of the work of these fine locomotives. The first one to go was *Tailte*, withdrawn in 1957; the other two lingered on without seeing much use until 1964. *Maeve* is preserved in the Belfast Transport Museum.

Right: *The Irish Great Southern Railways (later Coras Iompair Eirann) 4-6-0 No.800 Maeve as preserved. The locomotive is currently on display at the Irish Transport Museum in Belfast.*

FEF-2 Class 4-8-4

Tractive effort: 63,800lb (28,950kg).
Axle load: 67,000lb (30.5t).
Cylinders: (2) 25 x 32in (635 x 813mm).
Driving wheels: 80in (2,032mm).
Heating surface: 4,225sq ft (393m²).
Superheater: 1,400sq ft (130m²).
Steam pressure: 300psi (21kg/cm²).
Grate area: 100sq ft (9.3m²).
Fuel: 50,000lb (23t).
Water: 19,600gall (23,500 US) (90m³).
Adhesive weight: 266,500lb (121t).
Total weight: 908,000lb (412t).
Length overall: 113ft 10in (34,696mm).

The origin of the class occurred during the late 1930s, when rising train loads began to over-tax the 4-8-2s which were then the mainstay of UP passenger operations. One day in 1937 a "7000" class 4-8-2 had the temerity to demonstrate the lack of steaming power inherent in the type, on a train with UP President William Jeffers' business car on the rear. Even while the party was waiting out on the prairies for rescue, a dialogue by telegram went on with the American Locomotive Company (Alco) in far-off Schenectady, with a view to getting something better.

The result in due course was this superb class of 45 locomotives of which 20, numbered 800 to 819, were delivered in 1938. A further 15 (Nos.820 to 834) with larger wheels and cylinders as well as 14-wheel centipede tenders—instead of 12-wheel ones—came the following year and it is to these that the dimensions etc given above apply. This second batch was designated "FEF-2", the earlier ones becoming class "FEF-1". FEF stood for Four-Eight-Four!

A final batch of ten almost identical to the second one except for the use of some substitute materials, appeared in 1944. These were known as "FEF-3"s and were the last steam power supplied to UP. All the "800"s came from Alco.

The "800"s as a whole followed

—like Northumbrian 108 years earlier—the standard recipe for success in having two outside cylinders only, the simplest possible arrangement. That king of passenger locomotive wheel arrangements, the "Northern" or 4-8-4, was adopted and misgivings originally felt regarding the suitability of eight-coupled wheels for very high speeds were found not to be justified. The negotiation of curves was made easier by the fitting of Alco's lateral motion device to the leading coupled wheels.

The basic simplicity of so many US locomotives was often spoilt by their designers being an easy touch for manufacturers of complicated accessories. The UP managed to resist most of them

with the pleasing result that the locomotives had a delightfully elegant uncluttered appearance, unmarred by any streamline shroud. On the other hand, they rightly fell for such excellent simplifications as the cast-steel locomotive frame, which replaced many separate parts by one single casting. Another example was the use of a static exhaust steam injector instead of a steam-driven mechanical water-pump and feed water heater. A complication resisted by the UP was the provision of thermic syphons in the firebox; they held the view that on balance these quite common devices were more trouble than benefit. Even so, both common sense as well as Uncle Sam's rules meant power rever-

sing gear and automatic stoking, whilst electric lighting was something that certainly paid off in helping "800" crews to see what they were doing.

Perhaps the most original feature and one which contributed a good deal to the success of the "800"s was the main motion. Aesthetically, the main rods were pure poetry but there was a great deal more to it than that. Because of the speeds and forces involved, current technology was taken beyond the then accepted limits; at the same time, the magnitude of the stresses to

Below: *Preserved Union Pacific "FEF-3" class 4-8-4 No.8444 with a special train run for hundreds of enthusiasts a year.*

which those whirling rods were subject are very different to evaluate with any degree of confidence.

What a triumph for the designers, then, that these lovely tapered coupling and connecting rods were a resounding success even though frequently moved at revolutions corresponding to running speeds above the 100mph (160km/h) mark. The main principle of the new design was that the pulls and thrusts were transmitted from the connecting rods —and hence to three out of the four pairs of wheels—by separate sleeve bearings instead of via the main crankpins in accordance with convention. The result was that separate knuckle-joints in the coupling rods were replaced by making the centre pair of rods forked at both ends and combining the roles of crank-pins and knuckle-pins.

The results were superb and there are many reports of speeds being run up to the design limit of 110mph (176km/h). After the war there was a period when coal supplies were affected by strikes and, in order to safeguard UP passenger operations, the "800"'s were converted from coal to oil burning; a 6,000gall (27m³) tank was fitted in the bunker space. Otherwise only minor modifications were needed over many years of arduous service, a fact which is also much to the credit of the designers.

Normally the 4-8-4s were en-trusted with the many expresses formed of the then conventional heavyweight stock, but the new engines' arrival on UP coincided with the introduction of diesel-electric streamline trains on much

faster timings. In those early days the new form of motive power was not too reliable and "800" class locomotives frequently found themselves replacing a multi unit diesel at the head end of one of UP's crack trains. They found no problem in making up time on the tight diesel schedules sufficient to offset extra minutes spent taking on water.

The last service passenger train hauled by an "800" was caused by such a failure; it occurred when in autumn 1958, the last one built took the "City of Los Angeles" over the last stretch of 145 miles (232km) from Grand Island into Omaha. No.844 gained time on the streamliner's schedule in spite of the crew's lack of recent experience with steam. A year later there came a time

Left: *An "FEF-1" class 4-8-4 of the Union Pacific Railroad ready to leave Denver, Colorado. These locomotives had the smaller 12-wheel tenders.*

Above: *The last steam locomotive built for the Union Pacific Railroad, class "FEF-3" 4-8-4 No.844 (renumbered to 8444 to avoid confusion with a diesel unit).*

when all were out of service awaiting scrapping; it was a sad moment for all who admired these superb locomotives.

Since then No.844 (renumbered 8444 to avoid confusion with a diesel unit) has been put back into service by a publicity-conscious Union Pacific and frequently performs for her fans. No.814 is displayed across the Mississippi river from Omaha, at Dodge Park, Council Bluffs, and Nos.833 and 838 are also believed still to be in existence, the latter as a source of spares for No.8444.

Below: *A second section of "The Gold Coast" train behind class "FEF-1" (which appeared before "FEF-2"s) 4-8-4 No.826.*

Class 12 4-4-2
Belgium:
Belgian National Railways (SNCB), 1939

Tractive effort: 26,620lb (12,079kg).
Axle load: 52,000lb (23.4t).
Cylinders: (2) 18⅞ x 28⅜in (480 x 720mm).
Driving wheels: 82¾in (2,100mm).
Heating surface: 1,729sq ft (161m²).
Superheater: 678sq ft (63m²).
Steam pressure: 256psi (18kg/cm²).
Grate area: 39.8sq ft (3.7m²).
Fuel: 17,500lb (8t).
Water: 5,280gall (6,300 US) (24m³).
Adhesive weight: 101,000lb (45.8t).
Total weight*: 188,500lb (89.5t).
Length overall: 69ft 6¼in (21,190mm).
*(*engine only without tender)*

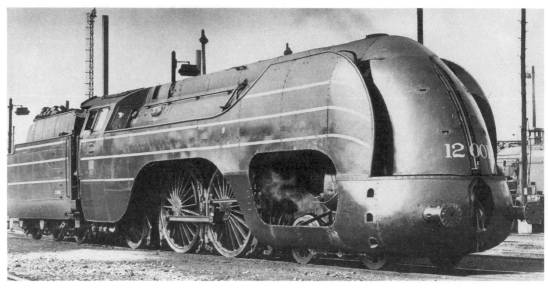

Most modern steam locomotives trace their descent more from *Northumbrian* than *Planet;* but here is an exception; and, moreover, one that was good enough for a world record for scheduled start-to-stop speed: Whilst the Belgian class "12" 4-4-2s were totally conventional as regards principles, the layout of their machinery was unusual if not unique—but then what other than original thinking would be expected of a country that produced both Alfred Belpaire and Egide Walschaert?

The concept was to operate frequent lightweight high-speed

Above and below: *Two views of the Belgian National Railways' class "12" high-speed 4-4-2 locomotives, built in 1938 to haul lightweight expresses between Brussels and Ostend.*

520 Class 4-8-4
Australia:
South Australian Government Railways (SAR), 1943

Tractive effort: 32,600lb (14,800kg).
Axle load: 35,000lb (16t).
Cylinders: (2) 20½ x 28in (521 x 711mm).
Driving wheels: 66in (1,676mm).
Heating surface: 2,454sq ft (228m²).
Superheater: 651sq ft (60.5m²).
Steam pressure: 215psi (15.1kg/cm²).
Grate area: 45sq ft (4.2m²).
Fuel: 22,000lb (10t).
Water: 9,000gall (10,800 US) (41m³).
Adhesive weight: 140,000lb (63.5t).
Total weight: 449,500lb (204t).
Length overall: 87ft 4½in (26,622mm).

trains, of three cars only, over the 71 miles (121km) between Brussels and Ostend in the even hour, including a stop at Bruges. Between Brussels and Bruges the timing was to be 46 minutes, giving an average speed of 75.4 mph (121.3km/h). The speed limit of this almost level route was specially raised for these trains to 87mph (140km/h). It was decided that four coupled wheels were adequate, whilst the power needed for the high speeds contemplated was best provided by a wide firebox. A leading bogie was certainly desirable and, to avoid oscillations inside cylinders were preferred, made reasonably accessible by the use of bar rather than plate frames. All this added up to the world's last 4-4-2s as well as the world's last inside-cylinder express locomotives. The tenders were second-hand, with streamlining added, and the locomotives were built by Messrs Cockerill of Seraing, Belgium.

Alas, the high-speed trains

only ran for a few months before war broke out in September 1939. One of the 4-4-2s (No.1203) has, however, survived and is preserved at the SNCB locomotive depot at Louvain. The best

timing by electric traction today between Brussels and Ostend is 11 minutes longer with one extra stop—an 18 per cent *increase* in journey time when steam gives way to electric traction is possibly

Above: *SNCB Class "12" 4-4-2 No.12.004, one of the world's last 4-4-2s.*

yet another record achieved by these remarkable locomotives.

South Australia certainly became 4-8-4 country in 1943 when the ten "500" class were supplemented by twelve "520" class. But there the resemblance ends because the "500"s had a lot of wheels in order to give brute force but the "520"s were many-wheeled so that they could tread delicately on the light 60lb/yd (30kg/m) rails of the remote branches in the State. This they did with great success.

All the locomotives were built at the SAGR's Islington shops between 1943 and 1947. The style of their streamlining was

clearly based on that of the "TI" class 4-4-4-4s of the American Pennsylvania Railroad. Unlike the contemporary "TI"'s though, they were starkly conventional under their shrouds—and, also unlike the "TI"'s had useful lives of up to 18 years. In 1948 all the locomotives of this class were converted to burn oil fuel.

Two "520"s are preserved; No.520 *Sir Malcolm Barclay-Harvey* is occasionally run. The other, No.523 *Essington Lewis*, is displayed at the Australian Railway Historical Society's site at Mile End near Adelaide.

Left: *Showing a fine plume of smoke, a "520" class 4-8-4 makes good time with an enthusiasts' special.*

Right: *One of the preserved class "520" locomotives* Sir Malcolm Barclay-Harvey *as built in 1943.*

Class C38 4-6-2 Australia:
New South Wales Government Railways (NSWGR), 1943

Tractive effort: 36,200lb
(16,425kg).
Axle load: 51,000lb (23.5t).
Cylinders: (2) 21½ x 26in
(546 x 660mm).
Driving wheels: 69in
(1,753mm).
Heating surface: 2,614sq ft
(243m²).
Superheater: 755sq ft (70.2m²).
Steam pressure: 245psi
(17.25kg/cm²).
Grate area: 47sq ft (4.4m²).
Fuel: 31,500lb (14.5t).
Water: 8,100gall (9,700 US)
(37m³).
Adhesive weight: 150,500lb
(68.5t).
Total weight: 451,000lb (205t)..
Length overall: 76ft 4½in
(23,279mm).

The last and best of Australian express passenger locomotives were the thirty "C-38" Pacifics of the New South Wales Government Railways, built between 1943 and 1949. They had been planned before the war but the majority were not completed until after it was over. The first five, built by the Clyde Engineering Co of Sydney, were streamlined. The remainder were not streamlined and built at the railways own shops at Cardiff and Eveleigh. The designers had not lost sight of the fact that simplicity was the steam locomotive's greatest asset and that its greatest handicap was the manual labour involved in keeping it running.

Hence only two cylinders, valve gear outside, all mounted on a cast steel locomotive frame with integral cylinders, air reservoirs, brackets, saddles, stays etc. All axles had roller bearings and there were rocking and dumping elements in the grate, power reverse and air sanding.

The "C-38" class could give

Above: Class "C38" 4-6-2 No. 38.01 hauling the "Western Endeavour" transcontinental special en route from Sydney to Perth. Note extra water tanks in the train.

Right: 4-6-2 No.38.06 on Sydney to Brisbane Day Express at Hawkesbury.

Class T1 4-4-4-4 United States:
Pennsylvania Railroad (PRR), 1942

Tractive effort: 64,700lb
(29,300kg).
Axle load: 69,000lb (31.5t).
Cylinders: (4) 19¾ x 26in
(501 x 660mm).
Driving wheels: 80in
(2,032mm).
Heating surface: 4,209sq ft
(391.0m²).
Superheater: 1,430sq ft
(131.9m²).
Steam pressure: 300psi
(21.1kg/cm²).
Grate area: 92sq ft (8.5m²).
Fuel: 85,000lb (38.5t).
Water: 16,000gall (19,000 US)
(72.5m³).
Adhesive weight: 273,000lb
(124t).
Total weight: 954,000lb
(432.7t).
Length overall: 122ft 10in
(37,440mm).

In the 1930s there was a notable increase in the use of 4-8-4 locomotives in the United States, both for freight and passenger service. There were, however, some problems with the very high piston thrust in these engines, and the resultant stresses in crank pins, while the balancing of the heavy reciprocating parts for high speeds also caused difficulties. All the problems could be solved, but R.P. Johnson, chief engineer of The Baldwin Locomotive Works suggested that they could be avoided by dividing the driving wheels into two groups in a single rigid frame, with separate cylinders for each, thus making the engine into a 4-4-4-4. Compared with the 4-8-4, piston loads were reduced, and it was easier to provide valves of adequate size, but the rigid wheelbase was increased by the space

required to accommodate the second set of cylinders. This increase was in itself sufficient to discourage some roads from further consideration of the proposal.

The first road to build a duplex engine was the Baltimore and Ohio, which made a 4-4-4-4 with an experimental water-tube firebox in 1937, but it was the Pennsylvania which first built a locomotive with a conventional boiler to this layout. In 1937, with the principal passenger services still worked by the "K4" Pacifics of 1914 design, the road's engineers embarked on the design of a locomotive to haul 1,090 tons at 100mph (160km/h), which was well beyond the capacity of any existing 4-8-4.

Johnson put the case for the duplex engine, and this appealed to the PRR men, but for the size of the engine required 16 wheels were insufficient, and the PRR took one of its most spectacular steps by adopting the 6-4-4-6 wheel arrangement. The locomotive was designed and built at Altoona, and it was the largest rigid-framed passenger engine ever built. It was numbered 6100 and classified "S1", and with driving wheels 84in (2,134mm) in diameter, a grate area of 132sq ft (12.3m²), and a boiler some 15 per cent greater than that of any 4-8-4, it was essentially an engine for developing high power at high speed. With a streamlined casing design by the fashionable stylist Raymond Loewy, its appearance was as striking as its dimensions.

No.6100 appeared early in 1939, but it spent much of 1939 and 1940 on display at the New

York World Fair and it was not until December 1940 that it entered revenue service. Although intended for use throughout the main line from Harrisburg to Chicago, in the event its great length led to its prohibition from the curved lines in the east, and this prohibition was further extended because the maximum axle load came out at 73,880lb (33.5t), against the figure of 67,500lb (30.5t) which had been stipulated to the designer.

As a result the engine was limited to the 283-mile Crestline to Chicago division, on which it proved capable of hauling 1225 tons at an average speed of 66mph (106km/h). With smaller loads it achieved very high speeds, and although the PRR and its official locomotive historian were silent on the subject, it was widely believed to have exceeded

Above: Class "T1" No.5537 leaving Fort Wayne, Indiana, with the eastbound "Fast Mail" express en route from Chicago to New York.

120mph (193km/h) on many occasions. There were, however, problems, particularly with slipping, not helped by the fact that only 46 per cent of the total engine weight was carried on the driving wheels, compared with 65 per cent in a "K4" Pacific.

Despite the limited and variable experience gained so far with the "S1", the PRR ordered two more duplex locomotives from Baldwin in July, 1940. The performance requirement was reduced to the haulage of 880 tons at 100mph (160km/h) and this could be met by a 4-4-4-4, with 80in (2,032mm) driving wheels, and a grate area of 92ft (8.5m²). The maximum

substantially higher power output than the "C-36" class 4-6-0s which the larger engines replaced. They were capable of taking the Melbourne Express loaded to 450 tons unassisted up the 1 in 75 (1.33 per cent) inclines of the main line to Albury. Their heavy axle-loading limited them to the principal routes of the state, but this still left ample scope for the class to perform with great ability on the majority of New South Wales' top passenger trains.

Withdrawal began in the mid-1960s and the class just lingered on in normal service until 1970. Several have been preserved and one or two are occasionally put into steam to give pleasure. The longest run of this kind ever made—or ever likely to be made—was when No.38.01 crossed the continent from Sydney to Perth and back on the "Western Endeavour" special train, to celebrate the day in 1970 when 4ft 8½in (1,435mm) metals became available over the whole 2,461 miles (3,961km) between the two cities.

axle load was 69,250lb (31.4t) compared with 73,880lb (33.5t) of the "S1". The two engines, classified "T1" and numbered 6110 and 6111 differed only in that 6111 had a booster. Apart from the inclusion of certain PRR standard fittings, Baldwin was given a free hand in the design. Franklin's poppet valves were fitted at PRR insistence, as these had produced a notable increase in the power of "K4" Pacific. Roller-bearings, light-weight motion, and disc wheels were amongst the modern equipment and the engine was clothed in a casing designed by Raymond Loewy, but quite different from that of No.6100. They were delivered in April and May 1942.

In 1944, No.6110 was tested on the Altoona testing plant and it produced a cylinder horse-power of 6,550 at 85mph (137 km/h) with 25 per cent cut-off. In service the engines worked over the 713 miles between Harrisburg and Chicago, but despite these long runs they built up mileage slowly and spent an undue amount of time under repair. Slipping was again the main trouble, although in these engines 54 per cent of the total weight was adhesive.

At this point the road took a fateful step. Ignoring its old policy of testing and modifying a prototype until it was entirely satisfactory, it ordered 50 almost identical engines. Nos.5500-24 were built at Altoona and 5525-49 by the Baldwin Works and delivered be-

tween late 1945 and early 1946.

With a shorter rigid wheelbase than the "S1" and a smaller maximum axle load, the "T1"s were allowed over the full steam-worked part of the PRR main line from Harrisburg to Chicago, and they worked through over the whole 713 miles. They took over all the passenger work on this route, including the 73.1mph (117.5km/h) schedule of the Chicago Arrow over the 123 miles (198km) from Fort Wayne to Gary, and four other runs at more than 70mph (112.5km/h). At their best they were magnifi-

Below: *Pennsylvania Railroad class "T1" 4-4-4-4 duplex locomotive No.5511, built at Altoona.*

cent, with numerous records of 100mph (160km/h) with 910-ton trains, including a pass-to-pass average of 100mph over 69 miles of generally falling grades with a load of 1,045 tons. They rode smoothly, and when all was well they were popular with the enginemen, but slipping remained a major hazard, not only slipping at starting but violent slipping of one set of wheels at high speed.

At this time the motive power department of the PRR was at a low ebb, both in equipment and in morale, and compared with the simple and well-known "K4" Pacifics, the "T1" was a complex box of tricks, particularly its valve gear. Maintenance of the big engines proved to be a difficult job, and their appearances on their booked workings became less and less regular. The faithful "K4"s were out again in force.

Various modifications were made to ease maintenance, mainly by the removal of parts of the casing, but one engine was rebuilt with piston valves. Eight engines had their cylinder diameter reduced in an attempt to reduce the tendency to slip but the problem was never solved. As time passed, the worsening financial state of the railroad led to the ordering of mainline diesels.

It was intended that the "T1"s should have a full economic life before succumbing to diesels. In the event, the serious and intractable problems with them had the effect of accelerating dieselisation, and by the end of 1949 most of them were out of service. So ended the most expensive locomotive fiasco of the century.

Challenger Class 4-6-6-4

Tractive effort: 97,400lb
(44,100kg).
Axle load: 68,000lb (31t).
Cylinders: (4) 21 x 32in
(533 x 813mm).
Driving wheels: 69in
(1,753mm).
Heating surface: 4,642sq ft
(431m²).
Superheater: 1,741sq ft
(162m²).
Steam pressure: 280psi
(19.7kg/cm²).
Grate area: 132sq ft (12.3m²).
Fuel: 56,000lb (25.4t).
Adhesive weight: 406,000lb
(184.3t).
Total weight: 1,071,000lb
(486t).
Length overall: 121ft 11in
(37,160mm).

On virtually all counts this loco-motive was the largest, heaviest, strongest and most powerful one which ever regularly handled express passenger trains. Its existence was only possible be-cause it was an articulated loco-motive, that is, there was a hinge in the middle.

Articulated locomotives were introduced early in locomotive history, but it was not until the full flowering of the narrow-gauge railway late in the 19th century that they were built in quantity. Many designs were tried, but the most popular was that of Anatole Mallet, a French consulting en-gineer. Mallet was an early advo-cate of compounding, and from 1876 a number of two-cylinder compound locomotives were built to his designs. In 1884, to cater for larger locomotives, he pro-posed an articulated design in which the rear set of driving wheels were mounted in the main frame, which supported the firebox and the rear part of the boiler. The front set of driving wheels were in a separate frame, the rear end of which was hinged to the front of the main frame. The front of the boiler rested on the hinged frame, and as the boiler swung across this frame on curves, a sliding support was needed. The high-pressure cyl-inders drove the rear set of wheels and the low-pressure cyl-inders the leading set. High-pressure steam was thus entirely on the rigid part of the locomotive,

and hinged steam pipes were needed only for the steam to and from the low-pressure cylinders.

The European engines built to this design were mostly for narrow-gauge railways. However, in 1903 the first American Mallet was built. Here the aim was to get the maximum adhesion, and as there were difficulties in designing a locomotive with six driving axles in a rigid frame, articulation was an attractive proposition at this stage. The American engine was an 0-6-6-0 built for the Baltimore and Ohio Railroad. It was the largest locomotive in the world and thereafter that distinc-tion was always held by an American member of the Mallet family.

More American Mallets fol-lowed, at first mainly for banking duties, but then for road work. However, with their huge low-pressure cylinders and the tor-tuous steam pipes between the cylinders, these engines were unsuitable for speeds above 30-40mph (40-50km/h). Above these speeds oscillations of the front frame developed leading to heavy wear on locomotive and track.

In 1924 the Chesapeake and Ohio Railroad ordered twenty 2-8-8-2 locomotives with four simple expansion cylinders. Al-though the main reason for this was that the loading gauge of C&O could not accommodate the large low-pressure cylinders of a compound, the change

brought the further benefit that more adequate steam pipes could be provided, and the engines were capable of higher speeds. Some intensive work was needed to develop flexible joints suitable for carrying high-pressure steam to the leading cylinders.

From this time onwards Ameri-can interest centred on the four-cylinder simple Mallet and suc-cessive improvements were made which upgraded the type from banking duties to main line freight work and, eventually, on a few roads, to express passenger

Below: *"Challenger" class 4-6-6-4 No.3985 at Cheyenne awaiting restoration to working order in 1981.*

work. Amongst changes introduced were longer travel valves and more complete balancing of the moving parts, but most important were the changes made to the connection between the leading frame and the main frame, and to lateral control of the leading wheels. It was these latter alterations which eliminated the violent oscillations which had limited the speed of earlier Mallets.

The Union Pacific acquired 70 compound 2-8-8-0s with 59in (1,500mm) driving wheels between 1918 and 1924. These were essentially hard-slogging, modest speed engines and in 1926, for faster freight trains, the railroad introduced a class which was remarkable in several respects. It was a three-cylinder 4-12-2 with 67in (1,702mm) driving wheels, and was the first class with this wheel arrangement. It was also one of the few American three cylinder engines and the only one to be built in quantity, a total of 88 being built. They were highly successful, but with their long rigid wheelbase and heavy motion they were limited to 45mph (72km/h), and with growing road competition a twelve-coupled engine was needed capable of higher speeds than the 4-12-2.

Experience with the compound Mallets had led to the decision to convert them to simple expansion and the way was then set for the railroad to make another important step forward in 1936 by ordering 40 simple-expansion 4-6-6-4s with 69in (1,753mm) driving wheels. They were numbered from 3900 to 3939 and designated "Challenger". The leading bogie gave much better side control than a pony truck and the truck under the firebox assisted the fitting of a very large grate. The engines were distributed widely over the UP system and were used mainly on fast freight trains, but the last six of the engines were ordered specifically for passenger work. The most obvious difference between these earlier "Challenger" locomotives and those depicted in the art-work above was the provision of much smaller 12-wheel tenders. Much of the coal which

the UP used came from mines which the railroad owned.

In 1942 pressure of wartime traffic brought the need for more large engines and the construction of Challengers was resumed, a total of 65 more being built up to 1944. A number of changes were made, notably an enlargement of the grate from 108sq ft (10.0m²) to 132sq ft (12.3m²), cast steel frames in place of built-up frames, and an increase in the boiler pressure to 255psi (17.9kg/cm²) accompanied by a reduction in cylinder size of one inch, which left the tractive effort unchanged.

A less obvious but more fundamental change from the earlier engines was in the pivot between the leading unit and the main frame. In the earlier engines there were both vertical and horizontal hinges, but in the new engines, following the practice adopted in the "Big Boy" 4-8-8-4s, there was no horizontal hinge. The vertical hinge was now arranged to transmit a load of several tons from the rear unit to

Above: *Union Pacific's "Challenger" 4-6-6-4 No.3964 takes on coal from an overhead coaling plant.*

the front one, thus evening out the distribution of weight between the two sets of driving wheels, and thereby reducing the tendency of the front drivers to slip, which had been a problem with the earlier engines. With no horizontal hinge, humps and hollows in the track were now looked after by the springs of each individual axle, as in a normal rigid locomotive.

All the engines were built as coal-burners, but in 1945 five of them were converted to oil-burning for use on passenger trains on the Oregon and Washington lines. Trouble was experienced with smoke obstructing the driver's view so these five engines were fitted with long smoke deflectors, and they were also painted in the two-tone grey livery which was used for passenger engines for a number of years, as depicted above.

A favourite racing ground for these monsters was the main line, mostly across the desert, between Salt Lake City, Las Vegas and Los Angeles, where they regularly ran at up to 70mph (112km/h) on passenger trains.

In 1952 coal supplies were interrupted by a strike and a crash programme for further conversions to oil-burning was put in hand, but the strike ended after eight engines had been converted. Rather perversely, in 1950 ten of the original series had been converted back to coal-firing, but in less than a year had been changed yet again to oil. Dieselisation gradually narrowed the field of operation of the "Challengers", but they continued to take a major share of steam working up to 1958 when the delivery of a large batch of diesels rendered them redundant.

The numbering of the Challengers was extremely complicated due to the practice of renumbering engines when they were converted from coal-burning to oil-burning or vice versa. Thus the original engines were renumbered from 3900-39 to 3800-39 and the three batches of the second series were numbered successively 3950-69, 3975-99 and 3930-49, so that 3930-9 were used twice but 3970-4 not at all. Furthermore, eighteen of the second series which were converted to oil-burning were renumbered from 3700-17.

Several other roads bought engines of the 4-6-6-4 wheel arrangement, generally similar to the "Challenger" and they also were used on some passenger work, but it was on the UP that the articulated locomotive had its most important application to passenger work, and a "Challenger" hauling 20 or more coaches was a regular sight. Fortunately one of the engines, No.3985 was preserved as a static exhibit, but in 1981 it was restored to working order, making it by far the largest working steam engine in the world.

Below: *Union Pacific Railroad "Challenger" 4-6-6-4 depicted in the two-tone grey passenger livery used in the late 1940s.*

Class J 4-8-4
United States:
Norfolk & Western Railway (N&W), 1941

Tractive effort: 80,000lb (36,287kg).
Axle load: 72,000lb (33t).
Cylinders: (2) 27 x 32in (686 x 813mm).
Driving wheels: 70in (1,778mm).
Heating surface: 5,271sq ft (490m²).
Superheater: 2,177sq ft (202m²).
Steam pressure: 300psi (21kg/cm²).
Grate area: 107.5sq ft (10m²).
Fuel: 70,000lb (31.75t).
Water: 16,700gall (20,000 US) (76m³).
Adhesive weight: 288,000lb (131t).
Total weight: 873,000lb (396t).
Length overall: 100ft 11in (30,759mm).

"Of all the words of tongue and pen, the saddest are 'it might have been'." In the USA, there was just one small (but prosperous) railroad that, on a long-term basis, came near to fighting off the diesel invasion. This was the Norfolk & Western Railway, with headquarters in Roanoke, Virginia, and a main line then stretching 646 miles (1,033km) from ocean piers at Norfolk, Virginia, to Columbus in Ohio. It had branches to collect coal from every mine of importance across one of the world's greatest coalfields. In the end steam lost the battle on the N&W and big-time steam railroading finally vanished from the United States—so dealing a fatal blow all over the world to the morale of those who maintained that dieselisation was wrong. But the Norfolk & Western's superb steam locomotives came close to victory; so let us see how it was done.

The principle adopted was to exploit fully all the virtues of steam while, rather obviously, seeking palliatives for its disadvantages. It was also a principle of N&W management that the maximum economy lay in maintaining the steam fleet in first-class condition, with the aid of premises, tools and equipment to match. All this is well illustrated by the story of the "J" class, Norfolk & Western's own design (and own

build) of express passenger super-locomotive.

Around 1940 the company's locomotive chiefs felt that it should be possible to have something better than the standard United States Railroad Association's design of 4-8-2 upon which N&W passenger expresses then relied. Very wisely, they accepted that Robert Stephenson had got the thermal and most of the mechanical principles right with the *Northumbrian,* but what needed attention was the cost and time involved in servicing and maintenance. This meant, for example, roller bearings to the axleboxes and throughout the motion, while an unparalleled number of subsidiary bearings, over 200 in fact, were automatically fed with oil by

a mechanical lubricator with a 24-gallon (110-litre) tank, enough for 1,500 miles (2,400km). Even the bearings of the bell were automatically lubricated!

There was another large lubricator to feed high-temperature oil for the steam cylinders; this is normal but the feeds from this lubricator also ran to the steam cylinders of the water and air pumps and the stoker engine. Hence the labour involved in filling separate lubricators at each of these was avoided. The basic simplicity of the two-cylinder arrangement with Baker's valve gear also had the effect of minimising maintenance costs.

Huge tenders enabled calls at fuelling points to be reduced to a minimum. Together with the usual

modern US features such as a cast-steel locomotive frame, all these things added up to a locomotive which could run 15,000 miles (24,000km) per month, needed to visit the repair shops only every 1½ years and had a hard-to-believe record of reliability.

During the period when steam and diesel were battling for supremacy on United States railroads, it was typically the case that brand new diesel locomotives were being maintained in brand new depots while the steam

Below: *A class "J" 4-8-4 of the Norfolk & Western Railway takes a fast express passenger train round a curve in the hills of Virginia.*

Above: *The superb lines of the Roanoke-built new Norfolk & Western class "J" 4-8-4 are exemplified in this artwork.*

engines with which they were being compared were worn out and looked after in tumble-down sheds. Often much of the roof would be missing while equipment was also worn out and obsolete. The filth would be indescribable.

On the Norfolk & Western Railroad during the 1950s, locomotives were new and depots almost clinically clean, modern, well-equipped and well arranged. A "J" class could be fully serviced, greased, lubricated, cleared of ash, tender filled with thousands of gallons of water and many tons of coal, all in under an hour. The result was efficiency, leading to Norfolk & Western's shareholders receiving 6 per cent on their money, while those of the neighbouring and fully-dieselised and electrified Pennsylvania Railroad had to be content with ½ per cent.

In the end, though, the problems of being the sole United States railroad continuing with steam on any scale began to tell. Even a do-it-yourself concern like N&W normally bought many components from specialists and one by one these firms were going out of business. In 1960 this and other factors necessitated the replacement of steam and the "J"s plus all the other wonderful locomotives of this excellent concern were retired.

One feels that the "J"s were the best of all the 4-8-4s, but that is a matter of opinion; in matters of fact, though, they had certainly the highest tractive effort and, as well, the class included the last main-line steam passenger locomotives to be constructed in the United States. They were built as follows, all at N&W's Roanoke shops: Nos. 600 to 603, 1941; 604, 1942; 605 to 610, 1943; 611 to 613, 1950.

No.604 had a booster engine on the trailing truck.

Nos.605 to 610 were originally unstreamlined and ran for two years as chunky but attractive

locomotives in plain garb.

In spite of having driving wheels which were on the small side for a passenger locomotive, speeds up to 90mph (144km/h) were recorded in service and 110mph (176km/h) on test. The latter was achieved with a 1,000 ton trailing load of 15 cars and represented the development of a remarkable 6,000hp in the cylinders.

With such power and speed capability available, the fact that overall speeds were not high reflected the hilly nature of the country served. For example, the coach streamliner "Powhattan Arrow" needed 15hr 45min for

the 676 miles (1,082km) from Norfolk, Virginia to Cincinatti, Ohio, an average speed of 43mph (69km/h). Whilst this train was not a heavy one, the overnight "Pocahontas" which carried through cars from Norfolk to Chicago via Cincinatti and Pennsylvania Railroad, could load up to 1,000 tons which had to be handled on ruling grades up to 1 in 62 (1.6 per cent).

Norfolk & Western also acted as a "bridge road" and their 4-8-4s hauled limiteds such as the "Tennessean" and the "Pelican"—the original Chattanooga Choo-choos—between

Top: *New class "J" 4-8-4 No.605, built at Roanoke in 1943, heads the streamliner "Powhattan Arrow".*

Above: *Another "J" built at Roanoke, No.607. Six of these locomotives originally ran unstreamlined.*

Lynchburg and Bristol, on the famous journeys from New York to Chattanooga and points beyond. No.611 was preserved at the Transportation Museum in Roanoke, Virginia, but in 1982 it was being restored to working order.

2900 Class 4-8-4

Tractive effort: 79,960lb (36,270kg).
Axle load: 74,000lb (33.5t).
Cylinders: (2) 28 x 32in (711 x 813mm).
Driving wheels: 80in (2,032mm).
Heating surface: 5,313sq ft (494m²).
Superheater: 2,366sq ft (220m²).
Steam pressure: 300psi (21kg/cm²).
Grate area: 108sq ft (10m²).
Fuel (oil): 5,830galls (7,000 US) (26.5m³).
Water: 20,400gall (24,500 US) (93m³).
Adhesive weight: 294,000lb (133t).
Total weight: 961,000lb (436t).
Length overall: 120ft 10in (36,830mm).

The Atchison, Topeka & Santa Fe Railway (Santa Fe for short) was remarkable in that it was the *only* railroad company which connected Chicago with California. Odder still perhaps that it was named after three small places in the southern Mid-West, while so many railroads with Pacific in their titles never got there. Even now it remains as it was in the great days of steam— solvent, forward-looking and with its physical plant in first-class condition. With a main line stretching for 2,224 miles (3,580km) across America (or 2,547 miles (4,100km) if you let the Santa Fe take you as far as San Francisco Bay) together, once upon a time, with some of the world's finest and most prestigious passenger services, you might think that the company's steam power must have been remarkable—and you would not be wrong.

Nearly all Santa Fe's steam locomotives came from Baldwin of Philadelphia. At one time it included briefly such exotic items as 2-4-6-2 and 2-6-6-2 superheated express Mallet locomotives with 73 and 69in (1,854 and 1,753mm) diameter driving wheels respectively. Six of the class of 44 of the 2-6-6-2s even had *boilers* with a hinge in the middle! Experience with these and a few other wild ideas

brought about a firm resolve to stick to the Stephenson path in the future and almost without exception all subsequent steam locomotives built for Santa Fe were "straight" (ie non-articulated) "simple" (ie non-compound) and with two cylinders only. The results of the slow-and-steady policy were magnificent.

The Santa Fe main line crossed the famous Raton Pass in the New Mexico with its 1 in 28½ (3½ per cent) gradient, as well as the less impossible but still severe Cajon Pass in eastern California. East of Kansas City across the level prairies 4-6-2s and 4-6-4s sufficed until the diesels came, but for the heavily graded western lines Santa Fe in 1927 took delivery of its first 4-8-4s. It was only by a small margin that the Northern Pacific Railroad could claim the first of the type as its own. These early 4-8-4s (Nos. 3751 to 3764) were remarkable for having 30in (762mm) diameter cylinders, the largest both in bore or volume in any passenger locomotive, apart from compounds.

This first batch burnt coal, subsequent 4-8-4s being all oil-burners. More 4-8-4s (Nos.3765 to 3775) came in 1938 and a further batch was built in 1941. The final group (Nos.2900 to 2929) on which the particulars

given in this description are based, were constructed in wartime. Quite fortuitously, they also became the heaviest straight passenger locomotives ever built, because high-tensile steel alloys were in short supply and certain parts—in particular the main coupling and connecting rods—had to be much more massive when designed to be made from more ordinary metal. They managed this feat by a very small margin, but when those immense 16-wheel tenders were included and loaded there were no close rivals to this title. The big tenders were fitted to the last two batches; and as well as being the heaviest passenger locomotives ever built, they were also the longest.

It must be said that Santa Fe would have preferred diesels to the superb last batch of 4-8-4s, but wartime restrictions prevented this. The company had been early into the diesel game with the now legendary streamlined light-weight de luxe "Super Chief" train, introduced in 1937, as well as the equally celebrated coach-class streamliner "El Capitan". But thirty years ago there were still trains such as the "California Limited", "The Scout" and the "Grand Canyon Limited" and, of course, the original "Chief", still formed of standard equipment. They were often then run in two

Above: *Atchison, Topeka & Santa Fe Railway class "3700" 4-8-4 No.3769 climbing the Cajon Pass, California, with the first part of the "Grand Canyon Limited", in June 1946. Note that the chimney extension is in the fully raised position.*

or more sections each and all needed steam power at the head end.

Apart from the early diesel incursions, these 4-8-4s that totalled 65 ruled the Chicago-Los Angeles main line from Kansas City westwards. It was normal practice to roster them to go the whole distance (1,790 miles—2,880km—via Amarillo or 1,760 miles—2,830km—via the Raton Pass); in respect of steam traction these were by far the longest distances ever to be scheduled to run without change of locomotive. Speeds up in the 90-100 mph (140-160km/h) range were both permitted and achieved.

This journey was not made without changing crews. In this respect feather-bedding union rules based on the capacity of the "American" 4-4-0s of fifty years earlier applied and crews were changed 12 times during the 34 hour run. Water was taken at 16 places and fuel nearly as often, in spite of the enormous tenders.

Below: *Santa Fe "2900" class 4-8-4. Note the chimney extension in the raised position, the handsome tapered connecting rods and the enormous tender with two eight-wheel bogies. Eight of these magnificent engines survive, but none is now steamable.*

Above: *Atchison Topeka & Santa Fe Railway class "3700" 4-8-4 No.3787 hauling the streamline cars of the legendary "Chief" express amongst the mountains of the Cajon Pass in California. This train ran daily over the 2,225 miles (3,580km) of Santa Fe metals between Chicago and Los Angeles.*

Left: *The impressive front end of a Santa Fe "2900" class 4-8-4.*

These magnificent examples of the locomotive builder's art were conventional in all main respects. One unusual feature was the 'hot hat' smoke-stack extension shown on the picture above; absence of overbridges and tunnels over many miles of the Santa Fe route meant that this could be raised for long periods with beneficial effect in keeping smoke and steam clear of the cab. Another detail concerned a modification to the Walschaert's

valve gear on some of the 4-8-4s. To reduce the amount of swing — and consequent inertia forces — needed on the curved links, an intermediate lever was introduced into the valve rod. This was so arranged as to increase the amount of valve travel for a given amount of link swing.

Santa Fe was generous in handing out superannuated 4-8-4s as not always properly appreciated gifts to various on-line communities. These included Modesto and San Bernadino, California; Pueblo, Colorado; Fort Madison, Iowa; Kingsman, Arizona; Alburquerque, New Mexico; and Wichita, Kansas. No.2903 is displayed in the Chicago Museum of Science and Industry, while No.2925 is still in the roundhouse at Belen, New Mexico. There was a rumour a year or so ago that Santa Fe might have intentions of entering the steam-for-pleasure business with this locomotive, like neighbour Union Pacific, but nothing came of the proposal.

West Country Class 4-6-2
Great Britain:
Southern Railway (SR), 1946

Tractive effort: 31,046lb (14,083kg).
Axle load: 44,500lb (20.2t).
Cylinders: (3) 16⅜in x 24in (416 x 610mm).
Driving wheels: 74in (1,879mm).
Heating surface: 2,122sq ft (197m²).
Superheater: 545sq ft (50.6m²).
Steam pressure: 280psi (19.7kg/cm²).
Grate area: 38.25sq ft (3.55m²).
Fuel: 11,000lb (5t).
Water: 5,500gall (6,600 US) (25m³).
Adhesive weight: 131,000lb (59.5t).
Total weight: 304,000lb (138t).
Length overall: 67ft 4¾in (20,542mm).

When Oliver Bullied from the London & North Eastern Railway was appointed Chief Mechanical Engineer of the Southern Railway in 1937 he affirmed his intention of contributing a major forward step in the art of steam locomotive design. He was a man of charm, ability, education and integrity and had never allowed the many years spent under Sir Nigel Gresley to blunt an extremely keen and original mind. The result so far as express passenger traffic was concerned was the building of 140 4-6-2s, which collectively were some of the most remarkable machines ever to be seen on rails. Bullied's locomotives were amazingly good in some ways yet almost unbelievably bad in others.

He began from the premise (often forgotten by others) that the prime task of the Chief Mechanical Engineer (C.M.E.) was to build locomotives which could run the trains to time, regardless of quality of coal, bad weather and the presence on board of the least skilled of qualified engine crews. On the whole he succeeded, except perhaps for the need of a certain specialised expertise on the part

of the driver; the fireman, on the other hand, just needed to throw the coal in.

Bullied also went to considerable pains to meet what should be the C.M.E.'s second objective: that the first objective should be met at minimum cost. Here one must say that despite the very considered and original approach adopted, these locomotives were disastrously more expensive than their rivals in first cost, maintenance cost and fuel consumption.

A third objective was achieved, however. Bullied belied his name by being most considerate toward the men who worked for him. He was an example to many of his peers through the care he took to add a number of far from costly features to the locomotives in aid of the convenience and comfort of his crews. They repaid him by doing their very best with the strange and unfamiliar engines he created.

Bullied's 4-6-2s all had three cylinders with three sets of patent chain-driven valve gear inside an oil-filled sump between the frames. Outside-admission piston valves were used, driven from the centre via transverse oscillating shafts. A large boiler was provided, with

a wide firebox tapered on the base line.

The first ones to be built were called the "Merchant Navy" class; the prototype of the 30 built took the rails in 1941. With the experience gained, some smaller 4-6-2s known as the "West Country" class were introduced in 1945. Over the next five years 109 more were built, making them the most numerous Pacifics in Britain. Southern Railway running numbers were 21C101 upwards; British Railways allocated Nos. 34001-34110. Names of west country locations were given to the first 48; most of the remainder were given names associated with the Battle of Britain and were sometimes known as the "Battle of Britain" class—but there was no technical distinction between the two series.

Other features included a multiple-jet blastpipe known as the Lemaître, disc type wheels with holes rather than spokes, and a so-called air-smoothed casing. Innovations (for the SR) appreciated by the crews included rocking grates, power (steam) operated fire-hole door and reverser, rocker grate and electric light. A French system of

Above: *"Merchant Navy" class 4-6-2 No.34002* Union Castle. *Note red-and-cream coaches of early BR days.*

water treatment known as *Traitment Intégral Armand*—which really kept the boilers free of scale even in chalky SR country—was used later. All except six were built at Brighton Works, an establishment that, apart from a few locomotives built during the war, had not produced a new one for many years. The odd six were built at Eastleight Works.

The very best features of the 4-6-2s were the boilers. They bristled with innovations so far as the Southern Railway was concerned—they were welded instead of rivetted, fireboxes were made of steel instead of copper and their construction included water ducts called thermic syphons inside the firebox. Yet in spite of these new features the boilers were marvellous steam raisers as well as being light on maintenance, thereby reflecting enormous credit on Bullied and his team.

An elaborate high pressure vessel, holding a mixture of water and steam at 280psi (19.7kg/cm²)

had been found easy, but one to hold oil a few inches deep proved to be difficult. The feature that did not work out was the totally enclosed oil-filled sump between the frames in which the inside connecting rod and three sets of chain-driven valve gear lashed away. Bullied expected that as in a motor car the lubrication drill would consist solely of a regular check of oil level with occasional topping-up. The motion would be protected against dust, dirt and water while wear would be small. Alas, it did not quite work out like this—the sumps leaked and broke and the mechanisms inside also bristled with so many innovations that they were never made trouble-free. The motion also suffered severe corrosion as the oil became contaminated. Hence there were appalling maintenance problems, never properly resolved in spite of many years of unremitting efforts to solve the difficulties.

Stretching of the chains which drove the miniature valve gears, plus the effect of any wear, all of which was multiplied when the motion was transferred to the valve spindles through rocking shafts, played havoc with the valve settings. This explained the heavy steam consumption. Oil leaking from the sump went everywhere, making the rails slippery and even adding a fresh hazard to railway working—the danger of a steam locomotive catching fire. This happened several times.

With outside motion in full view, drivers often spotted some defect before it had gone too far and something broke. But on these engines the first sign of trouble was often some extremely expensive noises, followed possibly by the puncturing of the oil bath as loose bits forced their way out. Incidentally, the price of all this complexity was very great even when development costs had been paid; the production

cost of a "West Country" was £17,000 at a time when even such a complicated locomotive as a Great Western "Castle" 4-6-0 cost under £10,000.

An unhandy throttle was another handicap and this, combined with the absence of any equalisation between the rear pony wheels and the drivers, made the locomotives liable to driving wheel slip both at starting and while running. On the other hand the performance which the Bullied Pacifics gave once they got going was superb.

Both classes were good but since the smaller "West Country" class seemed to be able to equal anything the larger "Merchant Navy" could do, one's admiration goes more strongly to the former. During the locomotive exchange trials which took place soon after nationalisation of the railways in

Above: *An unkempt "West Country" 4-6-2 No.34017 lays down a fine trail of smoke on a cold snowy day near Weald, Kent.*

1948, they put up performances equal or superior to any of their larger rivals from other lines. It is clear that the SR people knew their candidates were going to come out bottom in coal consumption anyway, so they were determined to show that they could perform instead. Elsewhere than on the SR punctuality in Britain at that time was dreadful and one cites a run on which No.34006 *Bude* regained 11 minutes of lateness on the level route in the short distance (about 40 miles, 64km) between Bristol and Taunton.

On another occasion in the Highlands of Scotland over 13

minutes time was regained in the famous ascent from Blair Atholl to Dalnaspidal; a drawbar horse-power approaching 2,000 was recorded on this occasion. The coal burnt per mile compared with the normal 4-6-0s on this line was 28 per cent more and the amount burnt per horsepower-hour developed was 22 per cent higher. It is also recorded that the consumption of lubricating oil was not 7 per cent but *seven times* more; but that was untypical—three times that of a normal engine was more usual! And remember that a normal locomotive was *intended* to be lubricated on a "total loss" system.

On their home territory the "West Country" locomotives were used on almost every Southern steam-hauled main line passenger working from the "Golden Arrow" continental express from Victoria to Dover, down to two and three coach local trains in Cornwall. Their maintenance problems were less apparent because the 140 Bullied 4-6-2s represented a huge over-provision of motive power.

Furthermore, in 1957-60, sixty "West Country" class were rebuilt with new conventional cylinders and motion; in this form and for the short period left to steam they were unambiguously amongst the very best locomotives ever to run in Britain. During 3 to 9 July 1967, the last week of steam on the Southern, these rebuilds worked the luxury "Bournemouth Belle" on several days.

Several both rebuilt and un-rebuilt have been preserved and restored; for example, unrebuilt No.21C123 *Blackmore Vale* on the Bluebell Railway and No. 21C192 *City of Wells* on the Keighley & Worth Valley Railway.

Below: *The impressive SR "Battle of Britain" class 4-6-2 Sir Winston Churchill now on display at Didcot.*

Niagara Class 4-8-4
United States:
New York Central Railroad (NYC), 1945

Tractive effort: 61,570lb (27,936kg).
Axle load: 70,000lb (32t).
Cylinders: (2) 25½ x 32in (648 x 813mm).
Driving wheels: 79in (2,007mm).
Heating surface: 4,827sq ft (4.48m²).
Superheater: 2,060sq ft (191m²).
Steam pressure: 275psi (19.3kg/cm²).
Grate area: 100sq ft (9.3m²).
Fuel: 92,000lb (42t).
Water: 15,000gall (18,000 US) (82m³).
Adhesive weight: 274,000lb (124t).
Total weight: 891,000lb (405t).
Length overall: 115ft 5½in (35,192mm).

Something has already been said of the New York Central Railroad's speedway from New York to Chicago, arguably in steam days the greatest passenger railway in the world, in terms of speeds run and tonnage moved. By the 1940s these speeds and loads were beginning to be as much as the famous Hudsons could cope with and the Central's chief of motive power, Paul Kiefer, decided to move on a step. He proposed a 4-8-4 with above 30 per cent more adhesive weight and tractive effort than the 4-6-4, together with a fire grate 25 per cent bigger. His aim was a locomotive which could develop 6,000hp in the cylinders for hour after hour and could do the New York-Chicago or Chicago-New York run of 928 miles day after day without respite.

The American Locomotive Company at Schenectady, proposed what was to be the last really new design of passenger locomotive to be produced in the USA. It owed something to the Union Pacific's "800" class; dimensionally, the two designs were very close and, in addition, the design of the 14-wheel Centipede or 4-10-0 tender was certainly based on the UP one. The NYC engines had something else unusual for America, in common with the "800"s—a smooth and uncluttered appearance but with no false streamlining or air-smoothing.

Because the NYC structure gauge only allowed rolling stock to be 15ft 2in (4,623mm) tall instead of 16ft 2in (4,928mm) as on the UP, the smokestack had to be vestigial and the dome little but a manhole cover. There were other differences such as Baker's valve gear instead of Walschaert's but in general the adoption of standard American practice led to similarities.

Naturally, the foundation of the design was a cast steel integral locomotive frame—nothing else could have stood up to the punishment intended for these engines. Also, as one might expect, all axles, coupling rods and connecting rods had roller bearings. Baker's valve gear has the advantage that it has no slides, so all its moving parts could, as in this case, be fitted with needle bearings. While speaking of the valves, an interesting detail was that the edges of the valve-ports were sharp on the steam side, but slightly rounded on the exhaust side. This eased the sharpness of the blast beats, thereby evening out the draught on the fire.

Although fundamentally the same design as that fitted to the UP locos, the tender had some interesting differences. The fact

Below: *Regarded by many as the Ultimate Steam Locomotive, the last of the Niagara 4-8-4s of the New York Central Railroad.*

that the NYC was one of the very few American railroads equipped with track pans (in Great Britain water troughs) meant that less water could be carried conveniently, leaving more capacity for coal. This in its turn enabled the New York-Chicago run to be done with just one intermediate coaling, while an improved design of power-operated pick-up scoop reduced delays by allowing water to be taken at 80mph (128km/h). Special extra venting avoided bursting the tenders (there had been cases!) when some 1,600cu ft (45m³) of incompressible fluid enters the tank all in a few seconds. Incidentally, the overhang of the tank over the running gear at the rear end was to allow the engines to be turned on 100-foot turntables by reducing the wheelbase.

Allocating the number 6,000 to a locomotive whose target was that amount of horse-power as well as that number of miles run per week might seem to be tempting providence, but all was well. The prototype had the sub-class designation "Sla", while the 25 production models (Nos. 6001-6025) were known as "S16" and there was also a single poppet-valve version known as "Slc" (No.5500). This greatest of steam locomotives got the class-name "Niagara" and when the word is uttered, no steam man worthy of the name ever thinks of a waterfall! Both targets were

Above: *A New York Central "Niagara" 4-8-4 on a westbound passenger train of standard heavyweight stock at Dunkirk, New York State, in March 1952.*

achieved—6,700hp on test and an average of 26,000 miles run monthly.

The original idea was that the prototype should be tested and then a production order confirmed, but before work had gone very far instructions were given for all 27 to be put in hand. This was reasonable because in fact the Niagaras were very much a standard, if slightly stretched, product of the industry, whereas what really needed attention was the ground organisation to enable the mileage target to be met. And this, of course, could not be tested until a fleet was available.

By an ordinance of the City of New York, steam locomotives were not allowed inside city limits. Trains therefore left Grand Central Station behind third-rail electric locos for Harmon, 32 miles out in the suburbs. It was here, then, and at Chicago that the Niagaras were, in their great days, kept in first-class condition for what was without doubt one of the hardest services ever demanded of steam, or for that matter, of any motive power.

World records are not achieved without extreme efforts, but excellent organisation allowed quick and thorough servicing. The

power production part of the locomotives had to be just-so to give such a remarkable performance out on the road and to achieve this the fire was first dropped with the engine in steam. Than a gang of "hot men" in asbestos suits entered the firebox — the size of a room — and cleared tubes and flues, did any repairs required to the brick arch, grate etc. Good water treatment ensured that no scale built up in the heating surface, preventing the heat reaching the water inside the boiler. On many railways steam locomotives were allocated one "shed day" each week for these things to be done, but running the 928 miles from Harmon to Chicago or *vice versa* each night, the Niagaras needed to do a week's work in one 24-hour period.

In those days there were 12 daily trains each way just between New York and Chicago — the Chicagoan, the Advance Commodore Vanderbilt, the Commodore Vanderbilt, the Advance Empire State Express, the Empire State Express, the Lake Shore Limited, the Mohawk, the North Shore Ltd, the Pacemaker, the Water Level, the Wolverine and, greatest of all, the 16-hour Twentieth Century Limited.

Even the most fanatical steam enthusiast would admit that other factors have contributed, but nevertheless the Day of the Niagaras did mark a peak. So low have things fallen ·that the best time by diesel traction today on this route between New York and Chicago is 19hr 50min and there is only one train.

The Niagaras also demonstrated once again that modern well-maintained steam power could be more economical than diesel. Alas, in those days, coal supplies controlled by miners' leader John L. Lewis were less reliable than oil supplies; moreover, most of New York Central's steam power was neither modern nor well-maintained. So, having run more miles and hauled more tons in their short lives than most locomotives which run out their term to obsolescence, the Niagaras went to their long home. None have been preserved.

Below: *New York Central Railroad "Niagara" No.6001 leaves Albany, New York State, for the south in April 1952.*

Right: *"Niagara" No.6018 leans to the curve at Peekskill, New York, with "The Missourian" from St. Louis to New York.*

242 A1 4-8-4
France:
French National Railways SNCF, 1946

Axle load: 46,500lb (21t).
Cylinders, HP: (1) 23.6 x 28.3in (600 x 720mm).
Cylinders, LP: (2) 27 x 29.9in (680 x 760mm).
Driving wheels: 76¾in (1,950mm).
Heating surface: 2,720sq ft (253m²).
Superheater: 1,249sq ft (120m²).
Steam pressure: 290psi (20.4kg/cm²).
Grate area: 54sq ft (5m²).
Fuel: 25,000lb (11.5t).
Water: 7,500gall (9,000 US) (34m³).
Adhesive weight: 185,500lb (84t).
Total weight: 496,000lb (225t).
Length overall: 58ft 3½in (17,765mm)..

By every competent authority it is agreed that André Chapelon should be included in the shortest of short lists of candidates to be considered as the greatest locomotive engineer of all. And this magnificent locomotive was his greatest work.

What is now the Western Region of the French National Railways had had a bad experience with a large 4-8-2 locomotive designed by a Government-appointed central design committee. It was a three-cylinder simple, but with poppet valve gear intended to give an expansion ratio equivalent to a compound. Alas, the mechanism never managed to achieve this, and moreover, there were other defects in the engine which caused bad riding and a tendency to derail. No.241.101 was laid aside after tests, an embarassment to all, particularly as it had been announced with tremendous fanfare as marking a new era in steam locomotive construction.

Chapelon had long wished to get his hands on this machine and to do to it what he had done before to the Paris-Orleans 4-6-2s. Official opposition took some years to overcome, but in 1942 his plans were agreed to, with a view of building a prototype for express passenger locomotives

to be constructed when the war was over. The work was put in hand by the Société des Forges et Aciéres de la Marine et d'Homecourt.

The chassis needed substantial strengthening and the extra weight involved in this and other modifications meant the need for an extra carrying wheel—hence France's first 4-8-4 tender locomotive. The de Glehn arrangement with two low-pressure cylinders inside would have involved a crank axle with two cranks and

rather thin webs (since there was no room for thick ones) and it is admitted that this was a source of maintenance problems. So the new engine was to have a single high-pressure cylinder inside driving the leading main axle and two low-pressure cylinders outside driving the second axle. All were in line between the bogie wheels.

Chapelon also moved away from poppet valves and used double piston-valves to give adequate port openings, as in his

Above: *A view of Chapelon's masterpiece, French Railways' 4-8-4 No.242.A.1, rebuilt from a pre-war 4-8-2.*

last batch of 4-6-2 rebuilds. The outside cranks were set at 90 degrees to one another, as in a two-cylinder engine; the inside crank bisected the obtuse angle

Below: *An overall view of the only standard-gauge European 4-8-4 steam locomotive, SNCF No.242.A.1.*

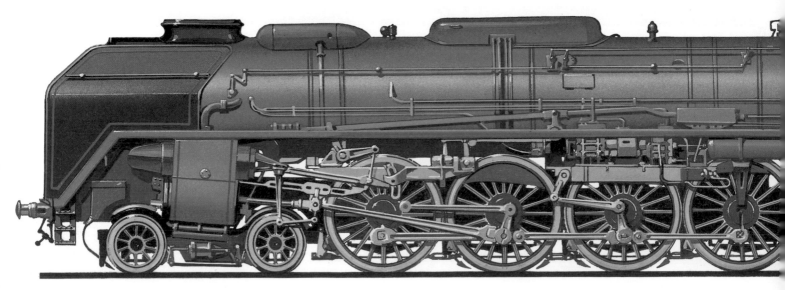

between the other two cylinders, being set at 135 degrees to each. The Walschaert's valve gear for the inside cylinder was mounted partly outside—the eccentric rod was attached to a return crank on the 2nd left-hand driving wheel. The bad riding was tackled with a roller centreing device for the front bogie as well as Franklin's automatic wedges to take up wear in the axlebox guides. Both were of USA origin.

The boiler had two thermic syphons in the firebox, concentric (Houlet's) superheater elements and a mechanical stoker. A triple Kylchap chimney and exhaust system was provided. When completed in 1946, the rebuilt locomotive (now No.242A1) indicated under test that it was by far the most powerful locomotive existing outside North America—the omission of the word steam is deliberate. It could develop a maximum of 5,500hp in the cylinders, compared with 2,800hp before rebuilding. This power output is similar to that of which a typical USA 4-8-4, perhaps 50 per cent, heavier than No.242A1, was capable of as a maximum when driven hard.

This sort of power output enabled then unheard-of things to be done. A typical performance was to haul a 15-car train of 740 tons up a steady gradient of 1 in 125 (0.8 per cent), at a minimum speed of 71mph (114km/h). A 700-ton train was hauled from Paris to Lille in 140 minutes for the 161 miles (258km), while the electrified line from Paris to Le Mans (131 miles—210km) was covered in 109 minutes with a test train of 810 tons weight; well under the electric timings even with this huge train. On another occasion a speed of 94mph (150km/h) was reached; this was also a special test, as there was a 120km/h) (75mph) legal speed limit for public trains in France at that time.

Alas for the future of No.242A1, the top railway brass of France were even more embarrassed by its outstanding success than they were by its previous failure. They

were engaged in trying to persuade the French government, at a time when the resources were at a premium, to underwrite a vast programme of electrification; and here comes a young man (Chapelon was only 58) with an engine which (a) could outperform any electric locomotive so far built and (b) was so economical in coal consumption as to nullify any potential coal saving through electrification. And *both* of these items were the corner-stones of the railways' case for electrification.

So it is not hard to understand why this great locomotive was never duplicated. In fact it was quietly shunted away to Le Mans depot where, turn and turn-about with lesser engines, it took over express trains arriving from Paris by electric traction. The potential of the 4-8-4 was still appreciated by its crews. When such trains were delayed they could use its great performance in earning

Below: *Chapelon's magnificent 242 A1 4-8-4, which was the most powerful steam locomotive to run in Europe.*

themselves large sums in bonus payments for time regained.

There was another potential question mark standing over a future for a production version of 242A1. It has been mentioned that the rugged American 2-8-2s showed an overall economy over the compounds because low maintenance costs more than balanced the cost of the extra coal burnt. Ironically, some of this was due to Chapelon himself, who had improved the valve events and reduced the cylinder clearances of the 141R so that the amount of this extra coal used was reduced from some 20 per cent to 10.

It should really then be no surprise that as revealed by Baron Gerard Vuillet in his authoritative *Railway Reminiscences of Three Continents*, there was an alternative proposal in the form of a two-cylinder simple 4-6-4 with cast-steel locomotive frame, roller bearings, mechanical stoker and a grate area of 67sq ft (6.2m²). Vuillet remarks, "this 147-ton locomotive would not have been much more powerful at the drawbar than the best

Above: *French Railways 242 A1 4-8-4 by Chapelon, a steam locomotive which, when it was built in 1946, outperformed any electric or diesel in existence.*

French Pacifics weighing 104 tons, but would have had a higher availability."

Chapelon was countering with proposals for three-cylinder compound 4-6-4s and 4-8-4s for express passenger work. He also had in mind a triple-expansion compound 4-8-4 with four cylinders, using steam at 584psi (41kg/cm²) generated in a boiler with a water tube firebox. The locomotive was intended to be capable of developing 8,000 hp. Confidently with the former, and it was hoped with the latter, Chapelon expected that maintenance costs of these modern compounds could be brought down close to those of simple locomotives. Alas, all this is now academic—the great 4-8-4 was withdrawn in 1960 and quietly broken up. Nothing now remains but models, memories and deep regrets for what might have been.

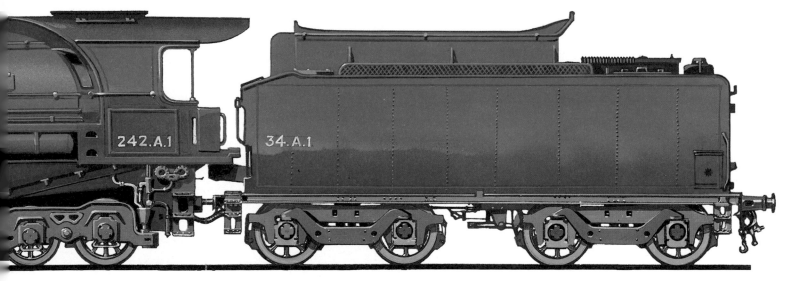

C62 Class 4-6-4
Japan:
Japanese National Railways (JNR), 1949

Tractive effort: 30,690lb
(13,925kg).
Axle load: 36,500lb (16.5t).
Cylinders: (2) 20½ x 26in
(521 x 660mm).
Driving wheels: 69in
(1,750mm).
Heating surface*: 2,640sq ft
(245m²).
Superheater: included above.
Steam pressure: 228psi
(16kg/cm²).
Grate area: 41.5sq ft (3.85m²).
Fuel: 22,000lb (10t).
Water: 4,850gall (5,820 US)
(22m³).
Adhesive weight: 142,500lb
(64.5t).
Total weight: 356,000lb
(101.5t).
Length overall: 70ft 5½in
(21,475mm).
(*including superheater)

Before they became world leaders in so many branches of technology, the Japanese were famous as imitators. In some ways—railway safety and signalling was one—they took British ways as their model, but as regards steam locomotives the basis of their practice was American. This has

applied ever since Baldwin of Philadelphia supplied Japan with some 2-8-2s in 1897, thereby giving the type-name Mikado to the most prolific of the world's wheel arrangements.

So in recent years Japanese locomotives have usually been neat and elegant miniature ver-

sions, to a scale of about three-quarters, of the typical US two-cylinder locomotive, to suit the 3ft 6in (1,067mm) gauge. The last word in express passenger locomotives in Japan were these forty-nine 4-6-4s of the "C-62" class and they were no exception to the rule; yet in details they

Above: *A pair of Japanese National Railways' "C62" class 4-6-4 locomotives head an express train in Hokkaido island.*

Below: *The bold lines of one of the Japanese railways "C62" class 4-6-4s, popularly known as the "Swallows".*

Pt-47 Class 2-8-2
Poland:
Polish State Railways (PKP), 1947

Tractive effort: 42,120lb
(19,110kg).
Axle load: 46,500lb (21t).
Cylinders: (2) 24¾ x 27½in
(630 x 700mm).
Driving wheels: 72¾in
(1,850mm).
Heating surface: 2,476sq ft
(230m²).
Superheater: 1,087sq ft
(101m²).
Steam pressure: 214psi
(15kg/cm²).
Grate area: 48.5sq ft (4.5m²).
Fuel: 20,000lb (9t).
Water: 7,000gall (8,500 US)
(32m³).
Adhesive weight: 184,000lb
(83.5t).
Total weight: 381,500lb (173t).
Length overall: 79ft 7in
(24,255mm).

In their short life of 60 or so years the railways of Poland have seen far too much history, yet their locomotive history shows a surprising continuity. The eight-coupled express passenger locomotive appeared early on in the form of the three "Pu-29" 4-8-2s built by the Cegielski Works of Poznan in 1929. The number in the class designation indicates the date of construction; the "P" stands for *Pospieszny* (Passenger) and the "u" means 4-8-2, "t" means a 2-8-2 and so on.

Since general usage of these lengthy locomotives would mean the renewal of many short turntables, second thoughts prevailed over making this 4-8-2 a standard class. It was considered that a 2-8-2 would do as well; the result

were very distinctive. They were the results of a rather substantial rebuilding of some Mikados of Class "D52"—a heavier version of the standard "D51" class—constructed during World War II. The work was done by outside firms, Hitachi, Kawasaki and Kisha Seizo Kaisha.

One suspects that this way of doing things was to circumvent some government or accountant's restriction on building new passenger motive power—little of the machinery could have been re-used and the saving of actual folding money must have been negligible. But such things are a familiar feature of locomotive practice the world over and, anyway, no one can complain about the results, which were superb in both practical and aesthetic terms. Train worship is even more of a religion in Japan than it is in America or Britain and the "C62"s, "Swallows" as they seem to have been (rather strangely) sometimes known, were certainly enshrined at the summit in this respect.

Features worthy of note provided as standard on the larger Japanese steam locomotive include electric light and a feed-water heater complete with steam pump. There are disc wheels all round, the driving wheels having rather prominent lightening holes. The steam dome is inside the sand dome, the latter keeping the former warm and dry. There is no footplate at the front end of the tender—the cab overhangs the leading pair of wheels, while a shovelling plate extends forward from the tender into the cab.

Twenty years ago they could be found hauling the top trains—such as the *Hatsukari* or Migratory Goose Express—out of Tokyo's main station, but now not only has steam locomotion disappeared from these narrow (3ft 6in—1,067mm) gauge lines but long-distance daytime passenger trains as well. They have migrated to the standard gauge electric Shin Kansen network on which the famous bullet trains provide 100mph (160km/h) service start-to-stop several times each hour.

The 4-6-4s, however, for a number of years found a haven in Japan's main northern island,

Hokkaido, working—often in pairs and occasionally in threes—the main expresses out of Hakkodate, the ferryboat port at its southern tip. When this finally came to an end two of these giants were set aside for preservation. One (No.C62-2) is on display at the Umekoji Museum Depot at Kyoto, on the Japanese

Above: *An express passenger train being double-headed by a pair of Japanese National Railways' "C62" class 4-6-2 "Swallows".*

main island, while the other (No. C62-3) is kept at Otaro on the northern island of Hokkaido and run on special occasions.

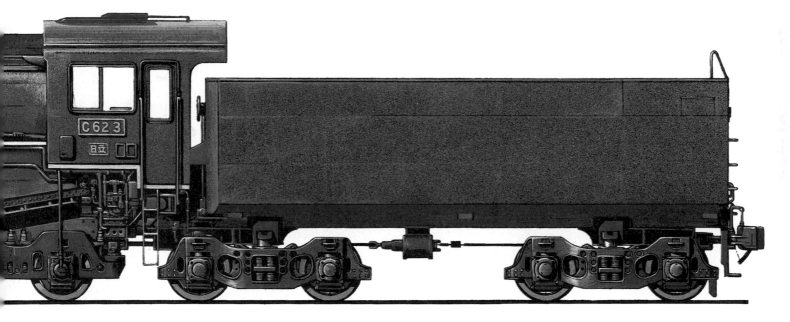

was the "Pt-31", which had the same cylinders, wheels and boiler pressure. Like most Polish locomotives, they were simple unrefined but rugged two-cylinder machines reflecting a country in which coal is plentiful, so that the pay-off of complicated refinements is at a minimum.

The German invasion of 1939 came before the whole 110 had been completed and the last 12 appeared as German State Railway class "39". Thirty of the

Left: *A Polish State Railways "P-47" class 2-8-2 at the head of a local passenger train. An interesting feature is the set of double-deck coaches, in order to maximise the seating capacity for a given length of train.*

"Pt-31"s stayed in the area taken over by Russia. After the war Poland again became independent but not all the surviving 2-8-2s came back into Polish hands. Many remained in the territory permanently ceded to Russia, while others worked in Austria for several years.

The recipe was so effective that further similar 2-8-2s were introduced in 1947. These were the class "Pt-47", of which 120 were built by the locomotive building enterprise Chrzanow of Warsaw and 60 by Cegielski. The main changes were from a rivetted to a welded firebox, from a separate steam and sand dome to a combined one and from hand stoking to automatic stoking. The new locomotives

were as handsome as the old ones and soon took over the haulage of Poland's principal express trains on non-electrified lines. All the 2-8-2s had a Krauss-Helmholtz leading truck, which to some extent has the effect of making the leading driving wheels part of the guiding system when running on curved track. Without some device of this kind, the riding qualities of locomotives with only a single leading guiding wheel have always been regarded as having a question mark applied to them—a number of serious derailments having occurred.

During the dawn of railways in their country, the Russian occupiers of Poland were responsible for not only the now defunct broad gauge there but also for a

tall structure gauge. Hence the "Pt-47" has an overall height of 15ft 4in (4,668mm), representing extra space which gave a welcome degree of freedom to the designers.

At the time of writing and by a factor of several times, Poland has more operational steam locomotives than any other country outside Africa or Asia. No doubt one factor in this decision to electrify gradually while keeping steam, lies in a preference for a transport system dependent on Polish coal rather than some other nation's oil, but another factor is certainly the overall economy and reliability of one of mankind's most faithful friends, the steam locomotive in its simplest form.

Class A1 4-6-2
Great Britain:
British Railways (BR), 1948

Tractive effort: 37,400lb (16,900kg).
Axle load: 49,500lb (22.5t).
Cylinders: (3) 19 x 26in (482 x 660mm).
Driving wheels: 80in (2,032mm).
Heating surface: 2,461sq ft (228.6m²).
Superheater: 680sq ft (63.2m²).
Steam pressure: 250psi (17.6kg/cm²).
Grate area: 50sq ft (4.6m²).
Fuel: 20,000lb (9t).
Water: 5,000gall (6,000 US) (22.7m³).
Adhesive weight: 148,000lb (67t).
Total weight: 369,000lb (167t).
Length overall: 73ft 0in (22,250mm).

When Sir Nigel Gresley died suddenly in office in 1941, The London and North Eastern Railway had 115 Pacifics and some 600 other three-cylinder engines of his design, all fitted with his derived motion, in which the inside valve took its drive from the two outside valve gears. In peace time this derived motion had been prone to failure, but under wartime conditions of maintenance the problem had become much more serious.

Gresley was succeeded by Edward Thompson, one of his most senior assistants, who had a particular interest in maintenance. Thompson foresaw that a large programme of locomotive building would be needed after the war to make good the arrears of locomotive construction, and in formulating this programme he was particularly concerned to eliminate the derived motion, in the large engines by fitting a third valve gear, and in the smaller ones by eliminating the third cylinder. As he was already aged 60 when promoted, he also felt the need to apply his ideas with urgency.

The opportunity to build a Pacific to his ideas arose from the poor availability of Gresley's "P2" class 2-8-2 locomotives, one of whose troubles was heavy wear of axleboxes due to the long rigid wheelbase on the sharp curves of the Edinburgh-Aberdeen line. By rebuilding these as Pacifics he hoped to improve their performance, and also to gain experience for further new construction. Elimination of

Above: *A Darlington-built British Railways "A1" class 4-6-2 No.60149* Amadis *ready to depart from Kings Cross station, London.*

Below: *British Railways "A1" class 4-6-2 No.60161* North British, *portrayed in experimental blue livery during BR's early days.*

Class WP 4-6-2
India:
Indian Railways (IR), 1946

Tractive effort: 30,600lb (13,884kg).
Axle load: 45,500lb (20.7t).
Cylinders: (2) 20¼ x 28in (514 x 711mm).
Driving wheels: 67in (1,705mm).
Heating surface: 2,257sq ft (286.3m²).
Superheater: 725sq ft (67m²).
Steam pressure: 210psi (14.7kg/cm²).
Grate area: 46sq ft (4.3m²).
Fuel: 33,000lb (15t).
Water: 6,000gall (7,200 US) (27m³).
Adhesive weight: 121,500lb (55t).
Total weight: 380,000lb (172.5t).
Length overall: 00ft 00in (00,000mm).

Of only three classes of express locomotive amongst those described in this book can it be said (with much pleasure) that most remain in service, doing the job for which they were made. One of them is this massive broad-gauge (5ft 6in—1,676mm) American-style 4-6-2, the standard express passenger locomotive of the Indian Railways. Class "WP" comprises 755 locomotives, built between 1947 and 1967, with running numbers 7000 to 7754.

The prototypes were a batch of 16 ordered from Baldwin of Philadelphia in 1946, well before Independence, so the decision to go American was not connected with the political changes. It was taken as a result of the satisfactory experience with the American locomotives supplied to India during the war, coupled with unsatisfactory experience with the Indian standard designs of the 1920s and 1930s.

Naturally, the locomotives supplied were built to the usual rugged simple basic USA standards. The provision of vacuum brakes, standard in India, made them even simpler, because a vacuum ejector is a vastly less complicated device than a steam air-pump. An air-smoothed exterior was provided for aesthetic rather than aerodynamic reasons, giving a solid dependable look to some solid dependable locomotives.

The original batch were designated "WP/P" (P for prototypes) and the production version differed in minor details. During the next ten years further members of the class were supplied from foreign countries as follows:

USA—Baldwin 100
Canada—Canadian Locomotive Co 100
Canada—Montreal Locomotive Works 120
Poland—Fabryka Locomotywim, Chrzanow 30
Austria—Vienna Lokomotiv Fabrik 30

There was then a pause until 1963, when India's own new Chitteranjan locomotive building plant began production of the remainder. Some further small modifications to the design were made to facilitate production at this works.

the Gresley gear involved arranging the inside cylinder to drive the leading axle, and as Thompson insisted on all the connecting rods being of the same length, an awkward layout was arrived at, with the leading bogie ahead of the outside cylinders.

Trouble was experienced with flexing of the frame, and loosening and breakage of steam pipes, but nevertheless the arrangement was applied to the "P2"s and to a further 19 mixed-traffic Pacifics with 74in (1,880mm) driving wheels. Before this programme was completed, Thompson also took in hand Gresley's original Pacific, *Great Northern*, and rebuilt it similarly, with separate valve gears, larger cylinders, and a grate area of 50sq ft (4.6m²), in place of the 41.3sq ft (3.8m²) grate with which all the Gresley Pacifics were fitted.

Before Thompson's retirement, his successor designate, Arthur Peppercorn, put in hand quietly in Doncaster drawing office a further revision of the Pacific layout, in which the outside cylinders were restored to their position above the middle of the bogie, and the inside connecting

rod was shortened to make the front of the engine more compact. Fifteen new Pacifics with 74in wheels were built to this design, classified "A2", and then 49 more with 80in (2,032mm) wheels were ordered, classified "A1". The *Great Northern* was absorbed into this class under the sub-classification "A1/1".

These engines were not built until after nationalisation, in 1948-49, Nos.60114-27/53-62 at Doncaster, and Nos.60130-52 at Darlington. They all had Kylchap

Above: *"A1" class 4-6-2 No. 60139 makes a fine show with the "Yorkshire Pullman".*

double blastpipes, and five of them had roller bearings to all axles. At first they had stovepipe chimneys, but these were replaced by chimneys of the normal Doncaster shape. They had assorted names, including locomotive engineers, the constituent railways of the LNER, some traditional Scottish names, some birds and some racehorses.

The "A1"s proved to be fast and economical engines, and they took a full share in East Coast locomotive workings, except for the Kings Cross-Edinburgh non-stops, for which the streamlined "A4"s were preferred. Their maintenance costs were lower than those of other BR Pacifics, and they achieved notable mileages. Over a period of 12 years they averaged 202 miles per calendar day, the highest figure on BR, and the five roller bearing engines exceeded that average, with 228 miles per day. Their riding was somewhat inferior to that of the "A4", as they had a tendency to lateral lurching on straight track, but nevertheless they were timed at 100mph plus (160+km/h) on a number of occasions.

These engines were a worthy climax to Doncaster Pacific design, but unfortunately they came too late in the day to have full economic lives. By the early 1960s dieselisation of the East Coast main line was well advanced, and the "A1"s were all withdrawn between 1962 and 1966. None of them was preserved.

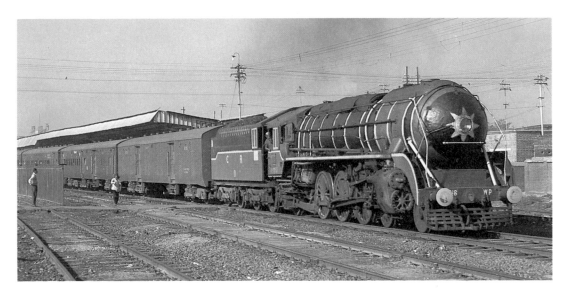

The fleet of "WP"s work in all parts of the broad gauge network and find full employment on many important express passenger trains, although they have been displaced from the very top assignments by diesels and electrics, also Indian-built. Enormous trains, packed with humanity, move steadily across the Indian plains each headed by one of these excellent locomotives. A crew of four is carried (driver, two firemen and a coal-trimmer) but even with two observers on board as well there is ample room in the commodious cab.

Left: *An Indian Railways class "WP" 4-6-2. The letters "CR" on the tender indicate it is allocated to the Central Railway.*

Class 241P 4-8-2
France:
French National Railways (SNCF), 1948

Axle load: 45,000lb (20.5t).
Cylinders, HP: (2) 17.6 x 25.6in (446 x 650mm).
Cylinders, LP: (2) 26.5 x 27.6in (674 x 700mm).
Driving wheels: 79.1in (2,010mm).
Heating surface: 2,633sq ft (244.6m²).
Superheater: 1,163sq ft (108m²).
Steam pressure: 284psi (20kg/cm²).
Grate area: 54.4sq ft (5.1m²).
Fuel: 22,000lb (11t).
Water: 7,480gall (8,980 US) (34m³).
Adhesive weight: 180,900lb (82t).
Total weight: 472,500lb (214t).
Length overall: 89ft 11in (27,418mm).

During the period in which André Chapelon was achieving unprecedented results by his rebuilding of Paris-Orleans Railway Pacifics, the total construction of new engines in France was small in proportion to the size of country. During World War II plans were prepared for a new fleet of high-powered steam engines, which it was confidently expected would be needed in large numbers to make good the arrears of new construction, and to provide for increase in the speed and weight of trains. For the heaviest express work a 4-8-4 was proposed, but construction of an experimental prototype by the rebuilding of an old 4-8-2 was slow. In the meantime construction of a modernised version of a PLM 2-8-2 was undertaken, and large numbers of 2-8-2s were ordered from North America.

Unfortunately in 1946 a national coal shortage caused the government to instruct SNCF to reduce its coal consumption, and the way was paved for a policy decision to electrify all main lines. Further development of steam engines was cancelled, but a case was made for the construction of a limited number of large passenger engines, particularly to cope with increasing loads on the old PLM main line to Marseilles, on which Chapelon 4-8-0s

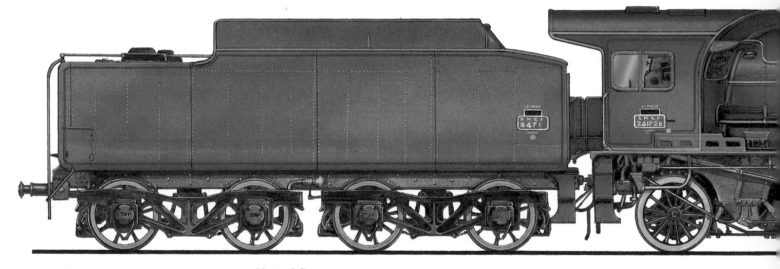

L-2a Class 4-6-4
United States
Chesapeake & Ohio Railway (C&O), 1948

Tractive effort: 52,1000lb (23,639kg).
Axle load: 73,500lb (33.5t).
Cylinders: (2) 25 x 30in (635 x 762mm).
Driving wheels: 78in (1,981mm).
Heating surface: 4,233sq ft (393m²).
Superheater: 1,810sq ft (168m²).
Steam pressure: 255psi (17.9kg/cm²).
Grate area: 90sq ft (8.4m²).
Fuel: 60,000lb (27.5t).
Water: 17,500gall (21,000 US) (80m³).
Adhesive weight: 219,500lb (100t).
Total weight: 839,000lb (381t).
Length overall: 108ft 0in (32,918mm).

It was a case of "last orders please" when in 1947 the Chesapeake & Ohio Railway went to Baldwin of Philadelphia for five 4-6-4s and to the Lima Locomotive Co of Lima, Ohio, for five 4-8-4s. They were to be the last steam express passenger locomotives supplied for home use by any of the big USA constructors, although naturally neither the customer nor the builders realised it at the time.

The C&O divided its routes into mountain and plains divisions and the eight-coupled engines were for the former, the six-coupled ones for the latter. There was, therefore, scope for the 4-6-4s, both north-west of the Allegheny mountains on the routes to Louisville, Cincinatti, Chicago and Detroit, as well as south-east of them in the directions of Washington and Richmond, Virginia.

In 1947 a man called Robert R. Young was in charge at C&O headquarters at Richmond and he believed the passenger train had a future. The Chessie ran through the big coalfields and at that time hauled more coal than any other railroad. It was therefore unthinkable that anything but coal-burning power should be used. Amongst his plans was one for a daytime streamline service actually to be known as The Chessie—and three steam-turbine locomotives with electric drive and 16 driving wheels were built in 1947-48 to haul it on the main stem and over the mountains. Conventional steam was to haul connecting portions and provide back-up. Alas, those whose concept it was had thrown away the steam locomotive's best card, that is simplicity, and in a short two years the turbo-electrics (Class "M-1", Nos.500-502) had been scrapped as hopelessly uneconomic.

In the meantime the whole C&O streamline project had been scrapped, but not before some older 4-6-2s (the "F-19" class) had been converted into streamlined 4-6-4s to handle the new train over part of its route. Furthermore, in the grand manner of a great and prosperous railroad, C&O considered hand-me-downs not be good enough for a prestige train and so had ordered these "L-2a" Hudsons, intending them to be streamlined. Running numbers were 310 to 314 and fortunately they were trouble-free as the turbines had been troublesome.

On various important counts the 4-6-4s were the top six-coupled locomotives of the world—in engine weight at 443,000lb (201t), 7½ per cent above those of the nearest rival, Santa Fe. In tractive effort, both with and without their booster in action, the latter worth 14,200lb

of Class "240P" were achieving prodigious feats of haulage. However, to reach this standard of performance with a grate of 40sq ft (3.7m²) required a high standard of fuel, and it was clear that for post-war conditions an engine with a much larger grate was desirable. Furthermore, the ex-PLM engineers who now influenced policy on SNCF favoured the simplicity of piston valves, rather than the poppet valves which were used in most of the Chapelon 4-8-0s. Authority was therefore given for the construction of thirty-five 4-8-2s, in place of the last forty 2-8-2s on order.

Time was short for the production of a completely new design, and Chapelon's 4-8-4 was not even completed, still less tested, so the only possibility was to modify an existing design. The design chosen was an ex-PLM

Left: *French National Railways class "241P" 4-8-2, a design based on some older 4-8-2 PLM locomotives of the same type.*

4-8-2 of a type of which one only had been built in 1930, but which gave the right basic layout and boiler size for the new class. This engine had the high-pressure cylinders inside the frames between the first and second coupled axles, and driving the third axle. The low-pressure cylinders were outside driving the second axle. The high-pressure and low-pressure valves on each side were driven from a common valve gear on the von Borries principle. Into this design were incorporated as many as possible of Chapelon's ideas on large superheaters and generous steam pipes and ports, whilst at the same time the PLM frame structure was strengthened in places where it was known to be weak. Mechanical stoker, feed water heater, and the French TIA system of water treatment in the tender were fitted; the TIA system in-

Below: *The complexity of the impressive SNCF class "241P" is well brought out in this superb drawing.*

creased greatly the time between boiler washing out.

Nevertheless the design was a compromise, a number of the parts which it inherited from the old design were overloaded at the power outputs which were now possible, and the mechanical performance left something to be desired. Despite the measures taken to accelerate production of the new class, which was numbered from 241P1 to 241P35, the engines were not delivered until 1948-9, by which time electrification of the ex-PLM main line was well in hand. Initially they worked on the former PLM and on ex-Northern main lines from Paris to Lille and Belgium. As electrification advanced, some of them moved to the Western Region, where they took over the heaviest trains to the Brittany coast from Le Mans onward. Under the enthusiastic regional mechanical engineer they were driven to their limits on these services, on trains which could load to 950 tons at busy times. With loads of 650 tons

they could achieve 60mph (96 km/h) from start to stop on short runs, and could reach the speed limit of 74mph (120km/h) with this load in six minutes. Their other speciality was the Bourbonnais line of the old PLM, on which they worked loads of up to 800 tons until displaced by diesels in 1968.

Although their power output in relation to their size never equalled that of the Chapelon 4-8-0s, it was at its best magnificent. They were worked more intensively than previous French passenger engines, and two of them once ran 19,900 miles (32,000km) and 18,578 miles (29,874km) in a month on trains averaging 585 tons, whilst working from Lyons Mouche depot.

The 241Ps managed a working life of nearly twenty years before they were finally displaced by diesels. Four of the engines have been preserved, including No. 241P16 in the French National Railway Museum at Mulhouse where the locomotive is one of the main exhibits.

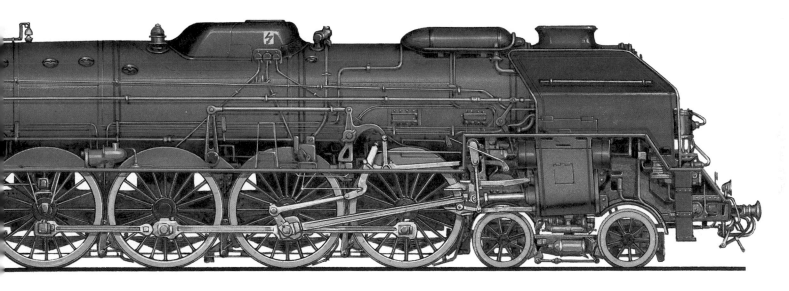

(6,443kg) of thrust, and adhesive weight, the figures are records. The massive qualities of C&O track are illustrated by the fact that their adhesive weight is also unmatched elsewhere.

Technically the engines represented the final degree of sophistication of the American steam locomotive that came from nearly 120 years of steady development of practice and details upon the original principles. The "L-2a" class was developed from the eight "L-2" class 4-6-4s of 1941 (Nos.300-307) and differed from them mainly in having Franklin's system of rotary-cam poppet valves instead of more conventional Baker's gear and piston valves. These locomotives also were notable for having

Left: *Although seemingly complicated, the C&O class "L-2a" 4-6-4 was fundamentally simple.*

unusually clean lines. The C&O once even had liked to hang a pair of air-pumps in the most prominent possible position on the smokebox door; now even the headlight was cleared away and mounted above the pilot beam.

The advantages of poppet valves have been mentioned elsewhere in this narrative, as have the problems involved in their maintenance. It would appear, though, as if manufacturers on both sides of the Atlantic had begun in this respect to offer a viable product—now that it was just too late to affect the outcome of steam's struggle for survival.

By 1953 Chessie's passenger service had become 100 per cent dieselised. Accordingly there was little work for the new 4-6-4s and all had gone for scrap before their seventh birthday.

Class 01.¹⁰ 4-6-2
Germany:
German Federal Railway (DB), 1953

Tractive effort: 37,200lb
(16,830kg).
Axle load: 44,500lb (20.2t).
Cylinders: (3) 19.7 x 26.0in
(500 x 600mm).
Driving wheels: 78.7in
(2,000mm).
Heating surface: 2,223sq ft
(206.5m²).
Superheater: 1,035sq ft
(96.2m²).
Steam pressure: 227.6psi
(16kg/cm²).
Grate area: 42.6sq ft (3.96m²).
Fuel: 22,000lb (10.0t).
Water: 8,400gall (10,000 US)
(38m³).
Adhesive weight: 133,000lb
(60.4t).
Total weight: 244,000lb
(110.8t) (without tender).
Length overall: 79ft 2in
(24,130mm).

Above: *Recently re-coaled German "01" class 4-6-2 surges through the countryside.*

Left: *German State Railway rebuilt class "01" 4-6-2 ready to leave Hamburg with a cross-border express for Dresden.*

At the end of World War II in 1945 the railways of Germany were devastated, and a large proportion of the express passenger locomotives were out of service. By the end of the decade services were largely restored, but by that time the partition of Germany had been formalized, and the railway system of the Federal Republic had adopted the name German Federal Railway, whilst that of the German Democratic Republic used the old name of German State Railway. The locomotive stock was divided between the two systems on the basis of where the locomotives were located at the end of hostilities.

By 1950 it was clear that both systems would extend their electrified networks, and introduce diesel traction on non-electrified lines, but both systems also made plans for limited construction of new steam locomotives for the interim period. In the event, new construction was confined to mixed-traffic and freight locomotives, and only two completely new express passenger engines were built. These were two three-cylinder Pacifics completed by DB in 1957, by which time the progress of electrification was so rapid that it was clear that there was no prospect of the class being extended.

Steam-hauled passenger trains therefore continued to be worked by the stock of pre-war Pacifics. To prolong their lives, many of these on both systems were rebuilt to varying degrees. Although each railway adopted its own scheme of rebuilding, they had much in common, and where any renumbering was involved, it was arranged that there was no duplication between DB and DR.

The first engines to be altered were the 55 three-cylinder Pacifics of Class "01.¹⁰", all of which came into DB ownership. These engines had been built in 1939 and 1940 with full streamlining, but by the end of the war parts of the casing had been removed, and many of the engines lay derelict for up to five years. Between 1949 and 1951 the class was given heavy repairs, in the course of which the streamlined casing was removed, and the engines acquired an appearance in accordance with post-war standards. Compared with the non-streamlined pre-war Pacifics, there was no sloping plate connecting the side running boards with the buffer beam, and the full-depth smoke deflectors were replaced by the small Witte pattern on the upper part of the smokebox. Removal of the casing around the smokebox revealed that the cylinder of the feedwater heater was mounted externally in a recess in the top of the smokebox, instead of being buried in the smokebox as in the "01" and "03" engines. The North American touch in the lineaments of the engines was thereby increased. Various parts which had been made of substitute materials during the war were replaced by normal parts.

The next rebuilding involved fitting new welded fireboxes with combustion chambers to five of the "01" Pacifics, the existing parallel barrel being retained. The original fireboxes without combustion chambers had been troublesome to maintain, despite Dr Wagner's intentions. The modified boiler could be detected by extra firebox washout plugs, but even more conspicuous was the fitting of Heinl feedwater heaters, with a raised casing ahead of the chimney.

Deterioration of the alloy-steel fireboxes of the "01.¹⁰" and "03.¹⁰" Pacifics then led to the design of a new all-welded boiler with tapered barrel, suitable for

Below: *German Federal Railway converted oil-burning class "012" 4-6-2 No.012077-4.*

fitting to all the large Pacifics; a smaller version of the same boiler was produced for the "03" and "03.¹⁰" classes. This new boiler was fitted to all the "01.¹⁰" engines between 1954 and 1956, and to the 26 "03.¹⁰" engines which had come into DB ownership between 1956 and 1958. At the same time new front end systems, with larger chimneys, were fitted, and a Heinl feedwater heater, with its tank concealed within the smokebox. The outline of the boiler was simplified compared with the pre-war types, as there was only one dome, and the sandboxes were on the running plates. The dimensions given above refer to these rebuilds.

The rebuilt "01.¹⁰" engines became the mainstay of heavy steam passenger workings on DB. As electrification spread northwards, they too moved north, and most of them ended their days at Rheine, where they

Class 231U1 4-6-4
France:
French National Railways (SNCF), 1949

were amongst the last DB steam engines to finish work in 1975. To increase the availability of the engines, 34 of them were converted to burn oil in 1957-58. These engines became class "012" under the 1968 renumbering, whilst the remaining coalburners were "011". In the latter days of steam operation on the Hamburg-Bremen line, these engines were hauling 600-tonne trains at speeds up to 80mph (130km/h), and were achieving monthly mileages of 17,000 (27,000km).

It was planned to fit the same type of boiler to 80 of the "01" Pacifics, but due to the increasing pace of electrification, only 50 were converted. Externally the engines were conspicuous by the large-diameter chimney, but as these engines worked over lines with a more restricted loading gauge than those on which the "01.¹⁰"s worked, the chimney was much shorter, and gave the engines a very massive appearance.

In East Germany, too, the slower pace of electrification led to the extensive rebuilding of 35 "01" Pacifics between 1961 and 1965. New all-welded boilers were fitted, but whereas on DB the new boilers had slightly smaller grates than their predecessors, those on DR had larger grates to cope with inferior coal. The external appearance of the engines was changed greatly by the fitting of a continuous casing over the boiler mountings, and a deep valancing below the footplating (later removed). Eight of the rebuilds were given Boxpok driving wheels, and 28 of them were later converted to burn oil. The rebuilt engines were classified "01". The rebuilding was so extensive that little of the original engine remained. They took over the heaviest DR steam workings, which included the international trains into West Germany, and they could be seen alongside the DB variants of Class "01" at Hamburg and Bebra.

Axle load: 51,000lb (23t).
Cylinders, HP: (2) 17¾ x 27½in (450 x 700mm).
Cylinders, LP: (2) 26¾ x 27½in (680 x 700mm).
Driving wheels: 78½in (2,000mm).
Heating surface: 2,100sq ft (195m²).
Superheater: 690sq ft (64m²).
Steam pressure: 286psi (280kg/cm²).
Grate area: 55.7sq ft (5.17m²).
Fuel: 20,000lb (9t).
Water: 8,370gall (10,000 US) (38m³).
Adhesive weight: 152,000lb (69t).
Total weight: 467,500lb (212t).
Length overall: 87ft 4½in (26,634mm).

This great engine was the result of the Northern Company's desire to improve upon their Chapelon 4-6-2s. An attempt was made to overcome the weakness of the plate frames by adopting cast steel bar-type ones. A higher power output was envisaged and this was taken care of by a wide firebox (instead of trapezoidal) and a mechanical stoker. Eight streamlined and partly experimental 4-6-4 locomotives were planned, four compounds (class 232S), three simples (class 232R) and one turbine. The idea was to work 200-ton trains at speeds up to 100mph (160km/h). Before the engines were completed in 1940 the railways had been nationalised and a disastrous war with Germany had begun, so the light high-speed trains envisaged for these locomotives to pull were replaced by immense slow ones. The turbine locomotive was never completed.

After the war the performance of the 4-6-4s was re-assessed. In the case of the compounds the designers had unfortunately tried to re-invent the wheel and had not been completely successful.

Below: *French National Railways 4-6-4 No.231U1 as restored for display in the museum.*

The rotary-cam poppet valve gear (instead of the oscillating-cam gear used by Chapelon) was troublesome and failed to meet its promise as regards economy in the use of steam. Even so, France was reluctant to abandon the compound principle and it was decided to finish off the chassis originally intended for the turbine locomotive in this manner. The result was the "232U1", completed in 1949 by the firm of Corpet-Louvet.

The purposeful clutter that was the Chapelon outline had been covered by a streamline shroud. Beneath it poppet valves had been replaced by piston valves. The four sets of valves were worked by two sets of outside Walschaert's valve gear. In an effort to reduce maintenance costs roller bearings had replaced plain ones on the axles, grease lubrication had largely replaced oil and again cast bar-type frames were used. The engine was successful; it was able to develop 4,500hp measured at the cylinders, about half way between that for a Chapelon 4-6-2 and the ultimate power of his "242A1" class 4-8-4. One drawback was the heavy axle load; this effectively confined the locomotive (and its fellow streamliners of the "232R" and "232S" classes) to the Paris

to Lille main line. Although the engines were designed for better things, the maximum permitted speed was kept at the standard French value of 75mph (120 km/h).

Efforts had also been made to simplify the controls—the complications of those implicit in the de Glehn system of compounding have been referred to earlier. In the "232S" and "232U" locomotives the changeover from simple working (used at starting) to compound was arranged to happen automatically, according to whether the reversing lever was set to give more or less than 55 per cent cut-off. So perhaps the supply of footplate wizards able to cope with the complexities of the typical French express passenger locomotive was not so inexhaustible as their admirers across the Channel thought!

By the time the virtues of the design had been assessed and the question of a repeat order arose, French Railways had turned to electrification. So No. 232U1 remained a solitary and is now displayed in superbly restored condition at the National Railway Museum at Mulhouse.

Below: *SNCF class "232U" 4-6-4 232U1 at the Gare du Nord, Paris in October 1959.*

P36 Class 4-8-4

USSR:
Soviet Railways (SZD), 1953

Tractive effort: 39,686lb (18,007kg).
Axle load: 41,000lb (18.5t).
Cylinders: (2) 22½ x 31½in (575 x 800mm).
Driving wheels: 72¾in (1,850mm).
Heating surface: 2,617sq ft (243m²).
Superheater: 1,537sq ft (142m²).
Steam pressure: 213psi (15kg/cm²).
Grate area: 73sq ft (6.75m²).
Fuel: 51,000lb (23t).
Water: 10,000gall (12,000 US) (46m³).
Adhesive weight: 163,000lb (74t).
Total weight: 582,000lb (264t).
Length overall: 94ft 10in (29,809mm).

Having by 1930 established an excellent class of passenger locomotive—the "S" class—and built about 3,000 of them, the Soviet Railways could sit back and consider the future of long-distance passenger traffic at leisure. Passenger traffic had so far always taken second place to freight but it was recognised that in due time higher speeds and more comfortable (and therefore heavier) trains would be needed for those whom the Soviet government permitted to travel in the future.

The first prototype came in 1932 and it was a logical enlargement of the 2-6-2 into a 2-8-4, combining an extra driving axle to give extra tractive effort and an extra rear carrying axle to give extra power from a larger firebox. The class was given the designation "JS" (standing for Joseph Stalin) and some 640 were built between 1934 and 1941. None is working today but a freight equivalent with the same boiler, cab, cylinders, tender and other parts was the "FD" class 2-10-2, many of which are still in service in southern China, after conversion from 5ft (1,524mm) gauge to standard.

Right: *Two class "P36" 4-8-4s stand nose-to-nose in a locomotive depot in icy Siberia.*

Above: *A class "P36" 4-8-4 of the Soviet Railways "on shed" somewhere in Russia.*

The episode was typical of a sensible and logical attitude towards the needs of the railway system, in respect of which the new socialist regime hardly differed from the old Czarist one. One small prestige extravagance did follow, however, with the building in 1937-38 of the first three of a class of ten high-speed streamlined 4-6-4s for the Red Arrow express between Moscow and Leningrad. It was hoped to raise the average speed for the 404-mile (646km) run from about 40 to 50mph (64 to 80km/h). The first two had coupled wheels 78¾in (2,000mm) diameter, but the third had them as large as 86½in (2,197mm). The latter machine again had boiler, cylinders and much else standard with the "FD" class. In the end the war put an end to the project, but not before the first prototype had achieved 106mph (170km/h) on test, still a record for steam traction in Russia.

World War II for the Russians may have been shorter than it was for the rest of Europe, but it was also a good deal nastier. So it was not until five years after it ended that the first of new class of passenger locomotive appeared from the Kolomna Works near Moscow. This prototype took the form of a tall and handsome 4-8-4, designated class "P36". The new locomotive was similar in size and capacity to the "JS" class but the extra pair of carrying wheels enabled the axle loading to be reduced from 20 to 18 tons. This gave the engine a much wider possible range of action, although this was never needed, as we shall see.

Whilst the locomotive was very much in the final form of the

Left: *Soviet Railways' class "P36" 4-8-4 No.P36-0148 arrives at Leningrad.*

steam locomotive, one feature which it had in common with many modern Russian engines was particularly striking and unusual; this was an external main steam pipe enclosed in a large casing running forward from dome to smokebox along the top of the boiler. This arrangement, excellent from the point of view of accessibility, is only made possible by a loading gauge which allows rolling stock to be 17ft 4in (5,280mm) above rail level. Roller bearings were fitted to all axles—for the first time on any Russian locomotive—and there was a cab totally enclosed against the Russian winter, as well as a mechanical stoker for coal-fired examples of the class. Many of the 4-8-4s, however, were oil-burning, particularly those in the west of the country.

After a cautious period of testing, production began at Kolomna and between 1954 and 1956 at least 249 more were built, making them the world's most numerous class of 4-8-4. Of course, compared with other classes in Russia, which numbered from more than 10,000 examples downward, the size of the class was miniscule.

In contrast, though, their impact upon Western observers was considerable because they were to be found on lines visited by foreigners, such as Moscow-Leningrad and between Moscow and the Polish frontier. Some of the class were even finished in the blue livery similar to the

streamlined 4-6-4s, but most looked smart enough in the light green passenger colours with cream stripes and red wheel centres.

For some 15 years the "P36" handled the famous Trans-Siberian express, the legendary Russia, from the end of electrification to the Pacific Ocean shore. The run took 70 hours and there were 19 changes of steam locomotive, so Siberia was paradise to at least one class of humanity. Steam enthusiasts had to show some subtlety in recording the objects of their love on film; the use of miniature cameras was very dangerous, but some success was achieved by people who set up a huge plate camera on its tripod, marched up to the nearest policeman and demanded that the platform end be cleared.

Steam enthusiasm was not without its dangers for those at home. In 1956 Lazar Kaganovitch, Commissar for Transportation and Heavy Industry, who had long advocated the retention of steam traction with such words as "I am for the steam locomotive and against those who imagine that we will not have any in the future—this machine is sturdy, stubborn and will not give up", was summarily deposed and disappeared. Steam construction immediately came to an end in the Soviet Union. Some twenty years later steam operation of passenger trains also ended and with it the lives of these superb locomotives.

Above: *A head-on view demonstrates the striking appearance of the "P36" class 4-8-4s, the last word in Soviet steam locomotion.*

Below: *Soviet 4-8-4 No.P36-0223 at the head of a local train (of the Trans-Siberian line) from Blagovetshensk, Siberia, to Vladivostok in November 1970.*

Gelsa Class 4-8-4 Brazil:
National Railways, 1951

Tractive effort: 29,857lb (13,547kg).
Axle load: 29,000lb (13t).
Cylinders: (2) 17 x 25¼in (434 x 640mm).
Driving wheels: 59in (1,500mm).
Heating surface: 1,826sq ft (169.5m²).
Superheater: 721sq ft (67m²).
Steam pressure: 284psi (20kg/cm²).
Grate area: 55.5sq ft (5.4m²).
Fuel: 40,000lb (18t).
Water: 4,850gall (5,850 US) (22m³).
Adhesive weight: 115,000lb (52t).
Total weight*: 205,000lb (93t).
Length overall: 81ft 7in (24,870mm).
*without tender

When it was formed in 1948, the Brazilian National Railways consisted of a grouping of various previously independent lines. Of a total route length of 24,000 miles (38,500km) existing in 1950, metre gauge accounted for 93 per cent. Two world wars and a long period of slump between them meant that much of the locomotive stock on these lines were obsolescent.

In 1949 a consortium of French locomotive manufacturers known as GELSA (Groupment d'Exportation des Locomotives en Sud-Amerique) was formed to tender for replacements and, having obtained a contract for 90 large metre-gauge locomotives, they engaged André Chapelon to take charge of design.

When it appeared that 24 of the locomotives were to be two-cylinder 4-8-4s, two treats were in store. First, of course, there was looking forward to seeing what the master rebuilder of compound locomotives would do when he tackled a brand new simple one. Second, there was to be the pleasure of seeing the world's first metre-gauge 4-8-4 locomotive in action.

Very great care was taken not only with the theoretical design but also with practical points such as the need to include many parts standard with existing spares and stores already used and in stock in Brazil.

The Belpaire type boiler was intended to provide steam for a power output of 2000 hp while

burning Brazilian coal of low calorific value—about half that of best Welsh steam coal—and with large ash content. The ash-pan floor had to be steeply inclined and there were four exterior chutes as well as a normal one in the middle to dispose of the amazing amounts of clogging residue formed. A mechanical stoker was needed.

Other equipment included power reverse, Worthington's feed water heater and pump and a double Kylchap blast-pipe and chimney. According to the practice of the particular line on which they were to work the engines were fitted either with steam brakes with vacuum for the trains or, alternatively, with air brakes. Rail greasing apparatus

Class YP 4-6-2 India:
Indian Railways (IR), 1949

Tractive effort: 18,450lb (8,731kg).
Axle load: 23,500lb (10.7t).
Cylinders: (2) 15¼ x 24in (387 x 610mm).
Driving wheels: 54in (1,372mm).
Heating surface: 1,112sq ft (103m²).
Superheater: 331sq ft (31m²).
Steam pressure: 210psi (14.8kg/cm²).
Grate area: 28sq ft (2.6m²).
Fuel: 21,500lb (9.75t).
Water: 3,000gall (3,600 US) (13.6m³).
Adhesive weight: 69,000lb (31.5t).
Total weight: 218,500lb (99t).
Length overall: 62ft 7½in (19,088mm).

A total of 871 of thes beautifully proportioned and capable loco-motives were built between 1949 and 1970 for the metre-gauge network of the Indian Railways. The newest members of the class, which still remains virtually intact, were the last express passenger locomotives to be built in the world.

It could be said that whilst

Britain's principal achievement in India was the construction of the railway network the greatest fault in what was done was the division of the system into broad and metre gauge sections of not far off equal size. Even so, 15,940 miles (25,500km) metre-gauge railways, including many long-distance lines, required to be worked and power was needed

to do it.

The strictures rightly applied to the standard "XA", "XB" and "XC" 4-6-2s of the 1920s and 1930s were not deserved by their metre-gauge counterparts, the handsome "YB" 4-6-2s sup-plied between 1928 and 1950. Nevertheless Indian Railways decided to do what they had done on the broad gauge and go

Above: *Indian Railways' class "YP" 4-6-2 No.2630. Note the four-man engine crew leaning out of the cab.*

American. Jodhpur, one of the princely states, in those days had still its own railway, and they had received ten neat 4-6-2s from Baldwin of Philadelphia in 1948. Baldwin was asked to produce

metre-gauge lines of the Brittany system. Brake locomotives were used to simulate the design loads and both French and Brazilian coals were tried. The results were excellent and by the end of 1952 all the locomotives had been delivered. In the meantime, Chapelon himself had visited Brazil—and been appropriately feted as the high priest of steam— to see the new locomotives into service.

Since that time all has been silence—and such small pockets of steam operation using large engines as now exist in Brazil seem to favour older US-built power, possibly just that bit more rugged than these otherwise superb and technically further advanced French machines.

was provided, automatically coming into use on curves, which could be negotiated down to 2,624ft (80m) radius (22 degrees).

The prototype was tested in Brittany on the heavily engineered

Above: *4-8-4 No.242N4 on test in Brittany with brake-test loco behind the tender.*

---

20 prototypes of class "YP", similar to those locomotives but slightly enlarged. The new locos were also a little simpler, with plain bearings instead of roller ones and 8-wheel instead of high-capacity 12-wheel tenders.

Production orders for the "YP" were placed overseas. Krauss-Maffei of Munich and North British Locomotive of Glasgow got production orders for 200 and 100 respectively over the next five years, but the remainder were built by the Tata Engineering & Locomotive Co of Jamshedpur, India. Running numbers are 2000 to 2870, but not in chronological order. The engines could be regarded as two-thirds full-size models of a standard USA 4-6-2. If one multiplies linear measurements by 1.5, areas by 1.5^2 or 2.25, weights and volumes by 1.5^3 or 3.375 the correspondence is very close. Non-American features include the use of vacuum brakes, chopper type automatic centre couplers in place of the buckeye type, slatted screens to the cab side openings and the absence of a bell.

With so many available, these

locomotives can be found in all areas of the metre gauge system; this stretches far and wide from Trivandrum, almost the southernmost point of the Indian railways, to well north of Delhi, while both the easternmost and westernmost points on Indian Railways are served by metre gauge lines. Recent allocation was as follows; Central Railway—9; Northern

Railway—101; North-Eastern Railway—235; Northern Frontier Railway—98; Southern Railway —199: South Central Railway— 72; Western Railway—155. The two missing engines were withdrawn after accident damage.

Diesel locomotives are now arriving on the metre-gauge network of India, but the "YP" class still hauls important trains.

Above: *An Indian Railways' class "YP" 4-6-2, allocated to the Southern railway system, lays down a fine pall of black smoke at the head-end of a metre-gauge express train.*

Below: *Indian Railways' class "YP" 4-6-2, the last express passenger-hauling steam locomotive to be built in the world.*

Class 11 4-8-2
Angola:
Benguela Railway (FCB), 1951

Tractive effort: 36,100lb (16,375kg).
Axle load: 29,000lb (13t).
Cylinders: (2) 21 x 26in (533 x 660mm).
Driving wheels: 54in (1,372mm).
Heating surface: 1,777sq ft (165m²).
Superheater: 420sq ft (39m²).
Steam pressure: 200psi (14.1kg/cm²).
Grate area: 40sq ft (3.7m²).
Fuel (wood): 650cu ft (18.5m³).
Water: 5,000gall (6,000 US) (25m³).
Adhesive weight: 116,000lb (53t).
Total weight: 295,000lb (133½t).
Length overall: 69ft 3in (21,107mm).

The Benguela Railway of Angola was one of the most remarkable (although not one of the most rapid) feats of railway-building in the world. It was the result of the enterprise of an Englishman called Robert Williams, who saw that a railway from the Atlantic port of Lobito Bay was the best way of transporting the copper mined in Katanga (in what is now called Zaïre), instead of sending it east across to the Indian Ocean at Beira for shipment.

Work began at Lobito Bay in 1904 and the 837 miles (1,340 km) to the border at Dilolo was completed in 1929. Through communication with the rest of the 3ft 6in (1,067mm) gauge southern African network was established in 1931; by this route Lobito Bay is 2,464 miles (3,965 km) from Cape Town.

Steam traction was (and largely is) used. In order to provide fuel, the Benguela railway planted eucalyptus forests close to suitable wooding points. These trees, imported from Australia, grow well in Angola and a sufficient area was planted to keep up a continuous supply of logs to fire the locomotives.

As in the case of other southern African lines, the first miles out of the port are the worst, concerned as they are with scaling the African plateau at a height of 5,000-6,000ft (1,500-2,000m). The steep grades of this section came to involve the use of Beyer-Garratt locomotives, but there was also a requirement for some smaller locomotives for the easier sections, particularly for hauling the passenger trains. In the early days 4-8-0s had been used, but in 1951 the Benguela Railway went to the North British Locomotive Co. of Glasgow for six 4-8-2 passenger locomotives, designated class "11".

The requirements were that trains up to 500 tons should be hauled up gradients of 1 in 80 (1.25 per cent) and that curves of 300ft (90m) radius could be negotiated. Axle loading was not to exceed 13 tons. This specification was met by taking the standard South African Railways "19C/19D" class 4-8-2 and making some modifications, mostly in connection with the burning of wood. The smokebox was fitted with an efficient spark arrester — for once without spoiling the elegant simplicity of the appearance of the front end — and a Kylala-Chapelon (Kylchap) exhaust system was provided. The boiler is pitched 7in (178mm) higher than on the SAR prototype, as permitted by the Benguela Rly loading gauge, and this gives room for a larger ashpan, for which drenching pipes are fitted. There was a large timber-holding cage on top of the tender.

That such sophisticated fittings were provided for an African railway may come as a surprise to people used to the primitive equipment provided as late as the 1950s on new locomotives for BR back home in Britain.

Selkirk Class 2-10-4
Canada:
Canadian Pacific Railway (CPR), 1949

Tractive effort: 76,905lb (34,884kg).
Axle load: 62,240lb (28.25t).
Cylinders: (2) 25 x 32in (635 x 813mm).
Driving wheels: 63in (1,600mm).
Heating surface: 4,590sq ft (426m²).
Superheater: 2,055sq ft (191m)m².
Steam pressure: 285psi (20kg/cm²).
Grate area: 93.5sq ft (8.7m²).
Fuel (oil): 4,100gall (4,925 US) (18.6m²).
Water: 12,000gall (14,000 US) (54.5m³).
Adhesive weight: 311,200lb (141t).
Total weight: 732,500lb (332t).
Length overall: 97ft 10⅝in (29,835mm).

Ten-coupled locomotives were used in most parts of the world for freight movement; in fact, the only steam locomotives in quantity production in the world today are 2-10-2s in China. Because the length of a rigid wheelbase has to be limited, five pairs of coupled wheels implies that they are fairly small ones and this in turn means (usually) low speeds. It is true that British Railways had some superb 2-10-0s that were occasionally used on passenger trains "in emergencies" and, in spite of having only 62in (1575mm) dia meter wheels, were timed up to 90mph (145km/h) whilst so doing, but these were exceptional. Perhaps the ten-coupled engines with the best claim to be considered as express passenger locomotives were the 2-10-4 "Selkirk" class of the Canadian Pacific Railway. Not only were they streamlined (in the way CPR understood the term) but the coloured passenger

Above and below: *Two views of the class "11" 4-8-2 of the Benguela Railway in Angola. The photograph above shows that the appearance of these engines in normal service came close to the ideal as drawn below.*

They included a pyrometer to check the steam temperature and a power reversing gear of the Hadfield steam-operated type. The firedoor was also steam operated, electric lights were fitted and there was a recording speedometer. Particularly important was the compensated springing; this feature avoided the trailing wheels stealing adhesive weight from the driving wheels at small track irregularities and so causing slipping—a facet of steam operation that had become chronic in Britain.

The Benguela line had the good fortune for many happy years to carry (mostly) one commodity, copper, from one source to one destination. Railways that do this tend to be prosperous and this was reflected in the fact that the locomotive fleet was well looked after and kept in first-rate condition, both mechanically and visually. Hence the fleet was very economic to run and so did its bit to make the concern even more prosperous—a benevolent rather than a vicious circle, in fact.

Independence from Portugal was followed by a civil war which is still continuing in 1981 and this has for some years now halted the copper traffic. Forestry operations have also been halted by guerilla activity; such trains as do run are mostly hauled by oil-fired steam locomotives, since the country does at least have its own oil supplies.

livery was also used for them; also, of course, they handled CPR's flag train, then called the "Dominion", across the Rockies and the adjacent Selkirks.

The overall story was very similar to that of the CPR "Royal Hudson". First came the slightly more angular "T-la" batch; 20 (Nos.5900 to 5919) were built in 1929. A further ten ("T-lb") with softer and more glamorous lines were built in 1938 and, finally, another six ("T-lc") came in 1949. No.5935 was not only the last of the class but the last steam locomotive built for the company and, indeed, for any Canadian railway. The "Royal Hudson" boiler was used as the basis, but

Left: *A Canadian Pacific Railway "Selkirk" class 2-10-4 runs alongside a turbulent river on the fabled Kicking Horse Pass route.*

enlarged and equipped for oil-burning, since all locomotives used on the mountain division had been fired with oil since 1916.

When one crossed Canada by CPR the whole 2,882 miles (4,611km) from Montreal to Vanouver was reasonably easy going apart from a section along the north shore of Lake Superior and, more notably, the 262 miles (420km) over the mountains between Calgary and Revelstoke. Until the 1950s CPR's flag train, the "Dominion", could load up to 18 heavyweight cars weighing some 1,300 tons and to haul these up the 1 in 45 (2.2 per cent) inclines required some fairly heroic measures. There was very little difference in the timings and loadings of the various types of train, even the mighty "Dominion" made 23 stops over this section.

The 2-10-4s were permitted to

haul loads up to about 1,000 tons on the steepest sections. Typically when hauling a capacity load up a bank of 20 miles mostly at 1 in 45, (2.2 per cent) the average speed would be 10mph. The booster would be cut in if speed fell below walking pace and cut out when the train had reached the speed of a man's run. Fuel consumption would be of the order of 37 gallons per mile up grade.

In the mountains downhill speeds were limited to 25-30mph (40-50km/h) by curvature, frequently as sharp as 462ft (140m) radius, but passengers hardly found—or find—this portion of the journey tedious having regard to the nature of the views from the car windows. On the few straight sections of line 65mph (108km/h) could be achieved by these locomotives.

The 2-10-4s were able to nego-

tiate these sharp curves by dint of widening the gauge on the curves from 4ft 8½in to 4ft 9¾in (1,435mm to 1,469mm), an exceptional amount, and by giving the leading axle nearly an inch (25mm) of side-play each way as well as providing it with a pair of flange lubricators. In other ways standard North American practice was applied, including a fairly early application of the cast steel one-piece locomotive frame, and the class stood up well to robust usage.

In 1952 diesels took over the running across the mountains and after the 2-10-4s had done a stint on freight haulage across the prairies, they were withdrawn. The last one was cut up in 1959, except for No.5931 (numbered 5934) in the Heritage Park, Calgary, and No. 5935 at the Railway Museum at Delson, Quebec.

Class 8 4-6-2
Great Britain:
British Railways (BR), 1953

Tractive effort: 39,080lb (17,731kg)..
Axle load: 49,500lb (22.5t).
Cylinders: (3) 18 x 28in (457 x 711mm).
Driving wheels: 74in (1,880mm).
Heating surface: 2,490sq ft (231m²).
Superheater: 691sq ft (64m²).
Steam pressure: 250psi (17.6kg/cm²).
Grate area: 48.5sq ft (4.5m²).
Fuel: 22,000lb (10t).
Water: 4,325gall (5,200 US) (20m³).
Adhesive weight: 148,000lb (67.5t).
Total weight: 347,000lb (157.5t).
Length overall: 70ft 0in (21,336mm).

The railways of Britain became British Railways on 1 January 1948 and naturally there was much speculation concerning the kind of locomotives that would succeed the "Duchess", "King", "Merchant Navy" and "A4" classes of BR's illustrious predecessors. In early 1951 it was announced that none was planned but instead, the first full-size Pacific for any British railway to have only two cylinders was unveiled. This locomotive class was intended to displace such second-eleven power as the "Royal Scot", "Castle" and "West Country" classes rather than the largest types.

Britannia was a simple, rugged 4-6-2 with Belpaire firebox and roller bearings on all axles, as well as many other aids to cheap and easy maintenance. It was designated class "7", and had a capacity to produce some 2,200 hp in the cylinders, at a very fair consumption of coal, amounting to some 5,000lb/h (2,270kg/h). This was well above the rate at which a normal man could shovel coal on to the fire but the large firebox enabled a big fire to be built up in advance when some big effort of short duration was required.

A total of 55 "Britannia"s were built between 1951 and 1953. They met their designers' goal of a locomotive that was easy to maintain, and also showed that they were master of any express passenger task in Britain at that time. They were allocated to all the regions, but the one that made the best use of the new engines was the Eastern. Their "Britannia"s were allocated to one line and put to work on a new high-speed train service specifically designed round their abilities. During the 1950s in most of Britain it could be said that 20 years progress had meant journey times some 20 per cent longer. On the other hand the new 4-6-2s working this new timetable between London and Norwich meant a 20 per cent *acceleration* on pre-war timings, in terms of the service in general.

In spite of being simple engines in both senses of the world, the "Britannia"s displayed economy in the use of steam. In fact they were right in the front rank yet there was always the nagging fact that the great Chapelon compounds across the Channel could on test do about 16 per cent better. This figure would be diluted in service by various

Above: *"Britannia" class 4-6-2 No.70039 climbing Shap in September 1965 with a Liverpool to Glasgow express.*

Below: *"Britannia" class 4-6-2 No.70020* Mercury *hauling the eastbound Capitals United Express in May 1959.*

factors but even so it was considerable, especially as within almost exactly the same weight limits they could develop nearly 1,500 more cylinder horsepower. There was, however, certain reluctance in Britain to go compound, because for one thing there was no counterpart to the French works-trained *mechanicien* drivers to handle such complex beasts. Past experience had also shown the extra maintenance costs implicit in the complexity to have over-ridden economies due to the saving of fuel.

A point was perhaps missed, though, that since the upper limit of power output was a man shovelling, a more economical machine would also be a more powerful one. And since more power involves faster running times and faster running times more revenue, a more efficient locomotive might be both a money saver and a money earner. But there is another way of obtaining some of the advantages of compounding and that is to expand the steam to a greater extent in simple cylinders. This in its turn means that the point in the stroke at which the valves close to steam (known as the cut-off and expressed in terms of per cent) must be very early. However, the geometry of normal valve-gears precludes cut-offs less than, say, 15-20 per cent. This is because, if the opening to steam is limited to less of the stroke than that, the opening to exhaust (the same valve being used for both) is also limited on the return stroke. This means steam trapped in the cylinders and loss of power. The solution is to have independent valves for admission and exhaust and the simplest way of doing this is to use poppet valves actuated by a camshaft. Alas, it cannot be too simple because the point of cut-off has to be varied and, moreover, the engine has to be reversed. Both these things are done by sliding the camshaft along its axis, bringing changed cam profiles into

action according to the position of the reversing control in the cab.

Permission was obtained in 1953 to build a prototype for future BR top-line express passenger locomotives. As a two-cylinder machine, the cylinder size came out too big to clear platform edges so, in spite of a yen for simplicity, three cylinders had to be used. Now it is a point concerning poppet valves that much of the mechanism is common, however many cylinders there are. So poppet valves of the British-Caprotti pattern were specified for this sole example of the British Railways class "8" locomotive. On test, No.71000 *Duke of Gloucester* showed a 9 per cent improvement over the

"Britannia" class in steam consumed for a given amount of work done. It was a world record for a simple locomotive.

Alas, although the boiler was of impeccable lineage, being based on the excellent one used on the LMS "Duchess" class, there was some detail of its proportions which interfered with economical steam production at high outputs. It would have been easy to correct the faults with a little investigation. Unfortunately (in the words of E.S. Cox, then Chief Officer (Design) at BR headquarters), "there were some in authority at headquarters, although not in the Chief Mechanical Engineer's department, who were determined that there should be no more development

Above: *Class "8" 4-6-2 No.71000* Duke of Gloucester. *Note the shaft which drives the rotary-cam poppet valve gear.*

with steam"; so nothing was done and no more class "8" locomotives were built.

So No.71000 spent its brief life as an unsatisfactory one-off locomotive. After it was withdrawn the valve chests and valve gear was removed for preservation, but that has not prevented a more than usually bold preservation society from buying the rest of the remains.

Below: *British Railways' ill-fated, one and only class "8" 4-6-2,* Duke of Gloucester, *No.71000.*

Class 25 4-8-4
South Africa:
South African Railways (SAR), 1953

Tractive effort: 45,360lb
(20,575kg)
Axle load: 44,000lb (20t)
Cylinders: (2) 24 x 28in
(610 x 711mm)
Driving wheels: 60in
(1,524mm).
Heating surface: 3,390sq ft
(315m²).
Superheater: 630sq ft (58.5m²).
Steam pressure: 225lb/sq in
(15.8kg/cm²).
Grate area: 70sq ft (6.5m²).
Fuel: 42,000lb (19t)
Water: 4,400gall (5,300 US)
(20m³).
Adhesive weight: 172,000lb
(78t).
Total weight: 525,000lb
(238t).
Length overall: 107ft 6¼in
(32,772mm).

Two successful departures from the fundamental Stephenson principles in one class of locomotive! South African Railways had a problem in operating the section of their Cape Town to Johannesburg main line across the Karoo desert. For many years they had lived with it, facing the expense of hauling in water for locomotive purposes in tank cars during the dry season, as well as the expense of maintaining deep wells, pumps and bore-holes in dry country.

For a long time steam locomotive engineers had toyed with the idea of saving the heat which was wasted in steam exhausted from the chimney. In power stations and ships this steam is condensed back to water and much less heat is wasted. The problem is that condensing equipment is bulky and complex; numerous experimental condensing locomotives had been built but savings in fuel costs were always swamped by higher maintenance costs.

In this case there were not only fuel costs, but there were also heavy water costs to be considered, so the SAR decided to look into the idea of condensing locomotives for the Karoo. Messrs Henschel of Kassel, Germany, had built a quantity of condensing locomotives during the war and in 1948 they were asked to make a class "20" 2-10-2 into a condensing locomotive. The condenser was mounted on a greatly extended tender, while a special turbine-driven fan took

care of the draught, now that there was no exhaust blast to induce it directly in the Stephenson manner.

Test indicated that the apparatus saved 90 per cent of the water normally used and 10 per cent of the coal, results that were promising enough to warrant SAR embarking on an unprecedented programme of introducing condensing locomotives. To that end came the class "25" 4-8-4 described on this page.

The 4-8-4s were up-to-date in all respects. Roller bearings were used not only for all the main bearings but also for the connecting and coupling rods. As can be seen, the latter were arranged as individual rods between adjacent crank pins thereby doing away with knuckle joints. The cylinders were cast integrally with the frames, using a one-piece locomotive frame—a similar one supported the equipment in the tender. The boiler was the largest possible within the SAR loading gauge and as a result the chimney and dome were purely vestigial.

In all 90 condensing locomotives were supplied, Nos.3451 to 3540, all except one Henschel prototype by the North British Locomotive Co. of Glasgow, Scotland. A further 50 non-condensing "25"s were also supplied, known as class "25NC" and numbered 3401 to 3450. Ten came from NBL and 40 from Henschel. The tenders hold 18 tons of coal and 12,000 gallons

Above: *Class "25NC" 4-8-4 takes water en route from De Aar to Kimberley on the main line from Jo'burg to Capetown. This loco was of non-condensing type when originally built.*

Below: *This superb drawing of a class "25" condensing locomotive gives a vivid impression of the extreme length of this "Puffer which never puffs".*

(54.5m³) of water and were some-what shorter than those attached to the condensing locos.

Once in service the class was in most respects very successful, but that usually fatal departure from the Stephenson principle of using the jet of exhaust steam to draw the fire—the Achilles heel of all condensing locomotives—at first nearly caused disaster. The fan blades of the blower that was used in place of the blast-pipe wore out rapidly, due to the ash and grit in the exhaust gases. Eventually with Henschel's help, the problem was overcome. As had been intended, over the "dry" section of the Cape Town to Johannesburg main line, between Beaufort West and De Aar,

Left, above: *A class "25" 4-8-4 with condensing tender.*

Below: *Class "25NC" No.3530 lays down a fine trail of smoke with a freight near Modder River in April 1979. The unusual shape of tender indicates where the condensing equipment was removed by conversion.*

these condensing locomotives enabled a number of costly watering points to be closed down as well as obviating the need to haul in water at others. Over this section they dealt with everything from the famous "Blue Train" to train loads of coal. It is a strange sensation to watch a "25" starting a heavy train; there is complete silence apart from the whine of the blower fan. The condenser silently absorbs those tremendous blasts of steam that so fascinate and thrill the ferro-equinologist.

By the 1970s, a better solution was on hand for the waterless Karoo—the diesel locomotive. So these strange "puffers that never puff" lost their justification for existence. It was therefore decided to convert the condensing engines to non-condensing, the main alteration consisted of converting the original condensing tenders to rather strange-looking long low water-carts. Currently only one condensing locomotive remains, kept really as a working museum-piece. It is a reminder of what is one of the

very few unconventional steam locomotive classes ever success-fully run in service and conse-quently a remarkable *tour de force* of locomotive engineering.

The fleet of non-condensing "25"s, however, remain, with the original 50 now increased to 139. They are now largely grouped at Beaconsfield Shed, Kimberley. At the present time they still work the main line south from there to De Aar, and also east to Bloemfontein and north-west to Warrenton. Many of them have regular crews and with official encouragement are speci-ally polished, decorated, and in some cases named.

More amazing than one could imagine at this late stage in the history of steam locomotion, is the fact that a South African class "25" is undergoing fundamental further development. The hon-oured name of André Chapelon is the source of a new way of burning coal in a locomotive firebox. The basis of the idea is to divert a proportion of the exhaust steam back into the fire. At the same time a high proportion of

the air needed for combustion is led in through short large-diameter tubes just above the fire. The result is that the firebed, behaving more like a chemical reaction than a furnace, reacts to give off producer gas, which mixes with the air being drawn into the firebox and burns cleanly there. The result—no more fire-throwing black smoke or clinker forming, coupled with a sub-stantial decrease in coal con-sumption. And all for the very minimum of expenditure.

The system suggested by Chapelon was used by a certain South American engineer called Da Porta on the locomotives of a coal-hauling line not far from Cape Horn; after years of suc-cessful use there, a small South African class "19D" was con-verted in 1979. During 1981, class "25NC" No 3450 was rebuilt to class "26" on the same lines as the class "19D". Success has been such that there is even a prospect that the use of these gas-fired locomotives might arrest the decline of steam in this, one of its last strongholds.

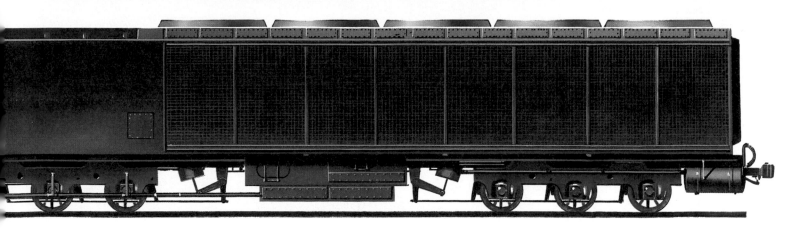

Class 59 4-8-2+2-8-4
Kenya:
East African Railways (EAR), 1955

Tractive effort: 83,350lb (38,034kg).
Axle load: 47,000lb (21t).
Cylinders: (4) 20½ x 28in (521 x 711mm).
Driving wheels: 54in (1,372mm).
Heating surface: 3,560sq ft (331m²).
Superheater: 747sq ft (69.4m²).
Steam pressure: 225psi (15.8kg/cm²).
Grate area: 72sq ft (6.7m²).
Fuel (oil): 2,700gall (3,250 US) (12m³).
Water: 8,600gall (10,400 US) (39m³).
Adhesive weight: 357,000lb (164t).
Total weight: 564,000lb (256t).
Length overall: 104ft 1½in (31,737mm).

Often in this narrative British climbs like Shap and Beattock have been spoken of with awe. Shap has 20 miles (32km) of 1 in 75 (1.3 per cent) but what would one say about a climb 350 miles (565km) long with a ruling grade of 1 in 65 (1.5 per cent)? But such

is the ascent from Mombasa to Nairobi, up which every night the legendary "Uganda Mail" makes its way.

The building of the metre-gauge Uganda Railway, begun in 1892, was a strangely reluctant piece of empire building, violently opposed at home, yet successful. One of its objectives was the suppression of the slave trade and that was quickly achieved; the second objective was to facilitate trade and that also was successful to a point where the railway was always struggling to move the traffic offering. By 1926 a fleet of 4-8-0s were overwhelmed by the tonnage and the Kenya & Uganda Railway (as it then was) went to Beyer, Peacock of Manchester for 4-8-2 + 2-8-4 Beyer-Garratts, with as many mechanical parts as possible standard with the 4-8-0s. It was the answer to mass movement on 50lb/yd (24kg/m) rails.

As the years went by, other Garratt classes followed and the K&UR became East African Railways. In 1954 with the biggest backlog of tonnage ever faced

waiting movement, the administration ordered 34 of the greatest Garratt design ever built. Whilst their main role was the haulage of freight, these giant "59" class were regarded as sufficiently passenger train oriented to be given the names of East African mountains. Also, of course, they

Above: *East African Railways class "59" 4-8-2+2-8-4 No.5904 Mount Elgon.*

bore the attractive maroon livery of the system.

By British standards their statistics are very impressive—over double the tractive effort of any

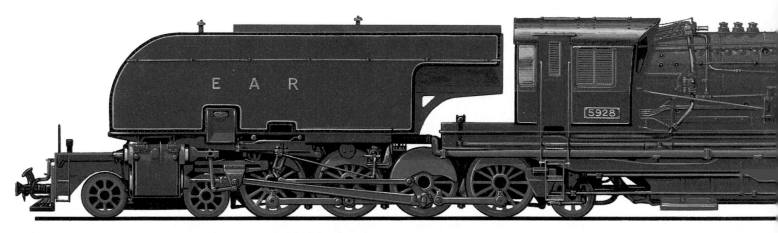

Class 15A 4-6-4+4-6-4
Rhodesia:
Rhodesia Railways (RR), 1952

Tractive effort: 47,500lb (21,546kg).
Axle load: 34,000lb (15.5t).
Cylinders: (4) 17½ x 26in (445 x 660mm).
Driving wheels: 57in (1,448mm).
Heating surface: 2,322sq ft (216m²).
Superheater: 494sq ft (46m²).
Steam pressure: 200psi (14.1kg/cm²).
Grate area: 49.6sq ft (4.6m²).
Fuel: 27,000lb (12t).
Water: 7,000gall (8,400 US) (32m³).
Adhesive weight: 178,000lb (81t).
Total weight: 418,000lb (190t).
Length overall: 92ft 4in (28,143mm).

A railway linking Cape Town up the whole length of Africa to Cairo was the impossible dream of an English clergyman's son called Cecil Rhodes, who eventually was to give his name to Rhodesia, now known as Zimbabwe. "The railway is my right

locomotive ever employed in passenger service back home, coupled with a grate area nearly 50 per cent greater. Oil-firing was used but provision was made for a mechanical stoker if coal burning ever became economic in East African circumstances. There was also provision for an easy conversion from metre gauge to the African standard 3ft 6in (1,067mm) gauge, as well as for fitting vacuum brake equipment, should the class ever be required to operate outside air-brake territory in Tanzania.

All the latest and best Beyer-Garratt features were applied, such as the self-adjusting main pivots, the "streamlined" ends to the tanks, and those long handsome connecting rods driving on the third coupled axle. Four sets of Walschaert's valve gear were worked by Beyer's patent Hadfield steam reverser with hydraulic locking mechanism. The virtues of the short fat Garratt boiler, with clear space beneath the firebox, made 14 or 15 hours continuous hard steaming no problem. Later, Giesl ejectors

were fitted to the class, with results that were controversial operationally, and quite unambiguously awful aesthetically.

One feature which did not work out was the tapered axle loadings, which gave successive axle-loads in tons when running forward of 15.4, 15.4, 19.0, 20.9,

Above: *East African Railways class "59" 4-8-2+2-8-4 No. 5916* Mount Rungwe.

Below: *East African Railways Beyer Garratt No.5928* Mount Kilimanjaro, *depicted in the superb crimson lake livery of the original.*

20.8, 18.8, 15.3; 15.5, 19.0, 21.0, 21.0, 19.0, 15.3, 15.3. The idea was that the gradual rise in axle-load should permit operation on 80lb/yd (38.6kg/m) rail north and west of Nairobi in addition to 95lb/yd (45.7kg/m) rail which was by then general between Nairobi and the coast.

The results of fresh motive power were very impressive, the backlog of traffic was quickly cleared and the new engines soon found themselves the largest and most powerful steam locomotives in the world. That they remained that way for 25 years was due to the economical use of well-maintained steam power long preventing any case being made out for a change to diesel traction.

Even so the diesel did win in the end, displacing the "59"s from the mail trains quite early on and gradually from the freights between 1973 and 1980. In addition a proposed "61" class 4-8-4+4-8-4 with 27-ton axle-loading, 115,000lb (52,476kg) tractive effort and 105sq ft (9.8m²) fire grate was shelved indefinitely.

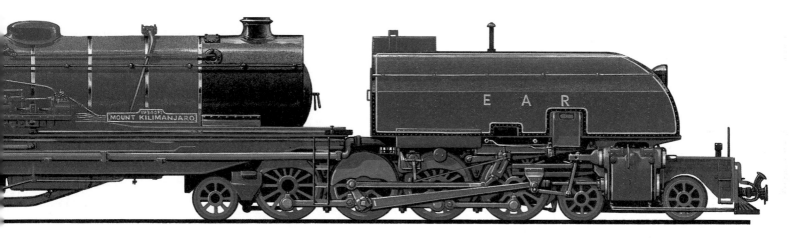

hand, the telegraph my voice" said Rhodes at the height of his power. When Rhodes died in 1902 his Cape-to-Cairo line had reached the River Zambesi, 280 miles (450km) north of Bulawayo, but there was sufficient impetus to reach Bukama, 2,700 miles (4,345km) from Cape Town in what is now Zaïre, by 1914.

In 1930, for working a 484-mile (778-km) stretch of this Cape-to-Cairo line between Mafeking and Bulawayo, what had now become Rhodesia Railways ordered four 4-6-4+4-6-4 Beyer-Garratts from England. They

Above left: *Class "15A" Beyer-Garratt 4-6-4+4-6-4 No.400 of Rhodesia Railways (now National Railways of Zimbabwe) under steam test at Bulawayo Works after overhaul.*

Left: *Rhodesia Railways Beyer-Garratt 4-6-4+4-6-4 No. 358. This class "15" is running bunker first on the Victoria Falls to Bulawayo train.*

were typical sound solid chunks of Beyer, Peacock engineering; they also showed the whole objective of the Garratt concept by having a tractive effort greater than and a grate area equal to the largest "straight" locomotive ever to run back in Britain, but within an axle-load limit 30 per cent less. Delays in completing bridge strengthening works denied the Cape-to-Cairo route to the new locomotives (known as the "15th" class) so they went into service on the Bulawayo to Salisbury main line; the haulage of the celebrated "Rhodesia Express" was entrusted to them. In service the class proved to be excellent runners and very light on maintenance. They played a large part in converting the RR management to the idea of a mainly Garratt-operated system and so, immediately after the war, a further 30 were ordered as all-purpose locomotives for the railway. Between 1949 and 1952 yet another 40 with slight modifications were delivered, known

as class "15A", and to which the particulars given here apply. A final 10 came from Messrs. Franco-Belge of France, Beyer, Peacock being then swamped with Garratt orders.

The resulting 74 locomotives were the largest class ever acquired by the RR. They were also the second most numerous design of Beyer-Garratt, as well as being the first Garratts to have the "streamlined" front tanks. On a 50mph (80km/h) locomotive, streamlining could only be for show, but the improved lines greatly ameliorated the rather severe looks of previous Garratts.

Their most notable assignment was the British royal family's tour in 1947, when two "15th" class decked out in royal blue handled the 730-ton "White Train". Not until 1963 was the class able to take over the work for which they were originally bought, and for the next ten years the "15" and "15A" classes monopolised the traffic between Bulawayo and Mafeking, through what is

now Botswana. The Bulawayo-Cape Town and Bulawayo-Johannesburg expresses were part of these duties; long-distance trains of this kind were worked on the caboose system, whereby two crews would operate the train, one in the cab on duty and the other taking their ease in a comfortable sleeping and eating van (the caboose) marshalled next the engine. The 970 mile (1,556km) round trip from Bulawayo to Mafeking and back would take three days and two nights.

When the railways in northern Rhodesia became Zambian Railways, a number of "15"s were allocated north of the Zambesi. A few others have been withdrawn, but some 50 remain. It is a pleasure to write not only that most of these are still in service but also that a policy has been adopted by oil-poor but coal-rich Zimbabwe to rebuild their fleet of Garratts. In this way these fine locomotives should be good for many more years of service.

Class 498.1 4-8-2
Czechoslovakia:
Czechoslovak State Railways (CSD), 1954

Tractive effort: 41,920lb (19,018kg).
Axle load: see text.
Cylinders: (3) 19¾ x 26¾in (500 x 680mm).
Driving wheels: 72in (1,830mm).
Heating surface: 2,454sq ft (228m²).
Superheater: 797sq ft (74m²).
Steam pressure: 228psi (16kg/cm²).
Grate area: 52sq ft (4.9m²).
Fuel: 33,000lb (15t).
Water: 7,700gall (9,200 US) (35m³).
Adhesive weight: see text.
Total weight: 428,500lb (194t).
Length overall: 83ft 11½in (25,594mm).

These remarkable locomotives in their handsome blue livery were some of the finest steam passenger express locomotives ever to be placed on the rails. Anyone with a gift for arithmetic could tell quite a lot about them by merely glancing at the number, which has the class designation as a prefix. The first figure gives the number of driving axles; take the middle figure, add 3, multiply by 10 and the answer is the maximum permitted speed in km/h; then take the last figure, add 10 and that gives the axle load to the nearest ton. So the 498.1 class had four driving axles, a maximum speed of 120 km/h (75mph) and a maximum axle load of between 18 tons and 19 tons. Fifteen were built by the famous Skoda Works during 1954-55.

Amongst things one can hardly tell from a glance would be the existence of a third inside cylinder, whose axis is inclined at 1 in 10 to the horizontal, driving, like the outside cylinders, on the second coupled axle. Roller bear-

ings were fitted to all the main axle bearings and also to the motion. Most remarkably the centre big end was also a roller bearing; the designers had sufficient confidence to wall up this bearing between the webs of the crankshaft.

Other sophisticated equipment included powered reversing gear, mechanical stoking, a combustion chamber, arch tubes and thermic syphons in the firebox, as well as axle load adjustment from 41,000lb (18.5t) to 37,000lb (16.8t) with corresponding reduction in adhesive weight from 164,000lb (74t) to 148,000lb (67.5t). The effect of this change was to transfer weight from the driving wheels to the leading bogie and rear pony truck. The alteration would enable the locomotives to be employed on the country's secondary main lines which would only accept the lower axle-loading, once the principal routes had become electrified. The change involved moving the position of the pivot points of the compensating levers, provision being made to do this without making any physical modifications. Incidentally, the three domes are, respectively from the front, for top feed, sand and steam. Amongst other unusual features are the ten-wheel tenders with one six-wheel and one four-wheel bogie. The three sets of Walschaert's gear are conventional except that the drive to the inside set is taken from a return crank mounted outside on the third coupled-wheel crankpin on the left-hand side.

This arrangement is similar to

Right: *A conspicuous red star decorates the front end of a Czechoslovak State Railways' class "498.1" 4-8-2.*

242 Class 4-8-4
Spain:
Spanish National Railways System (RENFE), 1956

Tractive effort: 46,283lb (21,000kg).
Axle load: 42,000lb (19t).
Cylinders: (2) 25¼ x 28in (640 x 710mm).
Driving wheels: 74¾in (1,900mm).
Heating surface: 3,161sq ft (293m²).
Superheater: 1,125sq ft (104.5m²).
Steam pressure: 228psi (16kg/cm²).
Grate area: 57sq ft (5.3m²).
Fuel (oil): 3,000gall (3,600 US) (13.5³).
Water: 6,200gall (7,440 US) (28m³).
Adhesive weight: 167,500lb (76t).
Total weight: 469,500lb (213t).
Length overall: 88ft 0¾in (26,840mm).

These magnificent locomotives, built to a gauge of two Spanish yards or 5ft 5.9in (1,674mm), were the final European express passenger locomotive class, the

only *class* of 4-8-4 in Western Europe and the ultimate achievement of Spanish steam locomotive engineering. They were descended from a long line of 4-8-2s dating from 1925. Those built before 1944 were compounds, but since then the world standard form of a two-cylinder simple has prevailed. In the case of these 4-8-4s the only departure from this has been the use of the Lentz system of poppet valves, with an oscillating camshaft actuated by a set of Walschaert's valve gear each side.

The ten locomotives were supplied by the Maquinista Terrestre y Maritima of Barcelona in 1956 and were numbered 242.2001-10. Details included a feed-water heater, equipment for the French TIA water-treatment system, a cab floor mounted on springs, and a turbo-generator large enough to supply current to light the train as well as the engine. Lights on the locomotive included one just ahead of the Kylchap

202

that found on Chapelon's "242A1" 4-8-4 and it reflects a good deal of contact between him and the CSD before politics put an end to such interchanges. It is interesting to find amongst the progenitors of the "498.1" class a group of three three-cylinder compound 4-8-2s very much in the French tradition.

These were built in 1949.

It was found, though, that the simple locomotive was better on an all-round basis and the "498.1" class followed directly on previous 4-8-2s, that is, the nine "486" class of 1933-38 and the forty "498.0" class of 1946-49. The new 4-8-2s, known as the "Albatross" class by their crews, were excellent performers both on heavy international expresses and lighter faster trains. On test speeds up to 93mph (149km/h) were achieved and in normal running the maximum permitted speed of 75mph (120km/h) was often achieved.

Steam traction has recently come to an end in Czechoslovakia.

It is understood that 4-8-2 No. 498.106 has been set aside for preservation but it is not known if the work has been completed.

Below: *A fine view of class "498.0" 4-8-2 No.498.82. Note the unusual design of tender with one four-wheel and one six-wheel bogie.*

double chimney, so that at night as well as in the daytime the fireman could judge by the colour of the exhaust whether he had adjusted the oil-firing controls correctly. All axleboxes had roller bearings. A special green livery —lesser Spanish steam locomotives were painted plain black —set off a truly superb appearance.

The 4-8-4s were built to work the principal expresses over the unelectrified section of the main line from Madrid to the French border at Irun, that is, from Avila to Miranda del Ebro. They had no problems in keeping time with such trains as the "Sud Express" loaded up to 750 tons, although really fast running was precluded by an overall speed

Left: *Note the small tender on this Spanish class "242" 4-8-4.*

Right: *Spanish National Railways class "242" 4-8-4 No.242.2001.*

restriction of 68mph (110km/h). Even so, the "242" class demonstrated on test an ability to run at 84mph (134km/h) on the level with 480 tons, as well as to develop 4,000hp in the cylinders. In service they could maintain a speed of 35mph (55km/h) with 600 tons along 1 in 100 (1 per cent) gradients. The tenders of the 4-8-4s were absurdly small for such a huge locomotive. No doubt the size of turntable available prevented any larger ones being attached, but in the absence of water troughs there was no possibility of making long non-stop runs in the face of a need for some 70 gallons (0.3m³) per mile with less than 6,200 gallons (28m³) available.

Steam has now been eliminated in Spain for normal use. Whilst various steam locomotives have been seen on special excursion trains, they have not so far included a "242", although one (No.242.2009) is set aside in the depot at Miranda del Ebro.

RM Class 4-6-2
China:
Railways of the People's Republic, 1958

Tractive effort: 34,597lb (15,698kg).
Axle load: 46,284lb (21t).
Cylinders: (2) 22½ x 26in (570 x 660mm).
Driving wheels: 69in (1,750mm).
Heating surface: 2,260sq ft (210m²).
Superheater: 700sq ft (65m²).
Steam pressure: 213psi (15kg/cm²).
Grate area: 62sq ft (5.75m²).
Fuel: 32,000lb (14.5t).
Water: 8,700gall (10,400 US) (30.5m³).
Adhesive weight: 137,750 (62.5t).
Total weight: 38,349lb (174t).
Length overall: 73ft 5½in (22,390mm).

This unusual but neat-looking 4-6-2 is thought to be the final design of steam express passenger locomotive in the world. There is another reason why it is treated as the last word in this book and that is because the country which produced it is also the last in the world to have steam locomotives in production. Those now being built are basically freight locomotives but are used for express passenger trains on certain mountain lines in the People's Republic of China. With many new lines under construction it is possible in China to ride a 1980s railway behind a 1980s steam locomotive.

The "RM"—"Ren Ming" or "People" class—4-6-2s are descended from some passenger locomotives supplied by the Jap-anese to the railways of their puppet kingdom of Manchukuo, otherwise Manchuria. The older engines in pre-liberation days were known as class "PF-1" ("PF" stood for "Pacific") but afterwards they became re-designated "SL" standing for "Sheng-Li" or "Victory". Loco-motive construction to Chinese design did not begin for several years after the Communist victory of 1949, but by 1958 the con-struction of the "RM" class was under way at the Szufang (Tsing-tao) Works. It was an enlarged version of the "SL" class, capable of a power output 12½ per cent greater.

The main difference between the "RM" and "SL" class—and indeed between the "RM" class and virtually all other steam loco-motives outside the USSR—was in the position of the main steam-pipe. This normally ran forward from the dome inside the boiler, but in these engines there was room for it to be situated much more accessibly in well-insulated trunking above the boiler. An interesting detail shared with other Chinese steam power, is the provision of an air horn, in addition to a normal deep-sounding dragon-scaring steam chime whistle. In other ways, though, these fine engines fol-lowed what had been for many years the final form of the steam locomotive. Thus we find two cylinders only, using outside-admission piston-valves driven by Walschaert's valve gear, coupled with a wide firebox boiler with no frills except a big

Above: *Brand new "Forward" class steam locomotive No.QJ 3404 on test at the People's Locomotive factory at Datong, China, in October 1980.*

superheater and a mechanical stoker. Apart from this last feature British readers could reasonably regard the "RM" class as what a class "7" 'Britannia' 4-6-2 might have been if the designers had had similar axleload limitations but another 3ft of vertical height with which to play.

Visitors to China report that these engines can frequently be encountered travelling at speeds

Below: *The world's final steam express design, a "People" class 4-6-2 No.RM 1201 near Jinan, December 1980.*

around 65mph (105km/h) on level routes hauling 600 ton passenger trains. There is reason to suppose that about 250 were built during the years 1958 to 1964 and that the numbers run from RM1001 to RM1250. Wide variations in the insignia and slogans which decorate present day Chinese steam locomotives introduce some variety into the plain (but always clean) black finish used. An "RM" class, specially painted in green, was used to haul the inaugural train across the great new bridge across the Yangtse River at Nanking.

The type of locomotive still being produced (and used on trains in the mountains) in China is the standard 2-10-2 freight locomotive of the "Qian Jing" or "March Forward" class. Even in 1982 they are still being produced at a rate of about 300 per year at a special factory at Datong in Northern China. Various reasons are given for this continued construction of steam locomotives, unique in the world and recently reprieved indefinitely, but the basis seems to be a combination of cheap indigenous coal and traffic rising at some 10 per cent per year. The construction of diesel locomotives in China absorbs five times as many skilled man-hours as steam locomotives of equal capacity so one can understand the reluctance of the Chinese railways to dispose of this cheap and reliable way of coping with their ever-increasing haulage problems.

It is very pleasant indeed to be able to end this book on such a satisfactory note, indicating a real possibility that our beloved steam locomotive might even now be brought back from brink of extinction. South Africa, India, Poland, Zimbabwe are, as we have seen, other places where the forces which toppled steam from its throne may yet be contained. But is there a possibility of any reconquest by steam in places where it had seemingly vanished from the commercial railway scene forever?

Britain, where steam began, is a poor prospect; a new and huge oilfield, combined with coal supplies that are expensive because of the small seams and old-fashioned pits from which it is mined, make it so. Any return to steam (apart from steam for pleasure) seems likely to take the form of steam turbines on the ground generating electricity for electric trains. It is some compensation to Britons though, that nostalgic steam activities exist in their country to an extent proportionately unparalleled elsewhere. The United States, on the other hand, presents a different aspect—indigenous oil supplies are now inadequate and, not only that, coal production and costs in a vast land are responding in an excellent style to characteristic American drive and know-how. Having demonstrated in the recent past that the steam

locomotive can match the diesel in performance and availability for service (see New York Central Railroad's "Niagara" class) and ease of servicing (see Norfolk & Western's "J" class) and being fully aware that it is now practical to make steam environmentally acceptable—as well as more efficient—by means of the producer-gas firebox (see South African Railways's class "26"), it is

not surprising that an American consortium is going ahead with the development of a steam locomotive for the 21st century.

Shall we in conclusion then, wish success to American Coal Enterprises, Inc., without being really sanguine that one day in the future steam could be found at the head of a luxury Twenty-First Century Limited running between New York and Chicago.

Above: *Displacing a fine plume of steam, "People" class 4-6-2 No.RM 1019 heads north through an autumnal snowfall from Harbin, Manchuria, with a passenger train in October 1980.*

Below: *A view of a beautifully cleaned "People" class 4-6-2, No.RM 1049 at Changchun Shed, northeast China, 1980.*

Index

Picture Credits

The publishers wish to thank the following organisations and individuals who have supplied photographs for this book. Photographs have been credited by page number. Some references have, for reasons of space, been abbreviated, as follows:

AAR = Colourviews
GFA = Geoffrey Freeman-Allen
MARS = Mechanical Archive & Research Services
PNWA = Peter Newark's Western Americana
VR = Vie du Rail

Page 6: top, B Stephenson; bottom, BBC Hulton Picture Library. **7:** CV; right, R Bastin. **8:** B Stephenson. **10:** top, C Gammell; bottom, N Trotter. **11:** left, B Stephenson; top right, B Hollingsworth; bottom right, CV. **12:** GFA; bottom, D Cross; top, Robert Barton. **13:** left, Robert Barton; top right, Union Pacific RR; bottom right, B Stephenson. **17:** CV. **18:** top, CV; bottom, CV. **19:** top, Science Museum/CV; bottom, CV. **20:** top, Science Museum; bottom, AAR. **21:** top, PNWA; bottom, PNWA. **22:** Science Museum/CV. **24:** top, R Bastin; bottom, PNWA. **25:** AAR. **27:** J Adams. **29:** Science Museum/CV. **30:** CV. **31:** CV. **32:** top, Swiss Federal Railways; bottom, CV. **33:** left, CV; right, O Bamer. **34:** top, CV; centre, VR/Henry; bottom, Science Museum. **35:** CV. **36:** AAR. **37:** J Winkley. **38:** top, CV; bottom, CV. **39:** CV. **40:** VR. **41:** J Dunn. **42:** CV. **43:** GFA. **45:** M Whitehouse. **46:** CV. **47:** CV. **48:** CV. **49:** top, CV; bottom, CV. **50:** DB Museum, Nurnberg. **51:** DB Museum, Nurnberg. **53:** top, CV; bottom, AAR. **54:** top, AAR; centre, Strasburg RR; bottom, Strasburg RR. **55:** Strasburg RR. **56-57:** GFA. **57:** GFA. **58:** top, Italian State Railways; bottom, GFA. **60:** VR. **62:** VR. **63:** CV. **64:** top, D Cross; bottom, GFA. **65:** D Cross. **66:** CV. **66-67:** J Winkley. **67:** top left, CV; top right, CV. **68:** Colour-rail. **69:** top, CV; bottom, CV. **70-71:** top, CV; bottom, CV. **71:** top, CV; bottom, CV. **72-73:** Colour-rail/RM Quinn. **74:** CV. **75:** top, CV; bottom, CV. **76:** CV. **77:** CV. **78:** top, CV; bottom, CV. **79:** top, CV; bottom, VR. **80:** top, Staatsbibliotek Berlin; centre, MARS. **80-81:** GFA. **81:** CV. **90:** bottom, Swiss Federal Railways. **90-91:** K Mills. **91:** bottom, M Whitehouse. **92:** CV. **94:** CV. **95:** top, Novosti Press Agency; bottom, Italian State Railways. **96:** top, Colour-rail/RM Quinn; centre, CV; bottom, Colour-rail/RM Quinn. **97:** top, Archiv Triebl; bottom, CV. **98:** top, CV; bottom, Swedish State Railways. **99:** Swedish State Railways/MARS. **100:** top, JM Jarvis; bottom, GFA. **101:** CV. **102:** CV. **102-103:** CV. **103:** LG Marshall. **104:** CV. **105:** CV. **106:** CV. **106-107:** GFA. **107:** D Cross. **108:** CV. **109:** CV. **110:** VR. **110-111:** top, C Gammell; bottom, CV. **111:** GFA. **112:** top, J Winkley; bottom, R Bastin. **113:** R Bastin. **114:** D Cross. **115:** R Bastin. **116:** Victorian Government Railways. **116-117:** Colour-rail/RM Quinn. **117:** top, CV; centre, GFA; bottom, Finnish State Railways. **118:** J Winkley. **119:** CV. **120:** Burlington Northern. **121:** CV. **122:** Southern Railway System/MARS. **123:** CV. **124:** JM Jarvis. **125:** top, GFA; bottom, AAR. **126:** South Australian Railways. **127:** top, D Cross; bottom, South Australian Railways. **128:** K Cantlie. **129:** top, C Gammell; bottom, D Cross. **130:** top, CV; bottom, CV. **131:** CV. **132:** CV. **133:** CV. **134:** top, JM Jarvis; centre, JM Jarvis. **134-135:** GFA. **135:** top, GFA; bottom, Canadian Pacific. **136:** top, CV; cente, CV; bottom, Colour-rail/HN James. **137:** top, CV; bottom left, CV; bottom right, CV. **146:** top, Bundarchiv; bottom, Norwegian State Railways. **147:** Norwegian State Railways. **148:** C Gammell. **148-149:** AAR. **149:** top, AAR; bottom, CV. **150:** GFA. **151:** CV. **152:** D Cross. **153:** top, CV; bottom, CV. **154:** CV. **155:** top, GFA; bottom, CV. **156:** British Columbia Railway/MARS. **157:** British Columbia Railway/MARS. **158:** Canadian National Railways/MARS. **159:** CV. **160-161:** Chicago & North Western/MARS. **161:** Colour-rail. **163:** top, CV; bottom, CV. **164:** C Gammell. **165:** top, JM Jarvis; bottom, JM Jarvis. **166:** top, CV; bottom, J Dunn. **167:** top, CV; bottom, SAR. **168:** top, CV; bottom, GFA. **169:** top, D Cross; bottom, CV. **170:** CV. **171:** Union Pacific RR. **172:** JM Jarvis. **173:** top, JM Jarvis; bottom, GFA. **174:** GFA. **175:** left, Santa Fe RR; right, GFA. **176:** CV. **177:** D Cross. **178:** JM Jarvis. **179:** top, GFA; bottom, JM Jarvis. **180:** top, VR/Fenino; bottom, VR. **181:** VR. **182:** top, K Yoshitani; bottom, C Gammell. **183:** K Yoshitani. **184:** Colour-rail/R Hill. **185:** top, CV; bottom, C Gammell. **186:** B Stephenson. **187:** C&O RR/MARS. **188:** top, R Bastin; centre, CV; bottom, M Whitehouse. **189:** top, CV; bottom, VR. **190:** top, CV; centre R Ziel; bottom, J Westwood. **191:** top, J Westwood; bottom, R Ziel. **192:** Colour-rail/RM Quinn. **193:** top, CV; bottom, Colour-rail/RM Quinn. **194:** Canadian Pacific. **195:** CV. **196:** top, D Cross; bottom, CV. **197:** Colour-rail/J Dewing. **198:** top, South African Railways/MARS; bottom, CV. **199:** C Gammell. **200:** top, CV; centre, CV; bottom, CV. **201:** CV. **202:** CV; bottom, Colour-rail/JG Dewing. **203:** top, CV; bottom, RENFE/MARS. **204:** top, Y Hollingsworth; bottom, C Gammell. **205:** top, R Gillard; bottom, CV.

PRINTED IN BELGIUM BY

proost
INTERNATIONAL BOOK PRODUCTION